Justice in Asia and the Pacific Region, 1945–1952
Allied War Crimes Prosecutions

This book explores a cross section of war crimes trials that the Allied Powers held against the Japanese in the aftermath of World War II. More than 2,240 trials against some 5,700 suspected war criminals were carried out at 51 separate locations across the Asia-Pacific region. This book analyzes fourteen high-profile American, Australian, British, and Philippine trials, including the Yamashita Trial (1945) and the two international proceedings (1948–1949) that followed the Tokyo Trial. By delving into a large body of hitherto underutilized oral and documentary history of the war as contained in the trial records, Yuma Totani illuminates diverse firsthand accounts of the war that were offered by former Japanese and Allied combatants, prisoners of war, and the civilian population. Furthermore, the author makes a systematic inquiry into selected trials to shed light on the highly complex – and at times contradictory – legal and jurisprudential legacy of Allied war crimes prosecutions.

Yuma Totani is associate professor of history at the University of Hawai'i. She is a recipient of the Postdoctoral Fellowship in Japanese Studies granted by the Edwin O. Reischauer Institute of Japanese Studies, Harvard University, in 2005–2006; the Abe Fellowship granted by the Social Science Research Council in 2010–2011; and the Frederick Burkhardt Residential Fellowship for Recently Tenured Scholars in 2012–2013, during which time she took up residence at the Center for Advanced Study in the Behavioral Sciences at Stanford University. She is the author of *The Tokyo War Crimes Trial: The Pursuit of Justice in the Wake of World War II* (2008) and rendered its Japanese-language translation, *Tōkyō saiban: dai-niji taisen go no hō to seigi no tsuikyū* (2008).

Justice in Asia and the Pacific Region, 1945–1952

Allied War Crimes Prosecutions

YUMA TOTANI

University of Hawai'i

CAMBRIDGE
UNIVERSITY PRESS

32 Avenue of the Americas, New York, NY 10013-2473, USA

Cambridge University Press is part of the University of Cambridge.

It furthers the University's mission by disseminating knowledge in the pursuit of education, learning, and research at the highest international levels of excellence.

www.cambridge.org
Information on this title: www.cambridge.org/9781107458086

© Yuma Totani 2015

First published 2015

Printed in the United States of America

A catalog record for this publication is available from the British Library.

Library of Congress Cataloging in Publication Data

Totani, Yuma, 1972– author.
  Justice in Asia and the Pacific region, 1945–1952 : Allied war crimes prosecutions / Yuma Totani.
    pages cm
  ISBN 978-1-107-08762-0 (hardback) – ISBN 978-1-107-45808-6 (paperback)
    1. War crime trials – Pacific area – History – 20th century. 2. World War, 1939–1945 – Law and legislation – Pacific area. 3. World War, 1939–1945 – Atrocities – Pacific area. I. Title.
  KZ1174.5.T68 2014
  341.6'90268–dc23   2014027891

ISBN 978-1-107-08762-0 Hardback
ISBN 978-1-107-45808-6 Paperback

To my parents, sisters, and brothers

Contents

Acknowledgments

This book project has been made possible with generous funding from various centers and organizations that have supported my research over the course of the last five years. As a recipient of the Abe Fellowship in the academic year 2010–2011 and the Frederick Burkhardt Residential Fellowship for Recently Tenured Scholars in the academic year 2012–2013, I would like to take this opportunity to express my heartfelt gratitude once again for the honor and privilege of the awards and for the generous funding. My gratitude goes also to the Center for Advanced Study in the Behavioral Sciences (CASBS) at Stanford University, which accepted my application and accommodated me during the Burkhardt fellowship year. I am grateful to my home institution at the University of Hawai'i, too, especially the Department of History, the College of Arts and Humanities, the Japan Studies Endowment, and the University Research Council, for providing me with critical research funds and other types of institutional support.

I have been fortunate enough to enjoy the friendship and moral support of the following individuals in recent years: Jerry Bentley (late), Mary Elizabeth Berry, David Cohen, Mark Drumbl, Fujita Hisakazu (late), Sheldon Garon, Andrew Gordon, Tim McCormack, and Richard Sousa. Each of these individuals has given me encouragement for my career development in general and this book project in particular. I am also indebted to Iriye Akira for his warm endorsement of my previous book on the Tokyo Trial, which, in turn, served as the critical foundation of the present book project. Of these individuals, Jerry Bentley was a star historian and a dear colleague of ours in the Department of History at the University of Hawai'i. He fell gravely ill at the end of 2011 and passed away on July 15, 2012. He used to be my go-to person when I needed some level-headed advice on career development, and his office door was always open for walk-in consultation, just a few doors down across the hallway. He is sorely missed in our department and in the larger community of world history of which he was a pioneer. I came to know Fujita Hisakazu as an authority on international humanitarian law and a professor emeritus at Kansai University in Kobe, Japan. An impactful intellectual, yet entirely unassuming and gentlemanly, he passed away rather suddenly, on November 7, 2012. He was working on a new project, which he mentioned to me when he stopped by to say hello during my visit to Kansai University in May 2011. I am saddened by the news that he is no longer with us, and he is sorely missed.

The post-WWII Allied war crimes trials as a field of study has been in the making for some time. But how it came about and why it grew the way it has in recent decades would be inexplicable if one fails to recognize the unique contribution of David Cohen. He began exploring the archives of former Allied Powers in earnest in the 1990s in order to locate the records of thousands of trials that the Allied authorities held in Europe and in the Far East. It was largely a solitary research activity in the early years, since few remembered that these trials had ever taken place or, even if some did, took little interest in that fact (with the exception, of course, of the people in Germany and Japan). His archival work culminated in the establishment of the War Crimes Studies Center at the University of California, Berkeley, in 1999, in order that the new center could give an institutional framework to his continuing effort to collect the trial records and build the archives of these trials. His research activities have branched out into other fields since, including monitoring programs of present-day international criminal proceedings and human-rights initiatives in Asia. Presently serving as director of the Worldwide Support for Development (WSD) Handa Center for Human Rights and International Justice (inaugurated in 2014) at Stanford University, Cohen remains the world's foremost scholar in historical studies of war crimes trials. This book is a tribute to his singular contribution in the field.

On September 3, 2013, I saw news footage of Diane Nyad, 64, wading out of the water to declare to the world that she finally did it – she swam across the Straits of Florida, between Cuba and Florida, without a protective cage, in her fifth attempt in thirty-five years. Her face sunburned and swollen after swimming in the open sea for nearly fifty-three hours, she seemed somewhat dazed but still lucid. She told the reporters that she had "three messages" for them, which were these: "One is we should never, ever give up. Two is you never are too old to chase your dreams. Three is it looks like a solitary sport, but it's a team." I have not had the honor of meeting Ms. Nyad, nor would I consider attempting long-distance endurance swimming myself. However, the third of her messages made a deep impression on me, as the same could be said of our profession. This field, too, is so gigantic, so complex, and so intractable that one person cannot handle it alone; it requires teamwork. I have discovered since I joined the studies of war crimes trials that there are many who feel the same. As I continue exploring this field, I look forward to working with present and future colleagues for the further advancement of war crimes studies.

What follows is a rather artless way of expressing my appreciation, but I would like to recognize the following friends and colleagues for sharing with me their research expertise in war crimes trials and related fields: Dean Aszkielowicz, Milinda Banerjee, Morten Bergsmo, Anja Bihler, Gideon Boas, Neil Boister, Timothy Brook, Steve Bullard, Chang Cai, Sharon Chamberlain, Wui Ling Cheah, Monique Cormier, Robert Cribb, Robert Cryer, Helen Durham, Sarah Finnin, Georgina Fitzpatrick, Cathy Hutton, Bing Bing Jia, Nina Jørgensen, Barak Kushner, Judge O-Gon Kwon, Konrad Lawson, Kerstin von Lingen, Suzannah Linton, Judge Liu Daqun, Mike Mochizuki, Jim Mornane, Narrelle Morris, Lisa Nguyen, Valentyna Polunina, Siegfried Ramler, Ann-Sophie Schoepfel, Lisette Schouten, Kirsten Sellars, Gerry Simpson, David Sissons (late), Beatrice Trefalt, Sandra Wilson, Daqing Yang, and Yi Ping. In addition to these individuals, I have come to know over the course of my research a number of students, historians, legal scholars, lawyers, and citizen activists who dedicate significant portions of their intellectual lives to researching war crimes and engaging in educational activities in Japan. I would like to acknowledge the following individuals in particular: Arai Shinichi, Awaya Kentarō, Hayashi Hirofumi, Higurashi Yoshinobu, Honda Katsuichi, Ikō Toshiya, Ishida Yūji, Kobayashi Motohiro, Kasahara Tokushi, Nakano Satoshi, Nakazato Nariaki, Philipp Osten, Saji Akito, Shiba Kensuke, Takeda Kayoko, Tanaka Yuki, Tawara Yoshifumi, Tōgō Kazuhiko, Udagawa Kōta, Ushimura Kei, Utsumi Aiko, Watanabe Haruki, Yamada Masayuki, Yoshida Yutaka, and Yoshimi Yoshiaki. I have had the privilege of meeting new friends and colleagues in China, too, while participating in the International Symposium on the Tokyo Trial on November 12–14, 2013, hosted by Shanghai Jiao Tong University and cohosted by Soochow University, and the Inauguration of the Fudan International Criminal Law Center and the Symposium on Old Evidence Collection and War Crimes Trials in Asia on March 5–6, 2014, hosted by the Fudan University Law School. I look forward to future opportunities to work with all of those who participated in these events. I would like to acknowledge the following individuals in particular: Chen Aiguo, Chen Haoran, Cheng Zhaoqi, Gao Hong, Jiang Fu, Ma Jing, Mei Xiaokan, Xiang Longwan, Yang Lijun, Zhang Lan, Zhao Yuhui, and Zhu Wenqi. Belatedly, I would like also to acknowledge the following individuals for providing me with invaluable guidance during my field research many years ago: A. M. Battacharjee, Sugata Bose, Partha Chatterjee, Rajeev Dhavan, Sudipta Kaviraj, Bart van Poelgeest, Ashis Nandy, Debi Prasad Pal, Prasanta Kumar Pal (late) and his brothers and sisters, Sumit Sarkar, and Peter Romijn.

I received invaluable technical support from Ryan Nakagawa at the College of Arts and Humanities, University of Hawai'i, and Todd Stock at CASBS, Stanford University. I would like to thank them once again for their generous assistance. I am grateful to Cambridge University Press for accepting this book manuscript and making its publication possible. I would like to express my special thanks to Lewis Bateman, Shaun Vigil, Shari Chappell, Saradha Chandrahasan, and Michael Toporek, as well as a whole crew that has taken charge of production and marketing. There are innumerable individuals whose full names I did not always learn but who nonetheless gave me tremendous help in researching archival materials at the following locations: the National Archives and Records Administration, College Park, MD; the National Archives of Japan, Tokyo; the National Diet Library, Tokyo; the National Institute for Defense Studies Center for Military History Archives, Tokyo; the National Archives, Kew, Richmond, Surrey, U.K.; the Imperial War Museums, London, U.K.; the National Archives of Australia, Melbourne; the Australian War Memorial, Canberra; and the Hoover Institution Library and Archives. My thanks also go to the Interlibrary Services staff at Hamilton Library at the University of Hawai'i and library staff at CASBS.

During the Abe Fellows' Retreat in January 2014, a number of fellow scholars generously offered me constructive feedback and words of encouragement concerning this book project. I would like to acknowledge the following individuals in particular: Araki Takashi, Thomas Berger, Paul Blustein, Joseph Coleman, Philip Cunningham, Linda Grove, Mary McDonnell, Melissa Melby, Nagase Nobuko, Leah Nylen, Nicole Restrick Levit, Fernando Rojas, and Tak Toda-Ozaki. I am also grateful to all Fellows and staff at CASBS for their moral support and friendship during my fellowship year in 2012–2013. I thank them all once again. The following individuals have been kind enough to invite me to, or join me at, various speaking engagements, panel sessions, and lectures pertaining to the studies of the Allied war crimes trials and related fields: Elizabeth Borgwardt, Lonny Carlile, Evan Dawley, Jon Van Dyke (late), Martin Dusinberre, Luke Franks, John O. Haley, Dorothy Hazama, Han Jung-Sun, Yoko Kanamatsu, Mark Levin, Tosh Minohara, Ti Ngo, Franziska Seraphim, Shibayama Futoshi, Seiji Shirane, Dan Sneider, Toyoda Maho, and Lori Watt. My acknowledgments would be incomplete if I fail to mention my dear students, colleagues, and staff at my present home institution at the University of Hawai'i (2008–present); my previous home institution at the Department of History at the University of Nevada, Las Vegas (2006–2008); the Edwin O. Reischauer Institute of Japanese Studies at Harvard University, where I spent one academic year as a postdoctoral Fellow (2005–2006); and the Department of History at the same university, where I was granted an opportunity in the same academic year to have a brief teaching stint. I am grateful to all of those who, without reservations, have extended to me at these campuses friendship, collegiality, and encouragement.

My final words of thanks go to Uncle Ryōji, my maternal great uncle, who presently lives in northern Japan within a few-hours ride of the bullet train from Tokyo. He took an interest in my book on the Tokyo Trial some years back and, despite his advanced age (at 94), he read through it and returned to me, by way of my mother, a short yet incisive comment in a handwritten letter. I am hoping that the Japanese translation of this book will make it to him by 2015 when he turns 101 years old.

Note to the Reader

All translations of Japanese-language sources into English are my own unless indicated otherwise. All Japanese personal and place names are transliterated in accordance with the standard style Romanization. But different types of Romanization may appear in historical sources, such as Tojo Hideki instead of Tōjō Hideki, Ohta Seiichi instead of Ōta Seiichi, Homma Masaharu instead of Honma Masaharu, Kato Rimpei instead of Katō Rinpei and *kempeitai* or *kempei tai* instead of *kenpeitai* (military police force). The former types of Romanization are retained in the case of direct quotes from sources. Most Chinese personal and place names are transliterated in accordance with the internationally accepted pinyin system of Romanization. Exceptions are made for those names that are better known with alternative Romanization, such as Chiang Kai-shek instead of Jiang Jieshi, and the Kwantung Army instead of Guandong Army. Japanese and Chinese names are given in the traditional manner throughout this book, that is, the family name precedes the personal name.

The Japanese word "*rikugunshō*" is commonly translated as the "War Ministry" in historical sources. But this book will use the "Army Ministry" as the translation of *rikugunshō* in light of the fact that this ministry was in charge of administrative matters of the army organizations only. For administration pertaining to the navy organizations, there was a navy counterpart, *kaigunshō* (the Navy Ministry). The English-language translation of words related to *rikugunshō*, such as its chief minister, vice minister, ministry officials, and documents issued by this ministry, will be similarly translated as army minister, vice minister of the army, army ministry officials, army ministry notifications, and so on, and *not* war minister, vice war minister, war ministry officials, war ministry notifications, and so on. Exceptions apply, however, in the case of direct quotes from sources where the terms, "War Ministry," "war minister," and so on, may be used.

Segments of Chapter 2 ("Prisoner-of-War Administration") and Chapter 6 ("The Navy High Command") in this book are incorporated in my forthcoming article, "International Military Tribunals at Tokyo, 1946–1948: Individual Responsibility for War Crimes," in Morten Bergsmo, Cheah Wui Ling, and Yi Ping, eds., *Historical Origins of International Criminal Law*, vol. 1 (New York: Torkel Opsahl Academic EPublisher, in press). A modified version of Chapter 4 ("In the Name of Asian Co-Prosperity") appears in Georgina Fitzpatrick, Timothy L. H. McCormack, and Narrelle Morris, eds., *Australia's War Crimes Trials, 1945–51* (Leiden, Netherlands: Brill, in press), under the title "Crimes against Asians in Command Responsibility Trials."

Introduction

"What kind of justice did the Tokyo War Crimes Tribunal render, victor's justice, or humanity's justice?" This question was posed to several dozen legal scholars, historians, military officers, and other professionals who gathered in November 2008 at the Melbourne Law School for a three-day international conference commemorating the sixtieth anniversary of the Judgment of the Tokyo Tribunal (hereafter referred to as the "Tokyo Judgment" or "the Judgment").[1] The Tokyo Tribunal – or the International Military Tribunal for the Far East (IMTFE) as it was officially known – was established by the Allied Powers as the eastern counterpart of the International Military Tribunal at Nuremberg. Vilified as victor's justice by its critics in Japan, or otherwise overshadowed by Nuremberg and largely forgotten by the rest of the world, the trial held before IMTFE (referred to as the "Tokyo Trial" hereafter) came to attain a new level of significance in the 1990s when the member states of the United Nations resuscitated the long-defunct international criminal justice system in order to have it play a central role in combating genocide, war crimes, crimes against humanity, and other international offenses occurring in the world today. Conference participants, this author included, ruminated over the striking parallel between past and present international criminal trials while also trying to find an answer to the foregoing question. It became increasingly clear, however, that even though a great deal of research has been done to date, our knowledge of the Tokyo Trial is still limited to reach a definitive assessment. The conference nonetheless served as a timely forum to consider afresh the significance of the trial and determine the future directions of war crimes studies.

Inspired partly by the Melbourne conference, this book explores a cross section of war crimes trials that the Allied Powers held in the Asia-Pacific region in the aftermath of World War II. This author's first book, *The Tokyo War Crimes Trial: The Pursuit of Justice in the Wake of World War II* (Totani 2008), focused on a single criminal proceeding, while this volume casts a wider net and explores several trials. There are two reasons for setting a broad analytical framework. First, despite its designation as the centerpiece of the Allied war crimes program in this region, the Tokyo Trial played a somewhat constricted role in documenting Japanese-perpetrated atrocities or, for that matter, in identifying and punishing the responsible individuals. This was due to the Allied Powers' intergovernmental policy at the highest level that following the example at Nuremberg, the Tokyo Tribunal should serve as a venue primarily to receive evidence concerning the Japanese planning and waging of aggressive war (the type of international offense then known as "crimes against peace") and secondarily to receive evidence of atrocities. In so planning, the Allied Powers aimed at securing a second ruling from an international tribunal – following Nuremberg, that is – that aggressive war constituted an international offense and that there was individual criminal

FIGURE 1. Suspected war criminals being photographed by an official photographer for the British Intelligence Branch, at Stanley Jail in British Hong Kong. © Imperial War Museums (SE 6510).

liability for those who planned and carried it out. As for the task of prosecuting and meting out punishment to those individuals who were responsible for the commission of atrocities, that was left mostly with fifty-one special war crimes courts that the Allied Powers concurrently operated across the formerly Japanese-occupied territories in the region (Figure 1). Given this type of division of labor, it is important that the latter trials come under scrutiny side by side with the Tokyo Trial.

Second, the Allied prosecutors at the Tokyo Trial did bring charges of atrocity against major Japanese war criminals notwithstanding the highest-level policy constraints. Their effort, however, met several obstacles, the notable

FIGURE 2. Exhumation of bodies of the Allied troops in the Singapore area. Capt. R. S. Ross of the Royal Army Medical Corps "examines a piece of cloth which looked as if it had been used to bandage the eyes." © Imperial War Museums (SE 6153).

ones being (1) chronic shortage of staff and resources when it came to investigating and collecting evidence of atrocities; (2) pressure to expedite the trial even if that meant shortening the time to present evidence on the charges of war crimes; and (3) postwar cover-up efforts by the Japanese government and military authorities. The former two obstacles stemmed from the structural constraints that are already pointed out, namely, the Allied Powers' intergovernmental policy that crimes against peace be the prosecutorial priority at Tokyo while charges related to atrocities be secondary. As for the third obstacle, it refers to attempts by the Japanese government authorities as well as individual army and navy units in theaters of war to destroy physical and documentary evidence of atrocities prior to the arrival of Allied war crimes investigators (Figure 2). It took months, if not years, for investigators to grasp the scope of Japanese obstructionism, uncover false stories, and track down war crimes suspects. The fruits of long and arduous investigations became available to the prosecutors at Tokyo only in part. The Tokyo Tribunal did make important legal and factual findings on charges of war crimes. If one is to have a full appreciation of the dynamic of the Far Eastern war crimes prosecution, however, it is vital to look beyond the Tokyo Trial and examine the Allied war crimes program as a whole.

As it explores the records of Allied war crimes trials with the foregoing theoretical considerations, this book pursues the following two specific research goals. First, it aims at bringing to light a large body of relatively underutilized oral and documentary history of World War II contained in the trial records. Sources in the trial records include affidavits, depositions, and sworn statements taken from the former members of the Japanese armed forces, Allied prisoners of war, civilian internees, and other noninterned civilians in Japanese-occupied territories; war crimes investigation reports produced by the Allied authorities as well as the postwar Government of Japan; Japanese army and navy military orders, directives, instructions, rules and regulations, and other operational and administrative records; and oral evidence taken directly from numerous Japanese and Allied witnesses in the courtroom, including from the accused themselves. This rich trove reveals firsthand accounts of the war as told in its immediate aftermath by the war victims, perpetrators of atrocities, eyewitnesses, and war crimes investigators. The analysis of these sources, in turn, will make it possible to produce a history of the Pacific War that pays close attention to the nexus of the operational aspects of the war and the occurrence of war crimes. There are innumerable publications to date that offer in-depth analyses of grand strategies, military operations, and military technologies.[2] Similarly, WWII-related publications are suffused with memoirs, diaries, and other personal accounts that elucidate personal experiences of combat missions, internment, Japanese military rule, resistance movements, and life at the home front. What this book will attempt is to focus on the intersection of these varied facets of the war in its endeavor to produce an interdisciplinary and integrative narrative history of the Pacific

War.[3] (There is controversy in the existing scholarship about the adequate definition and usage of the term, the Pacific War. This book will use the term when referring to the Far Eastern war that began with the Japanese invasion of American and British territories in the Pacific region on December 7, 1941. This Pacific War includes the war in the China-Burma-India (CBI) theater, but not necessarily the Sino-Japanese War that preceded the December 1941 attacks. When referring to the war that subsumes the Manchurian Incident of September 1931 and the Marco Polo Bridge Incident of July 1937, the term, the "Asia-Pacific War," will be used instead.)

Second, this book carries out a systematic analysis of the trial records with the view to bring out the Allied courts' findings on criminal liability of individuals accused of war crimes. This book is particularly interested in exploring cases against those persons who had held positions of authority in the wartime Government of Japan, the Imperial Japanese Army, and the Imperial Japanese Navy. How could a high-ranking government official or a military commander be held criminally accountable for occurrence of general and specific instances of atrocity? What methods of proof applied when the Allied prosecutors had little or no direct evidence of the accused's issuance of criminal orders or criminal knowledge? How did the doctrine of command responsibility, first introduced at the famous Yamashita Trial (1945) and subsequently applied broadly at other Allied courts, help the prosecution, the defense, and the judges resolve these knotty issues? By posing these questions, this book sheds light on the Allied courts' complex, and at times contradictory, findings on theories of criminal orders and knowledge, the Japanese system of command and control, organizational versus individual responsibility, and guilt or innocence of accused persons. A close inquiry into the jurisprudential legacy of the Allied war crimes trials will enable one to begin developing useful conceptual tools with which to tackle issues of Japanese institutional and individual responsibility for WWII-era mass atrocities.

This book is not the first to make an inquiry into the Allied Pacific-area war crimes trials. While publications are many, Philip Piccigallo's (1979) *The Japanese on Trial: Allied War Crimes Operations in the East, 1945–1951* deserves recognition as a pioneer English-language monograph that offers a comprehensive account of the Allied war crimes trials in this region. *The Japanese on Trial* continues to be key reference material to this day. But one shortcoming is that, in producing this monograph, Piccigallo had to rely heavily on secondary sources such as newspapers and law reports in lieu of the trial records themselves, due to limited access to the latter type of sources. From the standpoint of empirical research using the actual trial records, a landmark publication from early years is A. Frank Reel's (1949) *The Case of General Yamashita*. Reel analyzes the first of the war crimes trials that the U.S. Army held in the Asia-Pacific region. The accused was Gen. Yamashita Tomoyuki, the last general to command the Japanese armed forces in the occupied Philippines. (This case will be explored in Chapter 1.) Reel served as a member of the defense team representing the accused. Utilizing both his firsthand knowledge of the trial and the official transcripts of the court proceedings, he produced a well-grounded, analytically rigorous account of the Yamashita Trial. A pathbreaking piece that has advanced the study of war crimes trials in recent years is David Cohen's (1999) "Beyond Nuremberg: Individual Responsibility for War Crimes." This article is the first to make a systematic inquiry into the jurisprudential legacy of post-WWII Allied war crimes trials, with an emphasis on the Far Eastern cases. Informed by Cohen's unique expertise in law and history, this article offers a comparative study of the Nuremberg Trials, the Tokyo Trial, and the Yamashita Trial, thereby shedding new light on complex judicial opinions of the Allied courts regarding individual criminal liability of state and military leaders for WWII-era war crimes.[4]

The study of post-WWII Pacific-area war crimes trials has expanded dramatically in the last decade, especially in the field of law in English-language academia. This reflects growing interest among legal scholars today in researching historical trials to determine their significance in the subsequent development of international criminal law. One drawback of the recent research trend is that it has the tendency to fall within the confines of discipline-specific, nation-centric frameworks. It can also be weak in narrative integrity in the case of joint authorship. Two of the latest developments in the field help illustrate the point.

Hong Kong's War Crimes Trials, edited by Suzannah Linton (2013), is arguably the first in English-language scholarship to offer a comprehensive assessment of a series of Allied war crimes trials held at one location and to do so in an interdisciplinary manner. But a close look at the volume reveals that its contents are actually quite segmented due to multiple authors writing on discrete and often highly technical matters. No particular overarching theme exists to connect individual chapters, other than the mere fact that all the cases analyzed for the volume come from the U.K. Hong Kong trials. The interdisciplinary appearance of the volume is skin deep, too, as most contributors are scholars of law with limited background in the history of modern Asia or limited proficiency in relevant Asian languages. These features of the volume narrow the intended readership to legal scholars and practicing lawyers. *Australia's War Crimes Trials, 1945–51*, edited by Georgina Fitzpatrick, Timothy L. H. McCormack, and Narrelle Morris (in press), is comparable to *Hong Kong's War Crimes Trials*, but this volume deals with the entirety of the Australian war crimes trials instead of a trial group at one location only. This publication is designed as a thematic volume to accompany Narrelle Morris and Timothy L. H. McCormack (eds.), *The Australian War Crimes Trials Law Reports Series, 1945–51* (forthcoming). Owing to multiple years of teamwork among the core members, this volume has a far more comprehensive and better-integrated coverage of key themes as well as the right balancing of law and history. It is worth noting that some volume contributors have proficiency in the Japanese language, about a third of the volume contributors are historians with varying expertise in the Pacific War, and the remainder are scholars of law. That said, the fact remains that the nation-centric approach is the defining feature of the volume. This has the effect of placing Australia's national war crimes agenda in the front and center while sidelining the inter-Allied dimensions of the Australian war crimes program (such as Australia's close working relationships with American, British, Chinese, Dutch, and French authorities in war crimes policy formation, investigation, and trials) or overlooking legal, historical, and jurisprudential issues that grow out of war crimes trials beyond national boundaries (e.g., the emergence of case-law literature on command responsibility across the region).

The nation-by-nation approach is commonplace in Japan, too, but the scope of analysis, disciplinary emphasis, and narrative goals are different because of the far-richer tradition of war crimes studies on which the Japanese-language scholarship stands. Iwakawa Takashi's (1995) *Kotō no tsuchi to narutomo: BC-kyū senpan saiban* (Even if to become the soil of an isolated island: Class BC war crimes trials) and Hayashi Hirofumi's (2005) *BC-kyū senpan saiban* (Class BC war crimes trials) are two of the many foundational texts that define the Japanese-language scholarship on the Far Eastern war crimes trials today. These authors have analyzed the trial records by country as a practical way to organize vast archival materials at their disposal and to tell the complex history of the Allied war crimes program in a manner accessible to general readers. Hayashi Hirofumi's (1998) *Sabakareta sensō hanzai: Igirisu no tai-Nichi senpan saiban* (War crimes tried: The British war crimes trials against the Japanese) and Nagai Hitoshi's (2010) *Firipin to tai-Nichi senpan saiban, 1945–1953* (The Philippines and war crimes trials against the Japanese, 1945–1953) similarly adopt the nation-based approach as the main organizing principle in reconstructing the history of British and Philippine national war crimes programs, respectively. The Yokohama Bar Association's (2004) *Hōtei no seijōki: BC-kyū senpan Yokohama saiban no kiroku* (The Stars and Stripes in the courtroom: Records of Class BC war crimes trials at Yokohama) is somewhat of an anomaly, as its primary emphasis is not so much reconstructing the history of the Allied war crimes trials as probing thematically into an array of legal questions that arose from the U.S. Yokohama trials. The methodology adopted in *Hōtei no seijōki* is comparable to *Hong Kong's War Crimes Trials* and *The Australian War Crimes Trials, 1945–1951*, but one notable difference is the use of a single narrative voice in place of multiple authors speaking separately on topics of varied disciplines and focuses.

The Allied Powers formally assumed the power to try Far Eastern war criminals by signing the Instrument of Surrender on *USS Missouri* at Tokyo Bay on September 2, 1945. The surrender document required Japan to "accept the provisions set forth in the declaration issued by the Heads of the Governments of the United States, China and Great Britain on 26 July 1945 at Potsdam, and subsequently adhered to by the Union of Soviet Socialist Republics," and "to carry out the provisions of the Potsdam Declaration in good faith, and to issue whatever orders and take whatever actions may be required . . . for the purpose of giving effect to that Declaration."[5] The said declaration included the following provision:

We [The Allied Powers] do not intend that the Japanese shall be enslaved as a race or destroyed as a nation, but stern justice shall be meted out to all war criminals, including those who have visited cruelties upon our prisoners.[6]

Pursuant to this part of the surrender terms, nine nations that were represented at the surrender ceremony (Australia, Britain, Canada, France, the Netherlands, New Zealand, the Republic of China, the Soviet Union, and the United States) and two Asian nations that were about to gain independence (India and the Philippines) jointly established the IMTFE in the capital city of Japan.[7] Each of eleven participating nations supplied a judge and a prosecution team, and the Australian member, Sir William F. Webb, served as presiding judge of the Tribunal. The United States took on the additional burden of supplying court staff and about two dozen American attorneys to work with the Japanese defense counsel. A single joint trial against twenty-eight major Japanese war criminals (subsequently reduced to twenty-five due to two deaths and one case of mental unfitness to stand trial) was held between May 1946 and November 1948.

While less known, the occupation authorities established two other international military tribunals in Tokyo in late 1948 in order to hear additional cases against major Japanese war criminals still in their custody. The accused were Lt. Gen. Tamura Hiroshi and Adm. Toyoda Soemu, former high-ranking army and navy officers, respectively. The Legal Section of the occupation authorities originally planned to hold three additional trials subsequent to the Tokyo Trial, whose accused were to be (1) Tamura, (2) Toyoda, and (3) several members of the Japanese war cabinet during the Pacific War. The Legal Section ultimately decided against the joint trial of cabinet members, however, as Col. Alva Carpenter, chief of the Legal Section, concluded that the Tokyo Judgment failed to set out compelling precedents to justify further prosecution of the highest-ranking civilian members of the Japanese government for war crimes. Only two international proceedings thus followed the Tokyo Trial, viz., the Tamura Trial and the Toyoda Trial.[8] Incidentally, the international character of the two trials was significantly reduced because no Allied Powers other than Australia, China, and the United States took an interest in participating in further international criminal proceedings. James S. L. Yang of the Chinese Mission, Tokyo, served in the seven-member tribunal for the Tamura Trial, and Brig. John W. O'Brien of the Australian army served as presiding judge of the seven-member tribunal for the Toyoda Trial. The rest were Americans.[9]

In addition to the three international tribunals at Tokyo, seven Allied nations contemporaneously set up other special war crimes courts across the former theaters of war. According to data collected by the Ministry of Legal

Affairs of the Japanese government in the post trial period (1950s–1970s), a total of 2,244 trials were carried out against 5,700 individuals at special national courts that were located at 51 separate locations across the Asia-Pacific region.[10] These trials are generally referred to as Class BC war crimes trials for the reason that the Allied courts received evidence of wartime atrocity in the main (known then as "Class BC" offenses in the Far Eastern war crimes program) but rarely the evidence of crimes against peace (known then as "Class A" offenses).[11]

The breakdown of the Allied war crimes trials in this theater (based on the Japanese government data) is as follows: 456 American trials against 1,453 war crimes suspects at Guam, Kwajalein, Manila, Shanghai, and Yokohama[12]; 330 British trials against 978 suspects in formerly Japanese-occupied British colonies in Southeast Asia, namely, Alor Setar, Hong Kong, Jesselton (present-day Kota Kinabalu), Johore Baru, Kuala Lumpur, Labuan, Penang, Rangoon (present-day Yangon), Singapore, and Taiping[13]; 294 Australian trials against 949 suspects in several different Australian-controlled territories in the South Pacific as well as recovered British and Dutch territories, namely, Ambon, Darwin, Hong Kong, Labuan, Manus, Morotai, Rabaul, Singapore, and Wewak[14]; 448 Dutch trials against 1,038 suspects at 12 separate locations in formerly Japanese-occupied Dutch East Indies, namely, Ambon, Balikpapan, Banjarmasin, Batavia (present-day Jakarta), Hollandia (present-day Jayapura), Kupang, Makassar, Manado, Medan, Morotai, Pontianak, and Tanjung Pinang; 39 French trials against 230 suspects at Saigon; 72 Philippine trials against 169 suspects at Manila[15]; and 605 trials against 883 suspects by the Republic of China at 10 different locations, namely, Beijing, Nanjing, Guangdong, Hankou, Jinan, Shanghai, Shenyang, Taipei, Taiyuan, and Xuzhou.[16] Of these, the total number of convicted was 4,403 and the acquitted, 1,018. As many as 984 of the convicted war criminals were sentenced to death, although the actual number of the executed fell short of 934 because some cases were not confirmed or, alternatively, remitted to lesser penalties. There were also cases of escape and suicide.[17] All these trials were completed within the six-and-a-half years of the Allied occupation of Japan, between September 1945 and April 1952.[18]

The Soviet Union took part in the Tokyo Trial in its capacity as an Allied Power, having its nationals represented at both the bench and the bar. That aside, the Soviet government carried out its own criminal proceedings against the Japanese suspected war criminals in the Russian Far East. But no comprehensive data about these trials are available to date. Approximately 3,000 Japanese are believed to have been tried in closed session on charges principally of espionage or counterrevolutionary acts in violation of Soviet criminal law. A total of 2,689 convicted war criminals were eventually repatriated to Japan.[19] The only public trial that the Soviet authorities held was a week-long special military trial at Khabarovsk in December 1949. Based principally on confessions taken from the accused, the Khabarovsk Tribunal heard a joint case against twelve Japanese army officers on charges of developing, experimenting, and deploying bacteriological weapons. The Soviet authorities released the findings of the Khabarovsk Trial in its immediate aftermath to advocate the trial of Hirohito, the emperor of Japan. (Emperor Hirohito was not named as a war criminal due to an Allied joint policy decision, made back in April 1946, not to take any action against him.[20]) The Soviet initiative caused much consternation among other Allied governments, which preferred to adhere to the existing policy rather than opening up a new case. Nothing resulted from the Soviet initiative after all, however, as the Soviet Union dropped it out of diplomatic conversations by the end of 1950. No further talk of the trial of Hirohito occurred among the Allied Powers for the remainder of the occupation period.[21]

Quite apart from the Allied war crimes program, Communist Chinese are known to have undertaken their own proceedings against Japanese war criminals. Commonly referred to in the Japanese-language historical literature as "People's Trials" (*jinmin saiban*), some sorts of summary proceedings were carried out against suspected war criminals at the end of hostilities. These trials resulted in varying penalties in the case of convictions, including summary execution. Comprehensive data are not available to date. The only sources that shed light on the occurrence of these proceedings are retrospective accounts by repatriated Japanese accused.[22] Shortly after the founding of the People's Republic of China, the Communist Chinese initiated a new line of criminal proceedings against additional suspected war criminals that were transferred from the Soviet Union. A total of three cases involving forty-five accused were held at Shenyang and Taiyuan. The accused at these trials confessed to their own guilt and, in return, they received guilty verdicts and relatively lenient sentences.[23]

Of more than 2,240 trials held in this region, this book explores 14 only: the trials of Tamura and Toyoda and twelve others – mostly command-responsibility trials – that were held by American, Australian, British, and Philippine authorities. Several factors have influenced this author's decision to focus on a relatively small number of trials of high-ranking individuals and to do so with the Anglo-American proceedings only. First, research to date has revealed that the verbatim records of court proceedings are readily accessible with respect to the Anglo-American war crimes trials but not in the case of Chinese, Dutch, and French trials. At present, the latter nations' records are not open to public in their entirety due to various archival restrictions that apply at repositories of countries concerned. One could, for sure, make use of the National Archives of Japan, where the trial records collected by the Japanese Ministry of Legal Affairs in the early postwar decades are deposited. The Japanese collection is an incomplete set, however, and varying archival restrictions apply. (See the Conclusion for related discussion.) The limited access to the court records, in short, has made the Chinese, Dutch, and French trials a far less attractive option than the Anglo-American trials in pursuit of the research for this book. This author's lack of proficiency in Chinese, Dutch, and French has served as another disincentive for attempting a comparative study involving the Chinese, Dutch, and French trials. Second, this author has found the American, Australian, British, and Philippine trials to be highly comparable because regulations governing the court proceedings are almost identical. The British and American regulations appear to have served as models for all Anglo-American war crimes proceedings in this region. The same did not apply to the Chinese, Dutch, and French trials, where regulations governing the court proceedings were built on their respective nations' criminal-law practices.[24] The dissimilarity of court rules between the common-law nations on the one hand and the rest of the Allied Powers on the other has made it a complicated task for this author to carry out a comparative study that cuts across all seven national trial series.

As for limiting the number of case studies, there, too, are a few factors that influenced this author's thinking. First, the sheer volume of the trial records has made it impracticable to closely scrutinize every single trial. One case file can contain from a mere few pages to tens of thousands of pages of court record, and the sum total of the records of entire Allied war crimes trials could be much more than a million pages. In addition to court records, one also needs to explore voluminous investigative, administrative, and diplomatic papers concerning the trials. The unwieldy size of primary sources requires that a researcher determine key cases and delimit the scope of analysis so as to make his or her research practicable. Second, the Allied authorities usually planned the trials of those individuals in positions of authority as "capstone" cases, building on legal and factual findings already made at earlier trials where subordinates of the prospective accused had been prosecuted. These cases, in this regard, allow one to have an appreciation of the trial *series* as much as separate, individual instances of war crimes prosecution. In other words, focusing on the trials of high-ranking individuals allows one to see the larger picture of the Allied war crimes program as well as its elements. There were some exceptions to this norm, of course, where the trials of high-ranking political and military leaders of Japan *spearheaded* war crimes prosecutions rather than serving as capstones of a series of trials. The trials of Gen. Yamashita Tomoyuki and Lt. Gen. Honma Masaharu at Manila are representative examples (October 1945–February 1946). These trials were convened at the start of the American war crimes program and not at the end of a series of cases involving lower-ranking war crimes suspects. This book will examine a representative range of the spearheading type and the capstone type in order to see how the timing may have impacted the quality of justice rendered inside the courtroom. (The Yamashita Trial and the Honma Trial will be explored in Chapter 1.)

Third, and finally, this author has reviewed synopses of all Allied war crimes trials held in the Asia-Pacific region in order not only to identify the trials of high-ranking individuals but also to single out such cases that, on their face, were of great political import in the context of Asian decolonization.[25] The Ichikawa Trial (March–April 1946), the very first war crimes trial that the British authorities held at Rangoon is one such example. This trial served as a critical venue for showcasing "British justice" to the people of recovered territory and also for publicizing the heroism and sacrifices of the people of Burma. The Nishimura Trial (March–April 1947), held at British Singapore, is another example where the British authorities similarly showcased justice in the recovered colonial territory. (Both trials are explored in Chapter 5.) Trials such as these raise an interesting question about the historical role of war crimes trials not only in meting out stern punishment to individual war criminals but also in reestablishing the moral authority of colonial governments vis-à-vis Asian nations in the process of decolonization. (For a path-breaking study of postwar political realignment in the context of Asian decolonization, see Konrad M. Lawson's [2012] "Wartime Atrocities and the Politics of Treason in the Ruins of the Japanese Empire, 1936–1953." Lawson sheds light on the politics of retribution in postwar British Asia, China, and the Philippines, including the treason trials held against wartime collaborators of the Japanese.)

The remaining pages in the Introduction will clarify the basic institutional framework of Anglo-American war crimes proceedings by exploring the applicable rules and regulations.

MECHANICS OF THE TRIALS: AN OVERVIEW

Most trials analyzed in this book fell under the jurisdiction of respective hosting nations, and to that extent, they constituted national war crimes trials. However, they also took on certain characteristics as international – or to be more accurate, inter-Allied – events. For one thing, a significant part of pre-trial war crimes investigations was carried out multilaterally as well as nationally. The United Nations War Crimes Commission (UNWCC, 1942–1948) served in the early years as the hub of inter-Allied information-sharing and policy debates relative to war crimes prosecutions in both Europe and the Pacific.[26] In the aftermath of Japan's surrender, various liaison organizations began operating on the ground to link up the national-level war crimes investigations and facilitate inter-Allied evidence collection and apprehension of war crimes suspects. The Legal Section at the General Headquarters of the Supreme Commander for the Allied Powers (GHQ SCAP), based at Tokyo, Japan, functioned in part as one such liaison agency. It hosted five Allied divisions – Australian, British, Canadian, Chinese, and Dutch – so that the American members of the Legal Section could work with their Allied counterparts to coordinate war crimes investigations, transfers of suspects, and trials of war criminals as well as general information sharing.[27] Similarly, the War Crimes Coordinating Section at the Headquarters of the Allied Land Forces, South East Asia (HQ ALFSEA), based at first at Ceylon and subsequently at Singapore, dispatched seventeen war crimes investigation teams to Bangkok,

Batavia, Formosa (Taiwan), Hong Kong, Kuala Lumpur, Labuan, Medan, Penang, Rangoon, Saigon, and Shanghai as well as Tokyo. These teams are likely to have coordinated with their Allied counterparts working at the same locations.[28]

The overall policies on apprehension and trial of war criminals in the Asia-Pacific region were determined by the Far Eastern Commission (FEC, 1945–1952), the highest-level multinational policymaking body that came into being by U.S. initiative after the war. Representatives of the Allied Powers met on February 26, 1946, to begin "to formulate the policies, principles, and standards in conformity with which the fulfillment by Japan of its obligations under the Terms of Surrender may be accomplished."[29] Britain, China, and the United States (three powers that had jointly issued the Potsdam Declaration back in July 1945) and the Soviet Union (which adhered to Potsdam upon declaration of war on Japan, on August 8, 1945) maintained veto power. This arrangement displeased other member states and especially Australia, which quite legitimately considered itself "a major power so far as the Pacific and Japan were concerned."[30] That said, the Far Eastern Commission was a product of the U.S. administration's general policy on international cooperation in the post conflict peace settlement in the Far East. As such, it functioned to a significant degree on the principle of multilateralism on a wide range of issues, including matters pertaining to the Allied war crimes program in this region.[31]

The principle of inter-Allied cooperation was carried into the courtroom, too, by way of regulations allowing broad jurisdiction of the court, mixed courts, and mixed prosecution teams, or alternatively, accommodation as trial observers of officers representing nations other than the host country. These arrangements made it possible for individual Allied nations to have their own nationals represented when the trials at issue were of great national importance. By illustration, the "Royal Warrant: Regulations for the Trial of War Criminals (A.O. 81/ 1945)" of the British government (the "Royal Warrant" hereafter), dated June 14, 1945, stipulated that the convening officer of the trials – Lord Louis Mountbatten of HQ ALFSEA in this case – "may, in a case where he considers it desirable so to do, appoint as a member of the Court but not as President, *one or more officers of an Allied Force* serving under his command or placed at his disposal for the purpose, provided that the number of such officers so appointed shall not comprise more than half the members of the Court, excluding the President."[32] In addition, supplementary detailed guidelines titled "Allied Land Forces, South East Asia War Crimes Instruction No. 1 (2nd Edition)," dated April 1, 1946, set out that the U.K. military courts would have jurisdiction over any person "charged with any crime against nationals of any of the Dominions or Allied nations."[33]

A regulation to the same effect was included in "War Crimes: An Act to Provide for the Trial and Punishment of War Criminals (No. 48 of 1945)," dated October 16, 1945, and passed by the Australian parliament. More commonly known as the Australian War Crimes Act, the Australian regulations were modeled on the British Royal Warrant and the two resembled each other. Paragraph 5 (4) of the act read that "the Governor-General or any person authorized under this Act to convene military courts may appoint as a member (other than the President) of the court one or more officers of the naval, military or air forces *of any Power allied or associated with His Majesty in any war*, who are serving under his command or placed at his disposal for the purpose."[34]

The military commissions established by the U.S. Army at Manila and Yokohama similarly allowed the formation of mixed courts. "Regulations Governing the Trial of War Criminals," dated September 24, 1945, applied to the Yamashita Trial (the first U.S. war crimes trial to be held in this theater). It read that the commissions "may include, among others, *international military commissions consisting of representatives of several nations or of each nation concerned*, appointed to try cases involving offenses against *two (2) or more nations*."[35] (The actual military commission for the Yamashita Trial consisted of American members only.) This provision was carried over to revised regulations, dated December 5, 1945. The revised version also read that the Supreme Commander for the Allied Powers (SCAP) would serve as the convening authority in place of the commander-in-chief of the U.S. Army Forces (as had been stipulated in the original version of the regulations). Gen. Douglas MacArthur served in both capacities in any event,[36] but this particular modification had the effect of emphasizing the inter-Allied nature of the rest of war crimes trials to be held by the U.S. Army at Manila (1946–1947) and Yokohama (1946–1949). (To distinguish the two versions of American regulations, the original one will be referred to as "Pacific September Regulations" hereafter, and the revised one as "SCAP Regulations."[37])

The trials hosted by the U.S. Army at Shanghai (1946) and those by the U.S. Navy at Guam and Kwajalein (1945–1949), meanwhile, were strictly American events. The governing regulations allowed for Americans-only convening authority, jurisdiction, and composition of military commissions.[38] The Philippine war crimes trials at Manila (1947–1949) did not include any stipulations for mixed courts either, although the regulations issued by President Manuel Roxas as Executive Order No. 68 (July 29, 1947, hereafter referred to as the "Philippine Regulations") were otherwise the almost exact duplicate of SCAP Regulations.[39]

The Anglo-American war crimes authorities provided the accused with various fair-trial protections under their respective regulations, in apparent compliance with the Geneva Convention Relative to the Treatment of Prisoners of War, dated July 27, 1929 (also called "the Geneva Prisoner-of-War Convention" hereafter). The Geneva Prisoner-of-War Convention set out several rules for ensuring procedural fairness in the case of a detaining power opening a judicial proceeding against a prisoner of war.[40] The ones that the Anglo-American authorities incorporated in their trial regulations can be summarized by the following four points: (1) public hearing in a fair, expeditious manner[41]; (2) provision, when practical, of a legally qualified individual on the court as a law member or a judge advocate, who would make decisions on legal questions arising from the court proceedings[42]; (3) requirement of approval of all verdicts and sentences by the confirming authority, which was vested with the power "to approve, mitigate, remit in whole or in part, commute, suspend, reduce or otherwise alter the sentence imposed, or (without prejudice to accused) remand the case for rehearing before a new military commission"[43]; and (4) the accused's right to counsel.[44] The same principles generally applied to the Tamura Trial and the Toyoda Trial, too.[45]

Of these fair-trial protections, Japanese accused and Japanese defense lawyers often commented favorably on the rights to public hearing and counsel – the kinds of rights that had often been denied to criminal suspects under the prewar and wartime Japanese justice systems. For instance, Abe Tarō, a former army sergeant who volunteered to work as a defense lawyer at the U.S. Yokohama trials and the U.K. Singapore trials, stated at a post-trial interview in 1962, conducted by an investigative officer from the Japanese Ministry of Legal Affairs, that "it isn't right for the victors to try the defeated people at war trials," but agreed that the Anglo-American criminal trials had a better institutional safeguard to ensure procedural fairness. He thus commented:

For the sake of publicity perhaps, but they [the victors] took up expenses, held the trials in public, and made efforts to carry them out fairly, formalistic or otherwise. Would Japan have done the same or not? The Dark Chamber [*ankoku saiban*] instead, probably.[46]

Fujiiwa Mutsurō, another former defense lawyer at the U.S. Yokohama trials and the U.K. Singapore trials, similarly observed that "the idea of holding war trials itself is Anglo-American" and that if the host nation had been Japan or its wartime ally, Germany, the whole affair would have been simply disposed of "by the administrative fiat."[47]

Regulations governing the four Anglo-American trial series nonetheless suffered certain shortcomings. One of them concerned court interpretation. It was already a tremendous challenge at the Tokyo Trial as to how to overcome language barriers between English and Japanese so as to ensure fairness of court proceedings. The Charter of the Tokyo Tribunal required that "the trial and related proceedings shall be conducted in English and in the language of the accused,"[48] but it immediately became clear to the judges that this rule could not be fulfilled in any satisfactory manner. "Translations cannot be made from the one language into the other with the speed and certainty which can be attained in translating one Western speech into another," the Tokyo Judgment read. "Literal translation from Japanese into English or the reverse is often impossible." What *was* possible was "nothing but a paraphrase." But then, paraphrasing in place of word-to-word interpretation could not be satisfactory because "experts in both languages will often differ as to the *correct paraphrase*."[49] The Tribunal set up a Language Arbitration Board to resolve these problems, but as Kayoko Takeda's (2010) *Interpreting the Tokyo War Crimes Tribunal* shows, court interpretation remained a major challenge for the duration of the Tokyo Trial.

The language situations with respect to concurrent Allied war crimes trials in the Asia-Pacific region were somewhat simpler but no less problematic. Regulations governing the Anglo-American trials did not promise full bilingual proceedings and instead indicated that English was to be the only official court language. They recognized the accused's entitlement to interpretation, but there was no rule requiring complete or accurate interpretation of the entire court proceedings into the native language of the accused. For instance, the U.K. regulations stipulated little more than that an accused would have access to "services of an interpreter to enable him and his Counsel to understand the charges upon which he is to be arraigned and the rules of procedure etc., and to enable him to prepare his defence."[50] As for the American and Philippine regulations, an accused was entitled "to have the *substance* of the charges and specifications, the proceedings and any documentary evidence translated when he is unable otherwise to understand them."[51] The same regulation applied to the Tamura Trial and the Toyoda Trial.

The lack of a guarantee of full court interpretation may not have handicapped the accused greatly if they were fluent in English. For instance, Lt. Gen. Honma Masaharu and Maj. Gen. Tamura Hiroshi (analyzed in Chapters 1 and 2 in this book, respectively) were highly proficient in English, and they both chose to testify in English. (In the case of Honma, he had the questions put to him translated in Japanese from the midpoint of his testimony, but he continued to provide all his answers in English.) Lt. Gen. Kuroda Shigenori and Adm. Toyoda Soemu (analyzed in Chapters 1 and 6 in this book, respectively) were similarly fluent in English although both chose to testify in Japanese. (In the case of the Kuroda Trial, the court eliminated English-to-Japanese court interpretation in light of the accused's ability to comprehend spoken English.) For accused persons to have a high level of command in English was more a rarity than the norm at most trials, however, and one can reasonably assume that limited safeguards of adequate court interpretation undercut the fairness of proceedings in many cases.

It should be said that supporting full-fledged bilingual court proceedings was difficult for the Anglo-American authorities given their limited resources, especially court interpreters. What was more, they had to grapple with the same kinds of difficulty in court interpretation as the ones faced at the Tokyo Trial. "Rules of Procedure and Outline of Procedure for Trials of Accused War Criminals" (dated February 5, 1946), applicable to the U.S. war crimes courts, helps illustrate the challenges the Anglo-American authorities were confronted with when prosecuting non-English-speaking suspects. "Interpreting between oriental and occidental language is not comparable to coding and decoding cipher messages," article 6 of the rules read, "but requires a distressing amount of circumlocution and rearrangement of thought." The rules urged all participants in war crimes trials to forego oratory skills and instead take a pragmatic attitude when examining Japanese witnesses. The rules specifically advised that when speaking through an interpreter, counsel ought to "use short, simple questions as free from artifice as if examining a small child." It was advised further that certain types of questions were to be avoided, since they would lead to "misunderstanding and futile discussions."[52]

The rules gave the following list of the types of questions *not* to be put to Japanese witnesses:

a. Long questions. (Impossible for the interpreter and witness to remember.)
b. Complicated questions. (Dependent clauses confuse both interpreter and witness.)
c. Conditional questions. (Usually beyond comprehension of an oriental witness.)
d. Sarcastic questions. (Usually depend on untranslatable emphasis or play on words; waste [of] effort.)
e. Negative questions. ("You did not see them, did you?" Answer will be, "Yes, I did not see them" or "No, I saw them.")
f. Questions hinging on the precise meaning of a single word. (The interpreter picks from several choices that English word which he believes will most closely express his understanding of the witness. To question the witness about the English word is futile.)[53]

While reading somewhat comical and at times sounding condescending, the above list illuminates what kinds of practical difficulty the Allied authorities faced when trying to carry out trials in a "fair and expeditious" manner.

Another notable feature of the Anglo-American war crimes trials that casts a shadow over the general principle of fair-trial protection concerns the applicable rules of evidence. All American, Australian, British, and Philippine war crimes courts in this theater were vested with a broad power to determine admissibility of evidentiary materials in a manner that was prohibited at their own military courts. For instance, a pertinent provision in the Royal Warrant and the Australian War Crimes Act read as follows:

At any hearing before a Military Court convened under these Regulations the Court may take into consideration any oral statement or any document appearing on the face of it to be authentic, provided the statement or document appears to the Court to be of assistance in proving or disproving the charge, *notwithstanding that such statement or document would not be admissible as evidence in proceedings before a Field General Court-Martial.*[54]

The Australian and British military authorities, in other words, adopted a policy to allow looser rules of evidence at the trials of Japanese war criminals than those applicable at court-martial proceedings of their own soldiers. This violated the 1929 Geneva Prisoner-of-War Convention, and the Australian and British authorities must have known it. Article 63 of the convention required the trial of a prisoner of war be held "only by the same courts and *according to the same procedure as in the case of persons belonging to the armed forces of the detaining Power.*"[55]

Specific types of evidentiary material that the Royal Warrant deemed admissible were the following: (1) "secondary evidence of statement" in case of the death of a witness or unavailability of the witness to testify in court; (2) "any document purporting to have been signed or issued officially by any member of any Allied or enemy forces or by any official or agency of any Allied, neutral or enemy government . . . without proof or signature thereof"; (3) facts stated in reports by the International Committee of the Red Cross or any such persons in medical profession acting as *homme de confiance*; (4) facts stated in "any depositions or any record of any Military Court of Inquiry or (any Summary) of any examination made by any officer detailed for the purpose by any military authority"; (5) facts stated in "any diary, letter or other document appearing to contain information relating to the charge"; and (6) a copy of a document or other secondary evidence in case the original document either cannot be produced or "cannot be produced without undue delay."[56]

Rules applicable to the American and Philippine military commissions were substantially the same as those included in the Australian and British regulations, although phrased differently. A pertinent provision in Pacific September Regulations read: "The commission shall admit such evidence as in its opinion would be of assistance in proving or disproving the charge, or such as in the commission's opinion would have probative value in the mind of a reasonable man."[57] The same was repeated in SCAP Regulations, and a sentence was added that read, "The commission shall apply the rules of evidence and pleading set forth herein with the greatest liberality to achieve expeditious procedure."[58] The Philippine Regulations repeated the provision in SCAP Regulations verbatim, including the foregoing additional sentence, so did the regulations applicable to the trials of Tamura and Toyoda.[59]

Specific types of admissible evidence at the American and Philippine trials, too, were substantially the same as the ones already indicated in the Royal Warrant.[60] One notable difference is that SCAP Regulations contained the following additional rule:

All purported confessions or statements of the accused shall be admissible without prior proof that they were voluntarily given, it being for the commission to determine only the truth or falsity of such confessions or statements.[61]

This controversial provision must have come under criticism, however, as it was amended a year later to put limitations on the admissibility of confessions and statements. The second clause reading "it being for the commission to determine only the truth or falsity of such confessions or statements" was deleted, and instead replaced by a sentence that read, "If it is shown that such confession or statement was procured by means which the commission believes to have been of such character that they may have caused the accused to make a false statement, the commission may strike out or disregard any such portion thereof as was so procured."[62] This amendment is reflected in the Philippine Regulations.[63]

It should be pointed out on this occasion that comparable broad rules of evidence apply to present-day international criminal courts and that the post-WWII Allied war crimes courts, in this respect, are not necessarily a deviation.[64] The Anglo-American authorities could still face criticisms, however, as they adopted the foregoing rules of evidence with awareness of contradicting their own military courts' standard procedures and the 1929 Geneva Prisoner-of-War Convention. Why did they make this type of exception with the rules of evidence? There can be various possible explanations, but the main one would be general concerns among the Allied authorities that stringent rules of evidence could unduly prolong or otherwise complicate war crimes prosecutions.

The opinion of Louis Mountbatten, expressed during the planning for the British War crimes trials in late 1945, helps illustrate the point. In his capacity as commander-in-chief of ALFSEA and convening authority of U.K. war crimes trials in Southeast Asia, he articulated the goals of the British war crimes prosecution in a note, dated November 20, 1945. "War criminals must be tried in accordance with the best traditions of British justice," he wrote, but he also made the following point:

This does not mean tactics such as have been adopted by defending counsel at trials in Europe, which tactics aim at sabotaging a fair and quick trial.[65]

In so writing, Mountbatten had in mind the Belsen Trial (the trial of Josef Kramer and 44 others, September–November 1945) that had just come to an end in British-occupied Germany.[66] This trial turned out to be a far more protracted process than anticipated due to the formidable defense led by Maj. Thomas Winwood, defense counsel representing the chief accused, Josef Kramer, also known as the Beast of Belsen. A skilled orator and a deft trial lawyer, Winwood argued for the accused that "so far as concentration camps were concerned, it was the British who invented them, in South Africa during the Boer War," and that as for medical experimentation on live humans at Auschwitz, "some of the most famous doctors appear to have taken part in them, and we have no knowledge of what their value to humanity is." A comparable situation was developing at the on-going Yamashita Trial in Asia, too, where the defense team challenged the legitimacy of the American military commission and delayed the court proceedings. In light of these troubling situations at the initial Allied war crimes trials in both theaters, Mountbatten feared that the Japanese accused – especially those who had been in positions of authority during the war – might use the courtroom as "a platform from which they could boast of their policy and their actions, and would ensure them world-wide publicity, splendid Psychological Warfare for the Japanese." This was a prospect Mountbatten wished to avoid.[67]

With the foregoing considerations in mind, he brought to the attention of his subordinate officers a distinct feature of the rules of evidence contained in the Royal Warrant. He wrote:

These rules are in general those applied in the Field General Courts Martial, but they are specially modified in the Army Order in the interests of speed.[68]

He made frank admission of the fact that the modifications "constitute a considerable departure from our accepted standards of justice." But he justified the changes by stating that "the trial of war criminals was not in the ordinary run of justice; it was an endeavour to establish before the world that disregard of the laws of war did not pay." He instructed his subordinate officers to narrowly focus on (1) "the identification of the accused" and (2) "evidence that the accused committed, or aided, permitted or ordered the commission of a war crime" to achieve expeditious trial and punishment of war criminals.[69]

To sum up, all Anglo-American authorities provided the accused with various basic fair-trial protections, but they also made certain exceptions in the interests of efficiency and expediency. Should these exceptions be understood as having undercut the integrity of the Anglo-American war crimes trials? One can readily answer in the affirmative. However, it is also possible to say that written rules alone did not define the quality of justice at the Anglo-American war crimes trials. As the studies of individual cases in this book will show, various other factors also influenced the fairness of individual trials, such as (1) timing of the trials; (2) competence of the prosecution, the defense, and the judges; (3) competence of other court staff and especially court interpreters; (4) types of evidence introduced during the court proceedings; and, above all, (5) politics that defined the context of individual trials. Three landmark cases at the U.S. and Philippine war crimes trials at Manila – to which we now turn – will showcase a representative range of uneven manners in which the courts applied the principle of fair-trial protection at the actual court proceedings.

I

Justice at Manila[1]

"I stand here today with the same clear conscience as on the first day of my arraignment," read the prepared statement by the accused, "and I swear before my Creator and everything sacred to me that I am innocent of the charges made against me."[2] This day – December 7, 1945 – marked the end of the trial of Gen. Yamashita Tomoyuki, formerly commander-in-chief of the 14th Area Army (originally the 14th Army, but regrouped to form the 14th Area Army in July 1944), which fought the losing battles against American forces in the Japanese-occupied Philippine Islands between October 1944 and September 1945. Yamashita stood accused on the charge that he "unlawfully disregarded and failed to discharge his duty as commander to control the operations of the members of his command, permitting them to commit brutal atrocities and other high crimes against people of the United States and of its allies and dependencies, particularly the Philippines."[3] After hearing the last plea of innocence by the accused, the five-member U.S. military commission presided over by Maj. Gen. Russell B. Reynolds delivered the decision. It found Yamashita guilty and handed down the sentence of death by hanging. Execution was carried out on February 23, 1946, upon approval of the verdict and the sentence by Gen. Douglas MacArthur of the U.S. Army. This action was taken a little short of three weeks after the U.S. Supreme Court denied the defense application for leave to file petition for writs of habeas corpus and prohibition, as well as the defense application for leave to file petition for certiorari to review the order of the Supreme Court of the Commonwealth of the Philippines denying petition for the same. Two justices dissented.[4]

The U.S. Army hosted 86 additional war crimes trials at Manila between January 1946 and April 1947, signaling to the Philippine public the American authorities' continued commitment to war crimes prosecution in connection with the Japanese conduct of war in violation of laws and customs of war in the Philippine theater.[5] The post-Yamashita criminal proceedings were spearheaded by the trial of Lt. Gen. Honma Masaharu, formerly commander of the 14th Army that carried out the initial invasion and military occupation of the Philippine Islands starting in December 1941. Modeled on the Yamashita precedent, one of the two charges against him read that the accused "did unlawfully disregard and fail to discharge his duties . . . to control the operations of the members of his command, permitting them to commit brutal atrocities and other high crimes against the people of the United States of America, its allies and dependencies, particularly the Philippines."[6] The five-member military commission, with Maj. Gen. Leo Donovan serving as presiding officer and concurrently as law member,[7] found Honma guilty and sentenced him to be shot to death by musketry.[8] Execution was carried out on April 3, 1946, a little short of two months after the U.S. Supreme Court denied the defense application for leave to file petition for writs of habeas corpus and prohibition and for writ of certiorari petition, two justices again dissenting.[9]

The newly independent Republic of the Philippines subsequently inherited the American prosecutorial work and hosted a series of 72 trials at the same city, Manila, between August 1947 and December 1949. The centerpiece of the Philippine trials was the case against Lt. Gen. Kuroda Shigenori, yet another army officer who commanded the 14th Army (and later the 14th Area Army) – between May 1943 and September 1944. The charge against Kuroda read that the accused "did . . . unlawfully disregard and fail to discharge his duties . . . to control the operations of members of his command, permitting them to commit brutal atrocities and other high crimes against noncombatant civilians and prisoners of the Imperial Japanese Forces in violation of the laws and customs of war."[10] The five-member Philippine military commission in which Brig. Gen. Calixto Duque served as presiding judge pronounced at the end of the trial the verdict of guilty but spared the accused of the death penalty. It instead handed down life in prison. A petition for writ of prohibition that the defense had filed with the Philippine Supreme Court at the start of the trial was already denied,[11] but the Philippine government at a later date granted a presidential pardon to Kuroda. The same government also gave general amnesty separately to other convicted Japanese war criminals in the Philippine war crimes program. Kuroda returned home a free man and died in Japan in 1954.

What are we to make of these trials at which the American and Philippine authorities prosecuted three of the four successive commanding generals of the Japanese army that invaded and occupied the Philippines? (Gen. Tanaka Shizuichi, who led the 14th Army between Honma's and Kuroda's tenure, was not subject to war crimes investigation or trial, as he committed suicide at the end of the war.[12]) What was the extent of their power, authority, and duty as commanding general of the Japanese ground forces in the Philippines? Does the similarity of charges mean the application of a uniform theory of command responsibility, or were there some differences among them? What were the legal and factual findings that supported the guilty verdicts and varying sentences? Above all, how did the Yamashita precedent shape the prosecution's cases, the defense arguments, and the courts' findings at the Honma and Kuroda Trials?

As important as these questions are for our understanding of the history of post-WWII command-responsibility trials in this region, it is not easy to give them definitive answers. The assessment of the Yamashita Trial alone poses uniquely complex problems to begin with. As early as February 4, 1946, the judicial conduct of the U.S. military commission relative to the case against Yamashita came under scathing criticism of Justices Frank Murphy and Wiley B. Rutledge, two justices who dissented from the majority opinion of the U.S. Supreme Court. In their detailed, point-by-point discussion of the U.S. military commission's handling of the case, the two argued that the petitioner's fundamental right to due process as guaranteed under the U.S. Constitution was violated and that, moreover, the accused was convicted of a crime unknown in the history of the U.S. justice system.

The troubling legacy of the Yamashita Trial as elucidated by the two dissenting justices received immediate coverage in major national newspapers in the United States. "Gen. Yamashita Loses Appeal," the headline of a front-page article in the *Washington Post* on February 5, 1946, read. "But Justices Rutledge and Murphy, in two ringing dissents, branded the trial unfair and contrary to traditional American justice."[13] The *New York Times* similarly carried a front-page article the same day, the headlines reading, "Yamashita Appeal Denied, Six to Two, by Supreme Court," and, "Both Dissents Are Sharp – Murphy and Rutledge Declare That Guarantees under Our Law Have Been Violated."[14] The reporting on the contrasting judicial opinions of the majority and two dissenting justices, in this manner, raised awareness of the American public in days immediately following the trial about the nature of military justice that MacArthur's army was meting out to Far Eastern war criminals.[15] The Yamashita Trial came under further public scrutiny with the publication of A. Frank Reel's (1949) *The Case of General Yamashita*, a 324–page retrospective account of the controversial trial.[16] A number of studies were made in subsequent decades to assess the legacy of the Yamashita Trial, especially its implications to the issues of command responsibility that arose from war crimes committed by American military personnel during the Vietnam War. New studies similarly illuminated questionable legal and factual grounds on which Yamashita's guilty verdict stood.[17] Yet paradoxically, the trial of Yamashita gained stature as a landmark case and came to influence other command-responsibility trials of its time and beyond. Conflicting assessments of the Yamashita Trial have not been reconciled to this day.

Assessing the Honma and Kuroda Trials is also a difficult task, but not because they, too, provoked controversy. The problem has been rather a dearth of empirical studies and our limited knowledge of these trials resulting therefrom. Books and articles on the Yamashita Trial abound, but there are few publications that are devoted singly to assessing the Honma Trial or the Kuroda Trial. The Honma Trial certainly prompted Justices Murphy and Rutledge to produce dissenting opinions at the U.S. Supreme Court in the immediate aftermath (February 11, 1946), but they amounted to no more than restatements of criticisms they had already raised with respect to the Yamashita Trial, in a much-abridged form.[18] As for the Kuroda Trial, contemporaneous reporting in Japan and the Philippines may have kept the public abreast of the court proceedings and their outcomes, but the trial itself failed to generate interest in systematic analyses of legal doctrinal issues or the court's factual findings.[19] Unlike the case of Yamashita, the two trials barely made any mark in the case-law literature.

Recent progress in studies of the Philippine war crimes trials nevertheless suggests that imbalances in the existing scholarship are being addressed. Nagai Hitoshi's (2010) *Firipin to tai-Nichi senpan saiban, 1945–1953* (The Philippines and war crimes trials against the Japanese, 1945–1953) offers a comprehensive account of the institutional and political history of Philippine involvement in war crimes prosecutions, covering the period from the time of initial war crimes investigations and policy formation by the U.S. authorities to the release of convicted war criminals by the Philippine government. Sharon Chamberlain's (2010) "Justice and Reconciliation: Postwar Philippine Trials of Japanese War Criminals in History and Memory" takes a step further, delving into the transcripts of Philippine court proceedings to bring to light an array of procedural, legal, and factual questions that arose from the Philippine Manila trials. Taking its cue from these cutting-edge research pieces, this chapter will attempt a comparative study of the three high-profile trials in order to take a fresh look at the Yamashita precedent and its repercussions in the Far Eastern war crimes trials.

This chapter begins by reconstructing the history of the Japanese invasion of the Philippines on the basis of evidentiary materials presented at the three cases. It will then turn to the record of the Yamashita Trial and the U.S. Supreme Court opinions in order to determine the nature of the Yamashita precedent. An analysis of the records of the Honma Trial and the Kuroda Trial will ensue to elucidate differences and similarities on the prosecution's cases, the defense arguments, and the courts' findings.

WAR IN THE PHILIPPINES

"Now, using the map which is on the board, will you outline the essential elements of your campaign in the Philippines?"[20] Prompted during direct examination by Maj. Gen. John Skeen of his defense counsel, Honma began recounting in gripping detail the invasion of the Philippines that he carried out some four years ago. While his military campaigns were ultimately successful, Honma appeared to relive in the courtroom the frustration, bewilderment, and helplessness that he had experienced at various turns of event – botched landings, protracted battles, high casualties among his troops, and the enemy forces' unpredictable decisions on surrender.

The war in the Philippines began with the deployment of Japanese airpower, followed by the ground forces' land invasion of Luzon that Honma directed first from his headquarters in colonial Taiwan and subsequently on the island of Luzon itself.[21] "During all my campaign in the Philippines, I had three critical moments," Honma said as he set out in fluent English[22] the outline of his war story, "and this was number one."[23] By "this" he was referring to the landing of the main forces on December 22, 1941, at Lingayen Bay, west of central Luzon, coordinated with the landings of three detachments at north and southeastern approaches to Luzon Island.[24] Quite unexpectedly, transport boats at Lingayen got caught in the sand when taking the first party of infantry troops to the shore, leaving the rest stranded on board the mother ship. The fumbled landing turned out to be a comparatively minor glitch but this incident rattled Honma, who worried at the time that "if we were counterattacked we were almost helpless."[25] He managed to free the transport ships after the loss of one day and directed his troops to push southward as planned.

Honma's forces made a swift advance notwithstanding enemy's stiff resistance and reached the outskirts of Manila by January 1, 1942. This was made possible thanks largely to the 48th Division under his command, one of the only two divisions in the entire Imperial Japanese Army in those years with ample motor vehicle equipment, Honma explained.[26] Within days, however, this division was taken out of the Philippines by the order of the Imperial General Headquarters at Tokyo so that it could be utilized in the concurrent invasion of Java. Honma was given as a substitute an ill-trained, ill-equipped brigade that was originally meant for garrison duty and not for combat.[27] By the time of the Japanese descent on the Philippine capital, MacArthur, commanding the U.S. Army Forces Far East (USAFFE), had declared Manila an open city and withdrawn his troops to Bataan Peninsula wherein to continue the defense of the Philippines.[28] Based on this information, Honma headed off to Bataan with the main forces to engage the enemy troops while leaving the administrative matters of the newly occupied capital city with his deputy chief of staff, Lt. Gen. Hayashi Yoshihide.[29] Hayashi remained in Manila thereafter to serve concurrently as director of the Military Administration Section of the 14th Army.

The ensuing Battle of Bataan proved to be an arduous, long-drawn-out battle for Honma, where "the second one" of the three critical moments[30] in his Philippine campaign occurred. His forces were confronted with formidable resistance by the enemy. The 14th Army sustained heavy casualties due to "very powerful and accurate" artillery fire[31]; lost two battalions that were sent behind the enemy lines but that went missing "without a trace"[32]; and nearly suffered the complete loss of a third battalion, which was dispatched to locate the missing ones. According to the testimony of Col. Horiguchi Shūsuke, formerly chief of the Medical Section of the 14th Army, the total Japanese casualties in connection with the first Bataan campaign amounted to 2,700 deaths, 4,050 injured, and 15,500 sick cases suffering mainly from dysentery and malaria.[33]

Instead of having victory in sight, Honma by mid-February was compelled to withdraw his troops.[34] There was a rumor of the death of Honma at the time – "committal of suicide"[35] – on account his underperformance to that point in the Bataan campaign. "I could not ask for reinforcements from Tokyo," Honma explained to the court, since "it isn't considered in the Japanese Army for the Commander-in-Chief to ask for reinforcements; he must do with what he was given."[36] Honma further indicated that he was under tremendous pressure those days because "by the time – at the end of the first battle of Bataan, all other theaters of war – I mean, that is, the Dutch East Indies and the Malayan campaign – those campaigns came to an end while my campaign was delayed, and I knew that Tokyo was displeased with the tardiness of the progress of my campaign in the Philippines."[37] By this statement, he was referring to achievements of fellow army officers, Lt. Gen. Imamura Hitoshi of the 16th Army and Lt. Gen. Yamashita Tomoyuki of the 25th Army, who secured Batavia and Singapore, respectively, in spite of resistance from numerically superior enemy forces. Field Marshal Terauchi Hisaichi of the Southern Army – to which the 14th Army was then subordinate – soon decided to provide Honma with an additional division and three detachments, so that the latter could reorganize his forces and prepare for another offensive.[38] It was now scheduled to resume on April 3, 1942.

The second Bataan campaign paid its dividend rather quickly. Honma was anticipating a month-long battle at the least,[39] but Maj. Gen. Edward P. King, who commanded the forces defending Bataan, communicated on April 9 his readiness to surrender his troops. A total of about 70,000 American and Filipino soldiers – in place of 40,000 as had previously been estimated by his intelligence officer, so Honma informed the court – came into Japanese custody.[40] War being still in progress, Honma had these prisoners of war evacuated to the rear to an internment camp being prepared up north at Capas in Tarlac Province, in accordance with plans developed prior to the commencement of the second Bataan campaign.[41] (The infamous Bataan Death March occurred during the transfer of surrendered soldiers, as discussed shortly.) Honma then refocused on the remaining enemy forces under the command of Lt. Gen. Jonathan Mayhew Wainwright – reportedly acting as successor of MacArthur (who had by then left the Philippines to take up a new command in Australia) – and his headquarters on the small, tadpole-shaped island of Corregidor south of the Bataan Peninsula. At the same time, Honma ordered the Nagano Detachment, one of additional detachments that joined him in the second Bataan operation, to go to the Visaya District[42] – the island group that consisted of Bohol, Cebu, Leyte, Negros, Panay, and Samar – to engage the USAFFE in the southern region. As for Mindanao, another USAFFE-controlled island, a detachment under command of Imamura of the 16th Army in the Dutch East Indies was freed up to take charge.[43]

The "third critical moment" came at Corregidor in early May when Honma ordered his forces on Bataan to put into effect the planned military invasion.

This was originally scheduled to begin on April 25 but was postponed to May 5 due to delays in the arrival of landing boats and an outbreak of malaria.[44] Certain missteps were made at the start of the nighttime invasion on Day 1, exposing the Japanese landing troops to enemy torpedoes and heavy fire from artillery and machine guns. No news of progress was reaching his headquarters, and Honma "did not have a wink" that particular night.[45] The following morning, staff officers told him of the botched landing operation and the loss of thirty-one boats – more than half of the boats at Honma's disposal. Recalling his state of mind on that occasion, Honma told the court: "I thought, 'My God! I have failed miserably in this assault.'"[46] Agony was not to last too long, however. Wainwright initiated a meeting with Honma the same day to indicate his readiness to turn over his troops at the four fortified islands in Manila Bay, including Corregidor.[47] This Honma refused to accept, on grounds that his demand was surrender of the entirety of USAFFE in the Philippine Islands, not part of it. He ordered his men to resume attacks on Corregidor. On the following morning, Honma received definitive information that "General Wainwright came to the decision that he will surrender all of his troops under his command."[48]

With the Battle of Bataan and the Battle of Corregidor finally over, Honma on May 9 moved his headquarters from Lamao, southeastern Bataan, to the capital city, Manila,[49] to begin transitioning from being an operational commander to an occupation commander. The primary task for him was to establish a working relationship with the existing political authorities of occupied Philippines so as to consolidate Japan's control over the island nation, and at the same time to continue with unfinished pacification campaigns at pockets of resistance in the outlying areas.[50] The Philippines would be used thereafter for rear duties in support of the Japanese war effort elsewhere, serving as a major hub for transportation of Japanese troops, labor, raw materials, and other resources needed at diverse locations in Japanese-occupied territories throughout Asia and the Pacific region. Meanwhile, concrete steps would have to be taken in immediate weeks to ameliorate the conditions of prisoner-of-war internment at Camp O'Donnell. Honma knew based on reports from subordinate officers that the American and Philippine prisoners of war there were dying at an alarming rate.

At the time of surrender on April 9, defenders of Bataan were already in dire physical state, many suffering from malnutrition, exhaustion, malaria, injuries, and various other ailments resulting from these conditions. Some 200 or so officers transported in motor vehicles aside,[51] all surrendered soldiers were made to join waves of marchers to get to the location of internment, under the supervision of Japanese sentries. They were first routed to the "concentration area" or the "assembly point" at Balanga on the eastern coast of central Bataan,[52] and continued marching northward – passing through Orani, Hermosa, and Lubao – until they reached San Fernando, Panpanga. Thereupon they were made to take a four-hour train ride in overcrowded boxcars to Capas, Tarlac Province. After the final stretch of marching, they were taken in at Camp O'Donnell. Many died during the marches. Summary execution is believed to have taken place, too, of a group of Filipino officers and noncommissioned officers – between 350 and 400 of them – when being evacuated through the Bagac-Balanga route (cutting across Bataan Peninsula from west to east), on about April 12. The only two eyewitnesses and survivors of the massacre – Capt. Pedro L. Felix, of the Inspector General Service of the Philippine Army, and Maj. Eduardo T. Vargas, of the Engineer Corps of the Philippine Army – took the witness stand to offer oral evidence.[53]

The attrition rate of the Bataan Death Marchers remained very high at Camp O'Donnell. Inadequacy in food supplies, water, medicine, medical facilities, shelters, and sanitation facilities was commonplace during the marches, and they persisted at the camp with no improvement. Harsh treatment personally promoted by the first camp commander, Capt. Tsuneyoshi Yoshio, added to the hardship of prisoners of war. Nicknamed "Little Napoleon,"[54] Tsuneyoshi was remembered for having greeted every new group of prisoners of war with a speech emphasizing that they were mere "captives" and not "prisoners of war" because his government "did not acknowledge the existence of such a thing as prisoners of war." The prisoners were permitted to live "only through the kindness of the Emperor," Tusneyoshi purportedly told them.[55] According to the record kept by Col. Charles S. Lawrence, Maj. Gen. King's staff officer, the total number of surrendered persons at Bataan was "approximately 74,800," about 10,500 of which being Americans. The total number of Americans who reached Camp O'Donnell was 9,271 Americans and "the difference [of about 1,229] disappeared on the march out of Bataan." As for the remainder of surrendered individuals, "between 46,000 and 48,000 Filipinos reached O'Donnell," thus leaving between 16,300 and 18,300 unaccounted for.[56] The death rate at O'Donnell diminished beginning in the middle of June 1942 when Capt. Tsuneyoshi was replaced by a Col. Itō, a much more capable appointee, who brought about a measure of improvement to internment conditions.[57] Overcrowding was alleviated, too, as some prisoners of war were relocated elsewhere while some others were released on parole. Nevertheless, the substandard level of prisoner-of-war internment persisted in occupied Philippines for the duration of the war.

The likelihood of Honma's success as occupation commander, meanwhile, did not appear promising, as his occupation forces failed to retain some of the top political leaders of the preexisting Phlilippine government. President Manuel L. Quezon had gone into exile before the Japanese capture of the capital city. On the eve of his departure, Quezon appointed as presidential delegate Justice Jose Abad Santos Sr., chief justice of the Philippine Supreme Court and concurrently acting secretary of Finance, Agriculture, and Commerce.[58] Santos was unable to discharge his duty in full, however, as the Japanese expeditionary force in Cebu, the Kawaguchi Detachment, stumbled upon him on April 9, 1942, and took him in its custody. A month later on May 7, Judge Santos was executed by a firing squad reportedly for his refusal to co-operate with the Japanese occupation authorities.[59] The record of the Honma Trial indicates that execution was carried out at the discretion of a Lt. Col. Kawakami, director general of military administration in the Cebu area. He apparently took the time neither to inform nor to seek approval from his military superiors regarding the execution.[60]

In the absence of President Quezon, the Military Administration Section of the 14th Army set up a caretaker government – the Executive Commission – with a known Filipino nationalist, Jorge B. Vargas, as its chairman.[61] Honma appears to have developed a rapport with some members of the Executive Commission, and he particularly came to know "Mr. Vargas and Doctor [Jose] Laurel rather intimately," as Honma himself attested during the trial.[62] Whatever personal friendship may have evolved between him and some of the Philippine nationalist leaders, it was cut short when Honma was suddenly recalled to Japan and left the Philippines, on August 5, 1942.

The 14th Army had a rocky start with the Philippine general public, too. The aerial bombing of Manila in late December 1941 preceding the entry of the Japanese ground troops – which occurred despite the fact that MacArthur had already declared it an open city – could be construed as anything but a friendly gesture. As soon as Japanese troops set foot in Manila, the Military Administration Section of the 14th Army made clear to city residents the policy of zero tolerance of popular resistance against Japanese rule. A set of warnings from the Japanese military authorities adorned the front page of the local newspaper, *The Tribune* (Manila), in the morning edition on January 5, 1942. The top column of the front page (which the prosecution presented in evidence during the trial of Honma) read in full as follows:

WARNING
1. Anyone who inflicts, or attempts to inflict, an injury upon Japanese soldiers or individuals shall be shot to death;
2. If the assailant, or attempted assailant, can not [*sic*] be found, we will hold ten influential persons as hostages who live in and about the streets of municipalities where the event happened;
3. Officials and influential persons shall pass this warning on to your citizens and villages as soon as possible and should prevent these crimes before they happen on your own responsibilities;
4. The Filipinos should understand our real intentions and should work together with us to maintain public peace and order in the Philippines.
COMMANDER OF JAPANESE LANDING FORCES[63]

Honma attested to having no personal knowledge of the release of these warnings and suspected that the Bureau of Publicity of the 14th Army's Military Administration Section issued them without his approval, as "it was one of the bad habits of the Japanese troops that they use the name of the commander-in-chief when they wanted to put some importance on a statement of that kind."[64] That said, Honma could agree that "some kind of warning must have been needed at that time in Manila," even though the actual warnings in the *Tribune* were worded "much stronger than I might have wished."[65]

The residents of Manila soon learned that these warnings were not to be made light of, as the *kenpeitai*, or the Japanese military police force, were ready to give teeth to the 14th Army's zero-tolerance policy on Philippine resistance.[66] The *kenpeitai* set up its headquarters at Fort Santiago, a historic prison facility from the Spanish colonial era,[67] and used the prison compound as the main detention and interrogation center for those individuals whom it deemed threats to the Japanese war effort and military administration. Records of three Manila trials show that throughout Japanese military occupation, detainees were kept in shockingly filthy cells with little or no proper medical attention, food, water, or other minimum daily necessities for survival. Moreover, *kenpeitai* officers took the detainees out of the cells from time to time in order to extract confessions of the crimes they may or may not have committed. The *kenpeitai's* standard torture methods were applied freely on such occasions: "water treatment,"[68] electrocution, suspension from the ceiling by the wrists, cigarette-induced burning, knee splits, kicking, and beating with hands, clubs, whips, or other instruments. Some detainees at Fort Santiago were later released broken in body and spirit, while some others never returned alive. As an increasing number of public figures, family members and friends, and other personal acquaintances were taken behind the walls of Fort Santiago, the Philippine public came to regard it as the symbol of the fickle and vicious character of Japanese military justice.[69]

Among victims of the *kenpeitai* terror regime in early months were eight members of the Chinese consulate general at Manila: Clarence Kwangson Young, consul general representing the Republic of China, and seven other officials at the consulate. They fell under *kenpeitai* arrest on January 5, 1942, and were temporarily incarcerated at Fort Santiago in late March and early April on suspicions of their having connections with financial support by expatriate Chinese to the Chiang Kai-shek Government and the anti-Japanese boycott movement.[70] They were taken out of the fort on April 17, 1942, and summarily executed at North Cemetery, Santa Cruz, Manila.[71] This particular episode of killing was carried out without publicity (and apparently without Honma's knowledge[72]). The *kenpeitai* authorities refused to provide the wives of consulate members with information concerning the whereabouts of their husbands. The wives were only able to determine conclusively the fate of their spouses after the passage of nearly three and a half years. On June 14, 1945, they witnessed at North Cemetery the exhumation of the bodies of their late husbands, and identified the remains and personal affects.[73]

Other non-Filipino civilians who had taken up residence in the Philippine Islands were not out of harm's way either. Predominantly Americans but also including some non-American nationals, they were rounded up by the invading Japanese ground troops and placed at hastily established internment camps, initially at Camp John Hay in Baguio (central Luzon), the University of Santo Tomas (in the capital city), and Camp Bacolod (Negros Island), and later at other locations as well. The Japanese occupation authorities at first assumed no institutional responsibility whatsoever for the provision of food, clothing, medical supplies, or any other equipment necessary for the sustenance of camp life. Consequently, internees were left with few options but to rely on individual purchases, aid from Filipino friends, and Red Cross supplies. According to Honma's court testimony, the Foreign Relations Section in the 14th Army's Military Administration Section theoretically took charge of all matters concerning the handling of civilian internees. But he also understood from his subordinates' reporting those days that "they [internees] wanted to live in their own way under their own expense."[74] This state of affairs with varying degrees of improvement and aggravation persisted at civilian internment camps for the duration of the Japanese occupation of the Philippines.

With Honma's career as occupation commander cut short in early August 1942, the burden of improving the image of Japanese military authorities in the eyes of the Philippine public on the one hand and of strengthening the Japanese ties with the Philippine political leaders on the other fell on the shoulders of Tanaka Shizuichi, Honma's successor as commanding general of the 14th Army. But guerrilla activism was on the rise from the start of Tanaka's tenure, and he "had hardly any time to warm his seat [*seki no atatamaru hima mo nai*] as he himself went about leading tours of inspection and directing military expeditions," according to *Senshi sōsho: 2. Hitō kōryaku sakusen* (War history series: Vol. 2. The invasion of the Philippine Islands), the Japanese official history of the Philippine invasion.[75] Even so, Tanaka could not bring guerrillas under control due to diminishing fighting capabilities of the 14th Army. The prolongation of the Guadalcanal campaign required him to give up some of his best combat units and equipment for redeployment in the South Pacific. This, in turn, cut into the 14th Army's ability to tackle continuing security problems in occupied Philippine islands. Guerrilla fighters, for their part, were emboldened by the prospect of the U.S. armed forces' eventual return and by the simmering popular discontent and resistance against Japanese rule.[76]

Kuroda took up where Tanaka left off shortly after the assumption of command of the 14th Army, in May 1943. He resumed military campaigns against guerrillas in the outlying areas of Cebu, Mindanao, Negros, and Panay as well as within the island of Luzon. Pacification campaigns during Kuroda's tenure peaked in the months of July, August, and September 1943, when he "wanted to suppress guerrilla activities as early as possible and prior to the grant of Philippine independence."[77] By this statement (made during his court testimony), Kuroda was referring to Philippine "independence" that took effect in October 1943 in accordance with the promise previously made by Prime

Minister Tōjō Hideki on behalf of the Government of Japan. In its immediate aftermath, Kuroda ordered suspension of antiguerrilla military expeditions in the Luzon and Mindanao areas for three months, and also in the Visaya District in the months of January and February 1944. Its purpose was to let guerrilla fighters have a window of opportunity to surrender and to be reintegrated into the newly independent Philippines. "However, not all guerrillas came down during those months," Kuroda explained to the court, and "after the lapse of 3 months, it was again left to the discretion of the respective units to conduct punitive expeditions against guerrillas." The antiguerrilla pacification campaigns gained a greater sense of urgency in the spring of 1944 when the U.S. counterinvasion was turning into an imminent reality. In April, Field Marshal Terauchi of the Southern Army ordered Kuroda to carry out military expedition against guerrillas in Guimaras Island, in the south off Panay, "where the combined Japanese fleet was expected to anchor."[78] When Kuroda's tenure as occupation commander in the Philippines ended in September 1944, he left the island nation in a much more volatile condition than it was during his predecessors' tenures.

Yamashita arrived in Manila on October 9, 1944, to assume his new assignment as commander of the 14th Area Army. The Philippine Islands by then were a hotbed of guerrilla activism. "Among the Filipinos, there were considerable anti-Japanese feelings that existed,"[79] Yamashita told the court when testifying in his behalf, and "after the American landings on Leyte, the guerrilla actions increased more and more, and it became so that they interfered with military operations at quite a few places."[80] There was also a foiled attempt in the middle of November 1944 to blow up Yamashita's headquarters at Fort McKinley, south of Manila, by setting up dynamite in the basement of the officer recreation room.[81] This episode pointed to audacity of the Philippine resistance movement not seen in the early years of Japanese military occupation. The central Japanese government attempted to reverse the trend by cultivating pro-Japanese Filipinos by way of Gen. Artemio Ricarte, an old-time Philippine nationalist who had been in self-imposed exile in Japan to oppose American colonial rule in the Philippines. Ricarte formed a patriotic league, Makapili, purportedly to promote "a spiritual movement" of Philippine patriots and to work with the Japanese.[82] It was already a lost cause, however, in a country where the vast majority of the population stood firmly against the continuation of Japanese military rule.

What was left for Yamashita in those circumstances was to prepare the 14th Area Army for a protracted war at two fronts: one against guerrillas throughout the Philippine Islands, and the other against the U.S. assault forces. With respect to the former, he issued stern orders to his subordinates that guerrilla fighters be suppressed. He testified: "On October 11 of last year [1944], at a conference with the chief of staff, we discussed this matter, and I said that armed guerrillas, those guerrillas carrying weapons, must be suppressed by means of military action."[83] Meanwhile, he focused his attention on the defense of the Philippines in preparation for the impending landing of the U.S. assault forces.

The American invasion of Leyte began within nine days of Yamashita's arrival at Manila, allowing him no time to make a tour of inspection to familiarize himself with the position of vast military forces under his command. Field Marshal Terauchi ordered Yamashita to counter the enemy at Leyte although the original war plan was to focus on the defense of Luzon Island. Leyte was soon lost, necessitating Yamashita to gather up the troops at his disposal to prepare afresh for defensive war back in Luzon.[84] This he carried out with great difficulty. The forces under his command by then were a disorganized and ill-equipped lot. To complicate the matter, poor communication caused by incessant attacks from superior American aerial and ground forces, and from guerrilla fighters, made it impossible for Yamashita to stay in close contact with subordinate units. "When the Americans landed on Leyte, Mindoro and Luzon the situation came to a point where our communications were completely disrupted," so Yamashita informed the court.[85] He withdrew his headquarters from Fort McKinley to Baguio in the northern part of Luzon in order to concentrate the troops in the mountainous areas as a delaying tactic. Numerous instances of atrocity occurred over the course of the troop withdrawal and during the defensive battles for the remainder of the war in the Philippines. This included the Rape of Manila in February 1945, an instance of mass atrocity that took place in the capital city in the immediate weeks after the U.S. land invasion.

Yamashita came out of his hideout in Baguio on September 3, 1945, to formally surrender. In a month, he was taken before the U.S. military commission at Manila to be charged as a war criminal. The trial promptly began.[86]

THE YAMASHITA PRECEDENT

Yamashita faced a single charge of "willful disregard and failure to discharge his duty" to take control of troops under his command, thereby "permitting" his subordinates to commit war crimes. A total of 123 particulars enumerated concrete instances of atrocity for which he was held accountable. Each particular generally fell under one of the following categories of offense, in accordance with locations of the crimes and types of victims involved: (1) burning, pillage, looting and destruction of property, and killing, massacre, rape, attempted rape,[87] mutilation, and other forms of mistreatment of the civilian population over the course of the Battle of Manila; (2) destruction of property, killing, massacre, and extermination of the civilian population at locations other than Manila between October 1944 and May 1945[88]; (3) *kenpeitai*-related atrocities, including "brutal mistreatment, starvation, torture, wounding, maiming, burning alive, massacre and killing, without cause or trial, of more than 4000 unarmed noncombatant civilians" at Fort Santiago in February 1945[89]; (4) general mistreatment and specific instances of atrocity against civilian internees[90]; and (5) general mistreatment and specific instances of atrocity against prisoners of war.[91]

The prosecution undertook to document instances of atrocity stipulated in the particulars of offense by calling to the stand 254 witnesses – mainly civilian victims of atrocity, former prisoners of war, and former members of the Japanese military – and by presenting 401 court exhibits, including affidavits, sworn statements, sketches, diagrams, photographs, maps, films, Allied Translation and Interpreter Section (ATIS) documents containing confiscated Japanese army records in translation, records of Japanese courts-martial, certified documents describing the Japanese army command in the Philippines, a U.S. Army judge advocate general's report on war crimes investigations, and diplomatic records. The goal of the prosecution's case was to show "a wide pattern of widespread, notorious, repeated, constant atrocities of the most violent character" and to argue that given the notoriety and recurrence of war crimes, "they must have been known to the Accused if he were making any effort whatever to meet the responsibilities of his command of his position; and that if he did not know of those acts, notorious, widespread, repeated, constant as they were, it was simply because he took affirmative action not to know."[92] In other words, the prosecution aimed at establishing the guilt of the accused on inference of knowledge based on circumstantial evidence. No proof of actual knowledge was presented except on occasions described in the following.

Two prosecution witnesses, Narciso Lapus and Joaquin S. Galang, were wartime associates of Gen. Ricarte of Makapili, the pro-Japanese Filipino patriotic league. They claimed to have personal knowledge of Yamashita divulging to Ricarte the orders authorizing the wholesale destruction of the Philippines. For instance, Lapus attested to hearing from Ricarte in person that "there is a general order issued by General Yamashita all over the commanders of the military posts in the Philippine Islands to wipe out the whole Philippines, if possible."[93] Galang testified to a similar effect.[94] The credibility of their testimony was promptly put to doubt, however, in the face of defense counsel's able cross-examination and of other rebuttal evidence.[95] The prosecution's own witness, Capt. Norman J. Sparnon, a member of the ATIS, also cast doubts on the likelihood of Yamashita's issuance of alleged orders. Sparnon testified on his personal experiences as an intelligence officer of having handled "some hundreds of thousands" of captured Japanese documents.[96] He did not find during his intelligence work any orders by Yamashita authorizing the wholesale massacre of the people of the Philippines. His expert knowledge on the Japanese army's standard procedure in publication and dissemination of military orders also pointed to the very slim possibility, if at all, that such orders could have been issued by Yamashita and go down the chain of command of the 14th Area Army without leaving any paper trails.[97]

The prosecution nonetheless set out an important factual foundation, using other evidence and witnesses, to establish the possible link between Yamashita and the instances of mass atrocity during the Battle of Manila. Two witnesses were called to the stand to testify to the effect that even though much of the atrocities during the Rape of Manila were committed by naval ground troops, they had been taken out of the navy chain of command and instead placed under Yamashita's command at the beginning of 1945. One of the two key prosecution witnesses was Vice Adm. Ōkōchi Denshichi, formerly commander of the Southwestern Pacific Area Fleet, which operated in the Philippine theater. He attested in the main that there was a standing army-navy joint policy by which "navy personnel were required to join the ground forces"[98] in the case of army-navy joint operations. He accordingly turned over certain of the naval forces to Yamashita – approximately 20,000 troops in the capital city under command of Rear Adm. Iwabuchi Sanji (known as the "Iwabuchi Unit") – at zero hours on January 6, 1945.[99] On the same day the transfer was made, Ōkōchi left Manila and went to Baguio just like Yamashita, where the two established separate command posts about 500 meters apart but maintained contact intermittently for the remainder of the war.[100] Ōkōchi testified that as far as he knew, Yamashita's general plan for the defense of Luzon was "to evacuate Manila as fast as possible and make a stand on the outskirts of Manila," that is, in "the mountain terrain around Manila."[101] Ōkōchi also attested to learning in those days that the Iwabuchi Unit did not comply with Yamashita's orders of withdrawal and instead remained in the city. The witness could only guess as to why Iwabuchi should disobey the orders; he had no conclusive explanation. Iwabuchi himself was killed in action during the Battle of Manila, around February 20, and was thus unable to give his version of the story in the postwar war crimes investigation or trial.[102]

The other key prosecution witness to testify on related matters was Lt. Gen. Yokoyama Shizuo, formerly commander of the 8th Division of the 14th Area Army. Yokoyama assumed command of the "Shinbu Army," a composite army unit organized on January 2, 1945, which remained under command of the 14th Area Army. The mission of the Shinbu Army was "to offer token resistance and make a quick withdrawal" as the U.S. assault forces approached the capital city.[103] The Iwabuchi Unit was placed under the Shinbu Army around January 10, although Yokoyama attested that he did not have actual control over it until February 3 or so.[104] Yokoyama ordered on January 19 that the Iwabuchi Unit and part of the army forces make a stand against the U.S. forces while allowing all other troops in the city of Manila to gradually withdraw.[105] The Iwabuchi Unit, too, was later ordered to withdraw when Yokoyama received orders from Yamashita, on February 12 or 13, to evacuate the naval forces from the capital city.[106]

From the standpoint of the prosecution, testimony by Ōkōchi and Yokoyama was significant, since both confirmed that the Iwabuchi Unit had left the navy chain of command at the start of 1945 and that the naval ground troops came under the command of the 14th Area Army. In other words, the two witnesses established Yamashita's formal command authority in relation to the unit directly responsible for the Rape of Manila. That said, there was one complication in the prosecution's evidence.

According to Ōkōchi's testimony, what was transferred to the 14th Area Army was command of the said naval troops relative to matters concerning the land operation alone. Ōkōchi retained general administrative command over them, namely, on matters of "personnel, supply, supplies and so forth."[107] What this meant was if Yamashita was dissatisfied with, say, Iwabuchi, and wished to remove him, he could do so only "through me [Ōkōchi]." Similarly, Yamashita had no power or authority to court-martial members of other naval ground troops in Manila. Should a need for court-martial arise, "I [Ōkōchi] was to be notified, and I will punish them, and I would take necessary action."[108] Yamashita's power to command the Iwabuchi Unit, in this regard, was a limited kind, since he could give orders to the navy men only insofar as matters of military operation were concerned. He apparently had no power to remove subordinate navy officers without going through the navy chain of command.

Ōkōchi's foregoing testimony was perplexing enough to elicit the following exchange in the courtroom between Gen. Reynolds, presiding judge of the U.S. military commission, and the witness:

GENERAL REYNOLDS: Who was responsible for the discipline of Japanese troops in Manila after January 6th, 1945?

THE WITNESS: (Through the Interpreter) It was General Yamashita's authority to [discipline troops], in matters pertaining to operation; but in matters not pertaining to operation it was my responsibility.

GENERAL REYNOLDS: One more question: Was the witness responsible for the control and discipline of Japanese troops in Manila after January 6th, 1945?

THE WITNESS: (Through the Interpreter) I had the responsibility not pertaining to operations.[109]

Ōkōchi's responses above confirmed the existence of a bifurcated command structure in the case of army-navy joint operations. It was still unclear, however, as to how the two services could exercise separate authority on military discipline in terms of "matters pertaining to operation" and "matters not pertaining to operation." The exact nature of the army-navy agreement on joint operations continued to confound the judges at other trials, including the Toyoda Trial, where Vice Adm. Ōkōchi was called to the stand once again to testify on the same issues, both on behalf of the prosecution and the defense. (See Chapter 6 for details.)

The defense at the Yamashita Trial was highly critical of the prosecution's general method of proof in which the prosecution undertook to present no affirmative evidence of the accused's knowledge of war crimes. "In the first place, a man is not convicted on the basis of what somebody thinks he must have known," A. Frank Reel argued on behalf of the accused. "It must be proven beyond a reasonable doubt that he did know; the test known to criminal law is not negligence but intent."[110] In the defense opinion, the prosecution failed to establish the accused's knowledge of the crimes beyond a reasonable doubt. What was more, the defense pointed out that the general war condition made it impossible for Yamashita to *acquire* information about the crimes being committed. Beset with broad-based, disruptive attacks by American assault forces and guerrilla fighters, the accused was unable to ensure that his orders were being properly transmitted to the dispersed units or that the troop positions be fully reported to him. As Reel summarized the circumstances of the war, "Land communication was cut off early in the game, and Japanese wireless communication at its best was apparently somewhat worse than ours at its worst."[111] This state of affairs, in the defense opinion, could hardly be construed as a ground to convict the accused of willful disregard or failure to discharge his duty to take control of his subordinate troops.

The defense also questioned the prosecution's contention relative to Yamashita's command authority vis-à-vis the Iwabuchi Unit. The defense could agree that the naval unit came under command of the 14th Area Army, but it was "for tactical purposes during landing operations only,"[112] as the prosecution's key witness Ōkōchi had testified. Moreover, "the only important order he [Yamashita] ever gave them – the order to evacuate – they failed to carry out."[113] In other words, the Rape of Manila resulted from refusal of the Iwabuchi Unit to obey the first and the last military orders it ever received from Yamashita. Given these facts, the defense did not see how Yamashita could be held individually or criminally liable for atrocities committed by the Iwabuchi Unit.

As a further piece of exculpatory evidence, the defense pointed out certain "peculiarities" in the Japanese army's standard procedure on personnel issues. The defense explained that a Japanese army commander lacked the power to remove at his own will high-ranking subordinate officers whom he found to be underperforming or who otherwise failed to discharge duties.[114] In the case specifically of Yamashita's command in the Philippines, he tried to remove Col. Nagahama Akira, chief of the *kenpeitai* of the 14th Area Army, upon learning that Nagahama failed to address repeated protests from Jose Laurel of the Philippine caretaker government regarding the overzealous police actions taken by the *kenpeitai* (namely, general and specific instances of unjustified arrests). Yamashita had no power to dismiss the *kenpeitai* chief himself. All he could do was to recommend Nagahama's dismissal to military superiors in the Southern Army at Saigon and the army authorities at Tokyo. Yamashita made the recommendation, on December 1, 1944, and the official approval from the higher authority to remove Nagahama reached him, but with much delay, eight weeks later on February 1, 1945.[115]

During the trial, Yamashita took the stand to give his views on theories of liability applicable to a military commander. He agreed with the prosecution on certain fundamental issues, as he testified that "if the offender's superiors have condoned or permitted or ordered these offenses [wrongful acts], then, they, too, would be punished." But he maintained that if a commanding officer took "necessary precautions and means to prevent" the occurrence of wrongful acts, and if his subordinates still committed war crimes, the commanding officer should be "subject only to administrative reprimand."[116] He also held that to determine responsibility of a commanding officer for crimes committed by his subordinates, one must take into account "the location of the commanding officer and the time and the circumstances." No issue of responsibility should arise "if the conditions are such that it is utterly impossible for him to take any action."[117] Yamashita believed that in his case, his plea of not guilty was entirely justified given his wartime *location, time,* and *circumstances*. When the chief prosecutor, Maj. Robert Kerr, pressed the accused to explain how he could remain utterly ignorant of the killing of so many unarmed men, women, and children over an extended period of time, Yamashita testified that "under the foregoing conditions I did the best possible job I could have done." Atrocities occurred but he could not do anything about them, because he did not know of their occurrence. Organizational problems from within and military exigencies from without "were beyond anything I could have expected." He emphasized that the crimes were committed against his will, policies, and orders. "If the present situation permits it, I will punish these people to the fullest extent of military law," so he informed the court.[118]

The U.S. military commission seemed sympathetic to Yamashita's case, as its five-page decision took note of the defense evidence concerning "difficulties faced by the accused with respect not only to the swift and overpowering advance of American forces, but also to the errors of his predecessors, weaknesses in organization, equipment, supply with especial reference to food and gasoline, training, communication, discipline and morale of the troops."[119] The U.S. military commission also noted the Iwabuchi Unit's disobedience to Yamashita's orders. But the general tone of the commission's decision turned critical when it came to assessing the accused's knowledge of atrocities. It would be "absurd, however, to consider a commander a murderer or rapist because one of his soldiers commits a murder or rape," the decision read, but

where murder and rape and vicious, revengeful actions are widespread offenses, and there is no effective attempt by a commander to discover and control the criminal acts, such a commander may be held responsible, even criminally liable, for the lawless acts of his troops, *depending upon their nature and the circumstances surrounding them.*[120]

By "their nature and the circumstances surrounding them," the military commission meant "the tactical situation, the character, training and capacity of staff officers and subordinate commanders as well as the traits of character, and training of his troops and other important factors in such cases."[121] Instead of discussing the issues of "their nature and their circumstances," however, the military commission proceeded to reach the verdict of guilty based on the following two factual findings:

(1) That a series of atrocities and other high crimes have been committed by members of the Japanese armed forces under your [Yamashita's] command against people of the United States, their allies and dependencies throughout the Philippine Islands; that

they were not sporadic in nature but in many cases were methodically supervised by Japanese officers and noncommissioned officers; (2) That during the period in question you failed to provide effective control of your troops *as was required by the circumstances.*[122]

The military commission made a token reference to "circumstances" in the above findings, but not as a mitigating factor or a ground of exculpation as the defense had argued. Rather – and with a seeming twist of logic – the military commission held it as an aggravating factor, finding the accused guilty for the failure to control his troops *as was required by the circumstances.*

The findings of the U.S. military commission came under criticism when the Yamashita case was argued before the U.S. Supreme Court for leave to file petition for writs of habeas corpus. The two dissenting justices, Murphy and Rutledge, set out in their opinions point-by-point criticisms of procedural misconduct committed by the U.S. military commission, which they believed constituted violations of the Fifth Amendment guarantee of due process of law. Furthermore, Justice Murphy faulted the military commission for convicting the accused of a crime unheard of in American legal history. It was not that the justices disagreed with the applicable theories of liability in toto, as Murphy wrote: "No one denies that inaction or negligence may give rise to liability, civil or criminal." Besides, he could readily point out some precedents that dated back to the Philippine insurrection in 1900 and 1901. However, "it is quite another thing to say that the inability to control troops under highly competitive and disastrous battle conditions renders one guilty of a war crime in the absence of personal culpability."[123] Murphy knew of no examples in the history of U.S. military justice whereby a commander was held criminally liable for his inability to control his troops in such circumstances. In his opinion, the decision of the U.S. military commission was tantamount to convicting Yamashita on the following grounds:

"We, the victorious American forces, have done everything possible to destroy and disorganize your lines of communication, your effective control of your personnel, your ability to wage war. In those respects we have succeeded. We have defeated and crushed your forces. And now we charge and condemn you for having been inefficient in maintaining control of your troops during the period when we were so effectively besieging and eliminating your forces and blocking your ability to maintain effective control. Many terrible atrocities were committed by your disorganized troops. Because these atrocities were so widespread, we will not bother to charge or prove that you committed, ordered or condoned any of them. We will assume that they must have resulted from your inefficiency and negligence as a commander. In short, we charge you with the crime of inefficiency in controlling your troops. We will judge the discharge of your duties by the disorganization which we ourselves created in large part. Our standards of judgment are whatever we wish to make them."[124]

These trenchant remarks had no material impact on the fate of the accused. MacArthur confirmed the death penalty, and Yamashita was hanged within three weeks of the Supreme Court decision. Nevertheless, the dissenting opinions arising from the U.S. Supreme Court were not to end as mere foot-notes of the Yamashita Trial. Their substance was so weighty that it compelled the Allied prosecutors, defense lawyers, and judges elsewhere to ponder how advisable it would be to follow the footsteps of the Yamashita precedent. Some examples will be explored in Chapter 4, in connection with the Australian tri-als at Rabaul, and Chapter 6, in relation to the Toyoda Trial, as well as in the next two sections concerning the Honma Trial and the Kuroda Trial.

THE CASE OF HONMA

Honma faced two charges, one alleging that the accused "did unlawfully dis-regard and fail to discharge his duties" to take control of armed forces under his command, "permitting them to commit brutal atrocities and other high crimes," and the other that he did "on 6 May 1942 unlawfully refuse to grant quarter to the Armed Forces of the United States of America and its Allies in Manila Bay, Philippines, and did thereby violate the laws of war."[125] The charges were accompanied by forty-seven specifications. They can be divided into the following six categories by types of offense committed, locations of the crimes, and types of victims involved: (1) bombing of the city of Manila without military justification on December 27 and 28, 1941; (2) inhumane treatment of hospital patients at Bataan in the period between April and June 1942; (3) inhumane treatment of prisoners of war during their evacuation and especially during the Bataan Death March[126]; (4) inhumane treatment of prisoners of war at internment camps and during work details[127]; (5) mistreat-ment of civilian internees[128]; and (6) widespread atrocities against civilians in occupied territories, including "widespread raping and brutal mistreatment of American and Filipino women throughout the Philippines,"[129] execution of Chinese consulate members, and execution of the Philippine Supreme Court Justice Santos. Honma was found guilty of the first charge and thirty-six spec-ifications (eleven others were dismissed upon the defense motion), and was acquitted of the second charge.

The prosecution's method of proof for the first charge closely followed the one at the Yamashita Trial, namely, to document the geographic spread and recurrence of war crimes in territories under control of the 14th Army so that knowledge could be imputed to the accused. But there were also a few no-table departures from the Yamashita Trial. First, the prosecution highlighted the fact that Honma was a commander of a "victorious army"[130] that had "their line of communications intact, with their supplies, with a well-trained staff, with everything in their favor, pushing forward."[131] This statement can be understood as the prosecution's oblique reference to the Yamashita Trial, where the defense had referred to the disorganization of the Japanese armed forces as exculpatory evidence. Second, the prosecution showed that unlike the Yamashita case, this accused had the means to know and did acquire knowledge about the general conditions of prisoners of war in the 14th Army's custody. Finally, the prosecution's evidence pointed to commonplace indifference among the members of the 14th Army about the well-being of prisoners of war. Takatsu Toshimitsu, formerly a colonel serving under Honma's command at the time of the Philippine invasion, denied personal knowledge of prisoner-of-war mistreatment but "I can say that if these things happened, . . . it was due to the fact that at that time interest and consideration for prisoners of war was 'thin' from General Homma on down."[132]

The defense witnesses conceded that poor conditions of prisoners of war during evacuation from Bataan existed and were known to officers in the top echelon of the 14th Army. They included Honma, his chief of staff Lt. Gen. Wachi Takeji, and commander of the No. 3 Field Transportation Unit, Maj. Gen. Kawane Yoshitaka,[133] as well as other officers who oversaw the prisoner-of-war transfer. The 14th Army's operational headquarters those days was located at Balanga, where all prisoners of war were first assembled before marching to the transition point at San Fernando.[134] "On the southern side of Balanga," Honma testified in the courtroom, "there was an open field that was the concentration area where the prisoners were coming from all directions." He went on to testify that "as Balanga was a starting point for the evacuation, I saw the column marching from that concentration area toward San Fernando." He saw prisoners marching at other locations along the route, too, over the course of tours of inspection he carried out in the immediate aftermath of the fall of Bataan.[135] He denied seeing or knowing any mistreatment of prisoners of war by his subordinate troops, but described the prisoners as appearing "rather tired and haggard."[136] Honma professed powerlessness, however, since decisions on prisoner-of-war transportation those days were "left to the discretion of the commandant of the army transport" and "I was explained that there was no motor vehicles available, so the prisoners had to march as far as San Fernando."[137]

Honma also conceded his awareness of the dire circumstances of prisoner-of-war internment at Camp O'Donnell. For instance, he testified that Maj. Gen. Kawane "came to report to me that more than 100 a day were dying," which he believed to be "an excessive amount."[138] Honma confirmed that he was informed the total number of deaths at the camp exceeded 16,000 by June 10, 1942.[139] Reports of the condition at Camp O'Donnell were made to Honma from other subordinate officers as well. Col. Horiguchi, a prosecution witness who served as head of the Medical Section of the 14th Army, attested to having meetings personally with Honma "three or four times" and telling him "that within the prisoners there were many malaria, dysentery, beriberi, and malnutrition patients and that the condition was poor." Horiguchi testified that he made report on the number of deaths, too, whereupon Honma is said to have replied: "That is a very tragic situation, and it is necessary for the Army to put in much effort to improve this situation."[140] When Maj. Gen. Leo Donovan, presiding officer and law member of the military commission, asked if the court should infer from the witness testimony that "General

Homma was kept pretty well informed on the medical situation, deaths of prisoners of war, at all times," Horiguchi replied affirmatively.[141]

Honma took the witness stand in his own defense. The major problem during the Philippine invasion, he argued, was that he could not get cooperation from Tokyo in order for him to provide proper accommodation to prisoners of war. The 14th Army landed on the Philippine Islands with no personnel in charge of prisoner-of-war administration, due to the policy of Tokyo that there was "no basis" to prepare for it "until such time" arrived. Honma made repeated requests for staff, food, and medicine to both Tokyo and the Southern Army headquarters, and finally resorted to dispatching his chief of staff Wachi to Tokyo "to speed up the matters."[142] Much of the misery of prisoners of war having resulted from the "lack of foresight" on the part of higher authorities, the one to blame was not Honma but rather "the ruling powers in Japan" (the defense closing argument).[143]

The defense evidence also showed – and the prosecution's evidence partly supported – that, for his own part, the accused did do what he could within his power to improve prisoner-of-war conditions. Honma took the following concrete steps to address the problem: (1) relocating part of the prisoner-of-war population to a new internment camp at Cabanatuan, central Luzon, so as to relieve overcrowded conditions at Camp O'Donnell[144]; (2) securing approval of Tokyo to replace the camp commander, Capt. Tsuneyoshi, with a new one, Col. Itō, to improve the management of the camp[145]; and (3) releasing thousands of Filipino prisoners of war on parole from June 1942 onwards, first at his own discretion and subsequently with official approval from Tokyo.[146] These actions bore mixed results. The condition of Camp O'Donnell showed a measure of improvement due to the diminished prisoner-of-war population and the arrival of a more competent camp commander.[147] However, the overall conditions of prisoner-of-war internment in the Philippines remained poor during Honma's tenure as well as beyond.

With regard to general and specific instances of atrocity against civilians, the accused once again denied that he personally knew of their occurrence. The defense questioned the validity of the prosecution's method of proof, too, in the following two respects. First, the prosecution attempted to show recurrence of atrocities by presenting "typical" cases and urged the court to infer knowledge of the accused based on such evidence. But the defense doubted the prosecution provided sufficient documentation of general occurrence of war crimes, especially concerning specification 4, which alleged the occurrence of widespread rape during the initial invasion. "If widespread rape is alleged," Maj. Gen. Skeen argued on behalf of the defense, "it must be proved."[148] What actually took place in the courtroom was that the prosecution called to the stand a limited number of witnesses – it was so small in number that in the defense opinion, their testimony hardly added up to justify the prosecution's assertion of widespread rape. What was more, the court-martial reports of the 14th Army (introduced in evidence by the defense) showed that the 14th

Army meted out punishment to a number of its servicemen on rape in the first two months of 1942.[149] This piece of evidence indicated that "every effort was made to punish soldiers guilty of rape"[150] rather than tolerating it.

Second, the defense argued that the prosecution based its case on Homma's responsibility for war crimes on erroneous understanding of the actual command structure of the 14th Army. According to testimony of former 14th Army chief of staff Wachi, Field Marshal Terauchi ordered on the eve of the second Bataan campaign that duties associated with the administration of occupied territories be temporarily separated from operational command of the 14th Army. Its purpose was to relieve Honma of administrative burdens and instead enable him to devote all his attention to unfinished combat missions. To this end, the Military Administration Section of the 14th Army with deputy chief of staff Hayashi as its chief was placed under command of the Southern Army. Hayashi was thereafter made "responsible to the commander-in-chief of the Southern Supreme Army [Southern Army]."[151] Hayashi also took under his wing the 14th Army *kenpeitai* to exercise "wide authority to carry on his work freely." The separation of administrative and operational branches of the 14th Army remained effective until the end of June 1942.[152] Wachi contended that "at that time matters concerning the Filipino residents was [*sic*] not the responsibility of the Army commander [Honma]" but they were "solely the responsibility of the Military Administration Section."[153]

Col. Ōta Seiichi, a key defense witness and formerly chief of the *kenpeitai* of the 14th Army between January 11 and the end of September 1942, partly corroborated Wachi's accounts. Ōta testified that he "received orders from Major General Hayashi" as he was placed directly under the latter's command, although he also "received orders from General Honma" where matters of military operation were concerned. The latter included orders from the commanding general (Honma) to monitor the conduct of Japanese troops during the marching of prisoners of war from Bataan to San Fernando.[154] The chief of the 14th Army *kenpeitai*, in this regard, came under dual command. He was accountable to Hayashi on matters of military administration of occupied territories, and to Honma relative to operational missions.

Court testimony by the accused himself generally agreed with Wachi's and Ōta's accounts. Honma testified that after landing in the Philippines, he saw the necessity to separate the operational and administrative aspects of the Philippine campaign and that, for this reason, "I gave the authority to the Director of Military Administration [Hayashi] to give orders to the military police so far as the maintenance of peace and order and police matters are concerned." He sought approval of Terauchi on this policy, which was duly granted. Terauchi formalized the separation of command by issuing an order that Honma "transfer, to place General Hayashi, as Director of Military Administration, in full charge of the Military Administration."[155] Honma testified that under the new arrangement, "technically he [Hayashi] was under my control; but when he was placed in full charge of Military Administration by

[Field Marshal] Count Terauchi, his work was directly under Count Terauchi's headquarters until I came back to Manila."[156] Lt. Col. Frank E. Meek, chief prosecutor, sought further clarification by initiating the following exchange with the accused:

Q [MEEK]. You mean that military administration in the Philippine Islands was taken away from you for a period of time?
A [HONMA]. No, I shouldn't say so. That is a strong expression.
Q. It was always under you?
A. The orders came from the Southern Army Headquarters to place the Director of Military Administration for the time being under the Southern Army – to take the full charge.[157]

The above exchange indicates that the basic command structure of the 14th Army remained intact, but that as the accused had already testified, the Military Administration Section was temporarily placed under the Southern Army's command and that Hayashi was authorized to act under the latter's orders.

Summing up its case, the defense argued that "this entire case [against the accused] is an indictment not of an individual but of the system and background of the Japanese Army and Japanese theory of waging war." Many deaths of prisoners of war occurred, but not because of Honma's personal wrongdoing or because of his willful disregard or failure to discharge his duty. Rather, the Government of Japan and the Southern Army at the highest level were the ones responsible for repeated institutional failures to provide protection to prisoners of war. Similarly, instances of civilian-targeted atrocities occurred, but not on Honma's orders or knowledge. The accused, in any event, was temporarily relieved from duties pertaining to military administration; documented instances of atrocity mostly occurred in those months, including the killing of the Chinese consul general and Judge Santos. The defense concluded by urging the court not to judge the case against the accused "by the standards of our own army which are, despite frequent criticism, among the most efficient in the world." Instead, "we can only fairly judge this man by the standards established by the Japanese Army."[158]

The court dismissed the defense case for the most part and found Honma guilty.[159] No judgment accompanied the verdict, but a report produced by the reviewing authority allows one to have an insight into some of the court's thinking. The report was prepared by 1st Lt. Henry H. Willmott, assistant staff judge advocate of the Staff Judge Advocate's Office of the U.S. Army Forces Western Pacific.[160] He stated that the court's decisions were proper and that regardless of the accused's denial of knowledge of atrocity, "from the sheer number of incidents, his own physical proximity to some of them and their general notoriety, it can be concluded that he did know or should have known of them." Highlighting the difference with the case of Yamashita, the report added that no contention was made during the court proceedings that the "means of information were unavailable" to the accused.[161]

Willmott expressed dissatisfaction, however, on certain ambiguities in the court's verdicts. "It might be assumed," he wrote, "that in announcing no individual findings the Commission determined that all specifications not actually dismissed were satisfactorily proven." However, he took note that the prosecution offered "evidence of the rape of some thirteen women" instead of offering fuller documentation of alleged widespread rape. He wrote that "in view of the geographical area and number of persons under accused's command, . . . it is not sufficient proof by any standards of 'widespread rape or mistreatment.'"[162] The prosecution had asserted during the court proceedings that "we have many scores more" rape cases but that it was limiting itself to introducing "a typical group of cases" so as not to overburden the court. Willmott did not believe that simply stating there to be "many scores more" rape cases was satisfactory at all. As a matter of fact, "if made by a prosecutor before a jury in a court of law[, it] would be prejudicial error warranting reversal."[163]

A postscript to the Honma Trial: Three of Honma's former subordinates whose names have appeared in the foregoing discussion – Col. Ōta, Maj. Gen. Kawane, and Capt. Tsuneyoshi – were contemporaneously investigated, prosecuted, and convicted of war crimes. Their cases are summarized as follows:

- Col. Ōta Seiichi, formerly commander of the *kenpeitai* of the 14th Army: Ōta was arraigned at the U.S. Manila courtroom on December 21, 1945, on the charge that he "disregarded his duties as a commander" to take control of those subordinates of his, who committed beatings, tortures, and cruel and inhumane confinement of prisoners at Fort Santiago. Specifications included the killing of eight Chinese consulate members. The trial commenced on December 27, 1945. On January 5, 1946, the accused was found guilty and sentenced to death by hanging. The sentence was carried out on February 23 the same year.[164]
- Maj. Gen. Kawane Yoshitaka, formerly commander of the No. 3 Field Transportation Unit, 14th Army: Kawane was brought before the U.S. military commission at Yokohama in connection with the Bataan Death March and prisoner-of-war mistreatment at Camp O'Donnell. He was found guilty and sentenced to death by hanging. His sentence was carried out on February 12, 1949.[165]
- Capt. Tsuneyoshi Yoshio, formerly commanding officer of Camp O'Donnell between April 1 and July 5, 1942: Tsuneyoshi was tried by the U.S. military commission at Yokohama in connection with prisoner-of-war mistreatment at Camp O'Donnell. The trial took place between October 10 and November 21, 1947, with the outcome of guilty.[166] The accused narrowly escaped the death sentence and instead received life in prison. The reviewing authority of the U.S. 8th Army commented that "presumably this commission gave due consideration to theory of 'superior orders' and the higher responsibility for inadequacies in the camp facilities and supplies." Prior to

Tsuneyoshi's conviction, three of his military superiors in the chain of command – his immediate superior Col. Hirano Kuratarō[167] (Yokohama, Case Docket No. 304), Kawane, and Honma – had already been found guilty and sentenced to death.

"IF THEY WOULD NOT GIVE ME PLANES, I PLAY GOLF"

The charge against Kuroda Shigenori was phrased much the same way as those against Yamashita and Honma, as it read that while serving as "Commander-in-Chief of the Imperial Japanese Forces in the Philippines," the accused disregarded and failed to discharge his duties to take control of members under his command, thereby "permitting" them to commit war crimes. Specifications were divided into the American phase and the Philippine phase, enumerating general and specific instances of atrocities in which a large number of American and Filipino prisoners of war, civilian internees, and noninterned civilians in Japanese-occupied territories fell victim.

The prosecution followed the established method of proof when substantiating its case against Kuroda, namely, to document the broad geographical distribution and recurrence of atrocities committed by the members of army units under command of the accused. In the words of the chief American prosecutor S. Melville Hussey describing the American phase:

When the crimes of any army are extensive with its geographical distribution, and when the pattern is the same wherever you turn, then there is only one inference: the commander either has ordered the offense to be committed, or he just doesn't care.[168]

A total of 14 witnesses were called to the stand during the American phase to testify on mistreatment of prisoners of war and civilian internees. At least one witness, Maj. Willard H. Waterous of the U.S. Army Medical Corps, was already a familiar face in the Manila courtroom, as he had given testimony at the Honma Trial.[169] The American prosecution team also introduced in evidence 106 court exhibits so as to document prevalence of Japanese-perpetrated war crimes and to impute knowledge of their occurrence to the accused. The exhibits consisted mainly of affidavits, taken from former prisoners of war, civilian internees, and former high-ranking Japanese army officers including the accused, Kuroda and his chief of staff Wachi Takeji.[170]

Capt. Nicanor Marovilla–Seva, serving as chief Filipino prosecutor for the Philippine phase, similarly argued during his opening statement that atrocities "were committed over a vast area over an extended period of time and following a certain pattern as to preclude the possibility of any defense to the effect that the accused, even though he was the Commander-in-Chief, could not have known of the existence of these atrocities." But unlike the American prosecution team, and in tacit acknowledgment of Justice Murphy's stinging criticisms of the Yamashita Trial, Seva went on to indicate the prosecution team's readiness to show the *actual* knowledge of the accused of crimes committed by his subordinate troops. He thus stated: "The prosecution will even go further and prove beyond any doubt that in many cases of atrocities the accused did know of the existence of such atrocities, but that the accused refused or was indifferent in taking any steps to curtail the reputation of such atrocities."[171]

The evidence presented for the Philippine phase reflected the case Seva outlined in his opening statement, but the proof of the accused's actual knowledge of atrocities was, in fact, quite slim. Voluminous oral and documentary evidence – 34 witnesses and 118 court exhibits – was presented to show that atrocities targeted at the Philippine civilian population were widespread and that the perpetrators were members of army units under command of Kuroda. Records of trials that had been previously held by the U.S. and Philippine authorities proved useful for the prosecution, as certain members of the army units subordinate to Kuroda had been tried and convicted of war crimes. A substantial portion of the prosecution's court exhibits was extracts from those trials. As for proof of the accused's actual knowledge of atrocities, the prosecution's evidence was limited to one. It was an extract from the trial of Kōno Takeshi (one of the earlier U.S. Manila trials),[172] at which Dr. Fermin G. Carem, formerly governor of Iloilo, Panay, attested to having repeatedly made complaints about the killing of civilians to Lt. Gen. Kōno, then commanding officer of the Japanese expeditionary forces in Panay, and complaining of the same directly to Kuroda during the latter's visit to Iloilo City on an unspecified date. Kuroda is said to have replied in English to Carem, saying, "I am sorry, that is not my instruction."[173] But the prosecution stopped short of presenting further evidentiary materials to corroborate the occurrence of this particular episode. Kuroda, for his part, confirmed that he visited Iloilo in July 1943 but denied that this encounter ever took place.[174]

If proof of actual knowledge of atrocity was not forthcoming, the Philippine prosecution team nonetheless presented some evidence that pointed to the accused's shortchanging of his duty as a military commander. Testimony taken from two former members of the 14th Army *kenpeitai* is particularly noteworthy. 1st Lt. Kawai Tadaharu, a prosecution witness, who had served as adjutant of the *kenpeitai* command in the Visayan area (headquartered at Cebu), gave testimony on the accused's issuance of instructions prohibiting commission of atrocities against the Filipino civilian population. The gist of Kuroda's instructions was that "the purpose of the Japanese army was to conduct operations and the situation was such that pacification was necessary to be conducted to the inhabitants and therefore it was mandatory that illegal conducts should not be committed in the Philippines."[175] The issuance of such instructions was exculpatory on its face, but it could be considered incriminating if other evidence indicated Kuroda's failure to enforce these instructions.

The Philippine court, at least, appeared to weigh Kawai's testimony in this respect. For instance, the law member of the court, Maj. Federico Aranas, put questions to Kawai to bring out the following facts that could be salient in determining the accused's criminal liability: (1) that the said instructions were transmitted not only to the 14th Army *kenpeitai* units but also to "the entire 14th Army"; (2) that "illegal acts" under Japanese military law included killing of civilians without trial; and (3) that the witness knew of no one in the 14th Army who was punished for the commission of such.[176] Separate questioning from another member of the court, Col. Pedro F. Tabuena, elicited from the same witness an answer that during the period of the witness's assignment in Cebu, Kuroda never carried out tours of inspection relative to the Cebu military command.[177] The court could infer from these pieces of information that the accused may have been indifferent to ensuring his troops' compliance with his instructions.

Lt. Gen. Matsuzaki Hideichi, formerly commanding officer of the Davao *kenpeitai* (who had been tried and convicted of war crimes by the Philippine military commission[178]), was called to the stand at the Kuroda Trial to testify mainly on the chain of command between Kuroda and the 14th Army *kenpeitai* relative to guerrilla suppression campaigns. He attested that Kuroda in his capacity as commanding general of the 14th Army (and subsequently of the 14th Area Army) held direct command over the 14th Army *kenpeitai*.[179] When carrying out the pacification campaigns, he "would show the outline of missions to the army commanders or division commanders that were under him." The general outlines were thus "laid down by the Commanding General," while the details of individual operations were determined by each unit commander in charge of specific missions.[180] When questioned by Maj. Aranas as to who was the "immediate senior officer" with the power to discipline the commanding officer of the 14th Army *kenpeitai*, the witness testified: "when he was to be punished, he was to be punished by the commanding general of the 14th Army or 14th Army Group [the 14th Area Army]."[181] The court was interested on this occasion once again in Kuroda's personal commitment to ensuring his subordinates' compliance with his policies against illegal conduct. Coupled with evidence of commonplace occurrence of the *kenpeitai*'s acts of violence, and of absence of disciplinary actions by Kuroda against the *kenpeitai* chief, Matsuzaki's testimony could lead the court to infer that the accused tolerated *kenpeitai* atrocities.

The defense team countered the prosecution's case by first calling to the stand the accused person, Kuroda.[182] A total of 12 additional witnesses followed to testify for the defense. (Eleven defense witnesses were prominent Filipino political leaders.) Court exhibits – 108 of them – accompanied the defense case, to support witnesses' accounts.[183] Of these, Kuroda's testimony turned out to be a long and detailed affair. A total of 352 pages in the transcripts of court proceedings were spent on recording his testimony, as opposed to 208 pages and 183 pages for the testimony of the accused at the Honma Trial and the Yamashita Trial, respectively. The Philippine Manila court had to suspend the direct examination of the accused at one point, as Kuroda lost his voice from too much talking at the witness stand.[184] The Philippine court apparently was in no rush to reach its decision; it was rather keen to allow the accused an ample opportunity to speak in his own behalf, and to enable all other parties concerned to cross-examine the accused to their satisfaction. The Kuroda Trial indeed proceeded at a leisurely pace. The trials of Honma and Yamashita by the U.S. military commission lasted just about eight to nine weeks each, between the time of arraignment and the day of verdict and sentencing. The Trial of Kuroda, by contrast, lasted approximately thirty-one weeks, the prosecution and the defense spending about an equal amount of court time on making their respective cases.

The argument advanced by Kuroda himself was extensive, but the main points would boil down to the following: (1) that the Japanese military suffered from inherent institutional shortfalls in the areas of criminal investigation and enforcement of military discipline; (2) that he did discharge his duty to the best of his ability regardless of institutional shortcomings; (3) that he lacked command authority over at least some of those units that were directly responsible for the commission of atrocity.

On the first point, Kuroda argued that a commanding general in the Japanese Army suffered institutional constraints in acquiring information when disciplinary problems were concerned. The army procedure required subordinate commanders and the *kenpeitai* to make "true reports" of their respective activities, but "aside from such procedures, a commanding general of an army like myself had no other means of finding out defects in his army."[185] When asked by defense counsel about the availability of "Inspector General Service" as commonly found in the British or the U.S. Army, Kuroda replied that "there was no organizational set-up in the Japanese Army that was identical to such" and pointed out that the *kenpeitai* was the only army agent empowered to carry out investigation and enforcement of military discipline.[186] Kuroda testified that he had "complete confidence"[187] in the *kenpeitai* and that he would not go about inquiring into the *kenpeitai* compliance with the field service regulations anyway. "If I went out and tried to investigate about such details, even if there were several hundred army commanders like me, no operations could be carried out," so he testified.[188] He admitted to visiting the 14th Army *kenpeitai* headquarters at Fort Santiago, but it was only once, two weeks after his arrival in Manila. He stayed at Fort Santiago "for about half a day" or "2–3 hours" to acquaint himself with the 14th Army's *kenpeitai* organization and the units' disposition, but not to inquire about the conditions of detainees. "Matters about prisoners did not enter my mind at that time,"[189] he informed the court.

The foregoing testimony prompted Maj. Aranas to pose further questions to elicit the extent to which Kuroda may have been aware of the *kenpeitai* torture. Kuroda's reply was a flat denial of any personal knowledge. Quite interestingly, however, he offered to explain – based on pure guesswork, so he indicated to the court – as to why the Japanese military police might have been tempted to resort to torture when interrogating criminal suspects. "Our country was not one of democracies," Kuroda stated, and "according to our system adopted from the German system, the strongest and most important evidence is the confession of the accused or of the suspect." In those circumstances, Japanese police agents might well have found torture a convenient means with which to extract confession they needed. Kuroda claimed to have learned only "after the war" that torture was an interrogation technique widely applied by the *kenpeitai* officers and the civilian police alike.[190] These remarks led Aranas to initiate the following exchange with the accused:

Q [ARANAS]. You stated that you learned about these torture policies of the Kempei Tai [*kenpeitai*] and the civilian police only after the war, is that right?
A [KURODA]. Yes, of course, I never heard of the alleged torture policy.
Q. By 1945, you had 29 years of service in the Japanese Army, is that right?
A. Yes, more or less.
Q. And during all that period of time you were not given opportunity to look into the workings of the Kempei Tai?
A. Never. The military police in Japan were just outside of our knowledge as trials were.
Q. So when you were assigned as commander of the 14th Army, you had a unit under you the workings of which you were ignorant. I am referring to the Kempei Tai under the 14th Army.
A. That is right. It was the first time that I had MP [military police] as my subordinate unit.
Q. Did all combat officers of the Japanese army maintain the same ignorance as you about the Kempei Tai?
A. Yes, all.[191]

Kuroda held his ground in the above exchange, denying any personal knowledge whatsoever of the *kenpeitai*'s practice of torture. However, the tone of questioning by Maj. Aranas points to the law member's deeply skeptical views about the credibility of accused's account.

With regard to his second line of defense, Kuroda argued that far from being indifferent to the well-being of the people of the Philippines, he issued orders to his subordinate troops for proper treatment of civilians and, moreover, proactively sought information about his troops' conduct. Specifically, he gave instructions to his subordinate units "to report to me whatever ill conduct the troops might commit; especially the military police were instructed to be alert on this matter." He also made inquiries with Filipino officials and "asked these people to let me know as soon as possible whenever there was any illegal conduct committed by Japanese soldiers."[192] Similarly, and in connection with guerrilla suppression campaigns, Kuroda attested to having given instructions "strictly to comply" with the policy of taking precautions to protect lives and property of noncombatant civilians.[193] The outcome of these frequent instructions and inquiries was that the accused "did not receive any report, *at all*," either from his subordinates or from members of the Philippine government.[194]

In those circumstances, Kuroda believed that his plea of innocence was entirely justified.

Kuroda's argument was partly supported by certain Philippine nationals who took the stand as defense witnesses. Tomas Morato, formerly a congressman for Quezon Province and Marinduque, testified that Kuroda told Philippine political leaders to make report to him if the Japanese servicemen committed atrocities. So far as the witness's knowledge went, no Filipinos actually did so. When Col. Pedro Tabuena, a member of the court, asked why not, Morato replied that while they did bring up complaints to commanders of Japanese expeditionary forces, they were reluctant to press their cases because of "our fear of our lives."[195] When cross-examined further by Capt. Consolador R. Palad, an assistant Philippine prosecutor, the witness gave the following account:

Due to the debility [debilitation] that was caused by the punishment that was meted out to my person at Fort Santiago, got down his [my] morale, I did not believe that anyone who would be a victim in that place would ever have a courage to report these atrocities. Sometimes, they were also showed some pity but that fact alone would not make one have the courage to report the atrocities. Everyone, those who had been a victim of atrocities in Fort Santiago would have a feeling of fear to report those atrocities.[196]

Jorge B. Vargas, a defense witness and formerly chairman of the Executive Commission, similarly attested to falling short of making reports directly to Kuroda. Information of atrocities was "usually brought to the attention of the military administration," whereupon "they would invariably answer back that they were going to investigate or do something about it."[197] But the Japanese military violence remained prevalent. Vargas knew that a "lot of people were being dragged to Fort Santiago" and also heard news of "abuses in the provinces." The Japanese-perpetrated atrocities indeed were "so general" he could not remember each and every instance.[198] But the Philippine political leaders including himself rarely, if at all, went up to Kuroda to make complaints personally.

Testimony to the similar effect was made – although with a slight variation – by Camilo Osias, yet another Filipino defense witness and formerly education minister of the wartime Philippine government. He informed the court that Kuroda was "the most approachable, the most sociable and least stiff" of all Japanese generals serving in the occupied Philippines, standing in contrast to Honma, Tanaka, and Yamashita, whom Osias described as formal and distant.[199] Kuroda used to spend part of his time as occupation commander hosting social events in Manila and befriending Philippine political leaders. Osias himself used to meet with Kuroda "several times in his residence, at meetings in the Manila Hotel and at the Wack Wack Golf Country Club where we used to play golf."[200] Osias attested that he talked with Kuroda "very frankly" at least about the Japanese commonplace practice of slapping. To this Kuroda is said to have responded sympathetically, stating, "thank you, I will instruct my men."[201] Arguably, this piece of testimony was meant to be exculpatory of the accused. But the revelation of convivial socializing scenes in Manila led the court to form an impression that the accused "was not very active to his military duties." When asked by the court if this impression was correct, Osias replied affirmatively and added, "This is why he was called 'Play Boy' and he *himself*, said, 'if they would not give me planes, I play golf.'"[202] The final judgment of the court (as will be discussed shortly) suggests that this particular segment of the witness testimony served as incriminating evidence against the accused.

The third line of argument Kuroda advanced concerned the nature of his command authority in relation to Japanese military units in occupied territories. According to the defense, there were certain errors in the prosecution's comprehension of the organizational structure of the 14th Army (and later the 14th Area Army), one of which being the relationship between the commanding general and prisoner-of-war camp administration. The accused argued that under the Japanese Army Ministry's rules and regulations, the commandant of prisoner-of-war camps "made direct reports" to the army minister in Tokyo while the authority of the 14th Army commanding general was limited to "supervision" of the prisoner-of-war camps. Kuroda did have duties in relation to prisoner-of-war camps in the Philippines, but they were limited to deciding the location of prisoner-of-war camps, determining camp organizations, and distributing prisoners of war to those camps.[203]

Kuroda's testimony on limited authority of the 14th Army commander on prisoner-of-war management had supporting evidence in the "Collection of Laws and Regulations Concerning Prisoners of War" (*Furyo ni kansuru shohōki ruijū*, whose accurate translation would be "the compilation of various rules concerning prisoners of war") issued by the Army Ministry. The defense presented excerpts from the collection in evidence. One of the ministry regulations, "Ordinance Concerning POW [Prisoner-of-War] Camps," stipulated that the army commander, the army minister, and the camp commandant assumed separate duties in relation to prisoners of war in terms of "supervision," "control," and "administration" respectively.[204] Pertinent articles read:

Article 3

POW [prisoner of war] camps shall be under the supervision of the Army Commanders or garrison commander, as designated by War Minister [Army Minister], and shall be controlled by War Minister [Army Minister].

Article 5

The commandant shall be under the jurisdiction of the Army Commanders or garrison commanders, and shall administer the POW camps.[205]

According to the defense explanation, these terms – supervision (*kanri*), control (*tōkatsu*), and management of administration (*gyōsei o shōri*) – were used in army ministry rules and regulations to assign different types of authority among varying military superiors vis-à-vis prisoner-of-war camps.[206]

Other than the three types of defense argument outlined above, Kuroda also advanced a separate, broad-based cultural argument in which he disputed the applicability of the Western concepts of individual criminal responsibility. "We did not carry the concept of responsibility between individuals," he testified. "In our army, we never gave any thought to such things whether a person is responsible or not to his superiors."[207] In the face of rigorous questioning from Maj. Aranas, however, Kuroda conceded that a commanding general in the Japanese Army, in fact, would be held individually and legally responsible for shortcomings of his subordinate troops, such as poor discipline and unsanitary situations. He further conceded that "if I knew of such deficiencies, and I was in a position to be able to remedy such deficiencies, and I did not do so, then of course, I would have been legally responsible," and "it was the duty of the commander to carry out all means to know."[208]

The final decision of the court on the Kuroda case was guilty.[209] Factual findings of the court were broken down into three components: (1) mistreatment of prisoners of war and civilian internees; (2) mistreatment of unarmed noncombatant civilians; and (3) mistreatment of prisoners at Fort Santiago. On the first category of offense, the court found that "after the fall of Corregidor and formal surrender by Gen. Wainwright of the forces of the USAFFE in the Philippines, the American prisoners of war and civilian internees were distributed in the different camps," whereupon they were meted out "brutal atrocities, mistreatment, neglect and maladministration." The court was convinced of the occurrence of specific instances of atrocities and also of "their general pattern in all the camps and their monotonous consistency throughout."[210] The court noted that Japan was a signatory of the Hague Convention No. 4 Respecting the Laws and Customs of War on Land (1907, hereafter "Hague Convention No. 4") and the Geneva Convention Relative to the Treatment of Prisoners of War (1929).[211] The Japanese armed forces were known for exemplary treatment of prisoners of war during the Russo-Japanese War (1904–1905) and, above all, for having nurtured the "highest traditions of the Bushido." The nation with these model records, however, "visited death and brutality on all whom her warriors made contact"[212] during the Pacific War. With respect specifically to the accused's individual responsibility, the court concluded that he "permitted this state of affairs" by way of noninterference, and "to hide behind the defense of ignorance of these occurrences would be childish and incompatible with his powers and his position as commanding general of an army of occupation."[213]

On mistreatment of unarmed civilians, the court dismissed the accused's claim of utter ignorance. It tersely remarked: "Could we be so simple-minded as to believe that the accused in the comfort of his Manila headquarters was not aware, directly or indirectly, of the occurrence of these atrocities throughout the Philippines?"[214] This part of the judgment is likely to be grounded on

Osias's testimony that the accused was indifferent to military duties while having ample time for socializing with Filipino political leaders – including golfing, a time-consuming leisure activity indeed – in the capital city. The court emphasized that Kuroda as occupation commander had the responsibility to protect the people of occupied territories and, equally important, to ensure "due process of law" to captured guerrilla suspects. However, "the Japanese, not very much noted for his patience in the accomplishment of his military missions, most decidedly burned barrios and towns, killing men and women and children to strike terror in the hearts of the people so that the guerrilla movements would not gather substance or momentum." The court deemed that these were "all concrete violations of international law" for which Kuroda must be held individually and criminally accountable.[215]

With respect to *kenpeitai* torture, the court once again rejected Kuroda's assertion of utter ignorance. "This is surely a novel phenomenon which this commission is not prepared to believe," the court curtly remarked. Kuroda's explanations about inherent weaknesses of the Japanese military justice system did not impress the court either, as the judgment read, "This system, identical in the working of the sinister Gestapo of Nazi Germany and the ruthless Kempei Tai [*kenpeitai*] of Imperial Japan, is basically immoral, repugnant to the conscience of the ordinary man, and does violence to the laws and customs of civilized belligerents." The court was satisfied that the 14th Army *kenpeitai* did come under Kuroda's command and that the accused was individually and criminally liable for its criminal conduct "under the theory of command responsibility."[216]

Given the precedents arising from the Yamashita and Honma Trials, and given Kuroda's culpability as established by the court, one might assume that this accused, too, should receive no penalty other than capital punishment. The sentence the Philippine court handed down to him was life in prison, however, and even *that* Kuroda did not have to serve in full. The Government of the Philippines under President Elpidio Quirino (1948–1953) granted him a presidential pardon in December 1951, and let him return home a free man.[217] Two other convicted war criminals also received presidential pardons. The remaining war criminals who had been convicted by the Philippine court, too, received general amnesty. Why such leniency?

Sharon Chamberlain's (2010) "Justice and Reconciliation" brings to light a combination of personal and political reasons that influenced the Quirino administration's decisions. Based on the record of the Kuroda Trial, it can also be said that the young Philippine government was motivated to showcase to the world the Philippine commitment not only to the principle of justice but also to those of mercy and equanimity. Camilo Osias, for one, understood the significance of the Kuroda Trial in those terms. Having nearly completed his testimony during direct examination, Osias informed the court that he personally owed nothing to Kuroda and that he was not trying to take any position at this trial in one way or another. Rather, "it occurs to me that in this particular case not only General Kuroda is on trial but, *we Filipinos* are also on trial before the bar of public opinion." He went on to state:

I covet for my country, I cherish the fond hope of my people that out of these trials we may acquire a name and fame in the world of being a truly Christian Republic in the Orient, a people wedded to the ideals of justice, liberty and democracy as envisaged in the Constitution of the Philippines.[218]

It is possible that ten other Filipinos who testified as defense witnesses shared Osias's sentiments. Some of these individuals, including Osias, had been criticized for being collaborators of the Japanese and shunned from public offices in wake of the V-J Day.[219] In those circumstances, the way for them to win back the trust of the Philippine people might have been to testify against the former enemy commander, not *for* him, as in the case of Narciso Lapus and Joaquin Galang at the Yamashita Trial. But the times had changed, and so had the Philippine people's understanding of patriotism, justice, and the rule of law, apparently.

One may still question whether life imprisonment, followed by a presidential pardon, was too lenient form of punishment for Kuroda. But so far as the substance of the trial is concerned, the Kuroda Trial may merit recognition for its overall quality of fair-trial practice and well-reasoned judgment. MacArthur, the convening authority of the Yamashita and Honma Trials, may have meant these two trials to be the showcase of American justice on behalf of his beloved Philippine people. In retrospect, however, it appears that the nascent democratic nation of the Philippines was the one that did a far better job of living up to the high standard of justice, equanimity, and the rule of law.

2

Prisoner-of-War Administration

"Japanese Red Cross Orderlies Carrying a Wounded Russian to the Hospital," reads the caption for a 6- by 9-inch photograph in which two smallish Japanese men in uniform figure prominently, holding the front and back ends of a stretcher on which the injured Russian soldier in question rests. The midday sun must be shining bright on the patient, as he blocks his eyes with his left hand to protect them from blindness. His large body is curled up on the stretcher, covered with a dark blanket except for the lower half of his legs, which are exposed. The Japanese Red Cross orderly at the back end of the stretcher gazes into the distance, while the one at the front end slightly turns his head toward the camera, showing a faint smile on his face.[1] This photo was taken by a war correspondent reporting for *Collier's*, an American weekly magazine, in the aftermath of the Battle of Yalu River, the first major combat to take place in the Russo-Japanese War (1904–1905). This was one of several dozen photos that *Collier's* reproduced in its large-format commemorative photographic book, *The Russo-Japanese War: A Photographic and Descriptive Review of the Great Conflict in the Far East* (Davis et al. 1905), to showcase the "unique value and the comprehensive extent of *Collier's* Russo-Japanese War service."[2]

War correspondents and photojournalism were relatively new phenomena at the turn of the twentieth century, and the broad coverage of the war by the *Collier's* reporters is impressive.[3] Of relative novelty at the time of the Russo-Japanese War, too, was the Japanese participation in modern warfare. The western-style Japanese national army and navy came into existence after the downfall of the shogunal government in 1868. The Imperial Japanese Army and the Imperial Japanese Navy – as they came to be known – were put to use in major international armed conflict during the Sino-Japanese War, between 1894 and 1895. After a brief stint of joining the multinational forces to drive the Boxer rebels out of Beijing in Qing China, Japan deployed its army and navy forces afresh to fight another major war on the Chinese continent – this time, against the Russians – in order to resolve Russo-Japanese rivalry over the control of Korea and Southern Manchuria. The Russo-Japanese War was an important opportunity for Japan to showcase to the world not only its military might but also its respectability as a civilized nation, fully capable of waging war in compliance with the rules and customs of war. Japan earned an international reputation for its exemplary treatment of prisoners of war (POWs) precisely in this war,[4] and continued to live up to its reputation in the handling of surrendered German soldiers during World War I. Whatever happened, then, to the time-honored tradition of Japan's model treatment of prisoners of war? How did it come about that Japan gained notoriety for the general *mistreatment* of Allied prisoners of war during World War II?[5]

In the effort to address these questions, this chapter explores the Japanese government's policies on prisoner-of-war administration by way of the record of the trial of Lt. Gen. Tamura Hiroshi, one of two international proceedings held at Tokyo between 1948 and 1949 subsequent to the Tokyo Trial. Tamura was the last of three army generals who successively served as chief of the Prisoner-of-War Information Bureau and concurrently as chief of the Prisoner-of-War Administration Section of the Army Ministry. (Two predecessors of his, Lt. Gen. Uemura Mikio and Lt. Gen. Hamada Hitoshi, committed suicide in the aftermath of Japan's surrender.[6]) While holding these two high offices in the last nine months of the war (December 1, 1944–September 2, 1945), Tamura took on a variety of bureaucratic responsibilities pertaining to collection, maintenance, and transmission of information concerning the Allied prisoners of war on the one hand, and on the other, decision-making powers relative to prisoner-of-war internment, transfer, and employment. Due to the nature and timing of his service, Tamura was confronted in the courtroom with evidence of the systemic problems of Japan's prisoner-of-war administration as much as his own alleged personal wrongdoing in the exercise of his authority. The Tamura Trial, in this regard, serves as a useful window through which to probe into organizational dimensions of Japanese prisoner-of-war mistreatment as much as individual responsibility of the particular accused person. The prosecution's case at the Tamura Trial was limited to Japanese policies relative to prisoners of war arising from the Pacific War, however, excluding those concerning surrendered Chinese soldiers in connection with the concurrent Sino-Japanese armed conflict. Tamura's offices were vested with no institutional responsibility whatsoever of gathering information or managing captured soldiers insofar as war in China was concerned (for reasons to be explored in this chapter).

With the limitation of the Tamura Trial's coverage in mind, this chapter first makes a brief detour to segments of the Tokyo Judgment where the Tokyo Tribunal discusses its findings on the Japanese prisoner-of-war policies in relation to the Sino-Japanese armed conflict.[7] The main part of the chapter analyzes the organization of Japanese prisoner-of-war administration relative to the Pacific War and explores evidence against the accused person, Tamura.[8]

ARMED CONFLICT IN CHINA

According to the Tokyo Judgment, the war that Japan waged against China began with the invasion of the region of Manchuria in northeastern China on the night of September 18, 1931, and ended with the surrender ceremony held on the deck of *USS Missouri* at Tokyo Bay on September 2, 1945.[9] The wartime Government of Japan never recognized the existence of the state of war between the two countries, however, and it instead regarded the entire Sino-Japanese armed conflict between 1931 and 1945 as amounting to no more than an "incident [*jihen*]" to which no laws of war applied. "This war was envisaged by Japan's military leaders as a punitive war [*yōchōsen*]," the Judgment read, "which was being fought to punish the people of China for their refusal to acknowledge the superiority and leadership of the Japanese race and to cooperate with Japan."[10]

The general attitude of hostility among the Japanese political leaders against China is documented in various evidentiary materials received by the Tokyo Tribunal. For instance, there is a record of Hirota Kōki making a speech at the House of Peers of the Imperial Diet in February 1938 regarding the on-going Sino-Japanese conflict. One of the accused at the Tokyo Trial, Hirota had held key cabinet posts in the early years of the conflict (prime minister, 1936–1937; and foreign minister, 1933–1936, 1937–1938[11]). "Japan has been endeavoring to make the Chinese Nationalist Government make reflections, if possible, while chastising [*yōchō shite*] their mistaken ideas by armed forces," the record of Hirota's speech read. "Since they were facing Japan with very strong anti-Japanese feeling [*gankyō na hainichi shisō*], we decided on a policy whereby we had to necessarily chastise them."[12] Hirota delivered this speech shortly after his government – then led by Prime Minister Konoe Fumimaro – stated publicly that Japan would no longer seek a negotiated settlement to the armed conflict with Chiang Kai-shek's Nationalist Government. Konoe's government by then had decided on a policy to capitalize on the successful capture of Nanjing, the seat of the Nationalist Government, on December 13, 1937, and to try bringing the conflict to a decisive conclusion by the use of force. (The infamous Rape of Nanjing occurred in the wake of the fall of the city, as discussed shortly.) Chiang Kai-shek, meanwhile, abandoned Nanjing and reconstituted his government at Chongqing in inland China where he continued to direct the war against the Japanese.

Hiranuma Kiichirō was another accused at Tokyo, who formerly served as vice-president of the Privy Council (1930–1936), president of the Privy Council (1936–1939, 1945), and prime minister of Japan (1939). He, too, spoke at the Imperial Diet about a year later, on January 21, 1939, similarly justifying Japan's military action against China.[13] The tone of his language is harsher than that of Hirota, however, as Hiranuma articulated in a much more blunt manner the readiness of the Japanese government to authorize the use of force to destroy recalcitrant Chinese. The segment of his speech as quoted in the Tokyo Judgment appears in full as follows:

In regard to the China Incident upon which both the Cabinet and the people are concentrating their endeavors, there exists an immutable policy for which Imperial Sanction was obtained [*seidan o aogi tatematsuri*] by the previous Cabinet. The present Cabinet is of course committed to the same policy. I hope the intention of Japan will be understood by the Chinese so that they may cooperate with us. As for those who fail to understand, *we have no other alternative than to exterminate them* [*kore o inmetsu suru koto de arimasu*].[14]

Some eight years before Hiranuma's foregoing statement, the Government of Japan had already adopted a comparable policy in the handling of resistance movements in Manchuria. It notified the League of Nations that while agreeing to submit to the League-appointed commission of inquiry (the Lytton Commission) concerning the Manchurian Incident starting on September 18, 1931, Japan reserved the right to take action against "bandits [*hizoku*]", that is, "those Chinese troops who resisted the Japanese Army," whom Japan regarded as "not lawful combatants." According to the Tokyo Judgment, Japan acted on its reservations thereafter, and "a ruthless campaign for the extermination of these 'bandits' in Manchuria was inaugurated."[15] One of the early instances of extermination efforts took place on September 16, 1932. The Japanese garrisoned army in the region, the Kwantung Army (*Kantō gun*), carried out mass execution of the residents of Pingdingshan and two other towns in the vicinity of Fushun, claiming that civilians in these towns harbored "bandits." The Kwantung Army assembled more than 2,700 men, women, and children and summarily executed them by machine guns.[16]

The foregoing speeches by Hirota and Hiranuma, made after the outbreak of the Marco Polo Bridge Incident on July 7, 1937, indicate that the policy of denying China the status of lawful belligerence remained in effect after the start of undeclared yet full-scale war between the two countries. In November of the same year, the Japanese government established the Imperial General Headquarters to bring the Army and the Navy on a wartime footing. Nevertheless, and according to the findings of the Tokyo Tribunal, "no additional effort was made to enforce the laws of war in the conduct of the hostilities in China."[17] Lt. Gen. Mutō Akira, an accused at Tokyo and formerly chief of the Military Affairs Bureau of the Army Ministry, confirmed that his government made no policy change with regard to the status of the Sino-Japanese armed conflict. "MUTO says that it was officially decided in 1938 to continue to call the war in China an 'Incident' and to continue for that reason to refuse to apply the rules of war to the conflict." The Judgment also reads, "TOJO [Hideki] told us [the Tribunal] the same."[18] Tōjō concurrently held the positions of army minister and prime minister between October 1941 and July 1944.

Denying China the status of lawful belligerence did not necessarily mean that the Japanese government approved its servicemen's unprincipled actions against the Chinese people. The Tokyo Judgment illuminates that in the case of mass atrocity following the capture of Nanjing in December 1937, members of the Japanese diplomatic corps, the Japanese press, and the Japanese embassy in Nanjing were sufficiently alarmed by the scale of military violence that they "sent out reports detailing the atrocities being committed in and around Nanking [Nanjing]." The reports reached the Ministry of Foreign Affairs, whose chief, Hirota Kōki, forwarded them to Gen. Umezu Yoshijirō, another accused at Tokyo, who was then serving as vice minister of the army. The reports were referred to the Liaison Conferences that were attended by key members of the cabinet (the prime minister, the foreign minister, the finance minister, the army minister, and the navy minister) and the chiefs of the Army General Staff and the Navy General Staff. The fact that the reports of mass atrocity in Nanjing were contemporaneously brought to the attention of these top government and military leaders points to their weighty nature. As a matter of fact, and according to the Tokyo Judgment, "following these unfavorable reports and the pressure of public opinion aroused in nations all over the world, the Japanese Government recalled MATSUI [Iwane] and approximately 80 of his officers." But no further disciplinary steps ensued. The central government rather appeared to prefer papering over the matter than tarnishing the names of those war heroes already celebrated for their military achievements. Gen. Matsui Iwane, an accused at the Tokyo Trial and commander-in-chief of the Central China Area Army that carried out the invasion of Nanjing, was appointed to the position of a cabinet councillor upon his recall. On April 29, 1940, he was decorated for his "'meritorious services' in the China War."[19]

The government effort to reduce the Japanese military violence, if any, remained ineffective in the post-Nanjing period. "After the occupation of Hankow [Hankou, October 1938]," the Judgment read, "Japanese soldiers returning from China told stories of the Army's misdeeds in China and displayed loot which they had taken." In other words, those Japanese soldiers who completed their tour of duty were talking openly – and even bragging – about the acts of violence they committed in China. Troubled by the returning servicemen's loose talk, Gen. Itagaki Seishirō – an accused at Tokyo, who served as army minister between 1938 and 1939 – issued special orders to commanders in the field in February 1939 that this problem must be addressed immediately. "Not only does the improper talk of the returned officers and men become the cause of rumors," the orders stated, "but also impairs the trust of the people in the Army, disrupts the unity of the people supporting the Army, etc." The field commanders were thereafter to "make the control of instruction even more strict and consequently glorify the meritorious deeds, raise the Japanese Army's military reputation and insure [ensure] that nothing will impair the accomplishment of the object of the Holy War."[20] What is missing in the special orders, of course, was any indication that the Japanese servicemen must adhere to the laws and customs of war. The behavior of the Japanese troops was not going to change unless far more drastic steps were taken, not merely issuing orders to strengthen military censorship. But despite the general sentiments of disapproval in the Japanese leadership circles about their undisciplined troops, no powerful dose of preventative measures was forthcoming. The Tokyo Judgment shows that atrocities persisted instead.

The Japanese mistreatment of Chinese captives for the rest of the Sino-Japanese armed conflict is summarized in the Judgment as follows:

Many of the captured Chinese were tortured, massacred, placed in labor units to work for the Japanese Army, or organized into army units to serve the puppet governments established by Japan in the occupied territory in China. Some of these captives who refused to serve in these armies were transported to Japan to relieve the labor shortage in the munitions industries.[21]

This particular segment of the Tokyo Judgment indicates not only that the Chinese people continued to fall victim to Japanese military violence but also that they were systematically pressed into work parties to assist the Japanese armed forces with logistical work or, if not, were made to join armies of collaborationist governments in China.[22] Alternatively, they were deported to Japan for forced labor in support of Japanese war industries. Research to date shows that the Tōjō war cabinet adopted in November 1942 a formal resolution to authorize the mass transfer of Chinese civilians to Japan for labor. A total of 38,935 Chinese were deported to Japan in accordance with this particular cabinet resolution. Of these, 6,830 died due to cruel treatment, harsh work environment, substandard food and accommodation, and illnesses and injuries resulting from inhumane treatment.[23] In addition to those who were taken to Japan, a large number of other Chinese were deported to the South Pacific for forced labor. Their attrition rate was much higher than the one of Chinese forced laborers in Japan. (See Chapter 4 for related discussion.)

The Tokyo Tribunal in its Judgment documented some concrete instances of mass atrocity in the post-Nanjing period. The major ones are the following: mass execution of several hundred Chinese captives by the members of the Central China Area Army (under command of another accused at the Tokyo Trial, Gen. Hata Shunroku, Matsui's successor as commander-in-chief of the army) in the aftermath of the invasion of Hankou on October 25, 1938[24]; massacre by bayonetting of more than 600 Chinese men and women of various ages in the city of Weiyang in Guangdong Province toward the end of 1941; massacre of 700 civilians at the Taishan district, also in Guangdong Province, in July 1944; mass execution by artillery fire of 200 Chinese captured soldiers after using them for plundering large quantities of rice, wheat, and other goods during the military campaign to Changsha in September 1941; murder, rape, incendiarism, and other forms of atrocity against civilians in occupied Changsha; mass atrocity against residents of occupied Gweilin, including plunder, rape, and forced prostitution[25]; and deportation to Akita Prefecture, Japan, and forced labor of 981 Chinese captives, of whom 418 died of starvation, torture, and neglect.[26] The Judgment also recorded that a Japanese navy unit carried out massacre of 24 civilians and a French missionary in the town of Bowen, Hainan Island, in August 1941, apparently in retaliation for the death of a Japanese sailor although the actual circumstances of the sailor's death were never established. The number of the killed was relatively small but, according to the Tokyo Judgment, the reporting of this episode received wide circulation at Tokyo to the point of compelling the chief of staff of the Japanese occupation forces to make an on-site inquiry. Upon receipt of the final report in mid-October the same year, Gen. Kimura Heitarō – then serving as vice minister of the army, later an accused at the Tokyo Trial – "at once circulated the report for the information of all concerned to the various bureaus of the War Ministry [Army Ministry] and then sent it to the Foreign Ministry."[27] Yet just like any other episodes of atrocity in the Sino-Japanese armed conflict, the information of massacre on Hainan Island did not lead to any drastic policy change regarding the Japanese conduct of war and military occupation in the China theater.

It should be noted on this occasion that the Tokyo Judgment does not provide exhaustive documentation of Japanese military violence in China. It instead recorded samples of cases. The limited scope of documentation mirrored the original case made by the Chinese prosecution team, which restricted its task to showcasing only a representative range. (The sole exception is evidence relative to the Rape of Nanjing, which the prosecution documented extensively.) What was more, the prosecution's case at the Tokyo Trial was generally confined to atrocities committed in occupied territories and those combat zones in which the Japanese engaged Chiang Kai-shek's armed forces. When it came to atrocities elsewhere arising from conflict between the Japanese armed forces and the Chinese Red Army, the prosecution's case had no evidence to present.[28] This kind of prosecutorial imbalance at Tokyo reflected the complex situation of war crimes investigation in postwar China, where the civil war had already resumed before the termination of hostilities with Japan.

To summarize, the Tokyo Tribunal found (1) that the wartime Government of Japan from early on adopted the policy of denying the status of lawful belligerence to China and did not require the Japanese armed forces to comply with the laws and customs of war in the handling of surrendered Chinese combatants or civilians in their custody; (2) that the Japanese troops repeatedly committed atrocities against Chinese nationals; (3) that some instances of atrocity were systematic and highly organized, as evidenced in mass deportation, forced labor, and forced conscription; (4) that the Japanese leaders were informed of the prevalence of Japanese military violence from early on; (5) that they regarded it as a matter of great concern; but (6) that neither they nor field commanders took any decisive steps to bring to an end the repeated commission of mass atrocity by the Japanese servicemen.

THE WAR IN THE PACIFIC THEATER

A notable change was made in Japanese war policy with the outbreak of the Pacific War. The Government of Japan issued Imperial Ordinance No. 1182, titled "Prisoner-of-War Camp Ordinance" (*Furyo shūyōjo rei*) and dated December 23, 1941, to set out basic organizational principles concerning the establishment of prisoner-of-war camps in anticipation of enemy soldiers coming into Japanese custody. The ordinance stipulated that prisoner-of-war camps would be set up "whenever they are necessary" and in accordance with the decision of the army minister. Once established, "prisoner of war camps shall be administered by a commander of an army or a commander of a garrison under the general supervision of the Minister of War," and "the commandant shall be responsible to a commander of an army or to a commander of a garrison and he shall manage all the affairs of the camp."[29] Basic rules of prisoner-of-war camp organization were elaborated in Army Ministry Notification No. 29, titled "Detailed Regulations for the Treatment of Prisoners of War" (*Furyo toriatsukai saisoku*), and dated April 21, 1943. It designated the army commanders in the field as "chief administrators [*kanri chōkan*]" of prisoner-of-war camps with the power, among other things, to set up at their own discretion prisoner-of-war camp detachments and branch camps.[30] The issuance of new rules on prisoner-of-war camp organization indicates that the Japanese government since the start of the Pacific War considered itself bound by the laws and customs of war and that it felt obligated to take concrete steps to ensure Japan's compliance.

What exactly did it mean, though, for Japan to recognize prisoner-of-war status to captured soldiers and treat them accordingly? Army Ministry Notification No. 22, titled "Regulations for the Treatment of Prisoners of War" (*Furyo toriatsukai kisoku*), which dated back to the start of the Russo-Japanese War (February 14, 1904), defined a prisoner-of-war as "any enemy combatant who has fallen into the power of the Empire or any other person who is to be accorded the treatment of a prisoner of war by virtue of international treaties and customs." Such person "shall be humanely treated and in no case shall any insult or maltreatment be inflicted upon them."[31] These exact definitional stipulations were carried over in Army Ministry notifications in subsequent decades and remained applicable at the start of the Pacific War. In 1943, the Army Ministry affirmed its commitment to these principles by issuing another notification containing the same stipulations.

Continuing to fulfill its international obligations relative to prisoners of war, the Government of Japan issued another imperial ordinance, dated December 27, 1941, by which it established the Prisoner-of-War Information Bureau (*furyo jōhō kyoku*).[32] Maj. Gen. Sanada Jōichirō, a key prosecution witness at the Tamura Trial and formerly a top official of the Army Ministry and of the Army General Staff, explained that "the P.O.W. Information Bureau was organized and established immediately after the outbreak of war (about mid-Dec. [December], 1941) in conformity with the International Treaty, in order to take charge of the movement of war prisoners, their communications, the sending of their things."[33] The international treaty he referred to was probably the Hague Convention No. 4, dated October 18, 1907. According to article 14 of the convention, each belligerent state must establish an "inquiry office for prisoners of war" upon the start of hostilities. The function of a prisoner-of-war inquiry office should be "to reply to all inquiries about the prisoners" and "to make out and keep up to date an individual return for each prisoner of war" as well as "to receive and collect all objects of personal use, valuables, letters, etc., found on the field of battle or left by prisoners who have been released on parole, or exchanged, or who have escaped, or died in hospitals or ambulances, and to forward them to those concerned."[34] By issuing the foregoing ordinance, the Japanese government appeared to designate the Prisoner-of-War Information Bureau as such a central clearinghouse of information pertaining to prisoners of war. This bureau was thereafter to act "under the direction and supervision of the Minister of War" and was empowered to "demand information from any military or navy unit concerned."[35]

At the very time the new prisoner-of-war information agency was being instituted, the Japanese government received inquiries from the United States and the British Commonwealth of Nations via the Protecting Powers – governments not party to the war, representing the interests of belligerents to maintain diplomatic channels during the conflict – regarding its position on the Geneva Prisoner-of-War Convention of 1929.[36] Containing a total of ninety-seven articles detailing rights of prisoners of war, this convention gave comprehensive rules regarding protection of surrendered soldiers in custody of a belligerent state. Japan was a signatory of the Geneva Prisoner-of-War Convention but failed to ratify it, hence the Allied inquiries regarding Japan's policy on compliance with this particular international convention.

After conferring with the Army Ministry, the Navy Ministry, the Ministry of Home Affairs, and the Ministry of Colonial Affairs, the Ministry of Foreign Affairs communicated to the Allied Powers on January 29, 1942, that even though Japan did not consider itself bound by the Geneva Prisoner-of-War Convention by reason of nonratification, it "would apply 'mutatis mutandis' the provisions of that Convention to American prisoners of war in its power" and act similarly "toward the British, Canadian, Australian and New Zealand prisoners of war under Japanese control." Japan further notified that it would take into consideration "the national and racial manners and customs under reciprocal conditions when supplying clothing and provisions to prisoners of war."[37] In addition, the Japanese government offered to extend the Geneva Prisoner-of-War Convention to the Allied civilian internees in the spirit of reciprocity, viz., in return for the Allied Powers providing protection to Japanese nationals in their custody. The pertinent diplomatic message from the Japanese Ministry of Foreign Affairs, dated February 6, 1942, read that even though the Geneva Prisoner-of-WarConvention "has no binding power whatsoever on Japan . . . , this Ministry has no objection to applying the principles of the Convention to non-combatant internees within such limits as it is applicable, provided, however, that no person be subjected to labor against his will."[38]

A series of successful battles in the initial months of the Pacific War, meanwhile, resulted in very large numbers of the Allied troops falling into Japanese military custody. The Army Ministry's administrative responsibilities for managing the prisoner-of-war population dramatically increased as a result. According to the aforementioned prosecution witness Sanada, "because of enormous number of P.O.W., extensive occupied area and complexity of nationalities in this War, the hitherto-employed ways and means caused delay to the business of the central department." To tackle the backlog of mounting administrative tasks, the army minister and prime minister at that time, Tōjō, conferred with the vice minister of the army, Kimura, and the first chief of the Prisoner-of-War Information Bureau, Uemura. Tōjō decided at the end of March 1942 that the Prisoner-of-War Administration Section (*furyo kanri bu*) be newly instituted within the Army Ministry. Served concurrently by the same members in the Prisoner-of-War Information Bureau, this section was to act under orders of the army minister and take charge of all affairs concerning the management of prisoners of war as well as civilian internees.[39]

The Prisoner-of-War Administration Section took on greater responsibility eight months later when the army minister delegated to the section chief some of his decision-making power and authority. A notification from the army minister's adjutant, dated November 22, 1942, stated that the chief of the Prisoner-of-War Administration Section was now entrusted with decisions on a full range of issues of "minor importance," that is, from matters concerning prisoner-of-war and civilian accommodation, allowances, transfer, employment, punishment, correspondence, and relief, to matters concerning granting to foreign observers entry into internment camps to perform inspection.[40] As discussed later in this chapter, the exact scope of the section chief's decision-making power and authority became a point of contention when determining Tamura's culpability for prisoner-of-war mismanagement.

Once the two new prisoner-of-war affairs agencies were established, their members took on a wide variety of bureaucratic responsibilities in order to make the new prisoner-of-war information and administration system work. One of the first tasks they undertook was to host in the middle of 1942 group sessions for newly appointed prisoner-of-war camp commandants and their staff so that they would be fully acquainted with their duties. At the sessions, various printed materials were given out to them so that they would know the army minister's general policies regarding the handling of prisoners of war, the basic organizational structures of the new prisoner-of-war management regime, the uniform procedure for record keeping, and a full range of other rules and regulations pertaining to prisoner-of-war internment, allowances, relief, correspondence, transportation, employment, and punishment.[41]

Documents that were handed out at the instructional sessions were subsequently incorporated into "Laws, Rules and Regulations Concerning Prisoners of War" (_Furyo ni kansuru shohōki ruijū_, whose accurate translation would be "the compilation of various rules concerning prisoners of war"), so that its copies could be distributed as key reference material to all army ministry bureaus, government agencies, and army units concerned.[42]

Hosting training sessions and compiling the rule book aside, members of prisoner-of-war affairs agencies began carrying out on-site inspections of prisoner-of-war camps so as to fulfill their duties based on information of actual conditions on the ground. "Inspections were made mostly by the Chief of the P.O.W. Control Board [the Prisoner-of-War Administration Section] and members of the board," according to Sanada, but "I suppose members of other bureaus [of the Army Ministry] also often had opportunities of making inspections."[43] In this manner, the system of prisoner-of-war accommodation took shape in fits and starts under the direction of the Army Ministry. New regulations continued to be produced and some were amended well into 1943, but it appears that a standardized prisoner-of-war management system was in full operation by the later months of 1942.

One can surmise from the foregoing information that the Japanese government was mindful of its international obligations regarding protecting prisoners of war. However, it is doubtful that the new system helped Japan fulfill them. The record of the Tamura Trial and numerous other contemporaneous Allied proceedings, including the Tokyo Trial, attest rather to the prevalence of harsh discipline, privation, and physical abuses at the prisoner-of-war camps across the theater of war. What is more, the Allied prisoners of war were pressed into providing labor to support the Japanese frontline troops with logistical work or the Japanese war industries in the inner territories of the Japanese empire. As a result of severe and exploitative treatment, the Allied prisoners of war suffered from illnesses, injuries, and deaths. The Tokyo Judgment shows that the mortality rate among members of the U.S. and U.K. forces in Japanese custody alone amounted to 27%, or 35,756 deaths out of 132,134 prisoners.[44]

Why was there general mistreatment of prisoners of war notwithstanding Japan's formal commitment to treat them in accordance with the laws and customs of war? Explanations can be varied and complex. From the record of the Tamura Trial alone, one can point out a few possible explanations. First of all, the Army Ministry may be singled out for defeating the purpose of the new prisoner-of-war management system by adopting contradictory policies. The Army Ministry authorized as early as May 6, 1942, the use of prisoner-of-war labor for tasks connected with operations of the war in clear violation of the 1907 Hague Convention No.4 as well as the 1929 Geneva Prisoner-of-War Convention. Titled "Disposal of Prisoners of War" (_Furyo shori yōkō_), this particular policy document of the Army Ministry set out two separate rules regarding the use of prisoner-of-war labor. "Prisoners of war who are white persons [_hakujin furyo_] shall be imprisoned in Chosen [Korea], Taiwan,

Manchuria, and China successively," it read, so that they be "employed in the expansion of our production and or work connected with military affairs." In other words, Caucasian prisoners of war in the outlying areas were to be transferred and utilized in inner territories of the Empire of Japan. The same policy document endorsed the use of non-Caucasian prisoners of war labor, too, although on slightly different terms. It stipulated that "prisoners of war who are not white persons [*hakujin igai no furyo*] and who do not necessitate imprisonment shall immediately be released on parole and made to work in their present localities."[45] In other words, nonwhite prisoners of war (presumably of Asian origins) would be granted freedom on condition of parole, and their labor power would be put to use in occupied territories, not in Japan. The policy of applying differentiated race-based prisoner-of-war policy in all likelihood had propaganda purposes: to impress the Japanese people with their racial superiority vis-à-vis the white prisoners of war, and to convey the message of Asian solidarity to people in Japanese-occupied Southeast Asia.[46] The bottom line, in any event, is that the Army Ministry sanctioned from early on the use of prisoner-of-war labor in manners prohibited by the Hague Convention No. 4 and the Geneva Prisoner-of-War Convention, *while at the same time* overseeing the new prisoner-of-war management system purportedly to ensure Japan's compliance with the said conventions.

Second, Army Minister Tōjō may be held personally responsible for sending conflicting messages about his government's policy. When new prisoner-of-war camp commandants assembled in Tokyo in July 1942 for instructional sessions, he had the chief of the Prisoner-of-War Information Bureau read out his keynote address to convey his general policy views. In the address, Tōjō exhorted on the one hand that the new camp commandants must "adhere by the laws and regulations and apply them fairly and properly so that it will enhance and exhibit the prestige of our Empire." Yet on the other hand, he emphasized that "our country has a different conception of prisoners of war and consequently has different methods of treatment compared with those of American and European nations." Warning against leniency, he urged the camp commandants to "supervise them rigidly insofar as you do not become inhuman, and let them remain idle even for a single day." The prisoner-of-war labor would be put to use specifically "for the expansion of our industries and to contribute to the execution of the great Eastern Asia War."[47] The exhortation of fair and proper treatment notwithstanding, this address may have been construed as authorization to treat prisoners of war harshly to expand Japan's war production. At the least, the army minister's personal endorsement of Spartan austerity may have influenced the thinking and the behavior of individual Japanese servicemen in charge of managing the prisoner-of-war camps.

It did not take long for negative consequences of the Army Ministry's stringent prisoner-of-war labor policy to surface. Acting on the government decision to increase the use of prisoner-of-war labor in the inner circle of the Japanese empire, the Army General Staff planned and executed the transport of large numbers of prisoners of war across the Pacific Ocean. They did so on ships loaded beyond capacity and without ensuring adequate supplies of food, water, and sanitary arrangement. Many of the prisoners of war became too sick to be put to work when they disembarked at Japanese ports.[48] Deeply concerned about the deteriorated health of prisoner-of-war laborers, Vice Minister of the Army Kimura communicated to army units involved in prisoner-of-war transfer that necessary steps be taken. His message, dated December 10, 1942, read, "Recently during the transportation of the prisoners of war to Japan many of them have been taken ill (or have died) and quite a few of them have been incapacitated for further work due to the treatment on the way which at times was inadequate." Kimura urged that rules regarding the selection of prisoners of war for labor be far more rigorously enforced so as to minimize this type of undesirable situation, that is, rules concerning "medical examinations, distribution of the medical personnel, the medicine necessary during the transit, the preparation of provisions, administration during the transit, facilities to be provided at ports of call, supply of clothing, etc."[49]

Terrible health conditions of prisoners of war who were brought to Japan for labor received a much fuller commentary in a report completed by the Investigation Squad of the Army Medical College at an undated time (but presumably toward the end of 1942), titled "Suggestions Regarding Improvement of Health Conditions of Prisoners of War Camps."[50] The report began by affirming Japan's commitment to observing the laws and customs of war, but conceded the occurrence of "some regrettable events" in the handling of prisoners of war. The main reason, as the report identified it, was that "the persons concerned are not well acquainted with the customs of the enemy countries and often allow misunderstandings to arise." The report defended the policy of harsh prisoner-of-war treatment, stating that "the lowest standard of living allowable from the human standpoint" was sufficient for the Allied prisoners given the fact that "our people are going through hardship and deprivations." However, the poor health of prisoners of war worried the army investigators from the standpoints of labor efficiency and public health. The Army Medical College's own studies brought out that prisoners of war interned in the Tokyo area were generally malnourished. Many suffered from pneumonia and skin disease, as they were dressed in utterly filthy, lice-infested, tattered military uniforms. Should they have been in good condition, those uniforms would have been suited only for the tropical climate and not the bitterly cold winter in Japan. Medical examinations of feces samples taken from prisoners of war at Kawasaki, Tsurumi, and Yokohama showed that between 6.8% and 21.7% of prisoners of war at these locations were infected with amoebic dysentery. The evidence of malaria and instances of diphtheria were also recorded. "From the above facts, we greatly fear that if we let these carriers work outside the camps and allow them to come in contact with the Japanese people, there will be a great danger of spreading an epidemic in the country," the report of the Army Medical College concluded.[51]

Information regarding the troubling health conditions of prisoner-of-war laborers continued to reach the top echelon of the Army Ministry in the latter half of the Pacific War. In an effort to rectify the situation, the Army Ministry issued a notice afresh to army units concerned and urged that improvement be made. Dated March 3, 1944, the message from the vice minister of the army began with the statement that the use of Allied prisoners of war for labor remained central to the Japanese policy on prisoner-of-war administration. It went on to state that "although this [prisoner-of-war labor] has directly helped to increase our fighting strength and has produced other good results, the average PWs [POWs] health condition is hardly satisfactory due to the inevitable shortage of material etc." The Army Ministry's message stressed that "their high rate of death must be brought to our attention." The poor conditions of prisoners of war, not to mention their deaths, would negatively affect both Japan's international reputation and labor productivity. The vice minister warned that the information of prisoners' poor health in Japanese custody could fuel anti-Japanese sentiments to the point of making it "impossible for us to expect the world opinion to be what we wish it to be." From the practical standpoint of the Japanese war effort, it was also "absolutely necessary" to improve the health of prisoners of war so that they could be used "satisfactorily to increase our fighting strength."[52]

The examples of army ministry's internal records in preceding paragraphs show that the poor health of prisoner-of-war laborers persisted during the Pacific War and that the top officials of the Imperial Japanese Army were fully aware of this problem. It is clear, too, that they disapproved of the substandard treatment of prisoner-of-war laborers and a high death rate. Humanitarian consideration may not have influenced their policy views (although such possibility cannot be ruled out completely), but the pragmatic assessment of the Japanese war effort did. Nevertheless, they appeared utterly ineffective in tackling the problem. The repeated issuance of warnings and instructions is indicative of the Army Ministry's continuing failure to bring about material change in conditions of prisoner-of-war internment.

INDIVIDUAL RESPONSIBILITY

The accused Tamura Hiroshi served as chief of the Prisoner-of-War Information Bureau and concurrently as chief of the Prisoner-of-War Administration Section from December 1944 through September 1945. He faced a single charge of war crimes and eleven specifications.[53] Most of the allegations against him were "willful and unlawful disregard and failure to discharge his duties," drawing upon the doctrine of command responsibility that had by then become widely applied at contemporaneous Far Eastern Allied war crimes trials. Tamura also faced allegations of ordering war crimes. This indicates the readiness of the prosecution to take up the burden of proof not only of Tamura's disregard of duties but also of his possession of the power to issue orders. The latter could be a difficult task, however, since the two prisoner-of-war affairs agencies on their face were government officials without formal command authority. Much of the prosecution's evidence against Tamura focused on substantiating command authority nonetheless, which he allegedly possessed and exercised.

The breakdown of eleven specifications against Tamura is as follows. Four of them pertained to the accused's duties mainly as chief of the Prisoner-of-War Information Bureau. They read that Tamura "did willfully and unlawfully disregard and fail to discharge the duty" by (1) refusing and failing to investigate and collect full and accurate information of individual Allied prisoners of war; (2) obstructing the Protecting Powers and the International Committee of the Red Cross from performing their assigned tasks; (3) refusing and failing to transmit personal belongings of the deceased prisoners of war in Japanese custody; and (4) failing to preserve prisoner-of-war information for subsequent delivery to the interested Allied governments. The remainder of the specifications pertained to duties of the accused as chief of the Prisoner-of-War Administrative Section. They read that the accused "did willfully and unlawfully disregard and fail to discharge the duty" by (1) ordering and permitting prisoners of war to be exposed to the hazards of war; (2) ordering and permitting prisoners of war to be interned in inadequate and unsuitable accommodation; (3) compelling, permitting, and causing prisoners of war to be employed in manners in violation of the laws and customs of war including for work related to the operations of war; (4) ordering and permitting confinement of prisoners of war in unlawful cells or unlisted places; and (5) failing to control and restrain "persons under his supervision and control" by "permitting" them to commit atrocities. Tamura was further charged that he "did willfully and unlawfully order, direct, cause, incite, advise, and permit" (1) the mistreatment, abuse, torture, and killing of prisoners of war, and (2) the denial of prisoner-of-war status to the Allied airmen.[54]

When leveling these accusations against Tamura, the prosecution did not take much issue with inherent contradictions and institutional shortcomings of the Japanese prisoner-of-war management system. Rather, the main case against him was that he improperly exercised the power vested in him concurrently as chief of the Prisoner-of-War Information Bureau and chief of the Prisoner-of-War Administration Section. In the words of the chief prosecutor Robert H. Neptune, Tamura was brought to trial essentially on the grounds that he "denied prisoners of war the standard protection" as required by the laws and customs of war and that he moreover "frustrated the policy guaranteeing the control" even though the original purposes of offices he held were to guarantee the proper functioning of the system of prisoner-of-war protection.[55]

The major challenge for the prosecution at the Tamura Trial was to show that the accused not only failed to discharge his duty but also exercised command authority that allowed prisoner-of-war mistreatment to occur. The prosecution did not hesitate to concede that the accused was vested with no formal command authority, but argued that *in practice* he assumed such authority and exercised it. To demonstrate the adequacy of these allegations as well as those of disregard of duties, the prosecution brought to the courtroom a total of 22 witnesses and 459 court exhibits. The prosecution witnesses included former high-ranking army ministry officials who could testify on the de facto command authority that Tamura allegedly exercised as prisoner-of-war affairs chief. The defense, for its part, countered by arguing that Tamura "had no authority to issue an order of the type complained of by the prosecution in their charge and their specifications" and "consequently he could not have committed the crime."[56] With this as the baseline of the defense argument, E. N. Warren, a former defense lawyer at the Tokyo Trial who now represented Tamura, carried out relentless cross-examination of every prosecution witness that attested to the accused's ability to issue military orders.

One of the key prosecution witnesses to testify on Tamura's command authority as chief of prisoner-of-war affairs agencies was the aforementioned Sanada Jōichirō. He was a colleague of Tamura between December 1944 and March 1945, when he served as chief of the Military Affairs Bureau of the Army Ministry. Sanada did not contest that the chief of the Prisoner-of-War Administration Section was a government official and not a military commander. The section chief essentially served as "a direct assistant staff officer to the [Army] Minister."[57] In his capacity as "the only advisory staff of the Minister" on matters pertaining to prisoners of war, however, the chief of the Prisoner-of-War Administration Section assumed broad authority to manage prisoner-of-war affairs. Sanada pointed out that the section chief took charge, among other things, of (1) carrying out the inspection of prisoner-of-war camps or had his staff do so; (2) assembling and conveying to persons in charge of prisoner-of-war camps "the intention of the central government" under orders of the army minister; and, moreover, (3) "demand[ing] information from the army commanders" regarding prisoners of war by virtue of holding concurrently the position of chief of the Prisoner-of-War Information Bureau.[58] The chief of the Prisoner-of-War Administration Section did not have the power to issue orders, Sanada readily confirmed, but then he "frequently gathered the prisoner of war camp commanders for a conference and would transmit the opinions of the War Minister." Above all, this section chief was the only army ministry official with the power to make decisions on affairs of prisoner-of-war management. The authority of chiefs of other bureaus in the Army Ministry was limited to offering "advices [*sic*] and suggestions" within their respective job specializations.[59]

Sanada similarly brought out a complex picture about the power vested in the accused as chief of the Prisoner-of-War Information Bureau. He testified that the bureau chief had no authority to take disciplinary action against an army unit, say, for failing to provide requested prisoner-of-war information. However, the chief of the Prisoner-of-War Information Bureau concurrently held the office of the chief of the Prisoner-of-War Administration Section, and *in this capacity,* he could "request the War Minister to take appropriate action." The army minister in turn would issue orders on behalf of the bureau chief so as to require the army unit concerned to provide necessary prisoner-of-war information.[60] In other words, the chief of the Prisoner-of-War Information Bureau could make his demand binding on an army unit by having it conveyed through the army minister. Imposing disciplinary action, in this regard, was within his power so long as it would be enforced through the army minister. The defense lawyer Warren countered this witness by putting the following question: "The truth of the matter is, the POW Information Bureau was charged with the collecting of information and had absolutely no authority to do anything else, is that not correct?" This question met flat denial, however, as Sanada replied: "Not as you have stated."[61]

Sugai Toshimaro was formerly adjutant of the army minister between February 1943 and February 1945. He similarly took the witness stand for the prosecution. He confirmed that the chief of the Prisoner-of-War Administration Section was uniquely vested with decision-making authority on matters of prisoner-of-war management. The section chief would generally make decisions "after consulting with other bureau chiefs concerned" and issued them in the name of either the vice minister of the army or the army minister.[62] What was more, "if it was within his delegated authority, there were cases where he did not get the approval of the Minister,"[63] that is, he could make decisions on certain issues at his own discretion and transmit them to army units concerned in the name of the army minister. Regarding the section chief's relationship with army units in charge of prisoner-of-war camps, Sugai testified that he could "issue instructions and orders to the camp commanders after having received the orders from the War Minister." Upon cross-examination by the defense, Sugai revised his testimony by stating that "the word 'order' is not proper." But he held that it was a matter of little difference as to whether one should call them orders or instructions. "In substance they are the same. Both had to be carried out," he stated.[64]

Lt. Col. Hoda Haruo served as the third-ranking official of the two prisoner-of-war affairs agencies and was a former subordinate of three successive prisoner-of-war affairs chiefs. His court testimony generally fell in line with those offered by witnesses Sanada and Sugai. He recalled that the chief of the Prisoner-of-War Administration Section had the responsibility to report to the army minister and to receive the latter's authorization on "important matters." But the same did not apply when it came to "minor matters," because in late November 1942 the army minister delegated part of his decision-making authority to the chief of the Prisoner-of-War Administration Section. Ever since, the section chief "made decisions and approval[s] on behalf of the War Minister." Matters thus decided "were looked upon as the decision and approval and orders of the War Minister and carrying out of those was required."[65] When the defense suggested that the work of the Prisoner-of-War Administration Section was "merely a clerical duty," Hoda denied it. He reiterated that this office "had to make decisions" after consulting various government and military authorities concerned. Given the actual decision-making power, "you cannot say that it was an unimportant clerical duty."[66]

Hoda had additional information specifically about Tamura. He recalled that Tamura was "very strict on the prisoners of war," which he remembered as standing in stark contrast with Uemura and Hamada, two army generals who served in the same posts successively prior to Tamura's appointment.[67] The two predecessors, in Hoda's opinion, were more attentive to the welfare of prisoners of war than Tamura. By way of illustration, this witness related an episode in which Hamada had prisoner-of-war labor withdrawn from the Hidachi Production Company. Hamada is said to have taken this action upon receipt of an unfavorable report that his subordinate official filed after carrying out an on-site inspection.[68] Hoda did not recall comparable initiatives having been taken by Tamura. "To my knowledge he never sent a notification forbidding and prohibiting personal punishments as did both UEMURA and HAMADA," as he put it. What the accused did do, according to this witness, was to promote harsh treatment on prisoners of war. Specific instructions given out by Tamura included that prisoner-of-war confinement cells be made small and allow less sunlight; that complaints and petitions from prisoners of war be rejected; that relief goods be placed under strict control of camp commanders; and that Allied airmen be placed in a special compound at the Ōmori prisoner-of-war camp to prevent them from spreading to other prisoners the latest information about the state of the war.[69]

Lt. Col. Emoto Shigeo, 61, formerly area commandant of the prisoner-of-war camp group in Hokkaidō between May 1944 and April 1945, also took the witness stand for the prosecution. His testimony centered on his personal experience of being directed by the prisoner-of-war affairs agencies in general and by Tamura in person to increase severity in the handling of prisoners of war. A person with progressive streak and independent-mindedness, this witness appears to have been a known figure within the wartime Japanese army authorities as well as among the postwar Allied war crimes investigators. During his service as the Hokkaidō area camp commandant, Emoto overhauled the condition of prisoner-of-war camps and brought about dramatic improvement in the living conditions of prisoners of war under his control. He was taken to Sugamo Prison after the war but not as a war crimes suspect. Instead, he was treated as a material witness for the Allied war crimes investigators. He was summoned as a key prosecution witness at the trial of his predecessor as Hokkaidō camp commander, Col. Hatakeyema Toshio, at Yokohama.[70] The defense at the Tamura Trial had difficulty destroying credibility of this witness, since he was not only knowledgeable about the general problems of the Japanese prisoner-of-war camp regime but also highly experienced in court testimony by then. Coupled with the witness's impressive command of English (he chose to testify in English), and Warren's all-out effort to undermine his credibility, the cross-examination of this particular witness turned out to be a fast-paced, heated affair.

Mirroring the oral evidence offered in Hoda's testimony, Emoto testified on a major shift in prisoner-of-war policy since the time Tamura took up the position of chief of the prisoner-of-war affairs agencies. He could recall, for instance, that when Tamura's immediate predecessor, Hamada, visited the Hokkaidō camps in June 1944, Hamada expressed great satisfaction with exemplary improvement Emoto had brought about to prisoner-of-war conditions.[71] But once Tamura took office, Emoto received instructions from the prisoner-of-war affairs agencies that his camps should change course. The altered policy was passed to the witness when Hoda visited Hokkaidō in his official capacity. "The Allies are coming closer to Japan and we, the Japanese people, are not going to shake hands with the enemy after the war is over," he is said to have told Emoto. With this understanding in mind, "you must treat prisoners of war much more strictly." When Emoto countered that these instructions conflicted with the policy previously endorsed by Hamada, he was told that "now the situation had become different."[72]

The new prisoner-of-war affairs chief, Tamura, made a visit to the Hokkaidō camps shortly after Hoda in February 1945. Emoto attested to receiving various orders and instructions personally from Tamura on this occasion. Their gist was that a far more stringent management system should be imposed. Specifics of Tamura's instructions included that the Red Cross supplies be placed under far stricter control; that the guardhouse cells be reconstructed to make them smaller and afford less sunlight; and that all the posted placards indicating the rules and regulations concerning the proper treatment of prisoners of war in Japanese, English, and Dutch be removed from prisoner-of-war compounds.[73] The said placards had been prepared and nailed on the walls of prisoner-of-war barracks because of Emoto's decisions in preceding months, the purpose being to "enable all the prisoners of war, as well as my subordinates in the various prisoner of war camps, to know how prisoners of war should be treated." Tamura disapproved of the display of these placards, however, and told the witness that they "should be taken down and should not be put up thereafter."[74] When Emoto asked if there had been any policy change, Tamura is said to have replied that he "would require us [the Hokkaidō camp authorities] to treat prisoners of war very much more strictly because Maj. Gen. HAMADA's principles were very much too lenient."[75]

During extensive cross-examination that ensued, Warren interrogated the witness as to what steps he took to implement the orders that he allegedly received from Tamura. It soon became clear that while the witness made certain changes as told, he did not follow through with all of what Tamura had directed him to do. This revelation led Warren to suggest that notwithstanding the frequent use of the word "order," the witness actually never received any orders because Tamura, after all, was not vested with any authority to issue military orders. Alternatively, would the witness be prepared to say that

Tamura issued orders but that the witness disobeyed them? Emoto's testimony somewhat faltered when confronted with what amounted to personal attacks on his soldierly integrity. However, he held his ground by summarizing his position as follows:

So I say not all orders but some orders I couldn't obey. Not because of General TAMURA's order. Some of the orders issued by Northern Army Headquarters [the superior army unit of the Hokkaidō prisoner-of-war camps] I could not obey to the letter because the orders are wrong.[76]

By this reply, Emoto reiterated that Tamura had the power to issue de facto orders as much as other military superiors did, and that the witness did not follow some of them not on account of their originators but rather on their merit.

How did the defense respond to potentially incriminating evidence that arose from testimony by the prosecution's key witnesses? The answer is disappointingly straightforward. The defense chose to do nothing other than carrying out rigorous cross-examinations of these witnesses. Shortly after the prosecution's case rested and the defense motion for the finding of not guilty was rejected, Warren announced to the tribunal the defense decision that it would limit its case to calling to the stand the accused person alone. No other witnesses or court exhibits would be presented. He explained that this course of action was being taken as "the most expeditious way of proceeding." Moreover, "it gives the accused the opportunity to testify to the court on the matters on which the court wants clarification and gives the court the opportunity to go into any phase of the case which they may decide to ask the accused about."[77] Warren then called Tamura to the stand, and asked him some preliminary questions for the purpose of little more than establishing the witness's identity. No cross-examination followed as a result, nor was there any redirect by the defense. Some questions posed by the tribunal elicited follow-up questioning of the witness by the prosecution and the defense, but nothing much came out of that. The final arguments ensued, and the tribunal delivered its verdict and sentence. Tamura was found guilty of the charge and of all but three specifications. He received the penalty of eight years of hard labor.[78] The Tamura Trial, in this manner, came to an abrupt end on February 23, 1949.

While it cannot be independently verified, the Tamura Trial appears to have ended the way it did because of a behind-the-scenes plea deal of sorts, reached between the tribunal and the defense. Kanase Kunji, one of the two Japanese lawyers who served as members of Tamura's defense counsel, was interviewed by the Japanese war crimes investigation team of the Ministry of Legal Affairs on June 11, 1962, whereupon he related the following episode: The law member of the tribunal, J. Wordel Green, approached Warren in late January or early February 1949, inquiring into the possibility of bringing the trial to an early conclusion. The reason for requesting an early conclusion was purely personal. Green wanted the trial to end soon enough for him to secure an attractive job offer being made by the occupation authorities. The defense indicated its readiness to cooperate, so Kanase related, although on one condition, namely, "it will accept it [the request] if the verdict will be equivalent to Shigemitsu's [*Shigemitsu nami no hanketsu nara shōfuku*]".[79] By Shigemitsu, defense counsel was referring to Shigemitsu Mamoru, an accused at the Tokyo Trial. A former foreign minister during part of the Pacific War, Shigemitsu was convicted of war crimes and crimes against peace, but received an unusually light sentence of seven years in prison. According to Kanase's account, Tamura and his family generally supported the deal but Tamura cautioned that nothing undue should result from this "gamble [*bakuchi*]." "There probably cannot be a written agreement," Tamura is said to have commented, "but make sure that there is an assurance in the manner of a Gentleman's Agreement [*shinshi kyōtei to shite kakuyaku shite moraitai*]."[80] The fact that the trial ended speedily with the outcome of eight-years hard labor points to the likelihood that the alleged plea agreement was, in fact, reached and followed through.

The defense decision to decline the opportunity to meet squarely the prosecution's case is an unfortunate one, as it leaves some important questions about the issues of responsibility unanswered even though the trial reached its formal conclusion. Did Tamura have the power to exercise command authority? Was he a mere government functionary who undertook clerical duties alone, or did he assume and exercise some sort of command authority in relation to army units in charge of prisoner-of-war camps? A close look at the verdicts suggests that the tribunal rejected the prosecution's evidence on these issues, as it threw out of the charge all allegations that were suggestive of the accused's exercising of command authority. The only findings the tribunal made against Tamura were that he "willfully disregarded and failed to discharge his duties."[81] Since no reasoned judgment accompanied the verdict, one can only speculate that the tribunal was *either* unconvinced by the prosecution's evidence *or* did not bother to weigh in on the issue at all on account of the plea agreement. Whichever may have been the case, what this trial ultimately achieved was a guilty verdict on obscure legal and factual grounds, thus failing to make any marked contribution to advancing the understanding of individual responsibility of high-ranking government officials for war crimes.

3

The Deadly Construction Project[1]

The Japanese land invasion of British Burma, which began in mid-January of 1942, may not figure prominently in the general history of the Pacific War or for that matter, the subsequent routing of the Japanese armed forces in this particular theater. But the strategic importance of the Burma campaign can be hardly understated. The Japanese prospects for victory over China had turned into a distant hope rather than an imminent reality by the fall of 1939, as Japan failed to capitalize on its initial gains. Britain, France, the Soviet Union, and the United States, meanwhile, had begun actively supporting the Chiang Kai-shek Government by offering an array of economic and military aid shortly after the outbreak of the Sino-Japanese armed conflict in July 1937. The aid thus rendered included allowing passage of supplies to Chongqing through land routes via British Burma and French Indochina. Once drawn into the war against the Axis Powers in December 1941, the United States heightened its commitment to maintaining ground- and air-based supply lines in support of Chiang Kai-shek through the China-Burma-India (CBI) borders, so that China might eventually be utilized for the bombing of the Japanese homeland.[2] The war in two theaters now intricately connected, Japan had to find ways to interrupt the supply routes in the southern border region of China, isolate the Nationalist Government, and put an end to the prolonged conflict against China. In short, the war in British Burma came to constitute the heart of the Pacific War rather than a sideshow.[3]

This chapter brings to light the unique place Burma occupied in the Japanese war effort, through the lens of British war crimes proceedings at Singapore. It focuses on trials concerning Japanese construction in this theater of the transborder railway, known as the "Burma-Siam Death Railway."[4] Covering a stretch of 258 miles in forbidding, treacherous, malaria-prone jungles in the hinterlands of Burma and Thailand, the railway construction was ordered by the Imperial General Headquarters at Tokyo. Its purpose was to serve as the overland supply route so as to make up for the lines of sea communication that proved vulnerable to the Allied aerial and naval attacks. The railway would be utilized to transfer munitions, reinforcement troops, and other critical war supplies in the service of frontline Japanese troops in Burma. Estimated as requiring five to six years of construction work, the railway actually took no more than a year for completion and was operational by late October 1943. This impressive feat came at a high human cost, however. As many as 17,000 out of a total of 64,000 prisoners of war who were mobilized for the construction failed to return alive,[5] that is, approximately 26% died. There were innumerable deaths, too, among the estimated 75,000 to 250,000 Asian civilian laborers who were brought in for the construction work.[6] The civilian work force consisted not only of adult males but also their spouses and children. They were recruited or forcefully removed from their homes in Japanese-occupied territories across Southeast Asia. The exact number of civilian deaths cannot be established, but the British war crimes trial records point to a much higher mortality rate of civilian laborers than that of prisoners of war (as will be discussed in this chapter).

At the war's end, the British authorities took Field Marshal Terauchi Hisaichi, commander-in-chief of the Southern Army and the chief suspect in the Death Railway case, into custody. They were unable to proceed with a case against him, however, since he died in mid-1946 after suffering from brain disease for several months.[7] But a number of other key suspects were prosecuted in the U.K. Singapore courtroom. This chapter analyzes a representative range of three cases whose chief accused were the following: (1) Lt. Gen. Ishida Eiguma, formerly commander of the Railway Transport Unit of the Southern Army and the highest-ranking army officer overseeing the railway construction project between August 1943 and May 1944; (2) Col. Banno Hiroteru, formerly commanding officer of the 4th Branch of the Malay Prisoner-of-War Administration with responsibility to accommodate the "F" Force, one of the two reinforcement prisoner-of-war work parties that were brought to the construction zones in early 1943, whose mortality in eight months of employment was 44%; and (3) Maj. Kudō Hikosaku, formerly commanding officer of the 19th Ambulance Corps with duties to provide care to the sick and injured civilian laborers, but in reality someone who meted out abusive treatment including sexual violence against female laborers. This chapter will shed light on the grim reality of prisoner-of-war and civilian work conditions as documented in the records of three trials, and determine the courts' findings on responsibility of individual accused. Particular attention will be paid to evidence pertaining to command authority the accused allegedly assumed and exercised during the railway project. It will be explored how such evidence influenced the courts' final decisions on individual verdicts and sentences.

DOCUMENTING THE DEATH RAILWAY

One remarkable aspect of the U.K. Singapore trials on the Burma-Siam Death Railway cases is perhaps the availability of a detailed official report of the railway construction project, prepared by the postwar Government of Japan. Titled "Report on Employment of War Prisoners in SIAM-BURMA Railway," it consisted of a 78-page typescript narrative and appendices containing tabulated statements, diagrams, and sketch plans. This report was produced upon the initiative of the Government of Japan in the wake of surrender, in the apparent anticipation of postwar Allied war crimes investigation. The final version – completed in early January 1946 or possibly earlier – was voluntarily handed over to the British Liaison Mission in Japan. The report was then forwarded to the intelligence corps of the headquarters of the Supreme Allied Commander South East Asia (SACSEA) via the British War Office in London.[8] It was put to use at the British war crimes trials by the prosecution and the defense alike.

This report constituted an open admission by the Government of Japan that it had, in fact, planned and implemented a policy of large-scale use of prisoner-of-war and civilian labor for the railway construction, and that numerous deaths occurred as a result. The British prosecution team at the Ishida Trial readily recognized its truth value, deeming it "a full and, in many respects a frank, report" in which "very valuable information" was supplied.[9] What sorts of information, exactly, were provided in this report? How did the postwar Japanese government address the issues of Japanese organizational and individual responsibility for forced labor and many deaths? Did the Japanese official account differ in any material way from other accounts offered by the former prisoners of war and civilian laborers? The gist of the report centering on these questions can be summarized as follows.

According to the Japanese government report, the Southern Army began preparation for the railway construction in June 1942 upon the order from the Imperial General Headquarters at Tokyo. The actual construction started in November 1942. The purpose of the railway was to use it "as a ground supply route and a trade and traffic one" in the Thailand-Burma area, with the goal of completion by the end of 1943. The completion deadline was subsequently shortened, since "counter-attacks, particularly bombing, of the British Indian Army rapidly became fierce and the situations in this area considerably serious since the end of the rainy season of 1942." What was more, the British offensive severely strained "our sea-transportation from Malaya to Burma."[10] Alarmed by the improved British offensive and the increasing vulnerability of the Japanese sea supply lanes, the Imperial General Headquarters ordered in early February 1943 that the railway construction be expedited. The deadline was revised to be the end of the next rainy season, that is, before the end of the third quarter of 1943. It proved impossible to press on with the construction work, however, as the rainy season started "one month earlier than usual, i.e. it began towards the end of April in Thailand and in the middle of April in Burma."[11] The daily heavy rain inevitably slowed down the work. To make things worse, the cholera epidemic that had broken out in Burma in previous months spread among work parties on the Thai side. It peaked in June 1942 when, according to the Japanese report, there were a total of 6,000 cholera cases, of which about 4,000 died. The vast majority of cholera patients and the dead were civilian laborers. The report also explains that many frightened civilian cholera patients fled, only to complicate the effort to contain the disease as it created such situations that were "dangerous both from the view-point of epidemic prevention and the work itself." Torrential rain, meanwhile, destroyed parts of the railway and washed away bridges, causing tremendous disruption to overland transport. Delays of supplies necessarily "gave rise to malaria epidemic, and gastro-enteric disorder, together with malnutrition" as well as "difficulty in medical supply."[12]

The report indicates that the dramatic increase of the dead and unanticipated delays in construction caused much concern among officials at Tokyo, so much so that the Imperial General Headquarters dispatched Lt. Gen. Wakamatsu Tadaichi, chief of the Third Department of the Army General Staff for on-site inspections. Wakamatsu and accompanying army officers soon returned to Tokyo with recommendations that the deadline be extended so as to prevent further "unnecessary sacrifice." He also advised that improvements were being made with overland supply routes and that, therefore, the extension of the deadline was acceptable from the Army's overall operational standpoint as well. Acting on Wakamatsu's recommendations, the Imperial General Headquarters authorized the postponement of the completion date by two months. Ishida Eiguma was appointed at this juncture as new chief of the transport unit of the Southern Army. His mission was to bring the railway project to a successful conclusion.[13] The railway was completed about two months after the peak of the rainy season, in mid-October.

The general circumstances of the railway project aside, the Japanese official report contains information about the types of work forces deployed for the railway project. The Southern Army initially "levied labourers on the spot,"[14] the report reads, who were namely, "Thailanders, Malayians [*sic*], Burmese, Chinese, Javanese, Annamese." But local recruitment proved unsatisfactory in terms of both quantity and quality. The Southern Army was unable to secure a sufficient number on short notice, and civilian recruits were too "inferior in their physical conditions and ability" to serve as the "leading part of the labour for this construction which ought to be completed in a short time."[15] To overcome these problems, the Southern Army contacted the Imperial General Headquarters and "asked permission to employ POW's [*sic*]". The latter readily gave its approval, so the report reads, on the understanding that "the work was carried on in the rear far away from the first front, and that the railway would serve in the future as a trade route between Thailand and Burma."[16]

This particular passage in the report is interesting, for the postwar Government of Japan seems to take pains to emphasize the nonmilitary character of the railway project. The use of prisoners of war for war-related tasks was prohibited by the Hague Convention No. 4 (1907), and the Japanese government officials preparing this report must have been aware of it. Article 6 of the Hague Convention reads:

The State may utilize the labour of prisoners of war according to their rank and aptitude, officers excepted. The tasks shall not be excessive and *shall have no connection with the operations of the war.*[17]

A similar provision was included in the Geneva Prisoner-of-War Convention (1929), which Japan signed but did not ratify:

Article 31
Labor furnished by prisoners of war *shall have no direct relation with war operations.*[18]

There was controversy at the Tokyo Trial as to whether the 1929 Geneva Prisoner-of-War Convention was binding on Japan because of nonratification.[19] So far as the Japanese official report on the Death Railway is concerned, however, there apparently is no controversy on the matter. It recognizes the Geneva Prisoner-of-War Convention as applicable and thus writes: "At that time the army, as a whole, had a view that it is not against the Geneva Treaty on the War Prisoners to employ the prisoners of war in such work."[20]

The Japanese government report further outlines how the Southern Army went about organizing and sending prisoner-of-war work parties after receiving formal approval from the Imperial General Headquarters. To set up the basic institutional framework to accommodate prisoners of war, the Southern Army ordered the Railway Construction Unit under its command "to supervise as part of prisoners of war and to engage them in the preparation work." The initial task was to organize new prisoner-of-war camp administration and build the physical camp facilities in Thailand. Subsequently, the Southern Army brought on board two branches from the prisoner-of-war administration in Malaya so that they would be able to provide necessary accommodation to the reinforcement prisoner-of-war work parties.[21]

As for actual transfer of prisoner-of-war labor to the construction zones, the Japanese report shows that it took place in three waves. The first group – about 3,000 – was used for the "preparation work of each troop located at the bases for the railway construction," starting in August 1942. From October 1942 onwards, a much larger number of Allied prisoners of war in Java, Borneo, Singapore, and Indochina – a total of 50,637 – were transferred in separate groups. Three-quarters of them (38,000 men) were allotted to the 9th Railway Regiment under command of the Southern Army's railway unit and put to work on the Thai side. The remainder was taken to Burma under the 5th Railway Regiment – also falling under command of the Southern Army's railway unit – to build the other end of the railway. The last wave of prisoners of war arrived in Thailand in April 1943, totaling about 10,000 troops.[22]

The report admits that prisoners of war were made to march to their destinations most of the time – "walking a long distance under the burning sun-shine," as it states, and probably under torrential rain in the case of the rainy season – since transportation resources were meager. It also acknowledges that shelter, food, water, medicine, and so on, were generally inadequate. Health conditions of prisoners grew poor under those circumstances, or as the report puts it: "On their arrival at the destination, a little more than 30% fell ill, and in addition to that, the insufficient accommodations and the unsteady supplies by reason of the bad conditions of the transportation route, accelerated the increase of patients." Disruption of overland supply transport during the rainy season compelled some work parties to cut rations by half or even by two-thirds. "But the work was still continued," the report reads, "in accordance with the order which commanded to finish it [the railway construction] by the end of August." The deadline was later postponed, and the work conditions improved somewhat with the end of the rainy season. But the report offers a somber assessment of a high death toll. It reads: "However, owing to the fatigues accumulated within more than one year past, and the deployment in the remote places insufficiently equipped with the sanitary arrangements, the number of patients and the deceased *did not shrink.*"[23]

The total number of the dead and living that the postwar Japanese government listed is similarly sobering. The summary data appear in the report as follows:

	Total [number of workers]	Deaths
P.O.W.'s [*sic*]	about 50,000	about 10,000 (20%)
Japanese Army	about 15,000	about 1,000 (7%)
Labourers	about 100,000	about 30,000 (30%) (fugitives included)[24]

These data should be considered illustrative rather than exhaustive, as they do not appear to take into account the reinforcement work parties numbering some 10,000 or so prisoners of war that arrived late. The data pertaining to civilian laborers probably are inexact, too, as the U.K. trial records indicate that the Japanese authorities lacked the means or the will to maintain accurate counts of civilian dead. Nevertheless, the Japanese summary constitutes an open admission by the Government of Japan – as of late 1945 – that a very large number of Allied nationals perished for the sake of building the Burma-Siam Railway. It acknowledges that the losses among Japanese servicemen were much smaller than those of prisoners of war during the same period: a total of 10,000 Allied prisoner-of-war deaths versus 1,000 Japanese deaths.

To explain the high mortality rate among prisoners of war, the report makes the following three observations. First, the Japanese troops at the railway construction zones were "employed mainly for supervision of construction work and in the delicate technical work" while prisoners of war were "engaged in usual tasks," that is, digging and clearing the jungles, carrying the construction materials, building the bridges, and placing the rails. As a result of relatively light-duty work, "the decline of physical strength on the part of the Japanese army was not so remarkable as in the case of the prisoners of war." Second, the report speculates that the Japanese servicemen may have had a higher degree of tolerance for harsh climate than the Allied prisoners of war, presumably by physiological reasons or on account of rigorous military training, or both. It thus reads: "Compared with the Japanese, prisoners of war were not so well accustomed to the primitive life and had less powers of resistance." Third and finally, inadequate dressing of tropical ulcer – a prevalent disease that rotted affected areas on limbs and could be life-threatening if untreated – is singled out as another contributing factor to the weakening of the physical strength of prisoner-of-war laborers.[25] The same report, incidentally, offers no explanation as to why a much larger number of deaths occurred among civilian laborers. Perhaps the deaths of civilian laborers were of secondary consideration for the purpose of the report. It did refer to "local labourers" and "fugitives among the Native labourers suffering from cholera," but only for the limited purpose of explaining the spread of cholera across the construction areas. The cholera epidemic was brought under control by October 1943, so the report reads, owing to the Southern Army and the Army Ministry dispatching medical personnel to provide instructions on prevention.[26]

Based on the foregoing findings, the report concedes general shortcomings in the overall planning and implementation of the railway project. The pertinent part reads:

In the final analysis, causes of the tragedy may be traced principally to the placement of a time limit on the construction, the immense difficulty in making thorough preparation and to the precipitancy with which the Japanese soldiers, despite their lack of experience in such large-scale construction work and meagre scientific equipment, dared to carry on their work in strict obedience to orders which they characteristically regarded as imperative.[27]

In other words, the report acknowledges that the railway project was impractical to begin with, and that the ones who took charge of the project on the ground lacked foresight, experience and – above all – necessary equipment. One of the few assets the Japanese servicemen had in common, according to the comments above, was their commitment to single-minded pursuit of superior orders. But the report concludes with a tone of regret that this particular strength in military discipline of the Imperial Japanese Army served as an aggravating factor.

These admissions of institutional failure and expressions of remorse do not lead the report to apportion criminal liability to any particular individual. It instead asserts that that there was no "deliberate intention on the part of the Army authorities" to mistreat prisoners of war. The report emphasizes the bona fide belief among the wartime Japanese leaders that "the employment of prisoners of war in any work other than military operations was not a breach of the Geneva Convention." It is true that many deaths occurred, but not because of "the so-called maltreatment of prisoners of war."²⁸ But the report is prepared to name certain individuals as the ones in positions to take the burden of institutional responsibility. "The incident, already stated, was an inevitable outcome of the situation then prevailing," the report reads, but

if anyone is to be called to account for the dreadful death rate, the responsibility ought to be placed on the then Chief of the General Staff (General Sugiyama [Hajime]) who ordered the construction, the War Minister (General Tojo [Hideki]) who sanctioned the employment of prisoners and the Commander-in-Chief of the Southern Area Corps [Southern Army] (General Terauchi [Hisaichi]) who was entrusted with the construction on the spot.²⁹

Quite conveniently, the three named individuals were either dead or dying or otherwise in Allied custody pending trial when the report was prepared. Terauchi was already in British custody but gravely ill. (He died in June 1946.) Sugiyama was dead since mid-August 1945 when he committed suicide.³⁰ Tōjō, before turning himself over to the Allied occupation forces, also attempted suicide in September 1945 but failed, and was detained at Sugamo Prison in Tokyo pending trial.³¹ Yet by giving away the names of these three individuals, the postwar Government of Japan did not mean to be in complete denial of possible criminal charges. "As regards individual cases of maltreatment of prisoners of war," the report hastily adds, "it is desired that investigation be started upon the further receipt from the Allied Powers of a report of the details, particularly the ranks and names of the suspected offenders, *and if, as a result they should be found guilty[,] severe measures should be meted out to them.*"³²

A person whose name is conspicuously absent throughout the foregoing discussions, of course, is Emperor Hirohito. The Emperor of Japan had the "supreme command of the Army and the Navy" (article 11 of the Constitution of the Empire of Japan, 1889),³³ and was the one presiding over the Imperial General Headquarters with the ultimate decision-making power. What was more, and as shown in Yamada Akira's (2002) *Shōwa tennō no gunji shisō to senryaku* (Military thought and strategies of Emperor Shōwa), Emperor Hirohito took great personal interest in details of war policies, progress, and outcomes, from the start to the end of the Pacific War. He proactively sought information from subordinate army and navy chiefs, and played the decisive role in determining Japan's grand strategy.³⁴ He was kept up to date on the Burma-Siam Railway project, too. Ishida Eiguma, an accused at the U.K. Singapore war crimes proceedings, made an interesting remark in this connection. When interviewed by an investigative officer from the Japanese Ministry of Legal Affairs in 1960, he remarked that during his service in the Burma theater, "His Majesty passed down an inquiry as to whether or not the Burma-Siam Railway was completed yet [*heika kara, mada Taimen tetsudō wa dekinka to gokamon ga atta*]". Ishida followed up on the inquiry by submitting footage from the construction zones. "After the completion of this railway," he stated, "I had a moving picture made that showed the circumstances of construction and had it sent to Tokyo." Ishida believed that the film was subsequently "shown to His Majesty [*tenran ni kyōshita koto to omou*]".[35]

To sum up, the Japanese official report takes the following positions on issues of responsibility relative to the Burma-Siam Railway: (1) that the Army General Staff, the Army Ministry, and the Southern Army each had a share of responsibility in the planning and implementation of the policy to use prisoner-of-war labor for the railway project; (2) that Japan did not violate the Hague Convention No. 4 or the Geneva Prisoner-of-War Convention, or at least there was a bona fide belief in the leadership circles that the use of prisoner-of-war labor for the railway project was entirely lawful; (3) that, admittedly, the railway project was poorly conceived and poorly executed, as a result of which many prisoners of war died; (4) that no issues of criminal liability should arise, however, since prisoner-of-war mistreatment was never intended or authorized; (5) that if someone had to be held accountable for the prisoner-of-war deaths, chiefs of the aforementioned three main branches of the Imperial Japanese Army would be the right persons; and finally, (6) that the Government of Japan supports the policy to mete out stern punishment to perpetrators of individual instances of prisoner-of-war mistreatment. The report, in this manner, characterized the Burma-Siam Railway as a lawful construction project with unintended tragic consequences. Criminal offenders must be punished, the Japanese government readily agreed, but there was no case of prisoner-of-war mistreatment insofar as the Government of Japan or its constituent members were concerned.

The general chronology of the railway construction, organization of work forces, and woeful circumstances of work and accommodation as described in the Japanese official report fall largely in line with accounts that the former prisoners of war and civilian laborers, offered in their versions of official reports, affidavits, and court testimony. But there are also notable differences. First, accounts of Death Railway survivors show that Japanese mistreatment of Allied military and civilian work forces was far more widespread than the Japanese official report was prepared to admit. It is true that supplies of food, medicine, and so on, were generally short, but there were instances of man-made supply shortages as well, such as withholding by the Japanese camp authorities of supplies even when they were available in relative abundance. Second, life was further made difficult for the Allied military and civilian work parties as the Japanese authorities demanded a heavier workload from all workers during the so-called Speedo Period (when the amount of work was increased to meet the August 1943 deadline),[36] exacted labor from the sick, and tolerated habitual beatings by Japanese military personnel at camps and work sites alike. Third, prisoners of war managed to stave off some of the possible deaths of fellow soldiers by resorting to organizational skills and by individual acts of heroism. But the same cannot be said of civilian laborers; they lacked the means or expertise to protect themselves organizationally or collectively. As a result, they died in much larger numbers than prisoners of war. Witness accounts show that the Japanese military authorities exacerbated the situation by assuming little or no institutional responsibility to protect these most vulnerable populations.

The wide gap between the Japanese report and survivor accounts can be seen in how the efforts to contain cholera outbreaks are described. According to the Japanese official report, cholera spread across the construction zones during the rainy season but was brought under control in the second half of 1943, thanks to preventive steps taken by the Japanese medical staff. A fair number of former prisoners of war attested to the contrary. They instead pointed to neglect on the part of the Japanese to provide medical assistance to work parties and especially civilian laborers. Sgt. Harry Jones of the Royal Signals, for instance, testified that when cholera broke out at Tonchan South on the Thai side in June 1943, the Japanese guards "barricaded themselves in their own little compound" and left some 2,000 Asian civilian laborers without any medical attention. The Japanese camp authorities gave prisoners of war "a certain amount of lime" so that they could make saline solution, but did not do the same for civilian laborers. With utter lack of medical attention and without their own medical staff, civilian laborers died "at the rate of about 50 per day," Jones testified.[37]

Dr. Stanley Septimus Pavillard, formerly medical officer of the Straits Settlement Volunteer Force, offered an account to the similar effect. The prisoner-of-war battalion in which he served as chief medical officer sustained no more than seven cholera deaths due to the enforcement of a strict hygiene regimen, but prisoner-of-war battalions that did not take proper preventive measures lost "up to 50% of their strength."[38] As for civilian laborers, he saw them "dying like flies" and "many fled only to die in the jungle." The Japanese camp authorities at Tonchan South were insensitive enough to move the tent of civilian cholera patients "next to ours," where the patients had "no doctors or orderlies and were allowed neither food nor water." Medical orderlies – who were prisoners of war and not the Japanese camp staff – took pity on the dying cholera patients and brought over food and water. "The Jap guard was so terror stricken as to be useless," Pavillard commented.[39] John Kendal Gale, formerly a battery quartermaster sergeant of the Singapore Royal Artillery Volunteer, testified in this connection that the Japanese and Korean camp guards at Tonchan South "had bowls of disinfectants, changed many times a day, in which they washed their hands and their boots as they came in and out of the quarters." Some disinfectant was given out to prisoners of war but "it was badly damaged by water and its efficiency had been considerably reduced."[40]

Lt. Col. Charles Henry Kappe, formerly a member of the Signal Corps of the 8th Australian Division, arrived from Singapore at the railway construction zone in April 1943 as part of the third wave of prisoner-of-war labor. He served as senior officer of the Australian segment of the "F" Force, one of the two reinforcement prisoner-of-war work parties. (The other was known as the "H" Force.) The bulk of prisoners of war who formed the "F" Force were unfit to travel due to poor diet and illnesses to begin with, and many died as they were forced to march, sleep, and work under daily torrential rain without adequate supplies of food, potable water, medicine, or shelter. The survivors of "F" Force were subsequently brought back in batches to Singapore between November 1943 and April 1944. A total of 1,060 Australian men out of the original strength of 3,662 in "F" Force failed to return (29% died). The British component of "F" Force – some 3,300 men – died at a higher rate, losing more than half of its original strength (59%). Death did not stop there: "Many of them have died since," according to Kappe, and he believed "certain that many of them will feel the effects for the rest of their lives."[41]

Despite these terrible losses in the prisoner-of-war work party, Kappe noted in a final report on the Australian experience in "F" Force – which he completed shortly after taken back to the prisoner-of-war camp at Changi in Singapore in May 1944, titled, "'F' Force Report on Activities of AIF 'F' Force in Thailand by Lt. Col. C. H. Kappe" – that his account would be "incomplete were reference not made to the conditions surrounding the employment of native workmen by the I.J.A. [Imperial Japanese Army]." He estimated that 150,000 or so civilians – he identified them as Chinese, Malays, and Tamils who originated in Malaya – were put to work for the railway construction. So far as observations by him and other Australian members of the "F" Force went, "provision for medical attention seemed non-existent" to these people, although in June 1943, "English and Australian medical officers and attendants were sent from SINGAPORE to attend to the ravages of disease amongst their ranks." Kappe could agree that "the total absence of any hygiene arrangements amongst the native workers" directly contributed to the cholera outbreak, but he also believed that "the whole blame cannot be thrust on them." It was one thing for these civilian laborers not to be acquainted with elemental knowledge of hygiene; it was quite another when "absolutely nothing was done [by the Japanese] to teach them even the simplest rules of sanitation." In expression of solidarity with civilian laborers, Kappe included in his report the following remark: "It is interesting to note that officers and men who worked shoulder to shoulder with the natives ascertained by mean[s] of surreptitious conversation that they had much in common and that universally the natives hated the I.J.A."[42]

The Japanese official report on the Burma-Siam Railway admits the possibility that some of the Japanese servicemen may have inflicted violence against prisoners of war but also asserts that it was never sanctioned or prevalent. What the survivor accounts bring to light, by contrast, is that acts of violence were probably more a norm than an anomaly, although the severity of mistreatment could vary. Some prisoners of war offered insightful accounts on this particular topic. The aforementioned prisoner-of-war witness John Gale was once asked in the courtroom about the circumstances of widespread mistreatment of prisoners of war. Did it occur as a result of cruelty of individual Japanese servicemen, or was it sanctioned as a matter of policy? The following dialogue took place between defense counsel and the witness:

Q. [DEFENSE COUNSEL]. Now, about these beatings, etc., which occurred in camps. There were some guards who were more cruel than others?
A. [GALE]. Yes.
Q. There were some quite reasonable?
A. Yes, there was one man who said that as he was a Christian he never kicked with his boots on.
Q. And there were some who were quite good even?
A. I think one who was good throughout and there were some who only occasionally lost their tempers.
Q. So you mean to say that these cruelties were due to a sadistic temperament with some and with others due to losing their temper, and others were never cruel?
A. The big majority appeared to us to be very bad sadists. Some lost their temper extremely unnecessarily and frequently and others were fairly good.[43]

Maj. Rowland Lyne, formerly a member of the 2nd Battalion of the Straits Settlement Volunteer Force, attested to similar effect but his account had a slight twist. He referred to a camp guard known to prisoners of war as "Beardy" at Kanyu, a prisoner-of-war camp location on the Thai side. "That man tried to save us as much as he possible could," he testified, "but he became so afraid of his own people that he had become more or less the same as they were."[44] This episode points to tremendous peer pressure among the camp guards, not so much to protect the prisoners of war as to mistreat them.

Some other witnesses drew the court's attention to contrasting examples. "We were fortunate at Kanu [Kanyu on the Thai side] insomuch that our Jap Camp Comdr. was Lt. Hattori who had been with us at Wampo,"[45] Pavillard reported, crediting this particular individual, Hattori, for making personal commitment to providing better medical care to prisoners of war. Gale – who belonged to the same battalion as Pavillard – concurred and testified: "My battalion camps, owing to the energy of Dr. Pavillard and the assistance of Lt. Hattori, our hospital accommodation was probably the best there [at Wampo in Thailand]."[46] These accounts show that certain of the prisoner-of-war administration staff resisted the pressure from their peers and/or military superiors, and that in some instances, they were able to bring about material improvement to prisoner-of-war conditions.

The general state of prisoner-of-war treatment aside, the Death Railway survivors brought fresh insights into the ways in which the constructed railway was put to actual use. For instance, Gale attested to witnessing "a large number of Japanese military cars, pieces of artillery and general Japanese Army supplies" as well as "large numbers of Japanese troops . . . and food," thus affirming that the railway was used in the main to deliver military supplies and reinforcement troops. He went on to testify that as for personnel being transported by the rail, he saw "Japanese soldiers, British prisoners-of-war, Asiatic labor gangs, Japanese prostitutes for the Japanese troops and a few officials with the exception of now and then a few Siamese going up and down."[47] Pavillard similarly testified that he saw on board the railway "the Railway Engineers, the POW Government Administration Staff and certain number of Japanese civilians and comfort girls [i.e. comfort women]."[48] As regards comfort women, their final destinations appeared to include certain locations within the railway construction zones. Lt. Col. Yanagita Shōichi, formerly a prisoner-of-war camp commander and one of the accused at the Ishida Trial, made passing reference to comfort stations at Kanchanaburi in Thailand, the hub of prisoner-of-war administration in connection with the railway project. He attested to difficulties he used to have with recalcitrant Korean guards under his command. He gave them time off on one occasion to pacify them, only to learn that two of them "while going to the comfort house [comfort station] and so on" at Kanchanaburi got drunk and started sword fighting on some trifling matters.[49]

The gap between the Japanese official report and survivor accounts is arguably the greatest when it comes to reconstructing the Death Railway experiences from the perspectives of individual prisoners of war and civilian laborers. The Japanese report essentially offers a "top-down" account, whose purpose was to speak in defense of the Government of Japan. Survivor accounts, by contrast, were focused on documenting the actual conditions the individual victims had personally witnessed and experienced. On this particular matter, Lt. Col. Kappe of Australia took a moment to reflect and wrote in his report as follows:

It is necessary to say at this stage that no word picture, however vividly painted, could ever portray faithfully the horrors and sufferings actually endured. Incidents occurred repeatedly in which heroism and fortitude were displayed equalling the highest traditions of the A.I.F. [Australian Imperial Force] in war operations, but the written word again falls short in conveying to the reader what was in the minds of those witnessing the event. These men were not fighting a tangible enemy – they were fighting a far more sinister opponent in the form of starvation and disease.[50]

In the case of the "F" Force, the horror of the railway experience translated in the tangible outcome of the 44% mortality rate. But this figure, too, failed to convey tremendous mental and physical ordeals that the dying and surviving prisoners of war were made to go through.

Instead of dwelling on the indescribable horror of the Death Railway, however, Kappe concluded his final report by honoring the dead and paying tribute to meritorious deeds of his men. He wrote that "whilst the grim and trying circumstances . . . inevitably found out weaknesses in the character of some of the men, on the other hand that same set of adverse circumstances seemed to bring out the very best in others." He was satisfied to conclude that all in all, "the standard of morale and the behaviour of the larger proportion of the A.I.F. personnel left little to be desired."[51]

To underscore the exemplary behavior of Australian troops, Kappe inserted at the end of his report a quote from a letter he received in 1944 at Changi,

Singapore, from Lt. Col. S. W. Harris of the 18th Divisional Artillery of the Royal Army, the British senior officer commanding the British counterpart of the "F" Force.[52] In this letter, Harris expressed his heartfelt gratitude for the courage and devotion with which Australians "helped their sick cobbers and British comrades through long months of misery." He went on to compare the praiseworthy behavior of the Australian component of the "F" Force with the one of the Australian armed forces a generation before: back in the time of World War I. He reminisced over his personal war experience:

> I fought as a subaltern alongside the A.I.F. at Pozieres in 1916 [during the Battle of the Somme], and their gallantry during that battle is imprinted indelibly on my memory. The ordeal your men were called upon to endure in Thailand was, if possible, a higher test of courage and endurance as it took place, not in the heat of battle, but in the depths of the jungle when all hopes of survival seemed lost. They were challenged by circumstances of almost unbelievable horror; and they did not draw back from the challenge.[53]

The Battle of Pozières was a major turning point where a very large number of Australian lives were lost delivering a critical victory for the Allied Nations.[54] By recalling this particular battle, Harris acknowledged historical debts the British armed forces owed to fellow soldiers from Down Under since the time of World War I, and paid personal tribute to the Australian military's unparalleled tradition of perseverance, courage, and sacrifice.

THE CASE OF THE ISHIDA TRIAL

Lt. Gen. Ishida Eiguma (also known as Ishida Hidekuma) came on board the Burma-Siam Railway project late in the game. He was appointed commander of the Railway Transport Unit of the Southern Army in August 1943 and retained the command until March 1944. Two army generals who had successively served in the same position prior to his appointment died before the termination of hostilities: one in a plane crash during reconnaissance over the proposed railway construction zones in late December 1942, and the other due to malaria, falling ill in April 1943 and dying in February 1945.[55] Terauchi also being dead since June 1946, Ishida was the highest-ranking officer in the Southern Army with a connection to the Burma-Siam Railway project to survive the war.

Ishida was evidently displeased with both this particular wartime service and the postwar criminal prosecution against him. He informed the U.K. Singapore court that "I consider my appointment as a result of unreasonable personnel handling."[56] He was not a railway technician to begin with, he told the court, and he had already been serving the Southern Army in a different capacity with separate transport duties for the Army from earlier on – as commander of No. 2 Field Railway Headquarters since 1942[57] – but was "ordered to hold a dual position" as a result of the new appointment. "If I had been appointed to the position earlier, I would have had time to study all the requirements I had to meet," he stated, but he was given no such time in actuality. He was ordered to lead the railway project quite unexpectedly, hurried off to the Railway Transport Unit headquarters in Kuala Lumpur, which was "1,000 kilometres away" from the construction zones, and then traveled north to oversee the project in September 1943. He remained on site until the completion date, which was mid-October the same year.[58] In a word, he willy-nilly took up the command of the Railway Transport Unit.

Ishida was brought to the U.K. Singapore courtroom between October 21 and December 3, 1946, along with four other co-accused. They were Col. Nakamura Shigeo, commander of the Siam Prisoner-of-War Administration, and three former commandants of prisoner-of-war camp groups under Nakamura's command (Col. Ishii Tamio, Lt. Col. Yanagita Shōichi, and Maj. Chida Sotomatsu). Four common charges were leveled against them. The charge sheet read that the five "while engaged in the administration of Britain, Australian and Dutch Prisoners of War employed in the construction and maintenance of the BURMA-SIAM Railway were . . . concerned in the inhumane treatment of the said Prisoners of War resulting in the death of many of the said Prisoners of War and physical suffering by many others of the said Prisoners of War" (charge 1); that they were "concerned in the employment of the labour of British, Australian, and Dutch Prisoners of War in work having connection with the operation of the War . . . for the purpose of transporting supplies and munitions to the Japanese forces fighting in BURMA" (charge 2); that they were "concerned in the employment of the labour of the said Prisoners of War in work which was excessive having regard to the rank and capacity of the said Prisoners of War" (charge 3); and that they were "concerned in the internment of the said Prisoners of War in conditions which were unhealthy and unhygienic" (charge 4).[59] Theses charges aside, an additional four were leveled against the three former commandants of prisoner-of-war camp groups under the Siam Prisoner-of-War Administration (Ishii, Yanagita, and Chida) in connection with specific instances of war crimes.

At the Ishida Trial, the prosecution argued that the accused were criminally liable for commission of war crimes and disregard of duties, or as the prosecution put it: "Our case against these Accused is founded both on positive acts of inhumane treatment and on failure to do things which humanity demanded and which it was within their power to do so." The prosecution would concede that these accused "cannot be held responsible for conditions and shortcomings which were beyond their power to remedy," thereby pointing to larger problems of planning and implementation of the railway project. Nonetheless, "there was much which they could have done, should have done but failed to do so."[60] With respect specifically to Ishida, the prosecution recognized that "he came at a time when the condition and health of the POWs were already about as bad as they could be,"[61] but argued that he still had a share of responsibility to ensure proper treatment of prisoners of war during his tenure as commander of the Railway Transport Unit.

Yet paradoxically, the prosecution seemed to let Ishida off the hook in the actual presentation of evidence relative to charges of prisoner-of-war administration. The prosecution apparently concluded at some point during the trial that Ishida's duty was limited to overseeing the employment of prisoner-of-war labor and not the camp administration. The following dialogue during the court proceedings helps illustrate the prosecution's views. On this particular occasion, the prosecution is cross-examining accused Ishida concerning a two-week tour of inspection he carried out in Thailand in early September 1943. Ishida testified that, during the trip, he personally took concrete steps to ameliorate the conditions of prisoner-of-war internment even though it was not part of his job to do so. The prosecution followed up on the accused's testimony by putting further questions:

Q. [PROSECUTION]. So the position we have is this, that within three weeks after your arrival in Siam you set out on a tour of the camps, which lasted for 14 days, and you managed to effect some, at least, improvements in the conditions of the Prisoners-of-War although it was not your legal duty to bring about those improvements. Have I put it fairly?

A. [ISHIDA]. The date I started the tour of inspection was the 5th of September, and your summing up is correct.

Q. Yes. So does it not follow, if you could have done this, the Siam administration officers, *whose duty it was to see to it, and who had been there long before you arrived,* could easily have done the same thing themselves?

A. Of course they could have.[62]

In this dialogue, the prosecution appears to seek inculpatory evidence against other co-accused rather than Ishida. When questioned further, Ishida confirmed that "responsibility concerning the welfare of the prisoners rested with certain appointed persons other than myself," namely, members of the Siam Prisoner-of-War Administration.[63]

The U.K. Singapore court for this case produced no judgment but verdicts and sentences only. The final verdicts do indicate, however, that the court was persuaded by the prosecution's evidence of separate commands of the Railway Transport Unit and the Siam Prisoner-of-War Administration. It handed down to Ishida the verdict of guilty on charges of illegal use of prisoner-of-war labor (charges 2 and 3) but acquitted him of other charges relating to prisoner-of-war camp administration (charges 1 and 4). The co-accused were found guilty of all four common charges. Ishida received twenty years in prison, while Nakamura, commander of the Siam Prisoner-of-War Administration, and another co-accused (Col. Ishii) received the death penalty. The remaining two were sentenced to limited years of imprisonment (twenty years for Yanagita and ten years for Chida).[64]

THE CASE OF THE BANNO TRIAL

Lt. Col. Banno Hiroteru served as commander of the Medan prisoner-of-war camp in Sumatra until April 15, 1943, when he received an order by telegram that he take command of the 4th Branch of the Malay Prisoner-of-War Administration.[65] He promptly proceeded to the headquarters of the said prisoner-of-war administration in Singapore to receive from its commander, Maj. Gen. Arimura Tsunemichi, further orders and instructions.[66] The new mission for Banno – as he testified in the U.K. Singapore courtroom – would be "to supervise the 7,000 men now on the journey toward THAILAND, and bring them to THAILAND and co-operate with the construction of the BURMA-SIAM Railway with the force."[67] The prisoner-of-war work party in question was the "F" Force consisting of Australian troops under command of Lt. Col. Kappe and British troops under command of Lt. Col. Harris. Banno held the new command until October 30, 1943.

The record of the trial shows that Banno was by all accounts an ineffective commander. Garret George Richwood, formerly a staff sergeant in the 2/30 Battalion of the Australian Imperial Force and the first prosecution witness, attested to his impression of this accused when seeing him at the Upper and Lower Sonkrai Camps near the Burma-Thai border. He understood that Banno was general commander of the prisoner-of-war camps, but thought "he did not seem like the usual Japanese Colonel." When urged by the prosecution to explain, Richwood stated: "Well usually when a Japanese Colonel came every one was kept in huts and the place was all cleaned, but Col. BANNO, he didn't seem to have control of this Camp." In other words, Banno's own subordinates did not recognize his authority to the point of not bothering to make a pretense of good prisoner-of-war camp condition during tours of inspection. Richwood added that Lt. Fukuda Tsuneo – the camp commandant at Sonkrai and a co-accused at the Banno Trial – did not get out to greet his superior on such occasions. Banno was always "kind to the POWs," Richwood recalled, but "he had no power over his subordinates."[68] Lt. Col. Cecil Tats Hutchinson of the Royal Army similarly remembered Banno as being ineffective when dealing with those engineers who supervised the prisoner-of-war labor. "Col. Banno himself always expressed sympathy on the question of brutal treatment and told us again and again that he had seen the Engineer officer and that brutality would cease and shorter hours would be arranged." But Banno's words were not followed by results, or as Hutchinson puts it, "he was overruled and conditions did not improve until September [1943]."[69]

The senior officer of the Australian component of the "F" Force, Lt. Col. Kappe, was not impressed by Banno's leadership either. When appearing in the Singapore courtroom as a special court witness, Kappe attested to the accused's general failure to take personal initiative to protect prisoners of war from abusive work supervisors. Kappe stated that "after the failure of Colonel Banno to make the slightest improvement in our conditions in the early months, May, June and July, I came to the conclusion that he was completely incompetent and too weak-minded to fight the Engineers."[70] When the court put to the witness further questions regarding Banno's attitude toward prisoners of war, the following dialogue ensued:

Q. [THE COURT]. At heart did he appear to be sympathetic?
A. [KAPPE]. Yes, at heart I think he was sympathetic.
Q. And it is your opinion that he was an incompetent old man.
A. An incompetent fatuous old man.[71]

When asked to explain what he meant by "an incompetent fatuous old man," Kappe testified that Banno "behaved like a child when very serious events were occurring." To illustrate the point, he referred to two occasions when they personally met. About the only thing Banno inquired of him was "about my wife" in the first meeting, and "about my watch" in the second meeting. Kappe went on to state that Banno was a fool if he did not anticipate the possibility of the story of the "F" Force coming to light one day. "And he is also a fool," Kappe continued, "if he thought we, as trained soldiers, were not taking evidence against them even then, and in fact, preparing to over-throw [sic] their guards, and that there were British Forces near our area."[72] The "F" Force indeed kept detailed records of prisoner-of-war mistreatment by the Japanese. The records culminated in the compilation of a 135-page definitive account of the "F" Force's Death Railway experience (titled "The History of the 'F' Force"). Along with Kappe's report, "The History of the 'F' Force" served as key evidentiary material for the prosecution's case at the Banno Trial.[73]

When Banno proved himself to be a failed commander, Toyoyama Kisei – one of the six co-accused – made himself just the opposite example. He was a mere *gunzoku* (lit. "affiliated with the army"), a civilian who served in the Imperial Japanese Army without any military rank. He was one of many young men that the wartime Japanese government recruited in colonial Korea and Taiwan in order to put them to use for prisoner-of-war guard duties.[74] Despite being at the lowest rung of the prisoner-of-war camp administration and of the army, Toyoyama made a domineering presence. For instance, Capt. R. W. Pearce of the Royal Australian Army Service Corps related the first encounter he and his fellow soldiers had with Toyoyama at the transit camp past the railhead at Bampong in Thailand. "He was welcoming the troops to the camp, armed with a steel shafted golf club with the driver end sawn off," he stated, and "swinging this bludgeon with all his might, he was beating officers and men as they passed, on all parts of their bodies including the face."[75] Toyoyama would occasionally visit the prisoner-of-war hospital, where he would choose those prisoners of war "who were obviously dying" and beat them with a bamboo stick.[76] While committing these acts of violence, Toyoyama "made a practice of walking round the camp like a little god." Pearce observed that this particular Korean guard "appeared to give all orders in the camp and was apparently authorized to control rations."[77] When prisoners of war protested to him in person, Toyoyama is said to have rebuffed them by replying, "All Englishmen are dogs and only deserve to die."[78]

Lt. Col. Cyril Wild was a lead postwar British war crimes investigator in Southeast Asia and formerly a prisoner of war. Fluent in Japanese, he was put to use as an interpreter at the time of the British surrender to the Japanese in Singapore, and served in similar capacities during deployment alongside other prisoners of war for the Burma-Siam Railway construction.[79] According to his statements, the Australian component of the "F" Force had arrived at Bampong ahead of the British component, and upon the latter's arrival, informed the British that Toyoyama was "a complete menace to all the PWs [POWs]." Toyoyama retained his bad name when the reinforcement prisoner-of-war work party was moved up to Sonkrai and came under control once again of the same Japanese camp staff. Wild heard from Lt. Col. Harris that the camp at Lower Sonkrai was under a "reign of terror" due to Toyoyama's daily beatings. Harris is said to have made several complaints to Banno, who in turn assured him that steps had already been taken to contain the violence. Specifically, Banno told Harris that he gave orders to Lt. Fukuda "to control TOYOYAMA." Banno is said to have told Korean guards at large, too, that they were "positively forbidden" to beat prisoners of war. But nothing came of Banno's actions. Wild noted that the camp commandant Fukuda did "absolutely nothing in the camps which he is supposed to command, except to lie on his back and leave the running of the whole place to TOYOYAMA." To explain this state of affairs, Wild speculated that Toyoyama was Fukuda's "bugger-boy" and was thus allowed to do whatever he wanted while Fukuda simply looked on.[80]

Toyoyama stopped inflicting violence against prisoners of war from late August or September 1943 onwards, however, when stern warnings were transmitted from prisoners-of-war officers via Koroyasu Shunro, a Japanese interpreter. During his private conversation with Wild, Koroyasu is said to have agreed that "TOYOYAMA is a young man with an uncontrollable temper" and that while it was Fukuda's responsibility to control him, "I shall do my best" to stop the violence. He then passed on to Toyoyama a message from Wild that "Lt. Col. HARRIS has said that when we get back to Singapore . . . he intends to give Maj. Gen. ARIMURA a full account of TOYOYAMA's behaviour in Siam." This warning had an immediate effect. According to Wild, Toyoyama stopped the beating completely and instead began "going around giving them [prisoners of war] cigarettes and asking them to take note of his good behaviour." Toyoyama may have defied the authority of his immediate superiors such as Fukuda and Banno, but he apparently was afraid of Gen. Arimura, the highest-ranking commanding officer of the Malay Prisoner-of-War Administration. It is also possible that Toyoyama became worried about the possibility of postwar Allied war crimes prosecution; Wild transmitted a separate message to him that "through friendly Koreans" he had obtained information of Toyoyama's Korean name, home address, and army number, and "after the war I would see to it that he was severely punished."[81]

Banno was brought to the U.K. Singapore courtroom along with Fukuda, Toyoyama, and four other co-accused: Capt. Tamio Susumu, the former medical officer of the 4th Branch Malay Prisoner-of-War Administration; Capt. Maruyama Hajime and Lt. Abe Hiroshi, two former engineer officers in charge of supervising the construction work by segments of the "F" Force; and Ishimoto Eishin, another Korean guard. The seven accused were charged that they "in SIAM, between April 1st 1943 and December 31st 1943, in violation of the laws and usages of war, when engaged in the administration of a group of British and Australian Prisoners of War known as 'F' Force, employed in the construction of the Burma-Siam railway, were together concerned in the inhumane treatment of the said Prisoners of War, resulting in the deaths of many, and in the physical suffering of many others of the said Prisoners of War." Banno, Fukuda, Maruyama, and Tamio jointly faced another charge according to which they were also "concerned in the internment of the said Prisoners of War in conditions which were unhealthy and unhygienic."[82]

The findings of the U.K. Singapore court were guilty regarding all seven accused, but the sentences varied. The chief accused, Banno, received a penalty of mere three years in prison. The medical officer, Tamio, too, received a relative light penalty of five years in prison. The remainder of the accused uniformly received the death sentence except Ishimoto Eishin, whom the court found guilty of being "concerned in the inhumane treatment" but not for the resultant deaths or physical sufferings. Ishimoto received what appears to be a nominal penalty of eighteen months in prison.[83] What is the rationale behind these broad-ranging sentences? How can one explain, in particular, the court's leniency to Banno as opposed to its decision to mete out capital punishment to his subordinates such as Fukuda and Toyoyama? The court produced no judgment, but one can speculate its rationale on the basis of evidentiary materials in the record of court proceedings.

With respect to Banno's case, the court is likely to have accepted the overwhelming evidence that while having de jure authority over the prisoner-of-war administration, this accused lacked de facto authority to control his subordinates. Furthermore, Kappe's testimony of "an incompetent fatuous old man" may have influenced the court's thinking. The prosecution disputed during the closing statement the adequacy of the term "incompetent," arguing that Banno was not being charged with incompetence but rather with negligence.[84] "An officer, through incompetence, may make a wrong decision," the prosecution agreed, "but is this really a case merely of that?" The prosecution doubted that it was. As the prosecution saw it, Banno was sufficiently informed of existing prisoner-of-war situations to appreciate the "reasonable and probable consequence" of his own actions, or inactions for that matter.[85] For instance, the accused "must have known that by sending on the infected group he would be spreading the cholera among the Prisoners of War at Lower SONKRAI." He was, in fact, "expressly told by the Prisoner of War Medical Officer that that would be the consequence."[86] The fact being such, the prosecution contended that Banno "didn't carry out these duties properly not merely because he was incompetent, but because he was negligent," or rather, because he knowingly or recklessly disregarded his duty.[87] This was arguably a valid point. However, the lenient penalty of three years in prison for Banno seems inexplicable unless the court rejected the prosecution's contention.

As for the death penalties to Toyoyama and Fukuda, the court is likely to have taken grave views of overwhelming evidence that Toyoyama habitually and savagely inflicted violence on prisoners of war and that he did so on Fukuda's watch. Toyoyama declined to testify in the courtroom. Fukuda did not testify either. In a prepared statement, Toyoyama admitted that he was excitable and "especially during that period I am a bit off my natural condition." He also conceded that "I did many things that I should not have done in ordinary times." However, he pleaded in his own behalf two extenuating circumstances, namely: (1) that he himself had to endure severe beatings – "more than a thousand times," he informed the court – during two months of training in the Japanese military; and (2) that he did not think much of beating, as it was commonly practiced among "my own people" for the purpose of disciplining and education. He further stated: "I am uncultured and unacquainted with the customs of other races and tribes so I beat the POWs on impulse without reflection as I should have done."[88] These words of remorse failed to impress the court, however, as the stern punishment indicates.

The death sentences of Toyoyama and Fukuda nonetheless came under criticism of the reviewing authority. The review report read, "The sentence of only three years imprisonment in the case of BANNO has rendered more difficult a proper assessment of punishment in the case of his subordinates." The reduction of sentences was accordingly recommended: life for Toyoyama and Fukuda, and fifteen years in prison for the two other death-sentence cases. In the opinion of the reviewing authority, remission of sentences in this manner would enable the British court to adequately "meet the ends of justice."[89] The confirming authority accepted the reviewing authority's opinion, and all the death sentences were commuted as recommended.

THE CASE OF THE KUDŌ TRIAL

Maj. Kudō Hikosaku and eleven co-accused were all formerly members of the 19th Ambulance Corps, alternatively known as the "Kudō Butai" (the Kudō Unit). This corps originally served as a patient transport unit but came to take charge of providing care to hospital cases that arose among Asian civilian laborers in connection with the railway project. The origins and workings of the Kudō Unit as brought out in the court proceedings can be summarized as follows.

According to Lt. Col. Watanabe Mutsuo, the 19th Ambulance Corps was first organized in March 1943 with the "chief mission of transporting patients from the Field Hospital regions further down to the more settled parts of the country."[90] Watanabe commanded the medical corps of the Southern Army between December 1943 and March 1944. He took the witness stand to testify on behalf of the defense. Most of his account was devoted to explaining how the 19th Ambulance Corps ceased to fulfill its original mission and came instead to function as a medical unit with primary responsibility of providing care to civilian patients in the railway construction zones. He informed the court that the first commander of this ambulance corps, a Col. Dr. Kitagawa,[91] took the initiative of conferring with the Southern Army headquarters about the state of hygiene and sanitation of civilian laborers and suggesting that medical orderlies be recruited in Thailand to address civilians' poor health. No increase of medical personnel occurred in immediate months, however, and the duty to provide medical care to civilian laborers fell on certain divisional field hospital corps that were already stationed in the railway construction zones. The 2nd Field Hospital Corps of the 21st Division took charge first, and subsequently two of the field hospital units that belonged to the 2nd Division and the 54th Division. The duty to care for civilian patients finally fell on the 19th Ambulance Corps in about March 1944, as "all these field hospitals were eventually to go to Burma."[92]

The 19th Ambulance Corps thereafter took charge of caring for civilian patients in practically the entire stretch of the construction zones, or as Watanabe put it, "between Kanburi [Kanchanaburi] in Siam to Anaquin in Burma." There were six main hospital bases: Kanchanaburi, Wanyei, Kinsayok, and Niki on the Thai side, and Aperron and Anaquin on the Burma side.[93] The 19th Ambulance Corps did not have large staff – "approximately 55–60" members, according to Watanabe – but it was assisted by a much larger number of prisoners of war and civilian recruits. Watanabe estimated that the prisoner-of-war medical personnel numbered 345 strong and that the "Auxiliary Native Medical Unit" had about 400 members.[94] Lt. Gen. Ishida Eiguma, who took the stand as the first defense witness at the Kudō Trial, confirmed the addition of prisoner-of-war and civilian medical personnel. He testified that the Railway Construction Unit of the Southern Army adopted the plan in the latter half of 1943 of gathering "some 400 medical orderlies and doctors from Malaya" and transferring them to the construction zones to address the shortage of medical personnel. "Most of the medical orderlies consisted of Allied prisoners-of-war," Ishida explained, but there were also civilian assistants. In the latter case, they "had to be trained for a short time by the Japanese" before being put to use as medical orderlies.[95]

Lt. Col. Horace Claude Benson, formerly commanding the 27th Indian Field Ambulance of the Royal Army Medical Corps, was one such prisoner-of-war medical officer to come under control of the 19th Ambulance Corps. According to his affidavit, he became a prisoner of the Japanese when Singapore fell on February 15, 1942, and was transferred to Thailand in August 1943 to be placed at several different prisoner-of-war camps. He was moved to the "No. 2 Coolie [Laborer] Hospital (Dai Ni), Kanchanaburi," on March 27, 1944, and remained there until March 23, 1945. He recalled two prisoner-of-war medical parties under control of the 19th Ambulance Corps. One was the "L" Force of which Benson served as commanding officer. It consisted of 15 medical officers and 100 orderlies. They were "split up into small parties and employed by the Japanese mostly in Coolie Camps and Hospitals on the Thailand-Burma Railway." The other prisoner-of-war medical party was known as the "K" Force, and it was about twice the size of the "L" Force. It consisted of 30 medical officers and 200 orderlies. The commanding officer was Maj. Robert Crawford, formerly medical officer of the Johore Volunteer Engineers. He, too, became prisoner of the Japanese at the time of the fall of Singapore. The "K" Force was put to use the same way as the "L" Force.[96]

The No. 2 Laborer Hospital at Kanchanaburi accommodated a large number of civilian patients – varying "from 1,500 to 3,000," Benson stated – who were evacuated from other hospital camps of the railway up-country. They were commonly transported in overcrowded railway trucks over the course of two to four days, some of which were open and thus exposing the passengers to the sun and the rain, while some other compartments were closed and overheated. Consequently, many civilian patients reached their final destination "in a dreadful condition, and many of them were moribund." Their ordeal did not end there. Benson saw that upon arrival, batches of civilian patients were "herded together like cattle and made to wait in the sun without food or water until the records of each one had been taken." After hours of waiting, civilian patients would be "crowded into huts with no isolation of infectious cases and no segregation according to diseases," or rather, there was "very little" treatment given out to them to begin with.[97] Female patients were at the risk of sexual violence. Benson stated, "Any of the younger coolie women were always liable to be molested by the Japanese." He singled out Maj. Kudō Hikosaku (the chief accused in this case) and a Japanese private, Ishimura, as habitual sex offenders. These individuals were widely known at the No. 2 Laborer Hospital Camp for being "in the habit of taking women in to the Canteen despite their protestations." As a result of general neglect and mistreatment such as these, "quite a number of coolies committed suicide," Benson stated, "mostly by lying down on the adjacent railway lines during the night waiting for a train to come." He added, "Some hung themselves in their huts."[98]

Capt. Joseph Francis McGarity, a member of the "L" Force under Benson's command, revealed another piece of information regarding the ghastly treatment meted out to civilian patients at the No. 2 Laborer Hospital. As explained in court testimony by Watanabe and Ishida, a certain number of civilians were recruited as medical assistants and brought over to the railway construction zones to work for the 19th Ambulance Corps. In reality, and according to McGarity's personal observations, civilian assistants – or medical dressers, as they were referred to in the court records – were "completely apathetic" and "all they were concerned about was to get their work finished and keep the Coolies quiet." In actual terms, their apathy translated into declaring those patients too sick to walk as dysentery cases and promptly transferring them to the "Death House." The "Death House" at the No. 2 Laborer Hospital was a hut of about 12 × 6 meters where up to 50 gravely ill patients were crammed. According to McGarity, the patients were left to die there without food, water, or medicine. They lay on the bare floor immobilized, with no bedding whatsoever but instead "in unutterable filth." Two fit civilian laborers were assigned to the Death House but only for the limited purpose of pulling out the dead. "No attempt was made to clean the floor which was covered with blood, slime and excreta," McGarity stated. "The stench was revolting and flies were everywhere."[99]

The affidavit of Maj. Robert Crawford shows that McGarity's accounts were hardly an exaggeration. Based on observations made by himself and other members of the "K" Force, Crawford concluded that the conditions of civilian work and hospital camps across the railway construction zones were "so far below any standards of western civilization that they can be described as disgraceful and a grave danger to the lives of those living in them." He pointed out, by illustration, that all the civilian camps for certain durations had "no or quite inadequate sanitary arrangements," as a result of which the entire camp areas were "heavily contaminated with faeces." Not a single civilian camp was equipped with a satisfactory water supply. Civilian laborers instead drew water from "raw river," thereby making themselves vulnerable to cholera outbreaks. Supplies of tents, blankets, food, and clothing were also at a substandard level. Crawford noted that these unacceptable states of affair applied "not only to male coolies but also women and children who were brought by the Japanese to work on the railway."[100] In his estimation, a total of about 100,000 civilian laborers were brought over for the railway project although there were other estimates ranging between 75,000 and 250,000. He concluded that based on observations and estimations made by the "K" Force members, "it is certain that 50 per cent of the total labourers brought from Malaya to Siam and Burma died there in the period of 1943–45." Of these, he estimated that "by far the greater part of this mortality occurred in the last eight months of 1943."[101]

Maj. Kudō Hikosaku took command of the 19th Ambulance Corps by the time it had come to serve as a medical unit to provide medical care to civilian laborers as its principal duty. The prosecution charged that Kudō and eleven former subordinates while "being responsible for the medical care and attention of the civilian inhabitants of occupied territories employed in, and in connection with, the construction and maintenance of the Burma-Siam Railway, and the wives and families of the said civilian inhabitants, in violation of the laws and usages of war, were together concerned in the ill treatment of the said civilian inhabitants and their wives and families resulting in their physical suffering and the deaths of many of them."[102] Kudō and some of the co-accused also faced additional charges of killing civilian laborers and mistreatment of prisoner-of-war medical personnel. Voluminous oral and documentary evidence brought to light not only the general state of neglect but also numerous episodes of willful mistreatment of the sick by individual accused. Evidence against the accused is uneven, but sadistic behavior appears to have been prevalent in the Kudō Unit. A former prisoner-of-war medical orderly, Capt. Robert H. Cuthbert, made the following statement: "This unit was a collection of throw-outs, unfit for active service owing to their habitual drunkenness, disease, physical deformity or mental deficiency."[103]

The name of Kudō, the chief accused, stood out in the prosecution's case, as multiple witnesses attested to seeing him drunk, inflicting beatings, and sexually molesting female patients. The name of another accused Lance Corporal Onodera Shōji – or commonly known to prisoners of war by his nickname, "Green Pants" – also stood out for the extremity of violence he meted out to both male and female civilian laborers. The affidavit of Kenneth G. Prickett, formerly a member of the 197th Field Ambulance of the Royal Army Medical Corps and a medical offier at the No. 1 Laborer Hospital at Kanchanaburi, linked this accused to two specific episodes of rape. In one case, Onodera allegedly forced 20 male civilian laborers, including one with symptoms of syphilis, to rape a 19-year-old Indian female patient, and he allegedly inserted in her vagina lit pieces of bamboos afterwards. The victim died the same day. In another, Onodera allegedly raped a Burmese girl from the village of Mazeli, who came to the hospital camp to sell tobacco.[104] Furthermore, two other prisoner-of-war medical orderlies attested to having personal knowledge of Onodera orchestrating the killing of bed-ridden patients by way of poisonous injections and poisoned food.[105]

In the final decision of the court, one accused was acquitted but the rest were convicted. The sentences for the eleven convicted varied, ranging from death to six months in prison. The death penalty was meted out to two only: Kudō and Onodera.[106] While the court produced no judgment, evidence of rape against the two may have weighed greatly. The prosecution, at least, had urged in its closing statement that the court attach importance to evidence of rape, including the statement taken from a single witness against Onodera. It is true that "where the evidence consists of or comes from a single witness . . . you have to make a very careful scrutiny and consideration." Nontheles, "we [the prosecution] put these offences forward as brutal assaults which do constitute a war crime without embarking on the technical niceties of rape or the laws affecting it."[107] What was more, the key witness against Onodera – that is, prisoner-of-war medical orderly Prickett – not only gave a detailed account of the episode of rape involving the Indian female victim but also attested that "I was dead scared in case I was called to rape her myself."[108] The prosecution held that this kind of statement could be made by nobody but the one who personally witnessed the dreadful rape incident.[109] The court's definitive position on this matter cannot be established, but the admission of such evidence nonetheless made this trial another early historical example – along with the trials of Yamashita and Honma – in which evidence of sexual violence was received as a war crime.

4

In the Name of Asian Co-Prosperity[1]

If defeating the Chiang Kai-shek Government was the ultimate goal of the war in the CBI theater, the Japanese fought in the South Pacific for the fulfillment of a less definitive military objective: to keep at bay the Allied armed forces while maintaining Japan's control over the resource-rich British and Dutch colonial territories in Southeast Asia.[2] "The task assigned to 8 Army Group by G.H.Q.," according to Gen. Imamura Hitoshi, general officer commanding the 8th Area Army from the time of its formation in mid-November 1942 until the cessation of hostilities in September 1945, was "to co-operate with the Navy, [to] occupy the SOLOMONS, and to occupy strategic parts in NEW GUINEA and prepare for operations in that area."[3] Prior to Imamura's appointment, the Japanese had fought in the region costly battles that pushed their troops to the limits of human endurance for some four months, in the Battle of Coral Sea, the Battle of Milne Bay, the Battle of Guadalcanal, and the New Guinea campaign along the Kokoda Trail over the Owen Stanley Range between Buna and Port Moresby. The American and Australian forces resisted their foes with matching determination so as not to give away either Guadalcanal or Port Moresby, two strategic points of great importance for Australia and its allies in the region.[4] Within weeks of Imamura's assumption of the 8th Area Army's command at the Rabaul headquarters in New Britain, the Government of Japan reached the conclusion that the initial offensives in the South Pacific were a lost cause and that the troops in Guadalcanal and Buna must be withdrawn.[5]

The 8th Area Army thereafter engaged in a long drawn-out war against the American-Australian joint forces in order to resist the latter's further military advance. The enemy's ever-improving aerial, ground, and naval powers inflicted immense damage on the Japanese supply lines and troop movements, putting the 8th Area Army increasingly on the defensive. The 18th Army in eastern New Guinea – "120,000 strong,"[6] one of the two main armies under command of the 8th Area Army – incurred the greatest casualties due to relentless enemy attacks, so much so that it was almost annihilated. Combat-related deaths were many, but so were the deaths resulting from starvation. Dispersed and isolated, members of the 18th Army were left to fend for themselves in the hostile, unfamiliar vast stretch of land in northeastern New Guinea. There were instances of fratricide among the servicemen, too, in the name of mercy killing, in the name of the enforcement of military discipline, or in the name of sheer survival – by feeding on the dead, that is – as will be discussed in the section on the Adachi Trial in this chapter.

Meanwhile, the Allied forces pounded Rabaul with incessant bombing and carried out land invasion in parts of New Britain, although not necessarily to drive the Japanese out of the island. Rather, they aimed at reducing the 8th Area Army's fighting capabilities by striking at the core of its supply and communication network. All in all, "more than one half of the entire force of this army group were lost in the dense jungles or in the sea due to fierce battles or by disease" by the end of the war, according to Imamura's postwar account. About 100,000 of the army and navy servicemen stationed in Rabaul were among those who survived. These men were prepared for "a decisive battle with the Allied forces" and could have died, too, had the Australian forces chosen to carry out mopping-up campaigns against them in the remaining months of the war.[7]

The purpose of this chapter is to elucidate the circumstances of ghastly military campaigns that led to large casualties in this theater. Tragic as it may be, however, the primary concern here is not so much the Japanese, dead or alive. This chapter instead focuses on several thousand Allied nationals of ethnically Asian backgrounds who allegedly volunteered to cooperate with the Japanese to pursue the vision of Asian co-prosperity, served in this theater as members of special work parties attached to the 8th Area Army, and were nearly annihilated as a result. The Asian persons under consideration were a diverse lot: former members of the British Indian Army that surrendered to the 25th Army in British Malaya at the start of the Pacific War; former members of Chiang Kai-shek's armed forces, captured during the Sino-Japanese armed conflict; former Chinese guerrilla fighters, captured during the same armed conflict in China; noncombatant Chinese civilians, who fell under Japanese military control also in China; and some of those Indonesians who received training from the Japanese in the occupied Dutch East Indies so as to form the auxiliary troops, the *heiho*. The 8th Area Army put them to use at various locations in the southern theater for logistical work, such as loading and unloading supplies, building shelters and storage space, tending agricultural fields, carrying rations and other equipment during the troop movements, and digging tunnels, trenches, and gun emplacements for fortifications.

Over the course of deployment, Asian recruits were exposed to extreme conditions of the war as much as their Japanese military superiors were, such as air raids, long marches, disease, malnutrition, starvation, and other mental and physical hardships. They were also subjected to harsh military discipline of the Japanese army even though they were neither Japanese nationals nor members of Japanese combat units. The penalty of summary execution applied to them, too, when they were suspected of or found to have attempted desertion, when they committed insubordination, or when they committed other grave offenses in breach of the Japanese army's criminal code.

A cross section of the former members of the 8th Area Army faced prosecution at the Australian war crimes court at Rabaul, between 1945 and 1947. They were charged with – among other offenses – mistreatment of the Asian people employed in special work parties. Imamura was one of the accused,[8] so were a selection of other high-ranking officers of the same army, namely: Lt. Gen. Katō Rinpei, Imamura's chief of staff; Maj. Gen. Hirota Akira, formerly a colonel and commander of the 8th Area Army's supply depots, headquartered at Rabaul; and Lt. Gen. Adachi Hatazō, commander of the 18th Army in charge of the New Guinea campaign. One of the controversial questions at these trials was whether the Asian people at issue had attained membership of sorts in the Japanese armed forces so as to have fallen outside the purview of international law, or whether they retained their status as Allied prisoners of war or as noncombatant Allied nationals, and hence continued to be individuals protected under international law. The question, to put it differently, was whether their alleged volunteering to join hands with the Japanese effected any material change to their national affiliations. This chapter delves into competing arguments and supporting evidence that was presented at the Rabaul court, elucidates the court's findings, and considers their implications to the understanding of visions and realities of Asian co-prosperity during the Pacific War.

Quite apart from the foregoing questions, this chapter will investigate the trial records in order also to assess the findings of Australian Rabaul proceedings against individual accused, and specifically with respect to the doctrine of command responsibility. The cases against the aforementioned four individuals – Hirota, Adachi, Katō, and Imamura – were part of five capstone trials that the Australian military authorities held at the midpoint of their war crimes program, dubbed collectively the "responsibility trials."[9] After hearing some dozen related cases against lower-ranking war crimes suspects, the Rabaul court undertook to determine individual responsibility of the highest-ranking Japanese army officers for alleged offenses. Notably, the trial of Gen. Yamashita Tomoyuki at the U.S. military commission at Manila (October–December 1945) reverberated at these trials, as three of the four accused faced a charge that had a striking resemblance to the one leveled against Yamashita. This indicates Australia's policy to build its command-responsibility cases on the Yamashita precedent in view of the latter's historic importance. Lt. Col. J. T. Brock, judge advocate of the Rabaul court, also contributed to making the Yamashita Trial relevant although, as will be shown in this chapter, by way of highlighting the significance of the dissenting opinion of Justice Frank Murphy of the U.S. Supreme Court rather than the decision of the U.S. military commission. In effect, the judge advocate presented the Yamashita Trial more as a cautionary tale than a model to emulate. Consequently, the Rabaul proceedings took on the characteristics of as much a follower of the Yamashita Trial as its critic, adding another layer of complexity to its jurisprudential legacy.

The pages to follow will begin by exploring the records of four trials in order to determine the general circumstances of the Japanese formation and deployment of Asian work parties in the South Pacific. Specific issues concerning individual criminal liability of the four accused will be discussed in the second half of the chapter.

ORGANIZING ASIAN WORK PARTIES

According to statements taken from Japanese witnesses, the idea of making available supplementary work forces in the southern theater originated in the 8th Area Army. Faced from the start with an acute shortage of manpower for executing his operational missions in this theater, Gen. Imamura of the 8th Area Army "requested by wireless the Imperial GHQ in Tokyo that in future the units coming into this area should take with them as many labourers as possible."[10] The said request met prompt approval and generated two policy decisions. One was for the Imperial General Headquarters to direct the Expeditionary Forces in China to have one of their army divisions in transition to the South Pacific "take as many labourers as possible with them to New Britain and hand them over to the GOC 8th Army Group [general officer commanding the 8th Area Army]."[11] The proposed transfer of workers from China would serve as a stopgap measure to address the immediate needs on the ground. The other policy decision involved the Southern Army – the army group that assumed command over the Japanese armies deployed in British Malaya, the Philippines, and other parts of Southeast Asia since the start of the Pacific War. At the beginning of 1943, the Imperial General Headquarters ordered that "thirty special duty coys [companies] be organized and fourteen of them be transported to the area under the 8th Army Group immediately," each special-duty company consisting of "approx 60 Japanese soldiers as staff members and approx 720 inhabitants of occupied territories, with a captain as its commander." Field Marshal Terauchi Hisaichi, commander-in-chief of the Southern Army, would serve as the "supervisor of the organization."[12]

The Expeditionary Forces in China lost little time in implementing the above order. Lt. Gen. Kanda Masatane, general officer commanding the 6th Division in the process of transfer to the South Pacific, received the order to take "approximately 1,500 Chinese laborers to Rabaul by the same ship with the soldiers of 6 Division and deliver them to GOC 8th Army Group."[13] Kanda, in turn, had Col. Tomonari Toshi[14] – a subordinate of his, who was heading directly to Rabaul along with the army unit under his control – carry out the order. Kanda himself took the main strength of the 6th Division to Bougainville, where he assumed new operational missions under command of the 8th Area Army. Tomonari completed delivery of the Chinese work party "soon after his arrival at Rabaul at the end of Jan 1943."[15]

According to Imamura, those Chinese who were brought over to the South Pacific consisted principally of voluntary civilian laborers the Chinese government helped recruit – the government of China, that is, that the Japanese established after the capture of Nanjing in December 1937 and that subsequently invited Wang Jing-wei, political rival of Chiang Kai-shek, to assume leadership. "All political and military negotiations between Japan and China were carried out through the Wang Government," Imamura explained, and "it is a widely known fact that the Wang Government also, with the doctrine of the freedom of Asia, the unity of the Far East, fully took and maintained co-operative attitude with Japan."[16] Imamura allegedly discovered later on that "some ex-POW's [*sic*]" were among the Chinese laborers but deemed this finding a nonissue, the reasons being "that none of these labourers insisted on being POW's [*sic*] and that all of them were desirous of cooperating with the Japanese Forces faithfully."[17] In Imamura's opinion, these people in any case needed work amid difficult conditions of the war and, moreover, "considering the racial characteristics of the Chinese who like to work abroad, there is nothing to be suspicious of" about their willingness to make a long journey to the South Pacific for employment.[18]

Imamura's explanations above were meant to dispute the prosecution's allegations that a significant portion of the Chinese work force were, in fact, prisoners of war; that aside from the party of 1,500, there were other groups of Chinese people the 8th Area Army put to use in this theater; and that irrespective of their former status as combatants or otherwise, none of those Chinese individuals came to the southern region out of their own volition. In support of these allegations, the prosecution presented in evidence at trials of the four individauls named above (Hirota, Adachi, Katō, and Imamura) a total of just about a dozen statements in which survivors of the Chinese work parties related their respective circumstances of hiring and work conditions. Commonly offering concise but at times also formulaic accounts, and failing to indicate sources of information or provide corroborative evidence, these statements tended to give no more than sketches of discrete episodes of labor recruitment and deployment rather than offering exhaustive documentation. With this understanding in mind, the gist of survivor accounts at the Rabaul trials can be summarized as follows.

With respect to the aforementioned work party of 1,500 Chinese, Lt. Col. Woo Yien, a former member of that party, provided the pertinent accounts.[19] One of his statements read that a third of the work party – 504 including himself – were former members of the "Chinese National Army" (presumably of the Chiang Kai-shek Government) and the remaining two-thirds – 1,000 of them – were Chinese guerrilla fighters. He explained that both groups of people had been captured by the Japanese over the course of the Sino-Japanese War and kept under Japanese military custody as "Prisoners of War" until shipped from the port in Shanghai off to Rabaul at the end of the year 1942.[20] Maj. Chen Kwok Leong, who identified himself as a former "guerrilla leader of the Chinese National Army fighting against the Japanese in CHINA," confirmed that a group of 1,000 in the work party were guerrilla troops. They had fought against the Japanese, but became prisoners in March 1942 and remained in Japanese custody at Nanjing until taken to Shanghai for eventual transfer to Rabaul.[21] The former combatant status of at least a third of the Chinese work party is likely to have been evident to the 8th Area Army staffers at Rabaul since, according to Woo Yien, the former servicemen of the Chinese National Army were still dressed in their Chinese army uniforms at the time of arrival in Rabaul. They remained in the same uniforms until the "Japanese style uniforms without badges of rank" were issued to them a few months later.[22]

According to Woo Yien, over a half of this particular Chinese work party – that is, a total of 829 – was placed under control of the 8th Area Army's supply depots, commanded by the accused Hirota Akira. Of these, 315 died by the end of the war due to one or more of the following causes: aerial bombings, the harsh work regime, poor accommodation, insufficient food and medical supplies, and mistreatment by the Japanese, including summary execution. Eighty among the 315 dead are said to have been shot or decapitated "because they were sick" (i.e., presumably of no use as work forces). Woo Yien made the point that Hirota was the commanding officer of the supply depots and that his headquarters was "very close, never more than 2 miles from the Chinese camp." In this regard, Hirota "could not fail both to see and to hear of the ill-treatment we were receiving" for as long as "two and a half years."[23]

Apart from the work party of 1,500, various other small and large groups of Chinese civilians appear to have been used by the Japanese armed forces stationed in the southern region for miscellaneous tasks since prior to the formation of the 8th Area Army in mid-November 1942. Work locations included Palau, the capital of the Japanese colonial territories in the Central Pacific, then known as the South Pacific Mandate by the decision of the League of Nations after World War I, or *Nan'yō guntō* (the "South Sea Island Group") to the Japanese. Palau and other Japanese-controlled islands were put to use as key Japanese military bases during World War II.[24] The prosecution's evidence showed that the 8th Area Army continued to make use of existing Chinese civilian work forces in the South Pacific for the remainder of the war.

For instance, a group of forty two Shandong residents is said to have reached the southern theater as early as February 1942 and were put to work, first at Palau, unloading ships for five months, and subsequently at Wewak, New Guinea, tending gardens, apparently to help the Japanese troops with food supplies. A smaller party of twenty four Chinese from Canton reached this theater, too, in December 1942. This particular work party was taken to Rabaul and then to Wewak. Their main tasks were to build shelters for the Japanese army unit to which they were assigned. Witness accounts indicate that survival rates were extremely low in both work parties: all but four were dead or gone missing by the end of the war due to aerial bombing, disease, lack of food, killing by the Japanese, and desertion. It is alleged that one of the Shandong residents was killed and cannibalized by the Japanese.[25] There is no evidence to corroborate this particular allegation other than two witness accounts. A dire food situation did exist during the New Guinea campaign, however, which is known to have led some to commit cannibalism. (See discussion of the Adachi Trial in this chapter.) Luin Yun, 24, a civilian who used to make his living by rope-making in his hometown in Guangdong Province and who was the only survivor in the work party of 24 Cantonese, makes an interesting observation in this connection. Commenting on his own good luck to have survived the war, he stated: "At WEWAK I was finding food for the JAPANESE so my life was spared."[26]

A much larger group of civilians had been brought to this theater prior to the formation of the 8th Area Army as well. According to the statement of Woo Yien, he received a report from a Chinese civilian that a party of 2,880 Cantonese had arrived at Rabaul in September 1942, including "approx 50 boys under the age of thirteen years." Two-thirds of the work party, that is about 1,800 of them, was allotted to the 8th Area Army's supply depots under command of Hirota, of which 1,080 were said to have died due to mistreatment and neglect. Most of the boys died in the initial three months, leaving only eight surviving at the end of the war.[27] Ho Wen, a Cantonese man, offered an account concerning his experience. He and other male citizens of Guangdong became subject to forced labor after October 1939 when the Japanese Army occupied Guangdong. The common method of recruitment was that the "Japanese soldiers would round up citizens in the street and take them away on trucks by binding several men together." Alternatively, "the Japanese would contact the headman of a district and make him supply 20–30 men for labour." According to Ho Wen, he and fellow Cantonese "swore no oath of allegiance to the Japanese Force and the whole undertaking was against our will." Regardless, the Japanese transferred them to the Solomon Islands and made them work "in ration stores, gardens etc."[28]

At the time when the Expeditionary Forces in China secured and dispatched the reinforcement work party to the 8th Area Army, the Southern Army tried to implement orders from Tokyo but faced difficulties. One major challenge was to find as many as 21,600 individuals to form the required number of special-duty companies (= 720 laborers × 30 companies). Where to find so many people on short notice? Tokyo instructed the Southern Army to recruit people from among the "inhabitants in occupied territories," but who would be both willing and qualified to serve alongside the Japanese armed forces at some of the most dangerous combat zones in the South Pacific? According to

Col. Miyama Yōzō, who had held various high positions in the Southern Army, the Army General Staff, and the Army Ministry, and who served as chief of Archives and Documents Section of the First Demobilization Bureau after the war, the Southern Army initially planned to organize the special-duty companies by using the *heiho* – which translates as "sub-soldiers" or "auxiliary troops" (and which can also mean a single "sub-soldier" or "auxiliary troop") – but soon realized that there were not enough of them.[29] As a result, the Southern Army had to look elsewhere. What were the *heiho* exactly, though?

According to Col. Hosoda Hiromu, formerly a member of the Third Department of the Army General Staff, the *heiho* became a recognized category of combat troops in the Japanese armed forces after the enactment of the Heiho Regulation on September 23, 1942. A *heiho* is a "male other than a Japanese subject, who had volunteered, passed the examination for service provided by the C-in-C of the operational Forces, and trained after enlistment." Hosoda pointed out two specific conditions that led the central government to support the creation of non-Japanese special combat units. One was the vision of Asian solidarity and self-rule, which the Japanese authorities believed to have gained foothold among the Asian people in the years leading to the start of the Pacific War. "Recognizing the awakening of the Asiatic races to civilization, and their positiveness, the Japanese Government desired to organize these people as component members of the Japanese Forces, whereby more to urge their self-respect." The other condition that made the *heiho* an appealing concept was practical military necessities. With the Imperial General Headquarters demanding "a prompt increase for more armaments" in anticipation of prolonged war, the central government worried that "it would badly effect [affect] the national industries to call up many Japanese within a short period" for troop expansion. The idea of creating the Asians-only auxiliary troops emerged as a convenient solution to the two conditions mentioned by Hosoda.[30] Kaori Maekawa's recent research in Japanese army records documents the existence of Japanese prewar plans for the *heiho* organization.[31]

This was the backdrop against which the Southern Army turned to the *heiho* for recruitment purposes. As of early 1943, however, "the main body of the heiho's [*sic*] who were under Gen. TERAUCHI's command at that time were Indonesians" who were already "working in their native places" in Java, so explained Lt. Col. Kagoshima Takashi, formerly staff officer of the Southern Army in charge of "affairs concerning operation and organization." The Army could secure just about 1,000 *heiho* volunteers for the special-duty companies, falling far too short of the required number of 21,600. No dramatic increase in the number of the *heiho* troops was anticipated in the immediate future because, as Kagoshima explained, "it took several months, at least, to adopt heiho's [*sic*], because it was provided that they should have their characters tested, be supplied with clothing and arms, educated and drilled." Despite the urgent needs, "we could not give mere inhabitants the name of heiho's [*sic*] resorting to makeshift under the regulation."[32]

To overcome these hurdles, Field Marshal Terauchi is said to have consulted his legal advisor, Dr. Terajima, and decided to request that the Imperial General Headquarters approve the use of "volunteers among the Indian ex-POWs who have been released on parole" to make up for the shortfall. What this meant was that aside from the *heiho* troops, the Southern Army would recruit members of the British Indian Army, which had surrendered to the Japanese over the course of the 25th Army's invasion of the Malay Peninsula and Singapore. The target group would be ethnic Indians but not British prisoners of war, assuming Indian soldiers' willingness to work with the Japanese in the spirit of Asian solidarity. The Imperial General Headquarters duly granted permission. Terauchi thereafter directed general officers commanding the 16th Army (in Java) and the 25th Army to organize seven special-duty companies each and hand them over to the 8th Area Army.[33]

When recruiting Indian prisoners of war for the special-duty companies, the Southern Army adopted a policy not to recognize the recruits either as prisoners of war or as *heiho* troops. It instead decided to treat them as civilian laborers without any combat-related status. The 8th Area Army followed suit when it received the special-duty companies. Imamura instructed the units under his command that the Indians allotted to the 8th Area Army were "ex-POW's [*sic*] released on parole and labourers employed in the Japanese Forces," and that they were "to form part of the Japanese Forces and should be given the same treatment as Japanese civilians attached to the Army."[34]

Lt. Gen. Kuroda Shigenori appeared in the Rabaul courtroom in person as a defense witness, and testified on the formal position of the Southern Army. This Kuroda is the same Kuroda as the one discussed in Chapter 1. (He served as chief of staff of the Southern Army prior to his appointment as commanding general of the 14th Army.) Regarding the nonrecognition of prisoner-of-war status for Indian soldiers, Kuroda attested that the policy had its origin in the Government of Japan and that the Southern Army was "only working in accordance with that policy."[35] A policy document of the Army Ministry, dated May 6, 1942, and titled, "Disposal of Prisoners of War," can partly corroborate Kuroda's testimony. As already shown in Chapter 2 (but not introduced in evidence at the Rabaul trials), this policy document stipulated that while the "white" prisoners of war should be "employed in the expansion of our production and or work connected with military affairs" in the inner circle of the Japanese empire, those prisoners of war *"who are not white persons* and who do not necessitate imprisonment shall be immediately *released on parole and made to work in their present localities."*[36] Based on the existing policy of the central government, Kuroda in his capacity as chief of staff of the Southern Army issued a notification, marked Nan-Sō-San No. 1447 (Southern Army General Staff No. 1447). It instructed that prisoners of war released on parole should be treated as laborers.[37] When the Rabaul court questioned Kuroda whether he was aware that "according to International Law a Prisoner of War on parole still retains his status as a Prisoner of War,"

Kuroda replied that, as a matter of fact, "we have studied this with experts attached to the Army, and it was concluded that, when released on parole, they did not hold their status of a Prisoner of War."[38]

With respect to the Japanese policy to distinguish the Indian prisoners of war from the *heiho* troops and *not* to recognize the combat status of the former, Kuroda pointed to Nan-Sō-San No. 1470 (Southern Army General Staff No. 1470) as the key document that articulated the definitive position of the Southern Army.[39] Issued by himself on behalf of the Southern Army on April 22, 1943, the notification read in full as follows:

Matter of the Status of Indian Coolies as Substitute of Auxiliary Troops (*Heiho daiyō Indo-jin jinpu no ken*)

The Indians formed into the Special Land Service Coys No 1 to 7 inclusive, the Special Water Duty Coys No 10 to 20 inclusive and 26 and 27 Special Construction Coys, (Indian persons of war released on parole by Nan-So-San 1445), because heihos organising these coys cannot be provided, they (the Indians) are to be regarded as coolies [*jinpu*] supplementing labour power which should be supplied by the heiho, and in regard to their status and treatment, it is not to be the same as heiho or one who is similar to a heiho.[40]

Nan-Sō-San No. 1470 emphasized that even though Indians were recruited as substitutes of *heiho* troops, they should not be construed as having combat status but instead be understood as *jinpu* or laborers. Explaining the logic behind this policy, Kuroda testified that "Heiho are required from AHQ [Army Headquarters], that is, from the Imperial HQ, and are given training and are armed and may go into combat, but the Indians were non-combatants who were to service in the rear."[41] A former staff officer of the Southern Army and the aforementioned defense witness, Kagoshima Takashi, concurred. But he also testified that theoretically there was an avenue for the former Indian prisoners of war to attain *heiho* status, namely, to undergo the required recruitment and training process. Ambonese soldiers of the Dutch Army indeed became *heiho*s by this means. That said, Kagoshima doubted that Terauchi would have supported the refashioning of Indian prisoners of war into the *heiho*, the main reason being that Indians were already presented with the opportunity to join the "Indian National Army."[42]

The Indian National Army – or also known in abbreviation, INA – refers to a Japanese-sponsored Indians-only combat unit that came into being in Singapore in the wake of the Japanese invasion of the Malay Peninsula. Joyce Lebra, in her authoritative study, *Jungle Alliance: Japan and the Indian National Army* (1971),[43] credits two individuals for the creation of INA: Maj. Fujiwara Iwaichi, a Japanese intelligence officer and a member of the 8th Section, the Second Department of the Army General Staff, and Capt. Mohan Singh, second-in-command of a battalion under the command of the 15th Brigade, 1/14 Punjab Regiment, which surrendered to the Japanese at Alor Setar in British Malaya on December 11, 1941. The two met during Fujiwara's assignment in the Malay Peninsula to promote an anti-British independence movement among expatriate Indians. They are said to have established an instant rapport, and soon developed the idea of recruiting tens of thousands of Indian prisoners of war and other volunteers to organize an all-India combat unit. With support from Tokyo, the two worked closely to realize their idea until Fujiwara was taken off the INA project in the second half of 1942.[44] Mohan Singh was later thrown off the INA project, too, as he clashed with Rash Behari Bose, a Bengali revolutionary in self-imposed exile in Japan since 1915 in opposition to British colonial rule of India. Bose came to serve as head of the Indian Independence League – a Japanese-sponsored political association, comprised of expatriate Indians – in its formative months.[45] Mohan Singh also provoked the displeasure of the Japanese because he began to voice distrust of the Japanese leadership. Mohan Singh's arrest and imprisonment triggered mass resignation of INA members in protest. The Japanese authorities kept the INA alive, however, by bringing on board Subhas Chandra Bose, another charismatic Bengali nationalist (but no family relation of Rash Behari Bose). Subhas Chandra Bose in July 1943 took command of the INA and leadership of the Indian Independence League. He served in both capacities until August 1945, when he died in a plane crash.[46]

According to Kuroda's testimony, the Southern Army recruited Indian soldiers to use them as laborers in special-duty companies by getting help from the INA. Or as he put it, "All negotiations were made with the leader of the Indian National Army, and the Leader of the Indian National Army collected volunteers and handed them over to us."[47] This account stood at variance with testimony of the prosecution's witnesses, however, who attested to being first threatened into joining the INA and then, upon their repeated refusal, being packed off to the South Pacific as members of special-duty companies. Solicitation to join the INA continued afterwards, too, especially in the months following Subhas Chandra Bose's assumption of the INA command.[48]

Subedar Chint Singh, formerly an officer serving in the 2/12 Frontline Force Rifles and a prisoner of the Japanese in Singapore, appeared in the Rabaul courtroom as a key prosecution witness and testified on the general circumstances of recruitment.[49] He attested that initially, about 20,000 Indian prisoners of war joined the INA either on a voluntary basis or by force, of which 8,000 withdrew in December 1942. After being subjected to mistreatment, 3,000 rejoined the INA. The remaining 5,000 or so were "kept in a camp named SELETAR under the barbed wire fence guarded by the Japanese and the members of the Indian National Army."[50] The Southern Army appears to have used these 5,000 or so Indians to make up for the shortfall in the formation of required special-duty companies.

The 8th Area Army eventually received the reinforcement work parties, all arriving by the middle of 1943. But the number was reduced to thirteen regardless of the original order from Tokyo to provide fourteen.[51] The strength of each special-duty company was similarly reduced to around 560 or fewer in place of 720 as originally planned.[52] This suggests that the concurrence of the INA movement interfered with the Southern Army's assignment to create the special-duty companies but that the Japanese authorities chose to keep the movement alive, arguably for its propaganda value.

Of the thirteen special-duty companies allotted to the 8th Area Army, five were given to the 18th Army in New Guinea and the rest was distributed to other locations, including Rabaul. The members of the special-duty companies thereafter were exposed to the extremity of the war as well as subjected to mistreatment by the Japanese guards and their military superiors. Many deaths occurred as a result. The survival rate of Indian soldiers in New Guinea was particularly low, reaching barely 0.5%. According to testimony of Chint Singh, just about 12 out of the original strength of about 2,530 Indian soldiers brought over to New Guinea were accounted for as of September 30, 1945.[53]

Mohan Singh, the first INA commander, whom the Japanese forced out of power for his voicing dissent, learned about the tragic losses of fellow Indians in the South Pacific in the aftermath of the war. While still detained in Singapore at the start of 1946 (in British custody by then), he wrote:

I heard some details of the untold sufferings those beloved sons of Mother India had to undergo and of the price that they paid for the honour of our country – nearly 5,000 young, dauntless heroes – I became very bitter. I felt that those responsible for sending the cream of patriots to certain death in New Guinea and other South-East Asiatic islands, must be tried as war criminals.[54]

He expressed the same sentiments nearly thirty years later when he published a memoir of his INA experience. He wrote that those men were "very vocal and opposed to the policies of Rash Behari" and for that very reason "segregated and taken to New Guinea and other South Pacific Islands which turned out to be the most shameful and horrible death-trap." He continued: "Thrown into those forsaken islands with full wrath of vengeance of the Japanese, they perished there unwept and unsung, and now almost forgotten." For Mohan Singh, the history of the INA – and by extension, that of Indian independence – would be incomplete without remembrance of these brave Indian patriots. "History provides several instances where their adversaries go to the extent of not only maligning them, but also exterminating them," he wrote in conclusion, "and this is certainly one of those brutal instances."[55]

THE OPINION OF THE JUDGE ADVOCATE

Once in the courtroom, the accused at the Rabaul trials readily confirmed the difficult conditions of the war in the South Pacific but denied any targeted wrongdoing against the members of Asian work parties. The defense position was rather that the Asian recruits were treated in the same way as the Japanese civilians attached to the 8th Area Army. Because they enjoyed a status equivalent to the Japanese, so the defense logic went, the members of Asian work parties were subject to Japanese army rules and regulations while falling outside the protection of international law. No war crime, or no instance of violation of laws and customs of war, could occur in this situation. The court ultimately rejected the defense contention, however, or rather, Lt. Col. J. T. Brock, who served as judge advocate with responsibility to give legal advice to the court, rejected it. The opinion of the judge advocate on points of law was not binding but, according to the Rules of Procedure applicable to the Australian war crimes trials, "the court should be guided by his opinion, and not disregard it, except for very weighty reasons" and "must consider the grave consequences which may result from their disregard of the advice of the judge-advocate on any legal point."[56] The legal advice of the judge advocate was thus not to be made light of.

Brock's own advice to the Rabaul court on the issues of Asian work parties' status can be summarized as follows. Concerning first the status of Chinese civilian workers, Brock did not find any controversy so far as the issue of their nationality was concerned. "It has not been denied that these peoples were Chinese citizens," he stated, "nor does the allegation that they volunteered for service in the Japanese Army alter their nationality."[57] In those circumstances, there were no grounds to assume that the Chinese people attached to the 8th Area Army forfeited their status as noncombatant enemy nationals under international law. Furthermore, he pointed out that if evidence showed that Chinese civilians were put to work by the Japanese against their will, it would constitute a clear case of war crime in breach of article 52 of the Hague Convention No. 4. ("Requisitions in kind and services shall not be demanded from municipalities or inhabitants except for the needs of the army or occupation.")[58] Brock added that "deportation to slave labor" was a recognized category of war crime under article 6 (2) of the Charter of the International Military Tribunal at Nuremberg.[59]

With respect to Chinese and Indian prisoners of war, Brock enumerated seven methods by which, according to the existing literature on international law, a prisoner of war may be freed from captivity. They were: (1) release on parole; (2) prisoner-of-war exchange; (3) simple release or repatriation; (4) successful escape from captivity at the prisoners' own initiative; (5) liberation by the friendly forces; (6) transfer into "neutral territory by captors"; and (7) cessation of hostilities. As far as the Rabaul proceedings went, the primary concern was to determine whether the first method – that is, release on parole – should be construed as forfeiting of one's prisoner-of-war status. Brock was of the opinion that that was not the case. Insofar as a condition was attached to release on parole, he argued, a released person continued to retain the right to be treated as a prisoner of war. A person would lose his prisoner-of-war status if he breached the condition attached *but not before*. If one were to assume that a person forfeited his prisoner-of-war status upon release on parole, then that person would have nothing to forfeit if and when he should be found to have breached the condition of parole. "So far as the authorities on International Law at the moment are concerned, there is no method of release to take up voluntary service with the enemy as distinct from parole," Brock continued. However, "there is no need for any such distinct method, because the agreement to take service is merely a condition of parole," and therefore, "until he breaks that condition to serve with the enemy forces, he still remains a prisoner of war and is entitled to privileges."[60] The task still remained for the court to sift through evidence and determine whether there were actual cases in which prisoners of war did forfeit their prisoner-of-war status. Brock alerted the court that one could lose his status as a prisoner of war by committing espionage or a war crime, "and in the expression 'war crime' I include the words 'war treason.'"[61]

It is difficult to determine how the Rabaul court applied the legal opinion of the judge advocate, since it generated no judgments when reaching its final decisions. However, guilty verdicts for accused in three of the four trials in this chapter (as will be discussed shortly) indicated that the court found most, if not all, members of Asian work parties as having been protected individuals under international law. The correctness of this interpretation is partly confirmed in a memorandum, dated June 11, 1947, which the presiding judge of the court, Maj. Gen. J. S. Whitelaw, separately prepared for the benefit of the confirming authority. Whitelaw explained that the court indeed found Indians and Chinese as having retained status as prisoners of war. As for Indonesian *heiho*s, the court "was not satisfied on the evidence available" and "could not determine beyond reasonable doubt the status of these personnel at relevant times." The court thus "excluded" from its final consideration all alleged war crimes against Indonesians.[62]

Incidentally, the British government had its own ideas about the status of the former Indian prisoners of war under Japanese control and specifically those who joined the INA. Shortly after recovering its colonies in Southeast Asia, the British authorities prepared court-martial cases against former active INA members. The first trial was held between November and December 1945 against three commanding officers of the INA forces, which had been deployed alongside the Japanese to fight against the British in the CBI theater.[63] The venue of the first INA trial was Lal Qila (Red Fort), the historical Mughal fort located at the heart of Delhi.[64] The Red Fort Trial ended in utter public relations failure for the British authorities, however, as "a wave of resentment had already spread in the whole country like wild fire," according to Mohan Singh's retrospective account. "The entire nation stood solidly behind the cause of the INA and accepted this trial as a great challenge to the right of a subjugated nation to war for its liberation."[65] Ultimately, the Red Fort Trial did little to further the cause of British justice but instead tarnished it in the eyes of the Indian public. The image of the INA as the symbol of patriotism, meanwhile, was seared in the Indian war memory and is remembered to this day.

THE CASE OF HIROTA

Maj. Gen. Hirota Akira was commander of field supply depots of the 8th Area Army from December 10, 1942, until the cessation of hostilities in the summer of 1945. The prosecution alleged that the accused "unlawfully disregarded and failed to discharge his duty as such commander to control the conduct of the members of his command whereby they committed brutal atrocities and other high crimes against people of the Commonwealth of Australia and its allies."[66] The victim groups in the Hirota Trial were Chinese, Indians, and the local residents of New Britain, although the bulk of the prosecution's case focused on mistreatment and killing of members of the Chinese work parties. The statements by Lt. Col. Woo Yien and Maj. Chen Kwok Leong (which are discussed in the section, "Organizing Asian Work Parties") set out the general circumstances of recruitment and deployment of Chinese people in the Rabaul area, while the records of some thirteen war crimes trials that had been held before the Hirota Trial were introduced in evidence so as to document specific instances of atrocity committed by the accused's wartime subordinates. (The Hirota Trial took place between March 19 and April 3, 1947.) The prosecution additionally called to the courtroom five Taiwanese as witnesses. They were formerly members of the *hōkōdan* or the "Volunteer Group,"[67] another type of Asian work party that consisted exclusively of Japanese colonial subjects. These five had been tried, convicted, and sentenced to death alongside four others in March 1946 in connection with the killing of thirty sick Chinese in the work party. (The five death sentences were commuted to life a few months after the end of the Hirota Trial, on June 27, 1947.)[68] Their testimony concerned a conversation that allegedly had taken place at the War Criminals' Compound at Rabaul between their wartime superior officer, Pvt. Aizawa Harumoto, and Hirota, regarding the latter's share of responsibility in the killing episodes.[69]

Hirota did not contest the use of Chinese work parties under his command but denied that they were prisoners of war. They had been passed on to him from Gen. Imamura as *rōmusha* or laborers, he testified, and he treated them as such.[70] He also disputed the prosecution's allegation that he willfully disregarded and failed to discharge his duty as commander of the supply depots. He asserted that on the contrary, he regularly inspected the conditions of Chinese laborers – "I always made an inspection once a month," he testified – and that he "saw the defects and had them altered." When questioned for clarification, he attested that "whenever I would find a defect in an inspection, I would have it altered, and I always tried to find a defect during my inspection."[71]

Regarding his knowledge of specific episodes of atrocity, Hirota denied it and pointed out in his defense that most alleged killings took place in the early months of 1943, when he was yet to establish full control over his subordinate units. The 8th Area Army's supply depots underwent reorganization between the time of Hirota's appointment in December 1942 and February 20, 1943. The existing supply depots were consolidated to form the 26th Field Supply Depot in this period. It was not until "the latter part of Mar[ch] 1943 that I attained full command,"[72] he stated. "After the completion of disposition, with advance of my orders and instructions into them, such cases [of serious crimes] decreased in number gradually," Hirota asserted. "Especially during the years of 1944 and 1945 there happened only the minor cases originated in the individual antipathy, while wicked crimes were completely stamped out."[73] Hirota believed that he discharged his duty of maintaining his troops' discipline in the given circumstances. If any instances of atrocity occurred as alleged, he did not know of them and, in his opinion, had ample reasons for not being able to learn about them due to the organizational problems from within.

Gen. Imamura appeared in the courtroom as a key defense witness and led a spirited argument on behalf of the accused. He readily confirmed that as GOC 8th Area Army, he instructed Hirota to treat the members of the Chinese work party just like "the Japanese civilians attached to the Army" and "not POW,"[74] and that, therefore, Hirota could not be held liable for the policy that had already been set in place at a higher level. He also made the point – just as Hirota did – that most serious crimes as alleged by the prosecution "occurred during the first period when the command of Col HIROTA was not yet recognized thoroughly by his subordinates." He went on to argue that "in fact, at that time I myself directed the depots to maintain the military discipline among them. Such being the case, I, GOC the 8th Army Group, but not Col HIROTA should be held responsible for these incidents."[75] Imamura conceded that the accused continued to have difficulties enforcing discipline of subordinate troops due partly to chronic shortage of officers and "especially, that of leading staff." On this front, too, Imamura readily accepted personal responsibility by stating that "Col HIROTA was ordered by me to dispatch a part of his subordinates to Bougainville and New Guinea"[76] and that because of this order, the 26th Field Supply Depot could not maintain a sufficient number of officers to enforce discipline.

Quite apart from internal organizational problems and officer shortage of the 26th Field Supply Depot, Imamura urged the court to take into consideration the exigency of the war. "Rabaul was attacked every day and night by the powerful enemy Air Forces except in the worst weather," as a result of which the 8th Area Army "was obliged to move all of the stores and equipments [sic] under-ground."[77] The 26th Field Supply Depot was particularly in a vulnerable position because:

As the Supply Depot was in charge of foods [sic] for all units of 8th Army Group, the enemy Air Forces naturally concentrated their attacks on stores held by it and for about 1,000 days all members of the Supply Depot devoted themselves to protect the stores from enemy's attacks and consequently became exhausted physically and mentally.[78]

In Imamura's opinion, the combination of organizational and staff problems from within and ever-escalating Allied aerial attacks from without undercut the accused's ability to exercise in full his command authority.

The judge advocate for the court, Lt. Col. Brock, appeared to have sympathetic views on the defense case, especially where the defense argument on difficulties arising from military exigencies was concerned. Brock weighed in on this matter by referring to the dissenting opinion of Justice Murphy of the U.S. Supreme Court in the case of the Yamashita Trial. He recognized that the war crime charge Yamashita faced was not related to the Hirota Trial, but he considered a portion of Murphy's opinion as having "strong bearing on this case." Brock went on to quote from the dissenting opinion, a segment of which appears in the transcripts of the Rabaul court proceedings as follows:

> It seems apparent beyond dispute that the word "responsibility" was not used in this particular Hague Convention [No. 4 of 1907] to hold the commander of a defeated army to any high standard of efficiency *when he is under destructive attack*, nor was it used to impute to him any criminal responsibility for war crimes committed by troops under his command *under such circumstances*.[79]

Explaining his take on Murphy's opinion, Brock advised the Rabaul court that "unqualified responsibility, merely by reason of the fact of his appointment, is repugnant to the principle which requires that the individual should himself be possessed of a guilty mind."[80] In other words, Brock deemed it inadvisable for the Rabaul court to apply the standard of strict liability[81] by which the U.S. military commission found Gen. Yamashita guilty.

What he proposed instead was to consider "due diligence" as a key concept for determining the criminal liability of the accused. Brock drew upon the judicial opinion of the full court of the U.S. Supreme Court on this matter, explaining what he meant by "due diligence." The pertinent part of the Supreme Court decision he quoted in his summation read as follows:

> Hence the law of war presupposes that its violation is to be avoided through the control of the operations of war by its Commanders who are <u>to some extent</u> responsible for their subordinates . . . These provisions plainly imposed on the petitioner, who at the time specified was Military Governor of the Philippines, as well as Commander of the Japanese forces, an affirmative duty to take such measure <u>as were within his power</u> and appropriate in the circumstances.[82]

Highlighting the phrase, "to some extent," Brock advised that "the element of responsibility which is imposed on a commander in the field by International Law is *limited to a responsibility to exercise due diligence* to prevent his troops from committing offences and it is limited only to offences, so far as he is concerned as a commander, which it was *within his power to prevent*."[83]

The judge advocate's recommendations notwithstanding, the Rabaul court found Hirota guilty as charged but meted out a lenient sentence of seven years in prison.[84] There was no judgment that explained the grounds of conviction or the sentence. One can only surmise that in the court's opinion, there was

sufficient evidence to conclude Hirota as having failed to exercise due diligence and that, nonetheless, circumstances in extenuation led the court to
favor leniency in sentencing.

THE CASE OF ADACHI

Lt. Gen. Adachi Hatazō faced a charge that read substantially the same as the
one against Hirota, which was that the accused "unlawfully disregarded and
failed to discharge his duty" as commander of the 18th Army in New Guinea
between November 1942 and September 1945 "to control the conduct of the
members of his command whereby they committed brutal atrocities and other
high crimes against people of the commonwealth and its Allies."[85] The prosecution's evidence consisted of testimony by the aforementioned Indian officer
Chint Singh; records of fourteen Australian war crimes trials at which members of the units under command of the 18th Army had been prosecuted and
convicted; extracts from "Webb Reports" (war crimes reports produced by
Sir William F. Webb, three-time chairman of the Australian war crimes commission between 1943 and 1945, who subsequently served as president of the
Tokyo Tribunal); and statements taken from eyewitnesses and victims of war
crimes. By using these wide-ranging court exhibits and witness testimony, the
prosecution documented general mistreatment of Indian and Chinese work
parties, specific instances of killing of Indian soldiers and New Guinea inhabitants, and episodes of mutilation of the dead (Australian soldiers being the
primary victim group).

As was the case with the Hirota Trial, Adachi denied personal knowledge
of the alleged offenses, and argued similarly that he was limited in his ability to acquire information about them due to the dire circumstances of the
war. He stressed in particular the repercussions of the "'MO' Operation," an
eighty-day assault on the Allied forces that started in May 1944 and ended in
early August the same year. The gist of Adachi's extensive and often gripping
war narrative – which constituted the main defense argument in this case –
can be summarized as follows.[86]

Japan's vital defensive positions in the South Pacific were on the brink of
collapse in those months, he pointed out, because of the unexpected Allied
landings on Aitape and Hollandia on April 22, 1944. These landings effectively cut off critical supply lines of the Japanese troops in New Guinea while
enabling the Allied forces to prepare for the attack on Biak, the island off the
coast of northwestern New Guinea, which had served as a key air base for
the Japanese in the South Pacific. The major military engagements of the 18th
Army until then had focused on the northeastern part of New Guinea between
Buna and Madang, Adachi directing the military operations from his headquarters in the rear at Boiken, west of Wewak.[87] The opening of the new front
by the Allied landings from the opposite direction, however, changed the whole
dynamic of military campaigns, precipitating the collapse of what was then

considered the critical line of defense of the wartime Empire of Japan in this theater. "Anticipating a decisive battle by the Japanese main forces," the 18th Army thus planned and carried out an all-out attack on the Allied forces in the Aitape area with the goal "to facilitate the Japanese main operations, without regard to its success, and sacrificing the maintenance and self-preservation of the 18th Army, with the determination to fight to the last man."[88]

According to Adachi, the 18th Army managed to achieve its central objective in the "MO" Operation, namely, to harass the Allied assault forces. But the fulfillment of the operational mission came at a heavy human cost. As many as 10,000 officers and men were killed in action, and the remainder of the original strength of 30,000 deployed in this particular operation emerged in pitiable physical condition; they were a hungry, fatigued, disease-prone lot, having fought against better-equipped, better-fed enemy troops when they themselves had to live on half rations so as not to exhaust the limited food supplies. Even so, the 18th Army was left with barely enough food to feed its troops at one-third rations for less than a month when the battle was called off on August 4, 1944.[89] And yet, Adachi's account indicates that this was only the beginning of greater hardship that still awaited the 18th Army.

In light of the dwindling food supplies, Adachi is said to have ordered retreat of the troops in the month of August to prepare for "defense and counterattack based upon self maintenance." The rapid troop movement proved impossible, however. "The distance would take even a fit soldier two weeks to cover," Adachi explained, and "the physical standard of the troops were one fourth of the standard before the 'MO' Operation." These soldiers had to trek through inhospitable terrain while also carrying a 15-kilogram load (about 33 pounds) per person. The physical challenges were so great that "the actual pace could only reach 4 kilos [approx. 2.5 miles] a day" and "the actual trip took 8 to 10 weeks." Retreat was further slowed down because of Adachi's instructions to his troops that they be dispersed over a wide area "where local products were more abundant," thereby increasing the likelihood of their survival. An army of some 44,000 troops in total were thus turned into numerous small parties of tattered wandering scavengers in an unknown land, fending for themselves until they rejoined their fellow soldiers at the final destination. In the end, "the movement took 6 months from August 44 till January 1945 for the whole Army, and during this period 15,000 officers and men died of illness and starvation and the terrible misery along the route are beyond description."[90]

Once the retreat was complete, Adachi hastened to reorganize the remaining troops to prepare them for the defensive warfare. But then "in Dec 44 just when the preparations would be completed in a few months, the Australian 6 Division which had replaced the Americans commenced attack on our western front." The 18th Army engaged the formidable enemy for more than a half year, but this was entirely "a one-sided battle so far as artillery and airpower was concerned." Anticipating local food supplies and the stock of ammunitions to dry up by September, "the whole Army in July united in its determination to fight to the last man." They never saw the last battle of attrition, however, as the war abruptly came to an end in mid-August 1945. "The history of the 18th Army was truly tragic and it was only by unexpected happenings that we survived at all," Adachi said in conclusion, "Indeed, I am sure that if the war continued for another month the whole Army would have been annihilated, fighting to the last man."[91] It was against this backdrop, in his opinion, that the Rabaul court must evaluate his ability *in practice* to exercise command and control over his army.

With respect specifically to the allegation that Adachi willfully disregarded and failed to discharge his duty, the accused vehemently disputed it, arguing that in fact he did take concrete steps to maintain discipline of his troops and that such steps bore desired effects. In point of fact, he issued an Emergency Punishment Order in late October 1944 after learning that, since the end of the "MO" Operation, "the lack of food resulted in undisguised animal instincts and drove men into abnormal and insane conducts" and that "some gave full vent to their animal impulses."[92] If there is any ambiguity in the meaning of "abnormal and insane conducts," Lt. Gen. Yoshihara Kane, formerly chief of staff of the 18th Army, helps clarify it. "In Sep–Oct 44, we first heard of our men eating human flesh," thereupon Adachi promptly acted on his authority as commanding general and issued the Emergency Punishment Order.[93]

Swift justice could be achieved under the special order, as the commanding officer of an army unit was vested with power and authority to mete out the death penalty to a person found to have committed cannibalism. The court-martial process was not required under the Emergency Punishment Order, nor was a commander required to have legal qualifications to dispense justice.[94] Moreover, cannibalism was just one of many offenses that were made punishable by this order. The full listing, according to Adachi, was

a. rebellion;
b. resisting order in face of the enemy;
c. desertion in face of the enemy;
d. killing superior officers, and cannibalism, and murder with intent to commit cannibalism.[95]

Yoshihara testified that the higher authorities of the Army must have received the order contemporaneously in hard copy, so should the Imperial General Headquarters in Tokyo, by wireless.[96]

Adachi fully appreciated that the issuance of the Emergency Punishment Order was an extraordinary measure, but he also believed that the extraordinary circumstances of the war necessitated it. He was confident, in any event, that the Emergency Punishment Order did not deviate from the spirit of article 22 of the Army Criminal Code, according to which those who attempted rebellion or desertion under pressing circumstances could be summarily punished.[97] Above all, Adachi was of the opinion that this order saved his troops from falling into utter lawlessness and organizational breakdown. "If I had failed to take these measures at that time, discipline would have even more slackened and felonious crimes increased, affecting the operations disadvantageously and rendering the conduct of the operations difficult," Adachi observed. "In fact, the extreme circumstances under which the 18th Army was placed would have led to the collapse of any other ordinary army." He readily credited "the long-bred patriotism of the Japanese"[98] for the resiliency of his troops. Nevertheless, the Emergency Punishment Order, in his opinion, was the backbone of the 18th Army's organizational unity in the last year of war.

Was Adachi correct in this assessment? No one can tell. What one *can* tell based on the trial record is that quite a few individuals were summarily put to death under the Emergency Punishment Order. Lt. Col. Tanaka Kengorō, formerly a staff officer of the 18th Army attached to the Legal Department, testified that approximately seventy soldiers were executed under the Emergency Punishment Order from its issuance in October 1944 until the cessation of hostilities. About forty of them were "executed for desertion in face of the enemy or refusal of orders," and the remaining thirty or so "for cannibalism."[99] What was more, and by Adachi's own admission, members of Asian work parties attached to the 18th Army were subject to the same army rules including the Emergency Punishment Order,[100] although the number of executed among them was not shown in the defense or the prosecution's evidence. Maintaining discipline of Indians serving in the special-duty companies posed a great challenge for the 18th Army, so Adachi informed the court, for they "developed disaffection against the Japanese due to general hardships and their forecast of the war future." They resorted to "mass desertions" or "gave full swing to anti-Japanese conduct and speech."[101]

One particular episode of summary execution, which took place near Wewak on about April 22, 1944, was argued at length at the Adachi Trial with regard to its lawfulness. The case at issue concerned Capt. Nirpal Chand, the lead Indian officer of the No. 19 Special-Duty Company in the Wewak area. Adachi attested to receiving a report that Nirpal Chand was executed for reasons that he "did not obey the order to move to HOLLANDIA" and instead "instigated other Indians and gathered them and with machetes and axes in their hands, they tried to threaten Lt. MITSUBA [Hisanao] and others." Adachi testified that he subsequently had Mitsuba Hisanao, the Japanese lieutenant in charge of the said duty company, court-martialed concerning his handling of Nirpal Chand. But the 18th Army's Legal Department cleared Mitsuba of any wrongdoing, concluding that the killing was justified.[102]

Adachi's testimony on Mitsuba's court-martial was meant to dispute the prosecution's contention that Nirpal Chand was in fact killed unlawfully. Chint Singh offered the court extensive narrative accounts that traced the sequence of events leading up to Mitsuba's confrontation with Nirpal Chand.[103] He testified that the No. 19 Special-Duty Company originally had 529 men when it arrived at Wewak in mid-1943, but that by April 1944, as many as

130 men were dead due to disease and malnutrition. The same month, they received orders from their Japanese superiors to move from Wewak to Hollandia.[104] In order to stop further unnecessary deaths, Nirpal Chand conferred with other officer-class Indians (including Chint Singh), and they instructed their fellow Indian soldiers to desert the work party during the scheduled marching. Specific instructions were "to fall out in parties with any sick or weak Indians who could not go on and to attempt to escape into the hills," and "no one was to proceed beyond BUT [read "boot"]," – about 38 miles west of Wewak – and remain in the Wewak area "until the Americans whom we had heard had landed at HANSA BAY advanced to WEWAK."[105]

According to Chint Singh, the Japanese found just about 30 Indian officers including Nirpal Chand and Chint Singh when the No. 19 Special-Duty Company reassembled at But on April 20, 1944. The remainder of the work party was nowhere to be found. When questioned by Mitsuba, Nirpal Chand is said to have told him that most members "could not march with their heavy loads and had fallen out on the way" and that "the party could not proceed to HOLLANDIA until other arrangements were made for the carrying of these loads." Thereupon Mitsuba took away Nirpal Chand while other Indian officers were placed under guard. "I have not seen Capt. NIRPAL CHAND since that day," Chint Singh stated.[106] At a separate Australian war crimes trial at Rabaul, Mitsuba admitted that he carried out the execution of Nirpal Chand himself, two of the co-accused assisting him with the killing. They were found guilty, but spared of the death penalty. Mitsuba received 20 years in prison.The record of the Mitsuba Trial was presented as the prosecution's evidence at the Adachi Trial.[107]

The judge advocate's legal advice to the Rabaul court with respect to the Adachi Trial was substantially the same as the one he had already made at the time of the Hirota Trial. Making direct reference to the "previous trial," Brock argued that "the duty of a commanding officer is limited to the requirement that he 'must use due diligence' in the exercise of his duties." In other words, a commander "must use due diligence to foresee the possibility of crimes being committed under his command, or to take such action as is within his power, having regard to all the circumstances, to prevent those crimes being committed." Brock went on to quote once again from Justice Murphy's dissenting opinion in order to underscore his position. The Yamashita Trial "of course did not deal with the particular campaign with which you are concerned in this case," Brock prefaced, but he believed that how Murphy critiqued the Yamashita case was "particularly apposite."[108] A pertinent segment in the dissenting opinion, which Brock quoted at length for the Rabaul court (and also quoted in full in Chapter 1 in connection with the Yamashita Trial), read as follows:

In other words, read against the background of military events in the Philippines subsequent to October 9, 1944, these charges amount to this: "We, the victorious American forces, have done everything possible to destroy and disorganize your lines of communication, your effective control of your personnel, your ability to wage war. In these [those] respects we have succeeded. We have defeated and crushed your forces. And now we charge and condemn you for having been inefficient in maintaining control of your troops during the period when we were so effectively besieging and eliminating your forces and blocking your ability to maintain effective control . . ."[109]

Brock was of the opinion that the court should draw lessons from Murphy's foregoing observation when applying the due-diligence standard to the Adachi case. He added that with respect to Adachi's plea on extraordinary circumstances of the New Guinea campaign and especially the low morale of the troops resulting from starvation, he did not regard it as constituting a defense. However, he advised the court to take it into consideration in mitigation.[110]

The finding of the court was guilty as charged, and the punishment was life imprisonment, a far more severe penalty than the one the court meted out to Hirota.[111] There being no written judgment in this case either, one can only surmise that the court had some grounds to believe the accused had failed to exercise due diligence, and that the extent of Adachi's disregard and failure to discharge his duty merited him a tough sentence. If these indeed constituted the opinion of the court, however, it is doubtful that the record of the Adachi Trial (as analyzed in this section) justified it.

That said, the substance of the court's opinion may not have mattered much to Adachi personally. He took his own life by hanging a few months after the

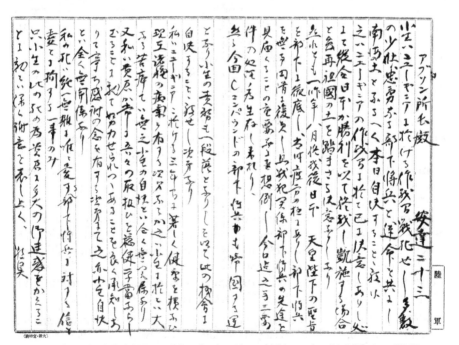

FIGURE 3. Lt. Gen. Adachi Hatazō's handwritten letter, addressed to Maj. Thomas W. Upson, commander of the War Criminals' Compound at Rabaul. MP742/1/336/1/1264/War crimes – Trial of Lt/Gen. Adachi Hatazo/1947–1950, National Archives of Australia.

end of the trial. Adachi was found dead on September 10, 1947, at the War Criminals' Compound at Rabaul. He left behind a short handwritten letter on a sheet from a regular Imperial Japanese Army writing pad, addressed to Maj. Thomas W. Upson, commander of the Compound (Figure 3). The letter explained that Adachi had planned from early on "to share the same destiny of my subordinates during the New-Guinea operations, for I had made up my mind not to tread on the earth of my father land [fatherland] even if Japan should have won the war." He held off his planned suicide for a while in order to assist repatriation of those subordinates who survived the war but who faced war crimes prosecutions. Now that his men were lately granted repatriation, "I felt my burden has somewhat been relieved."[112]

THE YAMASHITA PRECEDENT LIVES ON

Lt. Gen. Katō Rinpei served as chief of staff of the 8th Area Army since the time of its formation until the cessation of hostilities. The charge against him was framed differently from the preceding two trials, as it read that he "unlawfully employed persons of war on work having a direct connection with Japanese military operations."[113] In other words, he was charged with authorizing the commission of war crimes. The prosecution held Katō accountable specifically for the issuance of a military order to army units in Bougainville in December 1943, which allegedly authorized the killing of Indian and Indonesian members of special-duty companies in case of emergency, such as their engaging in "acts hostile or scheming to desert."[114]

The defense challenged the prosecution, arguing that far from proving the guilt of the accused, the prosecution failed to substantiate the power to command of the accused in the first place. The key defense witness was Imamura once again. He stated that "it is strictly prohibited by the Military regulations for the other persons to interfere in army commander's command and for any commander to invest his subordinates or his assistant with his own command." As far as the 8th Area Army was concerned, "I never allowed Lt-Gen KATO, chief of staff[,] or any other staff to issue orders or instructions to any units of the Army Group as proxy for me at their own will nor to issue their own orders or instructions to them."[115] Imamura's contention was partly supported by article 13 of the Japanese Army Regulations, which read:

It is the responsibility of the Chief of the General Staff to assist the Army Commander and moreover to arrange the duties within Army Headquarters.[116]

This article indicated that the chief of staff in the Japanese army functioned as secretary of sorts to the army commander and not as a second-in-command officer of the army.

In light of the foregoing evidence as presented by the defense, the judge advocate for the Katō Trial, Maj. H. J. Foster, advised the Rabaul court that "it would appear from the evidence that a Japanese Chief of Staff is not in the same position as a Staff Officer in the Australian Army." He further pointed out that insofar as international law was concerned, "no doctrine" existed to hold a staff officer accountable for crimes committed by subordinate members of the army "unless he himself is instrumental in the matter."[117] On this advice, the Rabaul court found Katō not guilty. Katō consequently joined 116, out of the total number of 408, suspected war criminals who were tried and acquitted of war crimes charges at the Australian Rabaul proceedings.[118] He was later brought before the U.S. military commission at Yokohama, however, on entirely different allegations. He was charged with the planning and implementation of prisoner-of-war transportation by sea in inhumane conditions – the so-called hellship cases[119] – while serving as chief of the Third Department of the Army General Staff of the Imperial General Headquarters in late 1942. Along with his co-accused, Katō pleaded guilty to the charge. He was sentenced to 18 years in prison.[120]

The trial of Imamura was arguably the centerpiece of the Rabaul proceedings, given the fact that the accused had been the general of the army overseeing the entire land operations in the South Pacific. In recognition of the singular importance of this case, a defense lawyer for Imamura stated: "This trial, though it is being held in this small hut in the corner of an island in the Pacific, doubtless is being watched closely by the unseen eyes of numerous persons the world over, especially by the students of International Law."[121] The judge advocate, Lt. Col. Brock, chimed in, stating during his summation as follows:

This trial is of far wider implication than the fate of the individual now before you. That alone is in itself a heavy responsibility. But heavier still is the weight of the opinion of the world, not only those unseen eyes, to which [Defense] Counsel referred, who were now throughout the World watching the result of this trial, but more particularly the eyes of the future.[122]

From the standpoint of law, however, the three preceding command-responsibility trials may have been of far greater significance. All the knotty legal questions had been raised and answered by the end of the trials of Hirota and Adachi (and, to a lesser extent, at the trial of Katō), namely, the status of Asian work parties under international law, criteria of command responsibility, and relevance of the Yamashita precedent to the Rabaul proceedings. The three preceding trials already covered all the key factual issues, too. The bulk of evidentiary materials that were used at the Imamura Trial were recycled from the preceding three.

That said, there is one legal question that the judge advocate raised with respect to the Imamura Trial alone. That is, whether Imamura had a case of superior orders as a defense. It was shown throughout the Rabaul proceedings that the policy to treat Indian and Chinese prisoners of war as "civilian laborers" was not the decision of GOC 8th Area Army but rather that it emanated from Tokyo. The judge advocate made the following observation on this point:

The accused says that, acting on the policy of the Japanese Government and of orders and instructions issued from time to time by the Imperial General HQ, he bona fide believed that these prisoners of war had changed their status and allegiance and had become part of the Japanese Forces.[123]

Brock was of the opinion that the existence of such policy, if established, could be considered as "the order of an authority superior to him [the accused], so that he could not, within the ambit of his command, depart from it unless that order was obviously unlawful."[124]

Issues of superior orders aside, the judge advocate also reminded the court to consider the defense argument disputing the prosecution's allegation that he "unlawfully disregarded and failed to discharge his duty . . . to control the members of his command."[125] The main points of the defense were: (1) that Imamura did not know the occurrence of alleged instances of war crimes; (2) that he did everything in his power to prevent the occurrence of war crimes; and (3) that all members of Asian work parties were voluntary civilian laborers and not prisoners of war.[126] The judge advocate's summation did not seem to influence the court's thinking much, however, as the final decision was a verdict of guilty. The sentence was nonetheless lenient: ten years in prison.[127]

The Rabaul court did not make any exception with the Imamura Trial when it produced no judgment to explain its rationale. However, the judges appear to have felt some degree of discomfort about the general lack of transparency in their verdicts and sentences in handling the high-profile cases involving Hirota, Adachi, and Imamura as accused. In the memorandum the court prepared for the confirming authority, the presiding judge Maj. Gen. Whitelaw offered a summary of the court's findings. The stated purpose of the memo was to provide relevant information to assist the confirming authority with determining the merit of petitions from accused regarding remission of sentences. On the issues of guilt of individual accused, Whitelaw had the following conclusion to convey to the confirming authority:

The Court is satisfied beyond reasonable doubt that the accused in each of the three trials knew that systematic acts of a criminal nature were taking place within his command, and that each culpably failed in his duty in that he took insufficient action to inform himself of particular incidents and to restrain and if necessary punish offenders as a deterrent to others who might commit similar offenses if they were to go unpunished. The Court is satisfied that the specific offences enumerated in each case directly resulted from the culpable negligence of the accused.[128]

This memorandum is interesting, for it sets out the grounds of conviction in an ambiguous manner. The court, on the one hand, declared that each accused was undoubtedly aware of crimes committed by subordinate troops but, on the other, it also concluded that each of them failed to acquire such knowledge on account of *negligence*. As for the judge advocate's recommendation to draw lessons from Justice Murphy's dissenting opinion, there is no indication that the court did so or, for that matter, gave any weight to the recommendation of adopting the due-diligence standard. The path the Rabaul court chose rather seems to fix the guilt of accused on the basis of "unqualified responsibility, merely by reason of the fact of his appointment" (to quote from Brock's summation at the Hirota Trial) or, to put it differently, the same stringent standard of strict liability as the one applied at the Yamashita Trial. If this assessment correctly captures the court's position, the trials of Hirota, Adachi, and Imamura may be understood as leaving for posterity another set of troubling historical precedents on command responsibility.

5

Kalagon and Singapore[1]

"There is just one thing that I am certain of about war crimes trials, that is, they are 'uncertain things' [*futashika na koto*],"[2] so Capt. Sumi Toyosaburō wrote as he reminisced over his experience of the British war crimes proceedings at Singapore. He had been a midlevel officer of the Japanese army-navy joint occupation forces on a remote island of Car Nicobar in the Indian Ocean. Formerly British-controlled penal colonies, the Andaman and Nicobar Islands came under Japanese military control during the Pacific War with the view to provide air and naval support in the CBI theater.[3] In March 1946, Sumi and fifteen others were brought to the U.K. Singapore courtroom on charges that in July and August 1945 they arrested, tortured, or otherwise mistreated a number of Nicobarese civilians in connection with spy allegations. The chief accused was Lt. Gen. Itsuki Toshio, formerly commanding officer of the Japanese occupation forces at Car Nicobar. He and two others also stood accused on allegations that they conducted illegal trials and executed eighty-three Nicobar islanders.[4] The Singapore court found all but one guilty. Lt. Col. Saitō Kaizō, Itsuki's chief of staff, was acquitted while the rest were convicted and received varying sentences: Itsuki was sentenced to death by shooting, five were sentenced to death by hanging, and the remaining nine received different terms of imprisonment ranging between three and fifteen years.[5]

Sumi was confounded by the outcomes of the trial and had an especially hard time reconciling himself to Saitō's acquittal. He remembered Saitō as a bully who ordered the arrest and summary execution of Nicobarese in his zealous pursuit of spy suspects. Nevertheless, he was let off scot-free, while Itsuki – a mild-mannered army commander who had little material part in orchestrating the spy hunt – was condemned to death. The *sanbō* (staff officers) theoretically had no power to command the armed forces, but according to Sumi, they were also "*sanbō*" – by which he meant "three brute forces" in the sense of *ranbō* (violent), *mubō* (reckless), and *ōbō* (arrogant) – who exercised de facto command authority to the point of eclipsing the de jure commander. This type of lopsided relationship between a commander and a staff officer was not uncommon, Sumi remarked, since a *sanbō* was the kind of person who rose to a high military post by merit while the position to command could be attained by sheer seniority. Sumi suspected the U.K. Singapore court failed to appreciate the theory and practice of staff officers in the Japanese military, presumably because of the prevailing notion in Western military organizations that staff officers were no more than functionaries of the commander of an army.[6]

Sumi deeply regretted Itsuki's guilty verdict and capital punishment in another respect. Although it was established at the U.K. Singapore trial that Itsuki served as presiding judge over unlawful trials of spy suspects and that he approved the imposition of the death sentences, truth be told, and according to Sumi's account, no such trials ever took place. The accused invariably attested to the occurrence of fictive judicial proceedings only to give the summary execution of the eighty-three Nicobarese an appearance of legality, and *the accused jointly told the false story upon Sumi's urging.* Sumi gained a smattering knowledge of international law when assisting the demobilization process at the war's end, and he later persuaded Itsuki, Saitō, and other fellow soldiers into subscribing to the idea that proof of judicial proceedings could absolve them of criminal liability for the summary executions.[7] The fabricated story only lead to Itsuki's death sentence, and other misjudgments and wrongful sentences resulted, too. Would it have been better if they had not concealed the facts and told nothing but the truth? Sumi was unable to judge. He felt that the guilty verdict and a penalty of ten-year imprisonment he himself received were unwarranted but, here again, he could not say that he would have received a lighter penalty or perhaps an acquittal had he told the whole truth. Unintended consequences of the Singapore trial continued to rankle him after his subsequent repatriation to Japan.[8]

The foregoing episode brings home a major challenge that the judges at the Allied trials commonly faced in the handling of war crimes suspects: how to determine beyond a reasonable doubt the guilt of an individual accused of the commission of alleged offenses. Eyewitnesses and survivors of war crimes may have helped establish the occurrence of alleged offenses, and they may even have helped identify some of those Japanese who were present at the crime scenes. But determining the share of responsibility of individual accused – and especially those who held positions of authority and who were not necessarily present at the actual crime scenes – was an entirely different problem. A paper trail of criminal orders was hard to come by, and the prosecution often had to rely on oral evidence of the accused themselves to establish the sequence of events leading up to the occurrence of offenses. The accused, for their part, may have readily provided pertinent information or may have gone so far as to admit personal guilt. However, their primary concern may have been less to assist the court with its fact-finding mission than to shift blame and protect someone from criminal accusations. False testimony made it difficult for the court to determine the guilt of individual suspects.

This chapter explores two case studies from the British war crimes trials in which the courts' decisions were based almost entirely on accused's testimony, including confessional statements. The 1929 Geneva Prisoner-of-War Convention stipulated that "no prisoner may be obliged to admit himself guilty of the act of which he is accused,"[9] but it was not uncommon for confessions by accused to be admitted in evidence at the Allied war crimes trials. The purpose of this chapter is not so much to question the admission of such evidence, however, as to probe into the ways in which the courts handled it in their effort to tackle the elusiveness of truth. It will be explored how the courts sifted through conflicting evidence, weighed veracity of one testimony against another, and reached the final decisions. Put it differently, this chapter inquires into the "oral history" methods that the courts employed in their quest to establish the nature of alleged offenses and to resolve the issues of guilt or innocence of accused persons.

One of the two cases to come under scrutiny is the trial of Maj. Ichikawa Seigi (Figure 4) and thirteen others, held at the U.K. war crimes courtroom at Rangoon, Burma, between March 22 and April 10, 1946. This trial was the first of a series of forty trials that the British authorities hosted in the CBI theater between March 1946 and November 1947.[10] The Ichikawa group was charged with the massacre of more than 600 inhabitants of Kalagon in the region of Moulmein on July 8, 1945, over the course of military expeditions the Ichikawa battalion led with the mission to decimate British parachutists and local guerrilla fighters. Kalagon was the only ethnic Indian village community in the Karen-dominated region in the border areas between Burma and Thailand.[11] The Japanese military authorities in the last months of the war suspected that the village was serving as a logistical base for the British and Karen guerrillas, and was possibly protecting deserters from the INA. Victims of massacre at Kalagon consisted solely of noncombatant civilians, however, including infants. The prosecution held all fourteen accused accountable for the mass killing as well as instances of beating, torture, and other forms of mistreatment of the villagers. The major task for the U.K. Rangoon court in this case was to resolve conflicting accounts about the nature of military orders Ichikawa is believed to have received from the regimental commander, Col. Tsukada Misao, concerning the attacks on Kalagon. In the absence of documentary evidence of orders, much of the court time was spent on examining and cross-examining Japanese witnesses including Col. Tsukada (who was called to the stand as a defense witness) so that the court could decide whether the killing of the entire village population was what Tsukada ordered, or if the operational mission he had given Ichikawa did not require mass, indiscriminate killing of the village people.[12]

FIGURE 4. Major Ichikawa Seigi, the first of the war crimes suspects to be tried at the U.K. war crimes court at Rangoon. © Imperial War Museums (SE 6880).

The other case to come under scrutiny is the trial of Lt. Gen. Nishimura Takuma and six others, held at Singapore between March 10 and April 2, 1947. This case pertains to a massacre of several thousand Chinese men, carried out by army units subordinate to the 25th Army in the first few weeks following the British surrender, between February 18 and March 3, 1942. Lt. Gen. Yamashita Tomoyuki, then general officer commanding the 25th Army directing the Malayan operation, is believed to have issued orders that those Chinese who posed a security threat be eliminated.[13] Just like the Ichikawa Trial, the main task of the court in this case was to determine what exactly was in Yamashita's orders regarding the handling of ethnic Chinese in occupied

Singapore. Yamashita would have made an excellent witness at this trial, but he had already been executed by American authorities in the faraway land of the Philippines in February 1946. The former chief of staff of the 25th Army, Lt. Gen. Suzuki Sōsaku, could not be brought over to Singapore either, since he was killed in action in the Philippines.[14] The court similarly could not reach two other key witnesses – Lt. Col. Tsuji Masanobu and Maj. Hayashi Tadahiko, formerly staff members of the 25th Army Headquarters – whom the Japanese witnesses at the Nishimura Trial repeatedly named as the ones who drew up the actual plan of massacre and oversaw its implementation. Tsuji eluded the Allied war crimes investigation by fleeing in Burma in the disguise of a monk, while Hayashi had been dead since a plane crash in 1944.[15] In the absence thus not only of documentary evidence of Yamashita's orders but also of key witnesses, the U.K. Singapore court had tremendous difficulty determining who issued what orders, and how they were transmitted for implementation down the military chain of command.

THE ICHIKAWA TRIAL

The Ichikawa Trial kick-started with the appearance in the courtroom in Rangoon of Havildar Saw Kaw Ku, 30, the first prosecution witness. Biographical information in the trial record indicates that this witness was an individual of Karen ethnicity and a former member of the 4th Battalion of the Burma Rifles, the British Burma Army. He ceased to be on active duty early in the war as a result of the British being driven out of Burma. He returned to civilian life but had a brief stint as an interpreter for the Japanese military police, the *kenpeitai*, in the last three months of the war. He became witness to the massacre in Kalagon as he was attached to a small *kenpeitai* contingent that accompanied the Ichikawa battalion at the time of the raid.[16]

The choice of this particular individual as the first prosecution witness is interesting, since court testimony by this witness and others revealed that Saw Kaw Ku was not only an invaluable eyewitness of the massacre but also a famous freedom fighter.[17] He began guerrilla activism in the second half of 1944, and in mid-1945 came to assist British parachutists, under command of a "Maj. Abbey," based in the area between Moulmein and the Dali Forest. According to the witness testimony, Abbey "wanted back all soldiers who were serving in the British Army before the war."[18] Saw Kaw Ku joined the *kenpeitai* specifically to gather intelligence information for the British and local guerrilla fighters behind the enemy lines. The Japanese military, for its part, was on high alert about Saw Kaw Ku's guerrilla activities but somehow failed to realize his presence from within. In all likelihood, the British authorities at Rangoon decided to proceed first with the Kalagon case to pay tribute to the sacrifice and heroism of the people of Burma, and to do so especially by giving due recognition to Saw Kaw Ku. It is worth noting that Saw Kaw Ku received at the war's end a "certificate of gratitude" personally from Abbey.

This matter was brought out during the court testimony, and the actual certificate – which the witness had on him – was shown to the court.[19]

The gist of Saw Kaw Ku's testimony can be summarized as follows. The battalion under command of Maj. Ichikawa carried out a sweep of Kalagon in June 1945 to search for the British parachutists that were known to have landed in the region. Saw Kaw Ku accompanied the sweep, serving as an interpreter for two *kenpeitai* members then assigned to the Ichikawa battalion. The *kenpeitai* interrogated some villagers, but without successfully locating parachutists, the battalion withdrew. The same battalion with a slightly larger contingent of about four or five *kenpeitai* members made a second sweep of Kalagon after a lapse of a few weeks, the witness again accompanying it as an interpreter. The exact purpose of the second raid was not disclosed to the witness, but he is said to have overheard Capt. Higashi Nobuo, officer commanding the Moulmein Kenpeitai Detachment (also an accused at the Ichikawa Trial), remarking on Kalagon assisting the British parachutists by "giving them rice, salt, and giving huts to live in" and the villagers having "joined the parachutists."[20]

The Ichikawa battalion reached Kalagon in the midmorning of July 7, 1945, thereupon W.O. Fujiwara Ryōzō (another accused at the Ichikawa Trial), a subordinate of Capt. Higashi and the officer in charge of the *kenpeitai* contingent in this raid, ordered that all villagers assemble or otherwise face death. The village headman being nowhere to be found, the next senior person of the village community made a round to summon everyone. The Japanese troops themselves went about to search and accost the villagers. Saw Kaw Ku personally witnessed these occurrences as he was "in front of the crowd of people that had assembled."[21] All adult males above the age of 15 were then put into the village mosque, while women and children were placed inside the structure next to the mosque.[22] The villagers remained in confinement throughout the night except eight men and one woman, whom the *kenpeitai* took out for questioning concerning the whereabouts of, and the village aid to, the British parachutists. Saw Kaw Ku served as an interpreter for all interrogation sessions and witnessed instances of mistreatment, such as slapping, beating with a stick, and hanging from the beam at the ceiling while the hands of the interrogated person were tied behind the person's back.[23]

The killing began in the late afternoon of the following day, on July 8. Saw Kaw Ku acquired partial knowledge of the massacre while crisscrossing the village. He first saw villagers being taken out of confinement in small groups, "their hands tied at the back with one long rope" and "about 25 to 30 villagers were tied together in one bunch."[24] Some were screaming while others tried to run away but were prevented by the Japanese soldiers. Men on the one hand and women and children on the other were taken in separate groups. "Some were about three years, and some were carried by their mothers,"[25] according to the witness testimony. Saw Kaw Ku sensed that something awful was afoot, as he himself accompanied a group of women and small children being taken to a village well. Once at the well, the Japanese soldiers began blindfolding the weeping and screaming women and children with pieces of rags. "I felt like going back," the witness testified, meaning that he wanted to leave the site and return to the temporary quarter that the *kenpeitai* had set up within the village of Kalagon. As interpretation was not needed on the spot, "I asked permission to go back, then I went back."[26] Consequently, the witness had no conclusive knowledge as to what happened to this particular group subsequent to his departure.

As he headed back, however, he encountered a scene of carnage in progress with a separate group of women and children by another village well, about 20 yards away from where the *kenpeitai* contingent was based. "I saw a Japanese soldier throwing down the children," he said, "he had a rod with him, and I heard a woman's screaming coming from inside the well."[27] The witness approached the well after the Japanese soldier finished pounding with the bamboo pole and left the area, and the witness saw stains of blood by the well. He conceded that he "dared not look down the well" to ascertain if there was indeed a woman inside or not, because "I was afraid to look down, as if that person had not actually died, she might ask for help. I was afraid what will happen to me. So I did not look down."[28]

Saw Kaw Ku's personal encounter with scenes of massacre was limited to these discrete episodes, but the extent of the massacre became known to the court from additional prosecution evidence (as will be discussed shortly). The following morning, on July 9, the Ichikawa battalion and the *kenpeitai* contingent headed off to Dali-kyowaing, the Dali reserved forest area, in search of British parachutists, but came back once again to Kalagon two days later on July 11. "The next morning they had breakfast early, and went out to the village, and set the village on fire," according to Saw Kaw Ku. Large-scale looting preceded the razing of the village, such as looting clothes, poultry, and about "70 cows and four horses." The Ichikawa battalion took away about eight village women, too, but Saw Kaw Ku did not know what became of the women afterwards.[29]

Nine residents of Kalagon took the witness stand after Saw Kaw Ku, testifying on their personal knowledge and experiences of mass atrocity. Some of the witnesses were directed to identify the accused in the dock by sight as well. Tara Bibi, 10, was a survivor of the massacre and one of the nine to testify at the Rangoon courtroom. With her father standing beside her, this witness attested to being taken to one of the village wells along with some 60 women, bayoneted in the head, and thrown into the well. The bayonet wounds were not fatal, however. She testified that she was able to climb out on her own, because the well was "almost filled with the human bodies and I was at the top."[30]

Mohd Eusof, 37, village headman, was not present at the time of the massacre – he and several other villagers fled upon information of the imminent Japanese raid – but he provided the court with the data of the dead and the missing resulting from the raid. The original population of Kalagon was "over

900 or may be [maybe] 1000," he testified, of which a total of 637 could not be accounted for at the war's end. They were either confirmed dead or believed to have been killed during the raid. The breakdown of the number was "about 195 women, about 175 or 176 men, and 266 or 267 children."[31] When cross-examined, Mohd Eusof confirmed that Kalagon under village elders' leadership provided nonmilitary aid to British parachutists, such as collecting provisions and providing labor for building huts for the British parachutists in the Dali Forest. He denied offering any military support, however, testifying that no firearms were ever stored in Kalagon and that he never carried firearms himself.[32] Regarding the abduction of women, Mohd Eusof testified that "12 women were taken away by the Japanese," two of whom managed to escape and returned home. One of the escapees, Akinabi, was brought before the court, although not to testify herself but merely for Mohd Eusof to identify her to be one of the two escapees.[33] The other one, Ulfa Bi, could not make it to the courtroom due to a recent childbirth, but her brother, Sulaiman, took the witness stand to testify on his own knowledge about the abduction and other matters related to the Kalagon raids.[34]

Evidence on massacre and abduction aside, one prosecution witness, Hakijan (also referred in the court record as "Akijan"), 18, took the stand to testify that she was raped.[35] 2nd Lt. Usui Kiichirō, a medical officer of the Ichikawa battalion and an accused, was identified by sight as the perpetrator. The defense counsel objected to admission of this witness's testimony on grounds that the charge sheet contained no specific allegation of rape. It is true that the charge of "beating, torture, *and other maltreatment*" was made against the accused, but "it is quite clear that when the charges were framed, there was no intention of accusing anyone of rape," the defense argued. "Rape is always considered a distinct and serious offence," the defense pointed out, and it was thus imperative for the prosecution to develop a separate charge if any evidence of rape was to be introduced.[36] After hearing the arguments from both sides, the court dismissed the defense objection and ruled that evidence of rape was admissible. The court also ruled that the press and spectators should be cleared of the courtroom so as to protect the witness from public exposure.[37] This witness's testimony turned out to lack credibility, however, and the court in the end acquitted Usui of the rape charge. The prosecution failed to prove the guilt of the accused "beyond reasonable doubt," as the court put it.[38]

The prosecution's case against the Ichikawa group concluded with the introduction of statements that the British war crimes investigators had taken from individual accused prior to the trial. The statements were largely confirmatory of the general sequence of events as already established by Saw Kaw Ku and the villagers. They nevertheless offered important details about the origins and the substance of military orders. For instance, Capt. Sakamaki Saburō, who served as an intelligence officer in the Ichikawa battalion and who had taken part in some of the interrogations on the eve of the massacre, explained in his statement that the first sweep of Kalagon came about on June 25 by the order of the regimental commander, Col. Tsukada, "in the nature of a recon-naissance, information having been received from the Kempei Tai [*kenpeitai*] that the Karen followers of SAW KU [Saw Kaw Ku] and British paratroops were constructing barracks and training the villagers as guerilla forces." But the battalion "obtained very little information and returned to HQ."[39]

Concerning the second raid, the battalion commander Ichikawa explained in his statement that the order of the raid originated in the divisional head-quarters. The order was passed on to him from the regimental commander on about July 2 or 3, during a meeting at a place called Chaungnakwa. Ichikawa was "to go KALAGON and DALI" and attack the enemy, based on intelli-gence information that Kalagon was supplying the British parachutists with weapons, provisions, labor, and guerrilla fighters. Moreover, "INA desert-ers were passing through KALAGON to liaise with BRITISH paratroops." Ichikawa is said to have inquired at the time "how far I could go," to which Tsukada allegedly replied that he "burn the village and kill the inhabitants." Ichikawa explained in his statement that, accordingly, he took his battalion of five companies at a paltry strength of just about 140 troops, plus four *ken-peitai* members. Three companies consisting of ninety troops took part in the actual killing, while two others were posted at the northeastern and eastern sides of the village "to prevent the paratroops from moving out of the area." The four *kenpeitai* officers, meanwhile, set up their field headquarters about 100 yards from the battalion headquarters inside the village of Kalagon and had no part in the actual killing.[40] He confirmed in the same statement that when leaving Kalagon, "we took away ten INDIAN women" and handed them over to the regimental headquarters except three, who escaped.[41]

Capt. Midorikawa Hisashi, an accused and an officer who formerly com-manded one of the three companies that took part in the massacre, explained in his statement that on July 8 he received the orders for the massacre. Specific instructions were "the villagers were to be divided out among the various coys [companies], and the coys were to kill them." He implemented the killing or-ders by taking the following steps:

I sent a squad to collect the villagers for our coy; the first batch of villagers I got was 25 or 26 people. I divided the villagers into three groups, and gave them to three squads, and told the soldiers to take them away. I warned the soldiers that the villagers were to be killed one by one: (they were to be blindfolded [,] taken away and killed by one thrust of the bayonet; there was to be no firing lest our positions be given away to the guerillas) . . . This was in the orders I received.[42]

Midorikawa had his company repeat this process as fresh batches of men, women, and children were allotted until no one was left in the mosque or in the adjacent structure. The two other companies presumably followed the same procedure. The killing continued well into the night of July 8.

When the defense case began, none of the accused contradicted their pre-trial statements insofar as the general sequence of events was concerned.

However, they invariably disputed that they were individually or criminally liable for the killing. Each of them asserted that their acts were entirely justified on one or more of the following grounds: (1) that they were merely following superior orders; (2) that the destruction of the Kalagon village was a military necessity; (3) that killing of small children was justifiable from the standpoints of mercy killing and of military expediency; (4) that the massacre was a reprisal measure against Kalagon, which gave aid to British parachutists and guerrillas; and (5) that some of the accused did not take direct part in the actual killing.

All of the foregoing lines of defense figured prominently in the testimony of chief-accused Ichikawa. He testified that he received from regimental commander Tsukada the orders to carry out the wholesale destruction of villagers. Ichikawa was allegedly told in the wake of the failed first raid that he would have to carry out another raid and that in the next one, he "must annihilate the villagers of Kalagon."[43] At the subsequent meeting at Chaungnakwa where the order for the next raid was issued, the regimental commander is said to have reiterated that he "must kill the villagers and burn the houses of Kalagon village."[44] The accused personally had nothing to gain by carrying out the massacre, so he informed the court, but he had a bona fide belief that the killing was a necessary part of the broader operational mission in the Burma theater. Children were not spared because if they were left to survive, "they would be orphans, and as such they could not have a living." It was also for the sake of "sav[ing] time and carry[ing] out my duties" that Ichikawa "could not help but killing them."[45] When cross-examined by the prosecution, he conceded that Japan as an occupying power might have had "some duties" in relation to the people of occupied territory. Nonetheless, he maintained that the massacre was entirely justified because "if the inhabitants [under control] of occupying power were acting in a hostile manner towards the occupying power[,] we should take retaliatory measure."[46]

As regards the charge of abduction of women, Ichikawa again admitted to having taken away some ten women and turning them over to the regimental headquarters except for a few who escaped. He defended this action, asserting that "I had orders from the Regiment to bring the women so that they could be used as spies."[47] When asked by the prosecution whether it was "customary with the Japanese Army to recruit local women for serve [sic] with the Japanese force as what is commonly known as 'Comfort Girls,'" Ichikawa attested to no knowledge of his superior's intention. He also denied entertaining any ideas of doing so himself. He stated: "In the Japanese army, unless the orders were received from the Division, we cannot employ girls in the service at brothels."[48] This part of the court testimony is interesting, as it constituted indirect admission of the army practice of sponsoring military brothels. That said, the court made no finding on this matter since the *purpose* of abduction was not required proof for the charge.[49]

When regimental commander Tsukada took the stand as the key defense witness, he readily accepted personal responsibility for the raids and resultant deaths of many civilians. He admitted that he was the one to order Ichikawa to carry out the first raid, based on intelligence information that "SAW KU and his dacoits were present in the neighbourhood of DALI Forest and these dacoits attacked the Japanese soldiers and lines of communications of the Japanese army."[50] He was also the one to order the second raid on the information that Kalagon was likely to be assisting Saw Kaw Ku, Abbey, and INA deserters with provision of supplies, labor, shelter, and intelligence. He passed on to Ichikawa a written order to blockade Kalagon and a neighboring village so as to decimate the enemy in the area. Furthermore, he gave Ichikawa verbal instructions during the meeting at Chaungnakwa that "in consideration of the lack of time and manpower this expedition should be thoroughly conducted even if they were to kill the KALAGON villagers." These words were meant to be "instructions," but Ichikawa may well have construed them as orders. If so, "Major ICHIGAWA [Ichikawa] had faithfully carried out his order."[51] The only point Tsukada disagreed with the chief accused's testimony concerned the allegation of abduction of village women. He confirmed that he gave approval to the idea of bringing back women for their possible use as spies, but not orders. What he gave was "not an order at all," he testified.[52]

As Tsukada publicly accepted personal responsibility for the causes and consequences of the Kalagon raids, cross-examination of this particular witness centered not so much on disputing his testimony as on clarifying the finer points of the substance of his orders. The prosecution was especially interested in eliciting whether Ichikawa was given any discretionary power in the implementation of orders. Was he vested with any authority to determine how extensively to mete out killing against the villagers? Did Ichikawa receive a "kill-all policy" as the accused himself appeared to argue, or was it a policy that did not make the wholesale killing of villagers the goal of the raid?

The court itself was greatly interested in this question and initiated the following dialogue with witness Tsukada:

Q [THE COURT]. If ICHIGAWA [Ichikawa] had returned and reported that he had executed a number of villagers who were definitely collaborating with the enemy and had burnt down the village of KALAGON would you have been satisfied with that.
A [TSUKADA]. Yes.[53]

This exchange is significant, as it indicates that Ichikawa may have in fact had discretionary power as to how he was to implement the orders in the actual raid. Tsukada at least seems to suggest that the destruction of active supporters of the enemy and their base was the operational mission, and not indiscriminate killing of the entire village population. The prosecution's further questions, shown below, brought out from the same witness that the killing of villagers was not the goal but rather a means toward the fulfillment of the larger operational mission, viz., the destruction of guerrillas in the Dali Forest area:

Q [Prosecution]. Did you at any time issue any order that the villagers will be killed.
A [Tsukada]. On the 4th of July I gave verbal order at CHAUNGNAKWA to that effect.
Q. That the villagers will be killed.
A. Yes, that they may be killed.
Q. I want to make perfectly clear, "will be killed."
A. Those who are hostile "may be killed."[54]

The repeated questioning by the prosecution reveals that Tsukada tolerated civilian deaths in pursuit of the operational mission, but not the killing of the entire village population as an end in itself.

This part of Tsukada's testimony proved contentious, as it conflicted with the accounts offered by the chief accused. Moreover, Capt. Katayama Tōru, Tsukada's former subordinate and staff officer at the regimental headquarters, took the witness stand to dispute its validity. He asserted that, as a matter of fact, Tsukada's orders were to kill all villagers and that Ichikawa had no discretionary power on the matter.[55] Contradictory testimony among defense witnesses was troubling enough to compel the court to have Tsukada recalled so that he would set the record straight. After making some equivocal statements, Tsukada finally requested that the key part of his previous testimony be withdrawn and substituted with the following: "I gave verbal orders that all the villagers of KALAGON *will* be killed."[56] This statement was supposed to put to rest any controversy over the substance of his military orders, but the court appeared to give no credence to it. The judgment read that Tsukada impressed the judges to be "a man of intellect and an ordinary honesty," whom they could not believe to have taken the witness stand at the first instance to "tell a lie to the Court in order to implicate Major ICHIGAWA further." The court concluded that the actual orders given to Ichikawa must have allowed him to "have some discretion as to what was to be done at KALAGON."[57]

THE FINDINGS OF THE RANGOON COURT

The U.K. war crimes courts produced no judgments by rule, but the Rangoon court for this case took an unusual step of writing a decision that articulated in some detail its legal and factual findings. In all likelihood, the court did so in recognition of the singular political importance of the Kalagon case from the standpoint of U.K.-Burma relations. This trial, after all, was the very first British war crimes trial to be held in the Burma theater. It would be fair to say that, by way of holding the Ichikawa Trial, the British authorities desired to impress the people of the recovered territory with the British commitment to justice and also to give due credit to contributions and sacrifices made by these people in the war against Japan.

The court's decision starts with the discussion of the Japanese rights of reprisal, one of the core arguments the accused had advanced during the trial. The court appeared quite sympathetic to this particular argumentation, as it concluded that the Japanese were indeed entitled to take a reprisal measure when confronted with hostile actions by the people in occupied territory. The court sought the legal basis of this ruling in *Manual of Military Law* of the British armed forces, which partly read:

Although collective punishment of the population is forbidden for the acts of individuals for which it cannot be regarded as collectively responsible, *it may be necessary to resort to reprisal against a locality or community[,] for some acts committed by its inhabitants[,] or members which cannot be identified.*[58]

The question for the court was what form of reprisal, then, should be considered justifiable. The *Manual* stipulated that "acts done by way of reprisal must not be excessive and must not exceed the degree of violation committed by the enemy." It further read that the kinds of reprisal measures that were historically recognized were "the burning down of buildings in a town, the burning down of an entire village, or heavy collective fines." The court ruled that when assessed against these standards, indiscriminate killing of more than 600 innocent civilians was "far in excess of what was reasonable and greatly exceeded the degree of violation committed by the villagers of KALAGON."[59]

The court went on to point out that the Kalagon Massacre was an excessive form of reprisal even by the Japanese own standard rules of engagement. Specifically, it had been brought out during the court's questioning of Tsukada that other regiments in the Burma theater resorted to razing the villages surrounding the Dali Forest in 1944 "because SAW KU's dacoit gang had their base nearby," but that none of these accompanied wholesale killing of the village population. "I did not hear that they were killed,"[60] so Tsukada testified. In this light, the Ichikawa battalion can be understood as having deviated from the standard practice of reprisal when it attempted to destroy the whole village population.

As regards the plea of superior orders as a defense, the court rejected it on grounds of "manifest criminality" of the killing.[61] To clarify the meaning of manifest criminality, the court referred to the legal opinion of Lord Wright – a recognized authority of international law in those years, who served as chairman of the United Nations War Crimes Commission between August 1945 and April 1946 – as expressed in an article he had contributed to *The Law Quarterly Review* of January 1946. A segment of Lord Wright's opinion appears in the court's decision as follows:

The true view is, in my opinion, that if what he ordered is a crime which is or ought to be a crime manifest to the subordinate soldier or Government agent, he cannot justify his obedience. It might be different if the criminality of the order is not reasonably obvious to the man; the order for instance might appear to him justifiable on the grounds of reprisal, or the nature and effects of the order might not be apparent, but even then the plea would not be a defence though it might go to extenuation. *But an order such as to burn the women and children of a village* in the village church or to machine gun a crowd of hostages, or to murder a number of airmen who had attempted to escape and being [*sic*] recaptured, or to inflict heaviest torture to extract information all instances are *manifest criminality.*[62]

In the quote above, Lord Wright held that a plea of reprisal may be considered in mitigation when the criminality of an order was not obvious. He did not believe the same logic applicable, however, in the case of the order to kill women and children en masse.

The Rangoon court followed Lord Wright's legal opinion and further pointed out that there was "some definite doubt in the minds of the [*sic*] number of the accused as to the propriety of this order for the wholesale massacre at KALAGON." However, "they stifled any doubts or misgivings with the idea that they were only carrying out the order of their superior officer which must be right and must be obeyed."[63] This part of the court's decision referred to certain segments in the trial, during which the court questioned individual accused to explore the latter's mind-set about the orders for indiscriminate killing.

For instance, Yanagisawa Izumi, a company commander and an accused, testified that, at the time of the Kalagon raid, he found the orders of massacre "slightly unusual" because until then "I received orders to attack directly the enemy and to deal with the enemy, but that was the first time when we had orders to destroy the village."[64] He admitted that some targeted for killing were children as young as "at the ages of 5 and 6."[65] The accused's seeming qualm over the killing of children prompted the court to initiate the following dialogue:

Q [THE COURT]. Have you ever heard of a principle known as to The Spirit of Bushido.
A [YANAGISAWA]. I do know.
Q. Is it a fact that officers in the Japanese army are trained in that code and trained to observe that code.
A. Yes.
Q. Is it a fact that one of the terms or part of the code of Bushido is to protect the weak and helpless.
A. Yes.
Q. Do you consider young children of 5 or 6 or little older as being weak and helpless.
A. Yes.
Q. So to massacre young children of that age of any addition is not against the spirit of Bushido.
A. I shall explain it.
Q. Is it against Bushido to kill the weak and helpless.
A. There are time[s] in the spirit of Bushido one has got to perform certain duties though he is quite unwilling to do.
Q. In other words you must perform the duty [if] you are ordered to *even if you think that it is wrong.*

A. Yes.

Q. In other words, military necessity may over-ride this moral code, the moral code of the army.

A. There are circumstances where such thing is done.[66]

In this dialogue, Yanagisawa took pains to explain that the Kalagon Massacre could be justified under the *bushidō* code, the putative Japanese martial ethos, in the name of military duty and military necessity. But what the court was inquiring on this occasion was not exactly whether the killing of children could be justified under *bushidō*. Rather, the court was interested in determining whether the accused thought the killing was morally wrong or, put it differently, manifestly criminal.

Capt. Midorikawa Hisashi, another accused and a former company commander that took part in the massacre, similarly attested to finding the order to kill villagers unusual. "This is the 1st time that I ever received an order to kill all the women and children and old people," he testified. This accused felt the killing to be "very pitiful" and he "cannot say whether it was a lawful order" either.[67] He conceded that the victims included small children "about 2 or 3 years old."[68] Regardless, he carried it out on the belief that it was the "right" thing to do given the "military necessity and force of circumstances."[69] Having thus admitted that he personally had qualms, Midorikawa tried deflecting criminal accusations against him and other co-accused by comparing the Kalagon Massacre with the destruction of Hiroshima by the atomic bomb. In both instances, innocent women and children were killed in the name of military necessity.[70] If so, and if no one was being held criminally liable for the dropping of atomic bombs, Midorikawa suggested that the same standard should apply to the members of the Ichikawa battalion.

The Rangoon court considered the accused's argument on atomic bombing, but dismissed it as being immaterial on the following three grounds. First, the defense argument struck the court as "an ingeniously worded plea against the jurisdiction of the court on purely moral grounds" although the court did not necessarily assume that the defense did so intentionally. The court declined to take issue with it in any event, for the reason that the Royal Warrant of 1945 was binding and that the court had no power or authority to inquire into validity of its own jurisdiction.[71] Second, the court deemed the defense argument on the atomic bombing immaterial if it was raised in connection with the doctrine of reprisal. The Ichikawa battalion carried out the Kalagon Massacre presumably to retaliate against the villagers for helping the British parachutists, and not in reprisal for the atomic-bomb attack on Hiroshima. The Kalagon Massacre preceded the bombing of Hiroshima by one month after all.[72] Midorikawa himself admitted that the two instances of mass killing had no connections:

Q [THE COURT]. At the time of those happenings in KALAGON did you hear about the atomic bomb being dropped anywhere?

A [MIDORIKAWA]. No, I did not hear.

Q. The order asking you to kill children had nothing to do with the atomic bomb.

A. It had no relation.[73]

Third and finally, the court acknowledged the implicit defense criticism about the gap between the humanitarian principles of international law on the one hand and, on the other, palpable disregard of such principles in the actual war. However, the court held that "a law does not cease to exist even though it is widely broken." It may be that the phrase "acts which outrage the general sentiment of humanity" lost much of its moral weight due to the unprecedented scale of destruction that the Allies and Axis Powers alike had wrought during this war. If so, the court still would hold that there would be "all the more reason to clarify and enforce" the laws of war rather than falling into cynicism about their efficacy.[74]

The final verdicts of the court were guilty for all except one. The medical officer attached to the Ichikawa battalion, Usui Kiichirō, was acquitted of all charges. Ichikawa and three company commanders who oversaw the massacre were sentenced to death by hanging, and the rest received varying terms of imprisonment.[75]

THE NISHIMURA TRIAL

"Shortly after the arrival of the Japanese Army in Singapore, do you remember certain security measures being laid down by General Yamashita's HQs?"[76] This question was posed to Col. Sugita Ichiji, the first of several Japanese to provide evidence for the prosecution on the massacre of ethnic Chinese that Yamashita's Army is known to have carried out in February 1942. Sugita was a key prosecution witness on account of having personal knowledge of the alleged instance of massacre as former chief intelligence officer of the 25th Army. What was more, he served in the aftermath of the war as head of the No. 4 Subcommittee of the Commission of Inquiry Relative to Prisoners of War, a government-sponsored committee that investigated the massacre at the war's end.[77] Sugita was by all accounts a reluctant witness; he attempted to kill himself by slashing his neck shortly after being brought over to Singapore. He left a note saying, "As I cannot bring myself to attest to the guilt of superior officers, I have chosen to commit suicide with good grace rather than presenting myself at the witness stand."[78] Having survived the suicide attempt, Sugita found himself taking the stand in the Singapore courtroom after all.

He responded to the foregoing question affirmatively, and revealed to the court the following sequence of events. The *kenpeitai* was first ordered to take up the guard duty of the occupied city on the night of the British surrender. "I think it was the next day," Sugita testified, "when there was an operational order issued to Gen. Kawamura [Saburō] stating that the city must be cleansed and in that order it stated that all the Anti-Japanese Chinese must be rounded up."[79] Lt. Gen. Kawamura (an accused) took the command of a freshly formed Singapore Guard Unit and was given control over the No. 2 Field Kenpeitai under command of Lt. Col. Ōishi Masayuki (another accused) and two auxiliary *kenpeitai* forces as well. Kawamura put to use the Guard Unit troops to implement the order in the town area of Singapore. The Guard Unit aside, two other formations took part in the implementation of the order in the outer flanks of Singapore: the Imperial Guards Division under command of Lt. Gen. Nishimura Takuma (chief accused) in the eastern flank of Singapore Island, and the 18th Division (not concerned in this trial) in the west. The ones to be targeted in the sweep of anti-Japanese Chinese persons "included the Communists, the Volunteer Force and any Chinese that were against the Japanese Army."[80] The purge took place in two waves. The first occurred on February 21 and 22 when the Guard Unit rounded up suspected individuals, screened them, and killed a total of "about 5,000." The second purge occurred in the "latter part of February" in the area under control of the Imperial Guards Division, and it resulted in the death of "about 300." They were all shot, Sugita testified, and "I have heard that they were buried at the sea shore."[81] The witness added that he had "never seen this order" himself, and "the information we got during the investigation in Tokyo was that this order was a general order." Specifics about the implementation of the order were said to have been determined when the order was passed down the chain of command.[82]

Some more details were provided in the statement of Col. Hashizume Isamu, a former member of the Second Section of the 25th Army in charge of the line of communication and a member of Sugita's postwar investigation committee. He confirmed that "no formal written order passed from the Army Commander [Yamashita] to the Defense Force Commander [Kawamura] regarding this operation." But according to the wartime diary (which the investigation committee received) of Kawamura, Yamashita visited the Guard Unit headquarters and said, "Naimen shido [*shidō*] dewa nai, tettei shite yare ('This is not a private instruction, make a thorough job of it')." The detailed plan of the purge was thereafter developed at the Guard Unit headquarters, two officers from the First Section of the 25th Army Headquarters – Lt. Col. Tsuji Masanobu and Maj. Hayashi Tadahiko – taking charge of the actual planning. Hashizume's statement read that "in the opinion of the Investigation Comittee[,] Lieutenant Colonel TSUJI's manner gave an impression of even greater strength of determination than General YAMASHITA's own (KOKORO TSUYOI)," thus suggesting that Tsuji may have been the driving force behind the actual planning and implementation of the massacre.[83] Meanwhile, Hayashi is said to have indicated to the *kenpeitai* chief Ōishi "roughly the number (GAISU [*gaisū*]) of Chinese who should be dealt." Ōishi at first allegedly protested against fixing a quota on grounds of impracticality, but he eventually relented. Ōishi's own estimate of the total number of the killed, as provided to the investigation committee, was about 5,000.[84]

The prosecution's case did not establish the number of the killed in any conclusive manner, but the statement taken from Hishikari Takafumi – a former war correspondent, who was embedded in the 25th Army at the time of the Malayan campaign – suggests that it may have been much larger than 5,000. According to Hishikari's recollection, in the initial days of occupation he learned from the chief of the Intelligence Section of the 25th Army, Sugata, that "50,000 Chinese were to be killed." On a later date, Sugita is said to have told Hishikari the overall result of the killing. The gist of the information was that "it had not been found possible to kill the whole of the 50,000 but that almost half had been dealt with." Hishikari received similar information from Maj. Hayashi a month later. Hayashi allegedly told him that the initial plan was to kill 50,000, but that the Guard Unit met the plan only half-way because of an order from a higher authority "to stop the massacre."[85]

The circumstances of the purge were also provided in the statement taken from Lt. Col. Ichikawa Tadashi, a former subordinate of Kawamura. He served as officer commanding one of the two infantry battalions that were allotted to the Singapore Guard Unit. According to his statement, he received an order to carry out "a vigorous house to house search" with the goal to identify and eliminate those Chinese who would fit into one of the following categories: those "hostile to Japanese will"; members of Chiang Kai-shek's Nationalist Party; or those in possession of arms.[86] This battalion duly searched the area under its jurisdiction, which "produced 300 Chinese of whom 14 were suspects." Further interrogation led to the identification of just a single individual as fitting into one category – having membership in the Nationalist Party. This person was promptly shot to death while the rest were set free. Ichikawa attributed the reason for a very small number of executed in the area of his search to "the fact that my area contained mostly European houses and very few Chinese ones."[87]

Former members of the 25th Army aside, the prosecution called to the witness stand Shinozaki Mamoru, a Japanese diplomat who had been based at Singapore and incarcerated by the British authorities in Changi Gaol prior to the Japanese invasion. He was freed by the *kenpeitai* of the 25th Army on February 16, 1942. According to his testimony, he learned soon after release that an order had been issued "by Gen. Yamashita to maintain peace and order for the occupation" and that all Chinese males were to assemble at "concentration areas" as designated by the *kenpeitai* authorities. While not apparent at first, Shinozaki figured out that "the purpose of this concentration was to find out anti-Japanese movements and elements and peoples."[88] He personally visited three of these concentration areas, whereby he witnessed the assembled people being subjected to some sort of screening process. He noted that "all the women and children had already been released and the remaining people were young men and men only."[89] Alarmed by the situation, Shinozaki secured approval from the Guard Unit commander, Kawamura, to issue two types of passes – "protection passes and transportation pass[es]"

– to save the innocent from the purge. Each pass read, "The bearer is a good citizen. So please look after him and protect him." Those individuals who could produce the pass were let go. In Shinozaki's own estimate, somewhere between 20,000 and 30,000 passes were issued and distributed freely.[90] "I did not care whether the person was good or bad or whether he was a communist," Shinozaki testified, and "anybody that came and asked for a pass I gave it to him." He also rescued some individuals by personally intervening in the screening process. Furthermore, he secured approval from the army to set up an Overseas Chinese Association in order "to protect the Chinese community and to rescue the powerful leaders who were still detained in [by] the Kempeitai." He estimated that an additional 2,000 or so were set free as a result.[91] Shinozaki noted with a tone of regret that the members of the Overseas Chinese Association were later criticized as collaborators of the Japanese.[92]

If the foregoing Japanese witnesses helped the prosecution establish the general circumstances of the purge, a total of twenty-nine citizens of Singapore took the witness stand to offer oral evidence on concrete instances of the roundup, screening process, and mass execution.[93] Khoo Ah Lim was one such person, himself being a survivor of the first wave of purge. He attested to going to the Telok Kerau English School (also spelled "Telok Kurau" in parts of the trial record) around February 20–22 for registration purposes, as instructed by the Japanese military authorities. He found "in the proximity of 3,000 to 4,000" persons gathered at the school, all males in the age between 15 and 50. The Japanese set aside about 200 of them on grounds of their having "property valued at 50,000" (presumably in Singapore currency) or being "volunteers, school teachers, Hainanese, and people who had been in Malaya less than five years." The witness himself fell under the category of the "educated class." These 200 or so were put on lorries the following day, taken to Siglap Road at milestone 7 ½, tied in pairs in a chain of rope, and made to go up a hill. The witness managed to free himself from the bind and fled the scene, but he did not know what became of three friends of his and two "cousin brothers" who were part of the crowd. They were presumed to have been killed at the hill.[94]

Lee Keng Jin offered additional testimony concerning the circumstances of the screening process at the Telok Kerau School. He and his son, Lee Chai Jiang, 18, went to the school grounds on February 18 "for the purpose of taking 'clearance permit' or pass" from the Japanese authorities.[95] At the school playground, the Japanese army authorities sorted out the assembled people and separated those who would fall under the following five categories: "one was lawyers and doctors, second merchants, third school teachers and students, fourth mechanics and labourers, and fifth British Government clerks or servants." The witness himself was let go but a total of about "600 to 700," including his son, were not. They were taken out of the school and detained at bungalows elsewhere. The witness tried to visit his son the following day twice, first in the morning when he was driven away by *kenpeitai* chief Ōishi, and second in the early afternoon by which time all the bungalows had been emptied. The witness attested to making "immediate enquiries in the neighbourhood," and found out that all the captives were taken away in lorries. "Ever since then I have not heard of the whereabouts of my son," the witness testified.[96] When cross-examined by the defense about the likelihood of his son being a member of the volunteer forces, the witness flatly denied it and instead replied: "He was only a clerk employed in the Seletar Naval Base, and he left school only about four or five months ago before his arrival [at the naval base]."[97]

A comparable sequence of events contemporaneously took place at a separate concentration area on Jalan Besar, according to testimony of some other prosecution witnesses. Lim Peng Koei testified that a few days after the fall of Singapore, he was called to serve as a Malay-Chinese interpreter for the *kenpeitai* unit at the Jalan Besar area, where he saw "well over 10,000 people" being assembled for inspection. The only question he was ordered to ask was about the people's occupation. In the end, about 600 who were identified as "the towkays [business owners], the bankers, banking clerks, detectives, volunteers, carpenters, and theatrical people – actors – as well"[98] were set aside for further detention. When the witness returned to the concentration area the following day, they were nowhere to be found. Chua Choon Guan, a taxi driver and a prosecution witness, was among those 600 or so individuals detained at Jalan Besar. He testified that the segregated group was put on lorries and taken to Tanah Merah Beach. They were then unloaded, their hands were tied behind their backs, and they were machine-gunned at the seaside. The witness luckily survived the killing; he was shot "on the side and legs" and the injuries were not fatal. He regained consciousness after nightfall, crawled out, and escaped from the killing ground.[99] The occurrence of this particular instance of massacre at the seaside was confirmed by Cheng Kwang Yu, a government employee and another survivor to testify for the prosecution.[100]

As regards the second wave of the purge, Low Sze Thang was the first to take the witness stand to give testimony. He informed the court that he and other male members of his family were taken by Japanese soldiers in the early morning of February 28 "at the point of bayonets and guns" to a tennis court, where about 1,000 others had already assembled. They were searched all over the body for tattoos, and about 300, including the witness and two of his elder brothers, were set aside for further detention, while others were set free. The witness was thereafter put on a lorry in a group of 22, who were dropped off at a bungalow at milestone 9½, Ponggol Road, stripped of their clothes in search of tattoos again, and accused of being the followers of Chiang Kai-shek. They were then put back on the lorry to be taken to milestone 11 on Ponggol Road, by the sea, where they joined "11 lorries full of Chinese and they were getting down from the lorries under the guard of 100 Japanese soldiers." Quite unexpectedly, the witness and eighteen others were taken to a rubber plantation and surreptitiously set free by a Japanese guard.[101] Ng Kim Song was one of the freed persons and confirmed the occurrence of the same sequence of events.[102] As for the fate of others in the group of some 300, testimony by Puay Ah Boh suggested they were likely to have been massacred. This witness was a fisherman living near milestone 11 on Ponggol Road and attested to seeing around 1500 hours on February 28 "trucks passing on the road towards the sea." There were about ten trucks, each carrying about thirty to forty and "all of them were males." While he did not personally witness the actual killing, he testified that he heard unusual sounds from the end of Ponggol Road, that is, "either crying or screaming sounds" and "'pop', 'pop'" sounds – presumably the sounds of gunshots.[103]

Other prosecution witnesses testified that the second purge continued well into the beginning of March. One witness, Yeo Hung Chung, informed the court that about 300 residents of Samba Ikat Village became subject to arrest and the screening process at a concentration area at milestone 8, Changi Road, on March 1. Those who had an identification paper "with the Japanese chop on it" – that is with some official seal or stamp by Japanese authorities – were freed (which included the witness), but those who did not possess one were kept at the concentration area. The witness attested to seeing three trucks carrying about forty persons – which included two female strangers – passing by his house "around 6 o'clock in the evening" the same day.[104] He heard the firing of machine guns afterwards. About half an hour later, he saw the three trucks returning empty. The witness also attested to seeing another batch of three lorries full of people passing by, although being already 7 o'clock in the evening, he could not see who exactly were loaded on the lorries. This time round, too, he heard the sounds of machine guns and saw three empty truck returning afterwards.[105] Another witness and a resident of Samba Ikat village, Tan Hai Suar, offered corroborative testimony, informing the court that a total of six trucks carrying Chinese persons under Japanese military guard arrived near his house on March 1. The occupants of the trucks were unloaded, directed to air-raid shelters previously built by the Allied forces, and massacred by machine guns. The witness later saw "heads protruding from the air raid shelters." He testified that the bodies "after a few days gave a very bad odor, so we farmers re-buried the dead."[106]

It is hard to tell if these ghastly accounts of massacre made any impression on individual accused. But this much is clear from the trial record: all accused were prepared to accept as factual the allegations that the 25th Army carried out mass killing of Chinese in the wake of the capture of Singapore. At the same time, all accused disputed their individual criminal liability for the massacre. They commonly testified that they had varying degrees of personal misgivings about the advisability of the order, but that they considered the order irrevocable and binding, and that they had no other options but to implement it given their respective subordinate positions vis-à-vis Yamashita. In short, they commonly pleaded superior orders as a defense.

Chief-accused Nishimura set the tone in this regard. He testified during direct examination that the operational order to kill the Chinese reached him on around February 23, just about six days after he received separate orders to prepare for the next operational mission in Sumatra. He found the new order "absolutely impossible," so he allegedly told his chief of staff, Obata Nobuyoshi, who brought back the order from the 25th Army Headquarters that day. Nishimura believed that the time allowed for the purge was too short, but Obata told him that Suzuki, chief of staff of the 25th Army, said the order was irrevocable and requested the dispatch of "a certain number of soldiers to do this work." Suzuki is said to have assured that the staff officer of the 25th Army, Tsuji, would take charge of the actual carrying out of the plan.[107] Nishimura explained to the court that he complied with the order in those circumstances, believing that his action amounted to no more than "loan[ing] the 25th Army some of my men."[108] When questioned by the defense counsel whether he considered himself responsible for the massacre, Nishimura replied no. "I have only obeyed orders and should these Army orders be illegal, the Commander-in-Chief [Yamashita] who issued this order is to be responsible," he testified. In any event, he "loaned these soldiers and the actual work was done under the supervision of Staff Officer Tsuji."[109]

When cross-examining Nishimura, the prosecution took issue with the term "loaning," as Nishimura seemingly distanced himself from the mass killing by making this particular word choice. Nishimura did admit that pursuant to Yamashita's order, he appointed a Maj. Gen. Kobayashi to head an infantry unit, and issued him the general order to screen and dispose of anti-Japanese elements among the Chinese population in Singapore.[110] If so, wouldn't that constitute his exercising of command authority and not just "loaning" of troops? The prosecution then asked as follows: "You agree, Gen. Nishimura, with me that for a Commander to allow his subordinate to use his discretion, he takes upon himself the responsibility for acts done in exercising that discretion?" To this Nishimura replied, "I do not think I have any criminal responsibility."[111] Under further cross-examination, he once again attributed the responsibility of the massacre to Tsuji and ultimately to Yamashita, stating "Gen. Yamashita, being a very intelligent person, and under the circumstances I do think that this order had to be issued by the Headquarters of the Japanese Army."[112] More specifically, "I do think that Yamashita was the responsible person."[113] As shown shortly, Nishimura's use of the term "loaning" did not exonerate him from the charge, but the court appears to have taken it into account when determining the penalty.

Kawamura Saburō, the next highest-ranking accused in this case, similarly defended his action by testifying that he received orders for the purge directly from Yamashita. The accused was general officer commanding an infantry brigade at the time of the invasion of Singapore. He was summoned to the 25th Army Headquarters on February 19, 1942, whereupon Yamashita ordered him to take the command of the new Singapore Guard Unit. Kawamura's mission was to carry out a "mopping-up operation" against anti-Japanese Chinese elements to improve the security situation in Singapore.[114] According to Kawamura's court testimony, detailed instructions were provided separately by the chief of staff of the 25th Army. The period of operation would be limited between February 21 and 23, and the targets of the mopping-up campaign would be individuals falling under the following categories: "(i) Former volunteer members; (ii) Communists; (iii) Looters; (iv) People having arms and harboring arms; (v) Elements obstructing the Japanese operation, and elements that are disturbing the peace and order and elements likely to disturb peace and order." As for the concrete methods of the purge, Kawamura attested to being instructed to cordon off the area under Japanese control, concentrate "all Chinese" at designated locations for the screening process, carry out the house-to-house search simultaneously, segregate the identified anti-Japanese elements, and eliminate them.[115]

Kawamura testified that he expressed to the chief of staff and an old friend of his, Suzuki, his personal doubts over the practicality of the order, but was told that "the shifting of the main body for the new operations was sooner than we had expected, and on the other hand the activities of the Chinese have become very serious in Singapore." Suzuki explained that, lacking sufficient guard personnel even for prisoners of war, "the Commander-in-Chief [Yamashita] made his final decision, and the time allowed to purge the Chinese is sufficient only for a few days." When Kawamura expressed additional concerns about the difficulty of identifying the "anti-Japanese" elements and particularly those who would fall under category (v) above, Suzuki alledgedly assured that "the general object of this purge are the Volunteers and the Communists." As regards the screening of those individuals who may fall under category (v), Suzuki told Kawamura that "I leave it [the decision] in your hands." Hearing this, Kawamura "was very glad to have this good understanding"[116] and prepared himself to implement the order.

Kawamura duly carried out the purge, and was ordered back to the 25th Army Headquarters on the afternoon of February 23 to report the progress. Based on information provided by his subordinates, he told Yamashita that between 4,000 and 5,000 Chinese were either executed or taken into Japanese custody. In reply, and according to Kawamura's testimony, Yamashita expressed words of appreciation but warned that Kawamura must remain alert, saying, "You must watch their movements carefully, arrest them when necessary, and continue the purge."[117] The second purge ensued five days after Kawamura's report, on February 28. The Imperial Guards Division carried out the mopping-up campaign, while the Singapore Guard Unit provided assistance, namely, to "fence the place and arrest anti-Japanese people who will try to escape from various places, and also purge the anti-Japanese elements in this area and dispose of them as before."[118]

The third accused, Ōishi Masayuki, also pleaded superior orders, although in his case, the plea was made relative to the Guard Unit commander (Kawamura) rather than Yamashita. He testified that Kawamura led a tour of inspection on February 18 to deliver the order regarding the mopping-up campaign. Ōishi attested to protesting at first, saying that "it was quite impossible to accomplish this in 3 days," but he soon backed down based on the information that the order was irrevocable. [119] He testified that he passed the order to two immediate subordinates of his – Lt. Col. Yokota Yoshitaka and Maj. Jō Tomotatsu (both of whom were co-accused at this trial) – as soon as he received it for implementation. When cross-examined by the prosecution, he confirmed that he received the order from Kawamura and then "passed it to my subordinates as it was," [120] namely, to Yokota and Jō. The two, in turn, "passed it over to the sector commanders" following "the usual Army method," he testified. [121]

The substance of Ōishi's testimony was confirmed by Yokota Yoshitaka, one of the subordinate officers, with control over three platoons and an infantry company of 200 troops at the time of the massacre. He attested to receiving the operational order "on the 18th at Fort Canning, from Col. Ōishi," and passing it on to his subordinate platoon commanders and auxiliary *kenpeitai* commanders. [122] Regarding the substance of the order, this accused indicated to the court his conflicted feelings at that time by referring to it as "an undesirable order." [123] When questioned by the prosecution for explanation, Yokota made the following remarks:

Q [PROSECUTION]. You say it was an undesirable order. Do you mean an undesirable order from a moral point of view?
A [ACCUSED]. I said from a personal standpoint.
Q. But why undesirable?
A. I am an honest soldier and in the operational forces to attack a position or an enemy is what a soldier would wish to do.
Q. Why do you think the order was undesirable?
A. Since this was not a gallant action I did not like it. [124]

The exchange above is interesting, since this was about the only instance during the Nishimura Trial when an accused expressed personal misgivings to the plan of massacre on moral grounds in place of reasons of impracticality.

A post-trial interview, conducted by an investigative officer from the Japanese Ministry of Legal Affairs in 1960, reveals that this accused actually found the order of purge so morally objectionable that he effectively boycotted its implementation. "There is controversy as to whether or not the Singapore Purge Case was a crime or not," Yokota told his interviewer, but he denied that there was any controversy at all. "In my opinion, it was a crime," he bluntly stated. [125] He went on to relate to the interviewer that the method of purge was "utterly non-sensical [*detarame*]" [126] and that as an officer on the ground, he was "absolutely staggered [*bikkuri shita*]" to hear the substance of the plan. [127] He had imagined that mass deportation of anti-Japanese elements to an isolated island or something of that nature was a possibility, but not summary, indiscriminate killing on a vast scale of the Chinese population. He was so astounded by the state of affairs that he dared not leave his headquarters. He instead kept himself busy meeting numerous Chinese, Indian, and Malay civilians, and British and Australian deserters, who came to him pleading for his help to save their lives. His immediate superior officer Ōishi found out about Yokota's inaction, and personally directed that he go out to lead tours of inspection. This Yokota refused, and the two almost got into a fight.[128] Yokota was subsequently removed from his post and sent back to Japan. This same Ōishi, however, made no mention when testifying at the U.K Singapore trial that Yokota disobeyed him or that he was later recalled to Japan. Ōishi instead offered erroneous testimony to implicate him. Yokota saw in this a "curious psychology [*myō na shinri*]" of his former military superior. Yokota himself ended up offering a false account, as he came under pressure from other Japanese assisting the defense case not to give self-serving testimony at the expense of co-accused.[129]

The Singapore trial must have been a bitter experience for Yokota, but he may have found some solace if he ever came across *Nihon kenpei seishi* (The official history of the Japanese military police), compiled and published in 1976 by the *kenpeitai* alumni association. While highly critical of Allied war crimes trials, the alumni association reflected on the *kenpeitai*'s wartime shortcomings and especially instances of *kenpeitai* officers' "pandering with the Army orders in excess to the point of overlooking the fundamental duty of the *kenpei*."[130] The alumni association singled out the Singapore Massacre as one regrettable example of the *kenpeitai* failure to fulfill its professional responsibility. "The mopping-up operation in Singapore, known as the largest one in the Malay area, was carried out in accordance with the hard-liner intention of the Army," *Nihon kenpei seishi* reads, and "the disgrace that blots the Japanese Army [ever since] cannot be cleared and continues to harm the friendships [between the Chinese and Japanese people]." Making a pointed criticism of *kenpeitai* chief Ōishi, the official history went on to read as follows:

The *kenpeitai* chief at the time ought to have stood firm in voicing objections; he ought to have done everything in his power and offered himself to stop this, by calling it wrong, even by placing his job on the line or by refusing to obey orders, etc. We ought to reflect on the easy compromise [the *kenpeitai* chief made] on the excuse that there was nothing he could do about military orders.[131]

Having stated thus, the alumni association expressed some sympathy with Ōishi's personal predicaments. It observed that few *kenpeitai* officers in those days could have stood up against Staff Officer Tsuji, a powerful army officer and a military hard-liner. What was more, there was a long tradition of rivalry between the *kenpeitai* and army staff officers. The deep-seated intraservice conflict created an environment where the *kenpeitai*'s advice could not be easily acceded to by army staffers, or vice versa, when determining operational priorities. Those *kenpeitai* officials who had to serve "reckless staff officers," in a sense, were "victims" themselves, so *Nihon kenpei seishi* reads.[132]

THE FINDINGS OF THE SINGAPORE COURT

The final verdicts of the court were guilty for all accused but sentences varied: life imprisonment for Nishimura; death sentences for Kawamura and Ōishi; and life imprisonment for the remaining four accused, all of whom were subordinate *kenpeitai* officers.[133] The U.K. Singapore court did not produce any judgment to explain these verdicts or sentences. But the report by the reviewing authority gives some clues as to how the court settled on these different penalties.[134] With regard to the four subordinate *kenpeitai* officers, the court appears to have taken into account the fact of their being "comparatively junior in the chain of command"[135] and took their plea of superior orders as a mitigating factor. As for chief-accused Nishimura, the court may have accepted in mitigation the plea that "the only active part he took in the massacre was to attach some of his troops to the authorities concerned under orders from Yamashita's H.Q., with knowledge of the use of which those troops were to be put."[136] In other words, it is likely that Nishimura's argument of "loaning" spared him capital punishment. (Nishimura was subsequently tried by Australians on an unrelated charge. He was found guilty and sentenced to death. His execution was carried out at Manus on June 11, 1951.[137])

The outcomes of the Nishimura Trial came under heavy criticism of the local Singapore press, as the city residents considered the two death sentences and life imprisonment for the rest too lenient. The reviewing authority justified the penalties on behalf of the court, however, commenting that life imprisonment "cannot reasonably be described as lenient."[138] Yet when compared with the outcomes of the Ichikawa Trial, the relative leniency of the U.K. Singapore court is undeniable. All the company commanders who had acted on Ichikawa's orders to kill Kalagon villagers were uniformly sentenced to death, while their counterparts at Singapore received life imprisonment. Should the same weighty penalty at the U.K. Rangoon court have been applied to those who were found guilty of the massacre of Chinese in Singapore? Or, could it be said that the U.K. Rangoon court was excessively stern to the Ichikawa group? There are no satisfactory answers to these questions.

The accused themselves had an entirely different assessment of the verdicts and sentences. Kawamura Saburō, for one, drew up a letter on the eve of the day of execution (addressed to "Mr. Supreme Commander of the British Army at Singapore" – presumably Mountbatten – and dated June 25, 1947) to criticize the British court's failure to administer justice properly.[139] Kawamura argued that if the purpose of war crimes trials was "deterrence [*yobō*]," the British authorities erred in trying the Japanese suspected war criminals to begin with.[140] The possibility of future wars loomed large among victorious Allied Powers, and not with vanquished nations such as Japan. If so, he argued that the Allied war crimes program should have been targeted at criminal offenders among the members of the Allied forces and not military personnel of a defeated nation. He also questioned the validity of the court's decisions, especially its rejection of the doctrine of superior orders as a defense. He doubted that the British Army had any different views about the centrality of strict obedience to superior orders, which, in his opinion, constituted the backbone of a strong army. Kawamura and other accused were thus "all flabbergasted [*ichidō no azen to suru tokoro*]" to find that the U.K Singapore court threw this principle out the window and freely handed down many convictions and death sentences to those who followed superior orders.[141] Above all, Kawamura was highly critical of the punitive nature of the British war crimes policy. He referred to "lenient treatment by the judges [*saiban-kan no onjō aru toriatsukai*]" of criminal offenders in the Japanese justice system, and maintained that the justice system in the British homeland surely must be "the same."[142] Based on this assumption, Kawamura would argue that attaching importance to retribution went against the humanist principle of the civilized world. It would follow that the British authorities ought to have emphasized not retribution but instead rehabilitation and reform of criminal offenders.

Having so argued, Kawamura appreciated the fact that the Singapore Massacre had done tremendous damage to Sino-Japanese relations. He thus prepared a separate short letter and requested that it be handed over to the representative of the local Chinese community. His intention was not to accept personal responsibility, however, but rather to seek some understanding from the local community that the entire episode was "fate and predestination [*unmei de ari, innen de ari*]." As a death-row inmate awaiting execution the next morning, he simply wrote that "if my death can in any way serve to mitigate your sentiments of hatred against the Japanese people in connection with this case, I will be deeply gratified and grateful."[143]

6

The Navy High Command[1]

"'War-crimes' trials have become a commonplace since the termination of the hostilities of the recent war, so much so that we forget easily, perhaps, that they are a novelty of these four or five years' standing."[2] With this statement on behalf of the accused, Ben B. Blakeney presented a detailed critique of the nascent jurisprudence of command responsibility that arose from European and Far Eastern war crimes trials. An American and formerly a lead defense lawyer at the Tokyo Trial, Blakeney headed the advisory counsel for the defense to represent Adm. Toyoda Soemu, the accused at one of the two international proceedings that followed the Tokyo Trial. It was August 9, 1949, when he began delivering the defense summation at the final stage of the trial. There were few spectators to hear the argument of the day, however, or even journalists. It had been like this for most of the last eight months, during which the court gallery remained virtually empty except for initial sessions in the fall of 1948.[3]

The problem was not that the court was outside the geographical reach of the general public. The occupation authorities set it up inside the Mitsubishi No. 11 Building at the heart of the government district in Maru-no-uchi, central Tokyo, which stood right behind the Meiji Building, the headquarters of the Legal Section of the Supreme Commander for the Allied Powers. Access was not an issue in this regard. The courtroom was later relocated to the Japan Youth Building (*Nippon seinenkan*) at Aoyama Gaien, which was another major structure under control of occupation authorities in the capital city and hardly an obscure location either.[4] Major difficulties – according to Shimanouchi Tatsuoki, one of the Japanese who served in Toyoda's advisory counsel – were rather that the charge leveled against the accused did not pique much interest among the public and that, moreover, the average Japanese would have had a hard time comprehending the English-only court proceedings.[5] The public curiosity about the trials may have waned, too, given how mundane – or "commonplace" as Blakeney put it – war crimes prosecutions had become.

Limited publicity does not necessarily mean limited significance of the trial, however. Having taken place when it did, the Toyoda Trial took on the characteristics of the summation of institutional and jurisprudential accomplishments of the Allied war crimes program in this theater. From the institutional standpoint, the Toyoda Trial inherited from the Tokyo Tribunal veteran court interpreters, translators, stenographers, typists, and other essential court staff with a proven record of competence.[6] The Toyoda Tribunal had full cooperation of the Japanese government and law enforcement authorities, too, for locating and producing witnesses needed for the trial without procrastination or obstructionism. The Government of Japan also took on the responsibility of paying travel and accommodation expenses for witnesses as well as salaries of defense lawyers.[7]

The prosecution and the defense teams, for their part, had substantial expertise in preparing their respective cases. At the prosecution's disposal were vast investigative and prosecutorial resources of the Legal Section of the Supreme Commander for the Allied Powers as well as those taken over from the International Prosecution Section at the Tokyo Trial. As for the defense, it had as its primary asset two-and-a-half years of practical experience in defending major Japanese war criminals at the Tokyo Trial. "The Toyoda Trial was in certain respects a microcosm of the Tokyo Trial," Shimanouchi wrote, "Or rather, to speak frankly as far as the defense was concerned, it was the rallying of its greatest capabilities [*sono saikō nōryoku no kesshū de atta*]."[8] Four of the five lead members of the defense counsel – Ben B. Blakeney, George A. Furness, Shimanouchi Tatsuoki, and Hanai Tadao – were part of the defense counsel at the Tokyo Trial. Furness had served also as a member of the defense team at the Honma Trial.[9] They were like-minded, had comparable intellectual capacities, and had known one another for long enough that, according to Shimanouchi, they could work together with complete seamlessness. The fifth member of advisory counsel, Baba Tōsaku, was not part of the defense at the Tokyo Trial, but proved to be an invaluable asset on account of his having been a top legal officer of the Imperial Japanese Navy.[10] What was more, and much to the chagrin of the prosecution, the Second Demobilization Bureau – the former Navy Ministry – threw its full weight behind the defense case so as to help clear the name of Toyoda of all criminal accusations. The prosecution's adversary at the Toyoda Trial, in this regard, was not just the joint advisory counsel of two Americans and three Japanese but the assemblage of the best and the brightest of the entire Japanese navy establishment.[11] The difficulty of ensuring "equality of arms" had been a chronic problem throughout the postwar Allied war crimes trials, but in this instance, the balance was possibly tipped in favor for the defense.[12]

From the jurisprudential standpoint, the Toyoda Trial can be again understood as the summation of the Allied war crimes prosecution efforts because of the ways in which the prosecution and the defense advanced their respective cases in the courtroom. The two sides argued at length on the applicability of precedents stemming from Nuremberg, the Tokyo Trial, the Yamashita Trial, the Honma Trial, and a cross section of other American, Australian, British, Dutch, and Philippine war crimes trials where high-ranking Japanese army and navy officers were tried. In turn, the Toyoda Tribunal – consisting of Brig. John W. A. O'Brien of the Australian Army[13] as presiding judge, five U.S. Army and Air Force officers as members, and Lt. Col. James O. Hamilton, an officer in the U.S. Army's Judge Advocate General's Department serving as the tribunal's law member – weighed these wide-ranging earlier cases so as to determine their relevance before reaching its final decision on the case of Toyoda.

The tribunal took note in its judgment this type of cumulative aspect of the Toyoda case by stating as follows:

Coming at the time that it does, and because of its nature, this trial was, in great measure, a Trial of Review. It has been necessary to examine, in varying degree, the "pros" and "cons," the charges, the judgments and the sentences of 32 earlier trials in which persons, who may or who may not have been connected with the accused in any way, were involved.[14]

What was on trial, in this respect, was as much the specific accused person, Toyoda, as judicial decisions of some thirty-two trials that preceded this case. "It is no small satisfaction to the members of the Tribunal," the judgment continued to read, "that, in every case, except one involving submarine atrocities, the verdict of this trial is not inconsistent with the findings in those cases in so far as they are co-related."[15] In other words, the tribunal apparently found a high degree of congruity between its legal reasoning that supported the final verdict and the emerging case-law literature from contemporaneous war crimes trials.

The Toyoda Trial convened on October 29, 1948, but the actual arraignment was postponed until November 26 so as to allow the hastily-appointed defense counsel "an adequate time for preparation of these motions [to be made in the accused's behalf] and the argument in support of them."[16] The Judgment of the International Military Tribunal for the Far East was delivered in the meanwhile, between November 5 and 12. All motions the defense eventually made were denied, whereupon the prosecution commenced its case and continued presenting evidence until January 26, 1949.[17] It was followed by arguments between the two parties over the defense motion to dismiss the charge and specifications, on February 7 and 8. The Toyoda Tribunal denied the motion in the end, on the ground that "sufficient substantial evidence has been submitted which, together with all reasonable inferences therefrom and all applicable presumptions, fairly tends to establish every essential element of the offenses charged in the five specifications."[18] The defense case began about three weeks later on March 7 and continued through July 20, consuming about twice as much court time as the prosecution. Rebuttal, surrebuttal, the further rebuttal, and the reply to the further rebuttal then followed, between

July 21 and August 3. An additional two weeks were spent on summations for both parties (that ended on August 17). The tribunal then adjourned. The trial resumed on September 6, 1949, whereupon the tribunal read out its decision. As a whole, the Toyoda Trial consumed some 300 sessions that "required the detailed and exhaustive examination of 121 witnesses and about 650 affidavits and other exhibits, as well as a record of proceedings and testimony covering 8000 pages," according to the Judgment of the Toyoda Tribunal.[19]

At the start of the trial, the prospect for the accused seemed hopeless. The defense team was well aware what the general trend of trials involving army and navy commanders had been like thus far. In the absence of evidence of criminal orders, the prosecution at earlier trials had commonly resorted to documenting numerous instances of atrocity by way of introducing voluminous affidavits, sworn statements, war crimes investigation reports, confiscated Japanese military documents, diplomatic records, eyewitness's court testimony, and so on. This method of proof would show broad geographical distribution and recurrence of war crimes, committed by troops under command of an accused. The tribunal would construe such evidence as sufficient grounds to infer the accused's knowledge and inaction toward fulfillment of his duties, finally to reach the verdict of guilty. It was not uncommon for such guilty verdicts to be accompanied by capital punishment. Toyoda's defense lawyers anticipated the same method of proof to be used against their client (which was in fact the case, as shown shortly in this chapter), with a likely outcome of conviction and capital punishment.

"My thinking when I became a member of the Toyoda defense," Shimanouchi wrote in his memoir published in 1984, "was simply, 'Toyoda probably would not escape the death sentence either but, since I have been asked [to act as counsel for the accused], I will do my best.'"[20] Other defense lawyers must have felt the same – especially Furness and Hanai, whose clients at the Tokyo Trial were convicted of war crimes just at the time when the Toyoda Trial was starting. Shigemitsu Mamoru, former foreign minister during part of the Pacific War (1943–45), and Hirota Kōki, former foreign minister at the time of the Rape of Nanjing (1937–38), were both found guilty of having "deliberately and recklessly disregarded their legal duty to take adequate steps to secure the observance and prevent breaches thereof, and thereby violated the laws of war."[21] The former received an unusually light sentence of a seven-year term in prison but the latter, death.[22] Hirota was executed on December 24, 1948, along with six other codefendants convicted of war crimes at Tokyo. This death must have weighed heavily on his chief Japanese defense lawyer, Hanai. In the case of Furness, he was able to stave off a stiff penalty against Shigemitsu, but was still disheartened by the death of Honma (whose execution had taken place at Manila in April 1946). Given these precedents, the prospects for Toyoda indeed looked ominous.

Initial fatalism was, however, replaced in the second half of the trial by a growing sense of confidence that the accused this time might prevail.

Throughout its presentation, the defense team stacked against the prosecution's case volume after volume of records, much of which had been drawn from the former Japanese Navy Ministry's archives. A number of former navy and army officers took the witness stand to support the defense case. They together showed (1) that the accused was vested with little or no command authority in relation to those navy servicemen directly responsible for committing atrocities; (2) that the accused did not know of the occurrence of documented instances of naval atrocities; (3) that he lacked the means to acquire such knowledge; and (4) that the prosecution's evidence in support of alleged broad geographical distribution and recurrence of naval atrocities was too spotty to warrant the imputing of knowledge to the accused. The defense evidence was voluminous, thoroughly researched, and well documented. By the time Toyoda took the witness stand in July 1949, the prosecution's case no longer stood on sure ground.[23] In a dramatic turn of events, the Toyoda Tribunal on September 6, 1949, declared the accused not guilty of all specifications and not guilty of the charge. A stir rippled through the unusually packed courtroom, so Shimanouchi observed, while Toyoda, deeply moved, shed tears. The accused was set free at the tribunal's adjournment. The day of the verdict thereafter remained unforgettable for Toyoda and his defense lawyers, who continued to meet on September 6 to reminisce over their well-fought court battles and ultimate victory. The annual private celebration came to an end with the passing of Toyoda four years later at his home in Setagaya, Tokyo.[24]

What are we to make of the Toyoda Trial that ended in the sweeping verdict of not guilty? How did the Toyoda Tribunal's decision was influenced by contemporaneous command-responsibility trials, if at all? Above all, what does this case tell us about the responsibility of the members of the Japanese navy high command for naval atrocities? This chapter explores the trial record in the effort to address these questions.

THE CHARGE

Toyoda had served as one of the highest-ranking officers of the Imperial Japanese Navy in the last phase of the war. He took charge of all Japanese naval operations in the Pacific theater from before the Battle of Saipan through the Battle of Okinawa as commander-in-chief of the Combined Fleet (May 3, 1944–May 29, 1945). He concurrently assumed other command posts, albeit briefly, in May 1945,[25] after which he left them to accept a new appointment as chief of the Navy General Staff of the Imperial General Headquarters at Tokyo. He continued to direct the Japanese naval operations as navy chief until the end of hostilities (May 30–September 2, 1945). These top positions aside, Toyoda had held for a year the command of the Yokosuka Naval District (May 1943–May 1944), one of four naval districts that provided coastal defense to the Japanese home islands. The case against Toyoda concerned an array of atrocities that the navy servicemen committed in the Indian Ocean and the Pacific Ocean areas as well as in Japan proper over the course of his assumption of these multiple top positions in the navy.[26]

The indictment contained a single charge, which read that the accused "at the times and places set forth in the specifications hereto attached and during a time of war between the United States of America, its Allies, and Dependencies and Japan, did violate the Laws and Customs of War." Five specifications accompanied the charge. Three of them read that while serving in the foregoing capacities, the accused "willfully and unlawfully disregard[ed] and fail[ed] to discharge his duties" by "ordering, directing, inciting, causing, permitting, ratifying and failing to prevent Japanese Naval personnel of units and organizations under his command, control and supervision to abuse, mistreat, torture, rape, kill and commit other atrocities and offenses against innumerable persons of the United States, its Allies, Dependencies and other non-combatant civilians" (specification 1), "to unlawfully rob, pillage, burn, and destroy buildings" (specification 2), and "to unlawfully use non-military objects and places, such as churches and hospitals as fortifications, thereby causing innumerable persons . . . to be maimed, wounded, killed, and subjected to the hazards of war" (specification 3). Toyoda was further charged with mistreatment of Allied prisoners of war interned at a special naval prisoner-of-war interrogation camp at Ōfuna, Tokyo, which came within jurisdiction of the Yokosuka Naval District (specification 4). Finally, he was charged with having "conspire[d] and enter[ed] into a common plan with other known and unknown persons to abuse, mistreat, torture, kill and commit other offenses" and "to conceal the aforesaid atrocities and offenses from the Government of the United States and its Allies" (specification 5).[27]

Concrete instances of atrocity for which Toyoda was held accountable were articulated in the bill of particulars.[28] A total of ninety particulars can be classified into seven categories depending on types of offense, locations, and victims: (1) mistreatment, torture, abuse, and killing of prisoners of war in custody of navy garrison forces in the outlying areas in the Pacific region; (2) mistreatment, torture, abuse, exposure to the hazards of war, and killing of noncombatant civilians in navy-occupied territories in the Indian Ocean and Pacific Ocean areas; (3) civilian-targeted mass atrocities by the navy ground troops over the course of the Battle of Manila, that is, atrocities committed by the Iwabuchi Unit; (4) mistreatment and killing of Filipino civilians by navy ground troops at locations other than Manila in the Philippines; (5) attacks on U.S. hospital ships; (6) "submarine atrocities," that is, killing of survivors of torpedoed Allied ships; and (7) mistreatment of prisoners of war at the Ōfuna naval prisoner-of-war interrogation camp in Tokyo, Japan.

The method of proof the prosecution adopted was a familiar one. Voluminous documentary evidence (a total of 490 court exhibits) was introduced to substantiate instances of war crimes articulated in the bill of particulars.

The vast majority of exhibits consisted of extracts from some twenty command-responsibility trials that had previously been held by American, Australian, British, and Dutch authorities at various locations in the Pacific theater. These exhibits showed that earlier war crimes trials elsewhere had already established the occurrence of alleged naval atrocities and that some of those who had been found guilty were members of the navy units under command of Toyoda. The remainder of the prosecution's court exhibits consisted of the following: organizational charts showing the Japanese navy command structure; the U.S. Army aeronautical approach chart maps; directives issued by the Navy General Staff; regulations issued by the Navy Ministry; Imperial Ordinances; Allied diplomatic records; Red Cross reports; the Japanese government's postwar war crimes investigation reports; excerpts from the U.S. Strategic Bombing Survey; captured German documents; sworn statements and affidavits by former members of the Japanese and Allied forces; letters and death certificates; and extracts from the record of the Tokyo Trial. A machine gun that was allegedly the same model as the ones used in submarine atrocities was also introduced in evidence, alongside drawings indicating how the machine guns were installed on the deck of Japanese submarines.[29] In addition, the prosecution called to the witness stand twenty-eight former Japanese navy officers. They either corroborated the occurrence of documented instances of atrocity or gave testimony on the navy chain of command. Some of the prosecution witnesses were convicted war criminals themselves, having been tried at other Allied war crimes proceedings.

The prosecution's documentary and oral evidence was impressive for its sheer volume, but it was characteristically devoid of proof of Toyoda's issuance of criminal orders or actual knowledge of naval atrocities. This feature was hardly a novelty. Preceding chapters have shown that the very same feature could be found in contemporaneous command-responsibility trials. It is nonetheless worthy of note that this state of affairs continued well into the late stage of the Far Eastern Allied war crimes program. Despite the passage of time, the Allied authorities at the end of 1948 were no better at securing proof to positively link the widespread Japanese-perpetrated war crimes with the highest-ranking individual Japanese commanders, either in the army or in the navy.

The prosecution at the Toyoda Trial justified the nature of its evidentiary materials by arguing that the legal doctrine of command responsibility made no requirement of proof of criminal orders or knowledge. "The accused has been charged with neglect of duty," Jesse Deitch, serving as lead prosecutor, explained to the tribunal, and made the following statement to clarify the prosecution's position[30]:

This is significant for it means that the prosecution need not prove that the accused ordered the commission of any of the incidents which resulted from his neglect of duty, and it means that the prosecution need not specifically prove that the accused knew of the impending commission of any incident before it occurred.[31]

Despite the above understanding of the standard of proof, the defense "has sought to confuse the Tribunal into believing that it is necessary to prove, either directly or circumstantially, that the accused had actual or constructive knowledge of the commission of an incident." Deitch asserted that all the prosecution needed to show, in fact, was merely the accused "neglected the duty to control his subordinates and the duty to protect prisoners of war."[32] As regards specifics of the accused's duty, the prosecution further held it unnecessary to inquire into the matter either. "That the accused had the duty as Commander-in-Chief and as Chief of the Naval General Staff [Navy General Staff] to control his subordinates . . . *is so elementary that it warrants no discussion.*"[33]

While crudely put, these statements may be understood as the expression of an influential strand of legal thinking about command responsibility in the postwar war crimes trials since the time of the Yamashita Trial. In a nutshell, a military commander would be held liable for war crimes committed by subordinate troops on account of his formal position as a commander, based on the principle of strict liability. All the prosecution needed to convict an accused, then, would be to show the position held by the accused in the armed forces under consideration, and to document the commission of war crimes by the members of the same armed forces. These were the kinds of proof by which Yamashita was convicted. The same arguably was the case with the trials of Hirota, Adachi, and Imamura at the Australian Rabaul proceedings, as already seen in Chapter 4.

That said, the prosecution's case against Toyoda did depart from contemporaneous landmark trials in certain other respects. Two notable aberrations can be pointed out. First, the prosecution at the Toyoda Trial disputed the validity of key factual findings concerning naval atrocities made at the Yamashita Trial and the Tokyo Trial, while *at the same time* they relied heavily on court exhibits and transcripts of court proceedings from these trials to substantiate its case against Toyoda. This led to an awkward situation in which the prosecution was simultaneously affirming and repudiating the two landmark trials. It is by no means unusual for the prosecuting agency, the defense, or the judges at any criminal trial to question the findings of earlier trials. What complicated the case at the Toyoda Trial, however, was the choice of evidence. The very evidentiary materials the prosecution used at the Toyoda Trial were the ones that had already come under rigorous scrutiny at the Yamashita Trial and the Tokyo Trial, where they were deemed exculpatory of the navy high command or otherwise insufficient to convict its members. It is difficult to tell why the prosecution at the Toyoda Trial complicated its case by using such evidentiary material against the accused; the chief prosecutor offered no satisfactory explanations. Specifics of the prosecution's case that led to this confounding situation may be outlined as follows.

With respect to the Yamashita Trial, the prosecution made extensive use of evidence of war crimes committed by the navy ground troops in the last months of the war in the Philippines, especially during the Battle of Manila. Notwithstanding the findings of the U.S. military commission, the prosecution argued that the naval ground forces in Manila (i.e., the Iwabuchi Unit) *actually remained under command of the navy and not the army*, and more specifically, under command of Vice Adm. Ōkōchi Denshichi of the Southwest Pacific Fleet. Ōkōchi in turn fell under command of the commander-in-chief of the Combined Fleet, Toyoda. In other words, the prosecution contended that Toyoda was the highest-ranking military officer to be held accountable for the occurrence of the Rape of Manila *and not Yamashita of the 14th Area Army*. "The Navy never intended to place their troops under the command of the Army,"[34] as lead prosecutor Deitch put it.

That stated, there was a significant degree of confusion in the prosecution's evidence. For one thing, the prosecution called to the stand Ōkōchi as its first witness, only to find that the witness was going to give more or less the same testimony as he had given at the Yamashita Trial.[35] The gist of his testimony was that the Iwabuchi Unit was *taken out of navy command* at the start of 1945 and *placed under command of the 14th Area Army* in accordance with the standing navy-army policy on joint operations. The prosecution could have well anticipated that Ōkōchi would testify so, and it must have also understood that such testimony would not be very helpful. Deitch ended up declaring Ōkōchi a "hostile witness,"[36] although he also conceded that he felt compelled to bring Ōkōchi to the courtroom given his unique wartime position and his deep knowledge of the navy organizations.[37] Toyoda's counsel subsequently called Ōkōchi back into the courtroom as a material witness for the defense. It will be seen that the prosecution's effort to give a new interpretation to the Yamashita Trial ended in utter failure.

The prosecution at the Toyoda Trial handled evidence of submarine atrocities at the Tokyo Trial in a somewhat similar manner. It had been alleged at the Tokyo Trial that upon urging from the German government, the Japanese navy high command secretly agreed, authorized, and implemented in the second half of the Pacific War a policy of killing survivors of torpedoed Allied ships in this theater. Yet the International Prosecution Section failed to substantiate this allegation to the satisfaction of the Tokyo Tribunal, and the defense presented a competent rebuttal to undercut the credibility of the prosecution's case. In the end, two individuals who had been implicated with submarine atrocities were acquitted (Adm. Shimada Shigetaro, navy minister, 1941–1944; and Lt. Gen. Ōshima Hiroshi, ambassador to Berlin, 1938–1939, 1941–1945).[38] The prosecution at the Toyoda Trial seemed unfazed, however, and it introduced afresh the very same evidence used at Tokyo to argue that the policy of submarine atrocities did exist at the highest level of the Navy. To strengthen its case, the prosecution drew upon evidence used at the concurrent trial of Vice Adm. Ichioka Hisashi and forty other navy officers before the U.S. Yokohama court (July–December 1948), where most were convicted on the charge and specifications related to submarine atrocities.[39]   The evidentiary value of the Ichioka Trial was reduced to nil in the eyes of the Toyoda Tribunal, however, as it was revealed that the defense lawyers at the U.S. Yokohama trial improperly advised the forty-one accused to plead guilty.[40] The information of procedural irregularities was sufficiently disturbing for the tribunal to conclude – as quoted earlier – that "in every case, *except one involving submarine atrocities*, the verdict of this trial is not inconsistent with the findings in those cases in so far as they are co-related."[41]

Another notable aberration in the prosecution case compared to contemporaneous landmark trials concerned the specification on conspiracy. The doctrine of criminal conspiracy had been introduced in the Charter of the International Military Tribunal at Nuremberg and later repeated in the Charter of the Tokyo Tribunal. This theoretically allowed the prosecuting agencies at both trials to help link major war criminals with a wide range of international offenses.[42] This was not so in practice. The Nuremberg Tribunal ruled that the Charter limited the applicability of conspiracy to crimes against peace and not in connection with war crimes or crimes against humanity.[43] The Tokyo Tribunal ruled the same.[44] Regulations governing the two international proceedings subsequent to the Tokyo Trial reflected the decisions of the Nuremberg and Tokyo Tribunals, and they explicitly limited the applicability of conspiracy to crimes against peace. In spite of this, the prosecution at the Toyoda Trial charged the accused with conspiring "to abuse, mistreat, torture, kill and commit other offenses" and "to conceal the aforesaid atrocities and offenses from the Government of the United States and its Allies" (specification 5).

Once in the courtroom, the prosecution used specification 5 mainly to hold Toyoda accountable for behind-the-scenes activities that it suspected the Second Demobilization Bureau was committing in the accused's behalf, such as possible fabrication of navy documents and coaching of Japanese navy officers who took the stand as either prosecution or defense witnesses. But these allegations did not go beyond the realm of speculation; the prosecution had no evidence to back them up. Cross-examinations of witnesses in those circumstances often descended into bitter acrimony, as chief prosecutor Deitch accused them of telling lies but without having laid proper foundation.[45] He reserved some of the harshest words for those who, despite their apparent proficiency in English, chose to take questions in Japanese and to testify in Japanese, using court interpreters. It was well within the witnesses' right to do so, and there was no legal requirement for them to testify in English unless the tribunal made specific rulings to that effect. Nevertheless, Deitch deemed these witnesses some of the worst prevaricators, arguing that they took advantage of court interpretation to gain extra time and to revise testimony under the pretext of translation errors.[46]

The foregoing features of the prosecution's case elicited caustic remarks from Toyoda's defense counsel. The defense particularly regarded with disdain the prosecution's contradictory use of evidence that arose from the Yamashita Trial. It pointed out that the prosecuting agency representing the United States at Manila had charged Yamashita with responsibility for atrocities committed by the Iwabuchi Unit. Now, another prosecuting agency *also representing the United States* effectively denied Yamashita's command over the Iwabuchi Unit in its attempt to convict Toyoda for the same instance of mass atrocity. This type of changeover was utterly unconscionable and, in the words of Blakeney, it amounted to "effrontery and impudent chicanery."[47]

The defense also received with scorn the prosecution's attacks on credibility of individual Japanese witnesses. Seeing Deitch spending much of his closing argument on summarizing the testimony of each witness he deemed untrustworthy and on calling each a "liar," Blakeney countered that such summation was "an utterly barren and profitless venture." Calling these witnesses a liar was nothing but "harangue."[48] The defense went on to point out that if one were to speak of impropriety, the prosecution itself was subject to censure. It was revealed during the Toyoda Trial that Deitch had knowingly withheld a certain document exculpatory of the accused[49] and that, moreover, he edited parts of the interrogation record of the accused instead of presenting it in its original form.[50] Prosecutorial misconduct such as these is likely to have made a negative impression on the tribunal. The tribunal ultimately threw out specification 5 by declaring that it "finds no evidence in the professional or personal activity of the defendant, from the 7th of December, 1941, to the present, which would justify a reasonable conclusion of guilt under the terms of this Specification."[51]

The prosecution's argument on the theory of command responsibility similarly came under harsh criticism of the defense. The prosecution had essentially argued that it "need prove nothing," Blakeney pointed out. It was "not that he [the accused] neglected his duty by issuing orders contrary to duty, not that he neglected his duty by approving the commission of acts which duty forbids, not that he neglected it by having knowledge of, and knowing, doing nothing to prevent or punish the commission of atrocities." If so, "what remains?" Blakeney asked. The answer was this: "Just that he neglected his duty by being Commander-in-Chief of the Yokosuka Naval District, Commander-in-Chief of the Combined Fleet, Chief of the Navy General Staff, or occupant of other high office."[52] What sort of *duty* did Toyoda have, then, which he allegedly neglected? The prosecution never gave a satisfactory explanation. It simply stated that the accused's duty to control subordinate navy units was "so elementary" as to require no proof. Consequently, the tribunal was left "to guess what power of command Admiral Toyoda possessed."[53]

The prosecution had insisted during its summation that the case against Toyoda had a firm ground in case-law literature that arose from contemporary European and Far Eastern war crimes trials. But Toyoda's counsel disagreed on this point. The emerging case-law literature was actually "mutually inconsistent and contradictory" to the point of making it difficult to single out a uniform theory of command responsibility. If one were to point out a common thread, however, the defense had the following to be said: to convict a person under the doctrine of command responsibility, the prosecution must at minimum take the burden of (1) proof of "orders for or at least of the possession of knowledge of the atrocities," and (2) proof of "the power to command."[54] Blakeney went on to illustrate the defense position by way of the examples of the Yamashita Trial and the Honma Trial:

General Yamashita was convicted of responsibility for the acts of the troops *under his command* as general officer commanding in the Philippines, . . . acts of which the Tribunal trying him found that he *must have had knowledge*. Lieutenant-General Homma was convicted of responsibility for the acts of the troops *under his command* when he occupied the same position, . . . acts of which the report of his trial shows that he *had personal knowledge* and for which he had given orders.[55]

In other words, the accused in both cases were convicted on the findings (1) that they knew or must have known of atrocities committed by the Japanese troops and (2) that the perpetrators of atrocities fell under the accused's command. Blakeney was quick to add that with both trials, "there was sufficient doubt" about knowledge of the accused to cause two justices at the U.S. Supreme Court to produce dissenting opinions.[56] But setting aside this particular controversy and limiting the discussion at a moment to purely theoretical issues, the guilty verdicts in both instances required proof of knowledge and of command authority. The case that the prosecution had made against Toyoda, however, proved *neither*. In those circumstances, the defense could only characterize the prosecution's case as having "no precedent."[57]

The final decision of the tribunal indicates that the defense argument convinced the judges. In the relevant segment in the judgment, the tribunal began by briefly referring to the Yamashita Trial and the Honma Trial. It was "not within the province of this Tribunal [Toyoda Tribunal]" to comment on the decisions of the U.S. Supreme Court, so the tribunal maintained, but "their lives were not forfeited because their forces had been vanquished on the field of battle but because they did not attempt to prevent, even to the extent of issuing orders, the actions of *their subordinates*, of which actions the commanders *must have had knowledge*."[58] The tribunal thus recapitulated the defense argument, summarizing that Yamashita and Honma were convicted essentially on (1) proof of knowledge (or "must have had knowledge") and (2) proof of command authority. The tribunal then segued to setting out its own criteria of responsibility.

Having "carefully studied" the findings made at Yamashita, Honma, and other contemporaneous war crimes trials, the tribunal ruled that the required elements to convict a military commander for war crimes should boil down to the following two sets of criteria, which are quoted in full. First:

1. That offenses, commonly recognized as atrocities, were committed by troops of his command;
2. The ordering of such atrocities.[59]

In the case that proof of orders could not be produced, a military commander may be still held liable for occurrence of war crimes under the second set of criteria of responsibility:

1. As before, that atrocities were actually committed;
2. *Notice of the commission thereof.* This notice may be either:
   a. *Actual,* as in the case of an accused who sees their commission or who is informed thereof shortly thereafter;
   b. *Constructive.* That is, the commission of such a great number of offenses within his command that a reasonable man could come to no other conclusion than that the accused must have known of the offenses or of the existence of an understood and acknowledged routine for their commission.
3. *Power of command.* That is, the accused must be proved to have had actual authority over the offenders to issue orders to them not to commit illegal acts, and to punish offenders.
4. Failure to take such appropriate measures as are within his power to control the troops under his command and to prevent acts which are violation[s] of the laws of war.
5. Failure to punish offenders.[60]

There are two notable features in the Toyoda Tribunal's criteria of responsibility. First, the tribunal rejected the prosecution's contention that no proof of knowledge, either actual or constructive, was required to convict an accused under the doctrine of command responsibility. The tribunal instead required proof of knowledge, namely, (a) proof that the accused was informed of atrocity or (b) proof that given a great number of offenses within his command, "a reasonable man could come to no other conclusion than that the accused must have known of the offenses or of the existence of an understood and acknowledged routine for their commission." Second, the tribunal similarly rejected the prosecution's contention that the power to command was inherent in any military commander and therefore needed no proof. To convict an accused under command responsibility, the tribunal held that the accused must be shown to have had the "power to command" and more specifically, "actual authority over the offenders to issue orders to them not to commit illegal acts, *and* to punish offenders."

The tribunal, in this manner, built on the defense argument and carefully delineated its positions on the doctrine of command responsibility. It is interesting to recall on this occasion, however, that when the prosecution's case rested seven months earlier in February 1949, the tribunal was satisfied to state that "sufficient substantial evidence has been submitted which . . . *fairly tends to establish every essential element of the offenses charged in the five specifications.*"[61] In other words, there was a time when the tribunal thought that the prosecution had a valid theoretical ground and that it had satisfactorily fulfilled its burden of proof. If so, what happened in the intervening months that led the tribunal to revise its views? What exactly was in the defense evidence that impacted the tribunal's thinking? To find an answer, one now needs to turn to the details of the defense case.

WHAT WERE TOYODA'S DUTIES, EXACTLY?

The heart of the defense case was to make thoroughgoing documentation of the unique command structures of the Imperial Japanese Navy. The goal was to refute the prosecution's presumption that Toyoda had the duty to control the subordinate units or the duty to protect prisoners of war. The bulk of evidence in support of this point was drawn from a large pool of navy documents in possession of the Second Demobilization Bureau. They consisted of ordinances pertaining to organization of navy fleets, navy guard units, naval districts, and navy prisoner-of-war administration; navy ministry notifications and orders also concerning organizational issues of the navy; directives on navy operational plans issued by the Navy General Staff of the Imperial General Headquarters; and directives on interservice agreements on the army-navy joint operations, also issued by the Navy General Staff. Some of these documents dated back to the Russo-Japanese War (1904–1905), as Toyoda's counsel attempted to trace the historical evolution of the unique system of command and control in the Imperial Japanese Navy. In addition, a number of former high-ranking navy officers took the stand, including a few septuagenarians, who provided personal insights into the complex historical evolution of the Japanese navy high command. The gist of the defense evidence can be summarized as follows.

The Fleet Ordinance, issued in November 1914, is arguably one of the most important evidentiary materials in the making of the defense case, as it brought to the front and center what the defense portrayed as the unique command structure of the Imperial Japanese Navy and especially that of the Combined Fleet.[62] According to this ordinance, and as the defense explained it, the commander-in-chief of the Combined Fleet exercised at least two distinct types of command authority vis-à-vis different subordinate elements. One was the *tōsotsu* power, whose rough translation would be "full command-power" and the other, the *shiki* power, whose translation would be something like "subject to the command."[63] The same English word "command" would apply but the two words purportedly carried different shades of meaning in the original Japanese. They were used in the Fleet Ordinance of 1914 and other navy regulations to define command authority to be vested in commanders of fleets, commanders of area fleets, the commander-in-chief of the Combined Fleet, the navy minister, the chief of the Navy General Staff, and the supreme commander of the Imperial Japanese Army and Imperial Japanese Navy, the Emperor of Japan.

With regard specifically to the commander-in-chief of the Combined Fleet, the Fleet Ordinance stipulated that he had the *tōsotsu* power in relation to his own home fleet in the Combined Fleet. He thus "control[led] and supervise[d] affairs of his organization pertaining to such command [*tōsotsu shi koreni kansuru taimu o tōtoku su*]" (article 10).[64] As regards the constituent fleets that came under the umbrella of the Combined Fleet, however, the chief of the Combined Fleet exercised the *shiki* power only, a little short of full command authority. This presumably allowed the commanders of individual subordinate fleets to retain and exercise the "full command-power" (i.e., *tōsotsu*) in relation to their respective fleet organizations and without interference from the chief of the Combined Fleet. According to defense witness Adm. Yoshida Zengo, what this meant in practical terms was the chiefs of constituent fleets would be subject to the command of the chief of the Combined Fleet "as far as concerned operational orders,"[65] but not concerning military administration. Each of the fleet commanders was instead "subject to the direction of the Navy Minister [*kaigun daijin no shiki o uku*]" in regard to military administration (article 11),[66] thus bypassing the commander-in-chief of the Combined Fleet. The Fleet Ordinance read that the commander-in-chief of a fleet "controls and supervises the military discipline, morale, education and training of his fleet [*kika kantai no gunki fūki oyobi kyōiku kunren o tōkan su*]" (article 12). The chief of the Combined Fleet himself, meanwhile, was also "subject to the direction [*shiki o uku*]" of the navy minister on issues of navy administration so far as his own fleet was concerned (article 10). To further complicate the matter, the Fleet Ordinance stipulated that the chief of the Combined Fleet and each of the commanders of constituent fleets *separately* and *individually* fell "under direct command of the Emperor [*tennō ni chokurei shi*]" (articles 10 and 11).[67] This stipulation had the effect of doubly undercutting the command authority of the chief of the Combined Fleet, who was vested in principle with the *shiki* power only (i.e., the power to issue operational orders) in relation to the constituent fleets.

The defense evidence shows that the next generation of navy authorities took additional steps to firm up the principle of vesting limited command authority in the commander-in-chief of the Combined Fleet. A notification issued by the vice minister of the navy in 1924, titled, "Regarding the Administrative Competence of the Combined Fleet," was one such step. It set out new guidelines to relieve the chief of the Combined Fleet of all administrative responsibilities relative to constituent fleets with the exception of matters closely associated with tactical and ceremonial matters.[68] The underlying idea was to allow the chief of the Combined Fleet to focus on exercising his *shiki* power – that is, coordination of naval operations of subordinate fleets – while leaving intact the *tōsotsu* power of individual fleet commanders in relation to their respective fleet organizations. Quite interestingly, the defense evidence revealed that accused Toyoda himself was instrumental in the making of this particular notification. Then an up-and-coming elite navy officer and a member of the First Section of the Navy Affairs Bureau of the Navy Ministry, Toyoda is said to have advocated that "the Commander-in-Chief of the Combined Fleet should not become deeply involved in operations within the constituent fleets, but should only have command and control of the operations initiated by the Combined Fleet as a whole as his main duty,"[69] according to defense witness Adm. Kobayashi Seizō. Toyoda himself corroborated Kobayashi's account as he stated: "Having participated at the time on the issuance of this notification, as one of the officers concerned, I am a man familiar with the situation of the time of its issuance."[70]

Another navy order to consolidate the divided system of command and control was issued on November 26, 1941, by the Navy Ministry (Restricted Order [*nairei*] No. 1538). This order required that "the fleet commanders and special guard district commanders shall control administration *by the order of the Navy Minister* [*kaigun daijin no mei o uke*]."[71] According to defense witness Rear Adm. Takada Toshitane, this order reflected the opinion of the then commander-in-chief of the Combined Fleet, Adm. Yamamoto Isoroku, who allegedly advised the Navy Ministry that "it is completely undesirable that the headquarters of the Combined Fleet have to do with military administration."[72] Another order by the Navy Ministry, dated April 10, 1942, reinforced the principle of separation of operational and administrative command. It stipulated that area fleets under the organizational umbrella of the Combined Fleet would be "subject to the command of the Commander-in-Chief of the Combined Fleet, *except for matters of military administration of occupied territory* [*tadashi senryōchi no gyōsei ni kansuru jikō o nozoku*]."[73] This order, in effect, reconfirmed the institutional arrangement that the chief of the Combined Fleet should exercise the *shiki* power alone over the subordinate fleets, thus staying away from administrative matters of occupied territories.

When taken all together, the foregoing navy ordinances, notifications, and orders brought out a unique evolutionary path of the Imperial Japanese Navy wherein separation of administrative and operational commands became the preferred mode of navy organization. The institutional propensity for narrowing, compartmentalizing, and redistributing different types of command authority was particularly pronounced in the Combined Fleet, seemingly to make command authority of the chief of the Combined Fleet ever smarter, leaner, and more agile for his execution of operational missions. The chief of the Combined Fleet by the early months of the Pacific War was stripped of all responsibilities pertaining to administration of area fleets, fleets, guard units, or navy-occupied territories. The only exception was his own home fleet in relation to which he retained the *tōsotsu* power. The logical end of all this was that the chief of the Combined Fleet could not be held liable for naval atrocities arising from navy administration in occupied territories, nor could he be held liable for failing to discipline the members of the constituent fleets, because his command authority in relation to them was limited to the *shiki* power.

If the institutional history of the Japanese Combined Fleet in the defense case pointed to the general trend toward division and compartmentalization of command authority, there was also a *countervailing trend* in the Japanese army and navy establishment as a whole – the trend, that is, toward the unification of command. The army and the navy had a long history of interservice rivalry, but exigencies of the war necessitated the two constituent departments of the Imperial General Headquarters at Tokyo – the core elements of which being the Army General Staff and the Navy General Staff – to reach a series of joint agreements to make the army-navy joint operations possible.[74] Among the first interservice agreements made during the Pacific War was articulated in Naval General Staff Directive No. 38, dated January 3, 1942. Issued in the wake of the capture of Manila, this directive was not so much a policy outline for the unification of the army-navy command as a joint agreement delineating separate jurisdiction of the two services in the Philippine theater. The directive indicated that the navy was to be responsible for sea areas, naval-installation areas and navy-assigned air bases, while the army would take charge of the rest.[75]

The plan for army-navy joint operations took a concrete form a year later to strengthen the defense of Japanese-occupied Southeast Asia in preparation for the Allied counterattacks. It read that "the Army and the Navy are to cooperate in the execution of the strongest possible offensive operations by ships and air forces and thereby strive to crush the enemy's attempts at counterattack."[76] The new directive also included the following stipulation:

Section V– Command Relations

10. When Army and Navy units are located in the same area, the highest commander [*saikō shiki-kan*] of the naval landing party is *subject*, in matters of land defense, *to the command* [*shiki o ukuru*] of the highest commander of the Army located in the same area. In case, however, the naval commander is higher in rank, the Army commander is subject, regarding the land defense, to the command of the naval commander.[77]

This directive required that the navy units were to come under command of the army in principle, but that the opposite should apply in the case of the navy commander on the ground being higher in rank than his army counterpart. The same directive additionally instructed that army and navy authorities with jurisdiction in the occupied Philippines were separately "at the earliest possible moment, to draw up their mutual agreements regarding defense." The chiefs of the Southern Army, the 14th Army, the Combined Fleet, and two subordinate area fleets were specifically named to work on the policy on the future army-navy joint operations.[78] According to Vice Adm. Ōkōchi, necessary interservice agreements were reached by the summer of 1944, and the transfer of naval forces to the army ensued in immediate months in Cebu, Leyte, Luzon, and Mindanao.[79]

The Navy General Staff issued in September 1944 a further directive to facilitate the unification of command between army and navy forces in other Japanese-occupied territories. It reconfirmed the existing policy that the navy would generally come under command of the army but that the opposite should apply when the navy commander was in the higher rank in relation to his army counterpart.[80] This policy was subsequently revised, however, and it was decided that the army would be given full command in the case of army-navy joint operations (irrespective of issues of ranks) so far as ground combat missions were concerned. The revised policy found its expression in Naval General Staff Directive No. 477, dated October 23, 1944:

It is to be the principle, however, that as to direct land defense, the Army is chiefly to be in charge.[81]

The policy to the similar effect was articulated in a separate directive, dated February 5, 1945, concerning the army-navy joint operations in Japanese-occupied British Malaya and the surrounding region. The commander-in-chief of the Southern Army thereafter "shall command [*shiki su*] the 10th Area Fleet and the 4th Southern Expeditionary Fleet," two area fleets that had come under the organizational umbrella of the Combined Fleet in this region.[82]

These directives on army-navy joint operations effectively removed from the chief of the Combined Fleet command authority over much of the constituent fleets and naval guard units in the last year of the war. This trend accelerated from October 1944 onwards when the aforementioned revised policy on army-navy joint operations made the army take charge of land defense. It is open to debate, however, as to how smoothly the unification of command was completed given certain ambiguities in the directives. It is instructive to note that, according to Naval General Staff Directive No. 477 (October 1944) quoted above, "it is to be the principle [*gensoku to shite*]" that the Army was "chiefly [*shu to shite*]" to be in charge of the direction of land defense. This suggests some wiggle room for the army and the navy to negotiate their respective areas of command and control. This type of ambiguity may well have caused interservice conflict in the actual army-navy joint operations.

The defense evidence concerning the command authority of the chief of the Yokosuka Naval District sheds another light on distinct institutional features of the Japanese navy that allegedly were overlooked in the prosecution's case. The principle of limited command authority applied here as well, but in a slightly different manner. The Naval Districts Ordinance, dated August 23, 1923, vested a naval district commander with what appears on its face to be an all-inclusive command authority. He had the duty to attend to "the defense and guarding of the area under its jurisdiction, and to matters concerning the mobilization activities assigned to charge" (article 2), and he was also responsible for "general affairs of his district and sees to the maintenance of the military discipline, morale, education and training of his subordinates" (article 5).[83] Yet a close look at the ordinance shows that it defined the administrative responsibilities of a naval district commander not in terms of *tōsotsu* but rather *kantoku* (whose English translation is "supervision") and *tōkan* (whose English translation is "general control"). A naval district commander was vested with the *kantoku* power on matters of military administration in general, and the *tōkan* power with respect specifically to maintenance of military discipline, morale, education, and training of his subordinates.[84]

According to Toyoda's testimony, these stipulations were included in the ordinance out of consideration for chronic institutional shortfalls of navy staff officers and resulting chronic difficulties for a naval district commander to exercise full command authority on all matters under his jurisdiction. The Yokosuka Naval District, for one, was a large naval organization that consisted of some 190 ships, units, offices, and schools, spread across "the entire Pacific coast of the eastern half of Honshū, extending as far south as the Bonin Islands."[85] The total strength of the Yokosuka Naval District was "more than 600,000." Nevertheless, its headquarters was by design staffed poorly, its regular members being no more than the commander-in-chief, his chief of staff, six staff officers, two adjutants, and four officers in charge of personnel, medical, supply, and legal matters.[86] Toyoda explained that due to the stripped-down nature of the command center, "the post of Commander-in-Chief of the Yokosuka Naval District war a busy one even in peacetime; during the war it was so to the extreme."[87] The idea behind the ordinance purportedly was to downgrade the command authority of the naval district commander on administrative matters to *kantoku* and *tōkan*, so that a naval district commander would be able to fulfill operational duties without being burdened by excessive responsibilities on noncombat missions. As Toyoda put it, a naval district commander thus served as "something like that of a comptroller to his commercial firm or of a superintendent to the school-dormitory under his charge"[88] so far as administrative matters were concerned.

The infamous Ōfuna prisoner-of-war interrogation camp in Tokyo (at which prisoner-of-war mistreatment was prevalent) was controlled by the Yokosuka Guard Unit, which in turn fell under command of the Yokosuka Naval District. There was no mistake, therefore, about Toyoda taking on command authority in relation to the Ōfuna camp. But if one were to follow the defense explanation, the Naval Districts Ordinance required that Toyoda exercise no more than the *kantoku* power on administrative matters in general, and the *tōkan* power specifically on matters pertaining to military discipline, morale, education, and training of his subordinates. What was more, the prosecution's case may have given the impression of this particular camp being "one of the major installations of the District." But Toyoda pointed out that if truth be told, the Ōfuna camp was "minor and incidental, or accidental, and one of the smallest installations, infinitesimally small in comparison with some of the others in a District which . . . had incident to its command very heavy responsibilities and very important duties in connection with the war which by then had reached its height."[89] In other words, Toyoda was of the opinion that the significance of the Ōfuna camp was blown out of proportion in the prosecution's case when, in reality, its importance in relation to the entirety of the Yokosuka Naval District's installations was marginal at best. Toyoda informed the tribunal that he did not have the knowledge of prisoner-of-war mistreatment at Ōfuna in any event, nor did the exigency of the war make it realistic for him to acquire knowledge about occurrences of prisoner-of-war mistreatment at a naval installation of such miniscule significance.[90] It will be shown that this line of argument succeeded in convincing the tribunal.

The defense's evidence concerning the Navy General Staff was relatively straightforward but it was by no means less revelatory. The Naval General Staff Ordinance, issued in 1933, stipulated that as an imperial appointee, the chief of the Navy General Staff fell "under direct command of the Emperor" and was responsible for "participat[ing] in the councils of the Imperial Military Command and supervis[ing] and control[ling] the Naval General Staff [Navy General Staff]." While the Combined Fleet and the Navy Ministry took charge of military operations and military administration respectively, the Navy General Staff as a whole was to have "control of matters of national defense and military tactics."[91] According to Toyoda, the Navy General Staff could thus be defined as "the highest staff-organ of the Emperor," which was vested with "the power to *instruct* the commanders-in-chief regarding operational plans, *but had no authority to command them in any way.*"[92] In other words, the Navy General Staff was an advisory body that facilitated the emperor with *his* exercising of command authority in relation to *his* subordinates. The Navy General Staff itself assumed no command authority whatsoever.[93] Defense witness Vice Adm. Ozawa Jizaburō concurred. He testified that the Navy General Staff served as "purely a staff organization" of the Emperor while the latter was "the Supreme Commander of the Armed Forces."[94]

Toyoda readily acknowledged, in this connection, that the navy chief had the power to draw up orders, known as *daikairei* (lit. "Grand Ocean Orders"; trans. "Naval General Staff Orders"). He explained, however, that he did so on behalf of the emperor to whom all orders were submitted for approval prior to their issuance in his name. The navy chief also took charge of drawing up and issuing directives, known as *daikaishi* (lit. "Grand Ocean Directives"; trans. "Naval General Staff Directives"). Their purpose was to give tactical instructions only, however, and they were not to be confused with military orders.[95] The bottom line was, the navy chief neither assumed nor exercised any type of command authority in the handling of *daikairei* or *daikaishi*.

In sum, the defense case showed that the Imperial Japanese Navy had taken on the institutional propensity for narrowing, compartmentalizing, and redistributing different types of command authority – as well as noncommand authority – for the ultimate purpose of maximizing the *tōsotsu* power in the person of the Emperor. To that end, the three branches of the navy under direct command of the Emperor separately took charge of navy administration (the Navy Ministry), navy operational planning (the Navy General Staff), and actual naval operation (the Combined Fleet), thereby making the functioning of the navy ever smarter, leaner, and agile in time of war. Was this system really workable, though? Wouldn't the complex intersection of different types of authority be so byzantine as to defy practical application? It is also worth questioning how the navy system of command and control jibed with that of the army at times of army-navy joint operations. Did the army counterpart intuitively understand the workings of the navy command and, therefore, readily accommodate them? Or, did the navy have to do much explaining in order to help the army grasp the unfamiliar system, and *then* to determine how to make the army-navy joint operation possible? Perhaps the Imperial Japanese Army had a corresponding complex system of divided command and control? The defense evidence gives no helpful clues to answer any of these questions.

THE TRIBUNAL'S OPINION

The defense case as outlined in the foregoing pages had a tremendous impact on the thinking of the Toyoda Tribunal. "In its initial stages, this case appeared to be but a simple one involving only direct command responsibility," the tribunal commented on its first impression of the case against Toyoda. But the complexity of the case dawned upon the members of the tribunal as new evidence on the workings of the Japanese navy was revealed to them. The judgment read:

When the enquiry reached into the highest strats [stratas] of the Japanese Navy, it became all-too-clear that *here was something that had little parallel to the systems of command familiar to Occidentals* and that the applications of such principles of command to the case was impracticable. A study had then to be made of what are, *to Western mentalities, amazingly complex and, at times, almost unbelievable principles of technical administration, authority and direction of a war effort.* This Japanese propensity for divided authority and control, for piecemeal responsibility and decision [making] has added tremendously to the task of this Tribunal in ascertaining the hidden truth.[96]

No explicit credit was given, but it is clear that the defense evidence carried great weight in the tribunal's understanding of the Japanese navy high command and, by extension, its final decision on the case against Toyoda.

In stating its factual findings, the tribunal divided the charge, specifications, and particulars of offense into the following six categories: (1) the Philippine phase; (2) naval land atrocities other than those committed in the Philippines; (3) air attacks on hospital ships; (4) submarine atrocities; (5) prisoner-of-war mistreatment at the Ōfuna interrogation camp; and (6) conspiracy charges. Of these, it has already been seen that the tribunal rejected the conspiracy charge. The tribunal also dismissed the first two in light of the overwhelming documentary and oral evidence that the accused held no command-power whatsoever over those navy units directly responsible for the commission of atrocities in the Philippines. It was either that wartime interservice agreements caused navy ground troops to come under the army command, or that the navy's system of divided authority and control gave the commander-in-chief of the Combined Fleet no authority regarding matters of military administration in navy-occupied territories. The tribunal went on to dismiss the third, fourth, and fifth categories of offense, the main reason being the prosecution's failure to show proof of either criminal orders or criminal knowledge, actual or constructive. In addition, the notion of proportionality weighed greatly in the tribunal's thinking. With respect to air attacks on hospital ships, for instance, the tribunal faulted the prosecution for the poor selection of evidentiary materials that failed to show broad geographical distribution or recurrence of alleged offense. A relevant section in the judgment read:

From the prosecution's oft-repeated "wide spread" angle, we need only to note that many Allied hospital ships conducted many hundreds of sorties within range of Japanese aircraft during the campaigns down the Paific from the Philippines to the Coral Sea, and back up in the fierce battles accompanying the island-hopping from Guadalcanal to Okinawa, and yet we are told in evidence of only three isolated attacks, although we are aware of two or three other incidents no way connected with the accused.[97]

The tribunal concluded that the Japanese attacks on hospital ships were not shown to be such routine occurrences as to warrant the inference of criminal orders or knowledge.

The concept of proportionality figured prominently in the tribunal's decision on the charge of prisoner-of-war mistreatment at Ōfuna, too, although in a different manner. The tribunal readily agreed that mistreatment of prisoners of war was commonplace at the Ōfuna camp and "it can find no major point of issue with those who have made it a 'cesspool of sadism.'" Mistreatment occurred indeed "over a considerable period of time, before and during this accused's period of command, as a result of which events Allied personnel suffered and died." The tribunal was also satisfied that the commander-in-chief of the Yokosuka Naval District assumed command authority concerning administrative matters at Ōfuna. However, the tribunal found no proof of reporting mechanisms or of actual reporting having been made to Toyoda regarding prisoner-of-war mistreatment at Ōfuna, that is, the types of evidence essential for imputing knowledge to the accused. What was more, the tribunal held that "the magnitude of the task which devolved upon him in those days"[98] must be taken into account when determining the guilt or innocence of the accused. Taking a cue from Toyoda's testimony, the tribunal made the following observations:

Then, in light of the magnitude of the task with which he was faced, we examine his opportunities for seeking objectively the information he needed in order to assure the proper conduct under law and regulation, and the discipline of those under his command to the lowest echelon. *We find that the Ōfuna Camp was insignificant in size and number*, and in purpose far removed from any position of contribution to the mission of the command. It was *incidental* to his responsibility, and served him no purpose. *It was under his command only as a geographical happenstance.*[99]

Toyoda surely held formal command over to the Ōfuna camp, but his "measure of guilt" must be weighed against his "measure of ability" to exert his control. In the tribunal's opinion, "it is a small and remote guilt indeed; and the Tribunal, in justice, does not find the Specification proved beyond reasonable doubt."[100]

The Toyoda Trial came to an end, in this manner, with the resounding victory of the defense case. Questions still remain, however, about individual and institutional responsibility of the navy high command for war crimes. One may ask once again: How practical was this seemingly byzantine system of navy command and control in the actual context of the war? How did individual Japanese navy officers discharge their duties amid these complexities? Or, was the Imperial Japanese Navy actually an entirely rational system that made full organizational sense, *regardless of the defense rhetoric of Japanese cultural peculiarities*? Toyoda, in reply, may simply direct us to study the trial record closely. "This trial I do not regard as a trial of myself as an individual – the fate of myself, the person, is of no moment," so he informed the tribunal when testifying in his behalf at the witness stand. "Hence I am making my greatest efforts to clarify the case, for I should not have the records of history to say that *even members of the high command of the Japanese Navy had been corrupt and depraved*, even at the denouement of the defeat inscribed on the last page of its history."[101] Toyoda appeared sincere in expressing these views, but the trial record is as much mystifying as illuminating as one endeavors to grasp the theory and practice of the Japanese navy organizations. This trial may have given the accused an unequivocal verdict of not guilty, but it left for posterity an opaque vision of the notion of responsibility in the Imperial Japanese Navy.

Conclusion

This book has explored the two international criminal proceedings that followed the Tokyo Trial and twelve other high-profile war crimes trials held by American, Australian, British, and Philippine authorities in the Asia-Pacific region. The goal has been to tap into the rich oral and documentary history of the war as contained in the trial records and produce a war narrative that aims at exploring the nexus between military operations and the occurrence of war crimes. This book has also elucidated the Allied courts' cumulative findings on the circumstances of war crimes, the Japanese system of command and control, and applicable theories of liability. Where relevant, the foregoing chapters have touched on the political significance of the trials in relation to the larger context of Asian decolonization.

What conclusions are we now to draw from these case studies? What kind of justice can one say has been rendered at these trials, and for whom? Should it be deemed "victor's justice," or should different kinds of historical assessment be made? How might one also assess the jurisprudential legacy of the fourteen cases analyzed in this book? Did they help clarify the issues of Japanese organizational and individual responsibility for war crimes, or did they rather confuse us by offering diverse and at times mutually conflicting decisions? Above all, what benefit is there to unearthing the records of historical war crimes trials, and that is, after the passage of seven decades since the end of World War II? Does such exploration help generate new knowledge about the war and the history of international criminal justice? Or does it only reveal inconvenient truths about Japanese wartime military violence and shortcomings of Allied justice, thereby reopening old wounds rather than bringing closure to them?

It is difficult to produce definitive answers to any of these questions, given the limited scope of analysis of this book. Nonetheless, one can still generate tentative assessments based on research done thus far. Let us consider first the nature of justice rendered at the Allied war crimes trials in general. It should be stated at the outset that none of these trials is free from accusations of victor's justice insofar as they were (1) planned and carried out by victor nations; (2) to prosecute the members of the vanquished nation alone; (3) for select instances of war crimes in accordance with the victor nations' logic of priorities and expediencies. The accusations of victor's justice may be raised also on the basis of information – offered by convicted war criminals themselves and their defense lawyers in memoirs, letters, farewell notes, and so on[1] – (1) that the trials generally suffered from biases, and at times incompetence of, the judges, prosecutors, court-appointed defense counsel, and court interpreters; (2) that there were cases of misidentification of accused persons; (3) that the court proceedings were commonly of summary nature; (4) that the accused were poorly advised and poorly fed to the point of undercutting their ability to defend themselves in the courtroom; and (5) that the Allied guards at prison facilities habitually inflicted vicious, vengeful violence against war crimes suspects pending trial, convicted war criminals, and even death-row inmates. All these accusations must be fully investigated and squarely taken into account as one seeks to reach a conclusive assessment of the Allied war crimes program as a whole.

Focusing more specifically on the quality of justice at the Anglo-American war crimes trials, it has already been pointed out that the Anglo-American courts in this region are subject to criticism for denying to the Japanese accused the due-process protection that their own servicemen were entitled to under their respective military justice systems, and for having done so in palpable violation of the Geneva Prisoner-of-War Convention of 1929. (See the Introduction.) This criticism may be tempered, of course, when one takes into consideration the fact that the principle of procedural fairness was hardly respected in prewar and wartime Japanese criminal justice systems.[2] As briefly discussed in the Introduction, even those Japanese defense lawyers who were critical of war crimes trials spoke approvingly of the Allied authorities' fair-trial practices, such as, rights to counsel and public hearings. These kinds of procedural fairness were not widely recognized in prewar and wartime Japan. The Allied war crimes trials may be considered as a step forward in the right direction in this regard. These trials potentially served as practical lessons on fair-trial practices, too, at the very moment when the Allied occupation authorities were carrying out an overhaul of the Japanese judiciary and law-enforcement organizations.[3] But insofar as the postwar Allied war crimes trials were meant as venues to showcase the *Allied* justice and not that of the Japanese, criticisms of victor's justice are not without merit.

It would be hasty, however, if one were to raise the criticism of procedural unfairness to the Anglo-American war crimes trials in toto. This book has shown that the types of fair-trial protection the courts accorded to the accused varied greatly from one case to another depending on (a) timing, (b) political context, and (c) competence of the prosecutors, the defense, and the judges serving the courts. By illustration, the Yamashita Trial, the Honma Trial, and the Kuroda Trial can be understood as a representative range of diverse ways in which the courts dealt with the issues of procedural fairness (Chapter 1). It has been seen in the case of the former two that, in a rush to showcase American justice to the Philippine public, the U.S. military commissions denied to both accused a sufficient time to prepare or present their respective cases. With the Yamashita Trial, the U.S. military commission took the additional trouble of delivering its decision – of all possible days – on December 7, 1945, thus making a symbolic gesture of avenging the Pearl Harbor attack. This type of choreographing might have been to the liking of Gen. Douglas MacArthur, the convening authority of the U.S. military commissions in this theater, but it was not the best public-relations choice given its obvious political overtone. Moreover, and as has already been seen, the two cases came under scathing criticism of two American judges – Justices Murphy and Rutledge – shortly after they were argued at the U.S. Supreme Court for leave to file habeas corpus petitions. Procedural shortcomings and other problems with legal and factual findings at these trials continue to cast a dark shadow over the history of U.S. military justice. The Philippine court for the trial of Kuroda, meanwhile, took far greater care than its American predecessors in ensuring that the accused had a fair opportunity to make his case in the courtroom. The relative exemplary conduct of the Philippine court merits appreciation, especially given the brief history of the Philippine nation's criminal justice in the postindependence era, and given the fact that the Philippine war crimes courts were bound by practically the same regulations as the ones applicable to the U.S. military commissions. As a side note, Kuroda was probably sincere when he expressed at the end of the trial his "deepest respect and admiration to the members of the Honorable Commission who conducted this trial not only with patience and tolerance but also with impartiality."[4]

The Tamura Trial and the Toyoda Trial represent other contrasting examples as to how differently the Allied judges acted on the principle of procedural fairness. In the case of the Tamura Trial (Chapter 2), the plea agreement that the law member of the tribunal is believed to have reached with the accused served to undercut the trial's integrity. The prosecution did make a valid case against the accused, and Tamura was found guilty presumably on sound legal and factual grounds. Nonetheless, the uncommonly light penalty of eight years of hard labor is inexplicable unless one gives credence to anecdotal evidence of procedural irregularity. The quality of procedural fairness at the Toyoda Trial was an entirely different affair (Chapter 6). A team of highly competent lawyers assisted the accused to ensure equality of arms between the prosecution and the defense. The Toyoda Tribunal, for its part, took great care to allow both parties to make their respective cases in full while taking stern positions on procedural misconduct at its or other courtrooms. The defense ultimately prevailed, earning a rare instance of acquittal for the accused in a high-profile command-responsibility trial when in most such cases, the verdict was guilty.

If the nature of Allied justice is to be evaluated from the perspective of victims of wartime Japanese military violence, one may reach other kinds of conclusion. The Allied war crimes trials took on the appearance of justice *in the service of victor nations* for several reasons that are already pointed out, but many of them also took on the characteristics of justice *on behalf of victims of atrocity* because of the types of offense that were brought to the attention of the Allied courts. It has been shown, for instance, that significant portions of the criminal accusations made at the Yamashita Trial, the Honma Trial, and the Kuroda Trial (Chapter 1); the Kudō Trial (Chapter 3); and the Ichikawa Trial and the Nishimura Trial (Chapter 5) concerned massacre, rape, torture, forced labor, and other types of mass atrocity committed by Japanese servicemen against innumerable unarmed civilians in occupied territories – men, women, and children of diverse age, race, and ethnicity – in the Philippines, Burma, Thailand, and Singapore. Similarly, four of the command-responsibility trials held at the Australian Rabaul courtroom brought to light systematic mass deportation and forced labor that the Japanese military authorities at the highest level planned and carried out against thousands of former Chinese combatants, Chinese civilians, Indian prisoners of war, and Indonesian *heihos*. Had it not been for these trials, the Japanese use of Asian work parties in the South Pacific – and many atrocities resulting therefrom – might have gone undocumented and largely forgotten, just the way Mohan Singh, the co-originator of the INA movement, feared that these cases already were (Chapter 4). Admittedly, not all trials were entirely successful in delivering the kinds of justice sought for or desired by victims of atrocity, as exemplified in the Nishimura Trial at the U.K. Singapore court (whose sentences came under criticism from the local Singapore citizens for being too lenient – see Chapter 5). Nevertheless, the case studies in this book show that the Allied war crimes trials offered unique opportunities for survivors of wartime atrocity to take part in war crimes documentation and seek retributive justice against responsible individuals. With respect to the Philippine war crimes trials, members of the local community took ownership of the trials at a heightened level, as they participated not only as witnesses and spectators but also as judges, prosecutors, and even as defense lawyers.

Turning now to the question as to how one might assess the jurisprudential legacy of the Allied war crimes trials, the sampling in this book is again too small to offer any satisfactory answer. Nevertheless, some tentative conclusions may be drawn from the case studies for future researchers' consideration. Generally speaking, it *is* a rather complicated task to try discerning jurisprudence that arises from the post-WWII Allied war crimes trials in this region, given the fact that the courts usually produced no reasoned judgments. It was because regulations governing the trials did not require the production of judgments – as opposed to the pronouncement of the verdicts and the sentences, which was required. A relatively large number of courts did express their opinions in writing in the cases analyzed in this book. Even so, the courts that produced judgments were limited to four out of fourteen cases: at the trials of Yamashita, Kuroda, Ichikawa, and Toyoda. Of these, the judgments for the Yamashita Trial and the Ichikawa Trial were so short – amounting to five and ten pages respectively – that they could barely expound on finer points of law or fact that supported the verdicts. In the absence of reasoned judgments in most cases, one may have to settle for a speculative conclusion rather than a definitive one when trying to determine the jurisprudential legacy of the Allied war crimes trials. Well-grounded conclusion *can* be reached, however, if one (a) carries out an exhaustive study of the Allied war crimes program as a whole; (b) compares cases to discern general patterns of the courts' decisions; and (c) refers back to the transcripts of court proceedings, court exhibits, and reviewing authorities' reports to determine the grounds of the courts' verdicts and sentences.

To limit our comments on case studies in this book, a couple of common doctrinal challenges can be identified as having arisen from the selection. One of them was the difficulty of determining the applicable criteria of individual responsibility in relation to command-responsibility trials, viz. those cases where a military commander was charged with the failure to fulfill his duty to control subordinate troops. It has been seen that the methods of proof the prosecuting agencies adopted were generally similar but also had slight variations. When it came to judicial decisions reached by the courts, *they varied greatly*. Specifically, the U.S. military commission convicted Yamashita on grounds of what amounted to strict liability. The Australian court at Rabaul followed suit even though the judge advocate repeatedly advised that the Yamashita case be treated as more a cautionary tale than a model to emulate (Chapter 4). Meanwhile, the prosecuting agencies for the trials of Honma and Kuroda seemed to distance themselves from the Yamashita precedent by insisting that their own cases were built on evidence of the accused's *knowledge* and not necessarily on strict liability. It is difficult to determine the court's exact position on this matter in the case of Honma, as the court produced no judgment. In the case of Kuroda, however, the court articulated the views that proof of knowledge was required to convict the accused. The judgment thus read in part: "Could we be so simple-minded as to believe that the accused in the comfort of his Manila headquarters was not aware, directly or indirectly, of the occurrence of these atrocities throughout the Philippines?"[5] The tribunal for the Toyoda Trial held a similar position and explained its rationale in some detail. Interestingly enough, the Toyoda Tribunal claimed to build its decision on historical precedents *including* the Yamashita Trial, but the actual criteria of responsibility it set out effectively rejected the principle of strict liability (Chapter 6).

Another doctrinal issue over which the Allied courts puzzled concerned the gap between the theoretical and actual workings of command authority in the Japanese military organizations. The Banno Trial (Chapter 3) is a revelatory case in this regard. It has been shown that his subordinates hardly recognized his authority as commander of prisoner-of-war administration and that they did not even bother to greet him or to try cleaning up the prisoner-of-war camps during his tours of inspection. Those Allied prisoners of war who testified against him readily agreed that Banno received little respect from his subordinates. The ones who exercised actual control over the camps were lower-ranking individuals, including *gunzoku*s, civilians attached to the Imperial Japanese Army with no military rank. One *gunzoku* by the name of Toyoyama was singled out at the Banno Trial as having a menacing presence, as he habitually beat prisoners of war with a golf club or a bamboo stick and "made a practice of walking round the camp like a little god" (Chapter 3). Another kind of contradictory relationship between superior and subordinate officers has been pointed out in connection with the Itsuki Trial, the case briefly discussed at the opening segment of Chapter 5. According to the personal recollection of the trial by Capt. Sumi Toyosaburō (a co-accused), Lt. Gen. Itsuki was commanding officer of the Japanese occupation forces at Car Nicobar but that the one who *in fact* exercised control over troops was his subordinate and chief of staff, Lt. Col. Saitō. Sumi maintained that this type of inversion of authority between superior and subordinate officers was commonplace in the Japanese military, since the ones who rose to staff-officer positions usually did so by merit, while command positions could be attained by sheer seniority. The *kenpeitai* alumni association made a related comment concerning Ōishi, the *kenpeitai* chief of the 25th Army in occupied Singapore. While faulting Ōishi for failing to resist unreasonable demands from the Army, the *kenpeitai* alumni association noted that it would have been difficult for Ōishi to stand up against Tsuji, a powerful staff officer in the 25th Army Headquarters, who did the actual planning and implementation of the Singapore Massacre (Chapter 5). If inversion of authority of this nature was indeed pervasive in the Imperial Japanese Army, however, the case of the Katō Trial at the Australian Rabaul proceedings offered a counterexample. Gen. Imamura, in this instance, vigorously defended the accused, testifying that "I never allowed Lt-Gen KATO, chief of staff[,] or any other staff to issue orders or instructions to any units of the Army Group as proxy for me at their own will nor to issue their own orders or instructions to them" (Chapter 4).

These three examples – the Banno Trial, the Itsuki Trial, and the Katō Trial – alert us that proof of the formal structure of the Japanese military chain of command may be insufficient to resolve the issues of individual responsibility, given the possibility that the inversion of superior-subordinate relations may have occurred. What is more, in Japan in the 1920s and the 1930s, there were many ambitious midranking army and navy officers as well as civilian officials who are known to have taken unauthorized actions – made independently of their superiors in the central government or the military high command – to instigate the invasion of Manchuria and to escalate it into all-out war against China. Given this particular historical context of Japan in the interwar period and beyond, it is vital that one inquire into not only the *formal* command structure but also the *actual* workings of superior-subordinate relations. Only then can one begin to develop much more satisfactory conceptual tools to determine criminal liability of individual Japanese for war crimes.

Another conundrum the Allied courts faced in some of the case studies concerned alleged peculiarities in the distribution of command authority in the Japanese military organizations. As one might recall, this issue has been raised as early as at the Yamashita Trial relative to personnel issues. The defense pointed out that Yamashita did not have the power to remove the underperforming *kenpeitai* chief, Nagahama, and that he instead had to seek approval from his military superiors in the Southern Army and at Tokyo. Kuroda similarly argued that his authority relative to handling of prisoners of war was a limited kind. He specifically pointed out that the Japanese army regulations vested a military commander with supervisory authority only and *not* the authority to exercise direct control over prisoner-of-war administration. The latter authority instead rested with the army minister. Yet having argued so, the defense in both cases stopped short of providing full documentation of alleged peculiarities of the Japanese army organizations. The courts, in turn, appear to have given no serious consideration to the matter. The situation was entirely different at the Toyoda Trial, where the defense made the uniqueness of the Japanese command structure the centerpiece of its case. Voluminous oral and documentary evidence by the defense brought to light the institutional propensity of the Imperial Japanese Navy for narrowing, compartmentalizing, and redistributing different types of command authority in the apparent effort to make the Japanese naval operations ever smarter, leaner, and more agile while ensuring that the integrity of command authority in the person of the Emperor would remain intact. If one is to give credence to the defense case at the Toyoda Trial, it raises new questions as to whether the corresponding institutional propensity might have existed in the Imperial Japanese Army, and if it did, whether such a possibility would require us to review afresh all the evidence submitted at command-responsibility trials involving army commanders.

Let us finally turn to the question as to what purpose it serves to unearth the records of post-WWII Allied war crimes trials just when we are marking the seventieth anniversary of the end of World War II. Why explore these historical trials at this late stage? Isn't it bound to reveal inconvenient truths about wartime Japanese military violence on the one hand, and shortcomings of Allied justice on the other? Doesn't such exploration merely reopen old wounds or, worse still, give rise to new animosities among the people of former foes? This author's response to these questions is threefold. First, insofar as World War II is recognized as a major historical event worthy of collective remembrance, historical inquiry should continue in order for one to have a better understanding of its historical reality and its present-day relevance. Second, the records of Allied war crimes trials constitute a uniquely rich body of oral and documentary history of World War II, and yet they have been underutilized to date. This author believes that investigating and interpreting these sources is key to advancing our knowledge of the war and to developing ever more meaningful ways of remembering this watershed moment in the modern history of humanity. Third, this author does not believe that probing into the trial records is about reopening old wounds – although some might think that way – but rather that such exploration offers an opportunity to learn from our predecessors about the challenges one faces when striving to achieve justice in the wake of mass atrocity. Put it differently, inquiring into these historical trials is about taking ownership of our historical heritage of war crimes prosecutions, and drawing lessons from them. Such endeavor will make it possible for one to build on it and strengthen one's commitment in the twenty-first century to furthering the principle of justice, accountability, and the rule of law.

The foregoing three-pronged answer aside, this author has another point to make to underscore the importance of continuing the research of the post-WWII Allied Pacific-area war crimes trials, namely: decades-long difficulties that researchers have had in accessing the trial records, and the limited scope of existing studies resulting therefrom. The origin of this particular problem can be traced back to the time of the Allied war crimes program. The Allied authorities were keen to hold the trials in public, but they indicated no interest when it came to sharing the trial records with the Japanese. The Allied governments transmitted to the Japanese government bare minimum information alone concerning the outcomes of the trials (such as the charges and sentences). They made no other arrangement of, for instance, transferring a duplicate of the trial records, or offering additional detailed updates.[6] If anything, they *positively banned* the accused Japanese war criminals, defense lawyers, or any other Japanese individuals concerned in the trials from taking back home copies of the trial records. Anyone who attempted to do so was subject to having them confiscated. (A few exceptions were the Australian Manus trials and the U.S. Navy trials at Guam, where such restrictions did not apply.[7]) Some information about the progress of the trials trickled out by way of limited news reporting and by word of mouth. But there was no other reliable source to inform the Japanese public contemporaneously as to what kinds of justice were being meted out against its own people at the special Allied courtrooms.[8]

As if to fill in the information void, first-person accounts of the trial experiences by individual convicted war criminals, defense lawyers, and Japanese prison chaplains began appearing in print as early as 1948, and they multiplied by the time the Allied occupation of Japan ended in 1952. A prison diary kept by Kawamura Saburō – one of the accused in the Singapore Massacre case – was one such example. It was printed under the title, *Jūsan kaidan o agaru: senpan shokeisha no kiroku* (Going up the thirteen steps: Records of an executed war criminal) (1952). A number of other personal accounts were also published contemporaneously to offer insider views of the trials. The bulk of publications in early years contained letters, diaries, memoirs, and farewell notes by those who had been convicted of war crimes and who were already executed.[9] The effort to get the voices of the dead heard culminated in the publication in 1953 of *Seiki no isho* (The will of the century). A 740-page magnum opus of sorts, this volume contained in fine print 701 pieces of wills, memoirs, essays, poems, letters, and various other writings of executed war criminals. *Seiki no isho* was put together at the initiative of volunteers among war criminals serving sentences at Sugamo Prison in Tokyo and with cooperation from bereaved families.[10] This publication was not a monolith that spoke in one voice. However, its overall effect was to humanize the convicted war criminals and to sanctify the last words from the departed souls, regardless of the nature of charges or findings the Allied authorities made against them.[11]

If the primary purpose of *Seiki no isho* and related publications was to honor the dead war criminals, a separate line of publications was introduced concurrently to inform the Japanese public of injustices done to Japanese nationals in the hands of Allied authorities. The organization that spearheaded this effort was the nine-member Sugamo Legal Affairs Committee (*Sugamo hōmu iinkai*), established by inmates serving sentences at Sugamo Prison. This committee collected as much oral history of the Allied war crimes trials as possible from fellow war criminals and produced *Senpan saiban no jissō* (Reality of war crimes trials). A hefty 700-page publication, this volume gave detailed accounts of abusive treatment that the Allied personnel meted out to individual war criminals over the course of apprehension, investigation, trial, and imprisonment.[12] It also included a chapter on predicaments of the family members of war criminals, who were made to live with stigma as personal relations of war criminals.[13] Characteristically, all information contained in this publication was based entirely on the memories of individual war criminals, because the Sugamo inmates had "not even a single piece of trial record, the [defense] counter evidence, materials on operations, logs of directives, or maps."[14] *Senpan saiban no jissō* nonetheless became a critical source material, and along with *Seiki no isho*, it came to set the foundation of the Japanese people's knowledge of the Allied war crimes trials.[15] These publications constitute a rich body of social and cultural history of the trials, and their significance as such should not be discounted. In the absence of corroborative documentary source materials and specifically the trial records, however, they can elucidate the historical reality of Allied war crimes prosecutions only in part and from the limited perspectives of Japanese accused only.[16]

The Japanese government authorities, for their part, tried to take their own initiatives to address the information void. Toyoda Kumao was a former high-ranking navy officer and one of the original members of the war crimes research section in the Second Demobilization Bureau (the former Navy Ministry), which had been responsible for assisting the postwar Japanese government with investigation and administrative tasks in connection with the Allied war crimes trials. He and his army counterpart in the First Demobilization

Bureau (the former Army Ministry) came to worry that they "had no trial records in their possession" and that "unless some steps were taken, there would be a hole in the important period of history [*jūyō na rekishi no ichijiki ga ketsuraku*]."[17] They were generally critical of Allied war crimes prosecutions, but they regarded the trial records as unique historical sources that deserved preservation for posterity. Further discussions and administrative actions culminated in the establishment on May 15, 1958, of the Judiciary and Legislation Investigation Bureau (*shihō hōsei chōsabu*) under the Secretariat of the Ministry of Legal Affairs. This bureau thereafter worked on a multiyear project to collect as many trial records as possible for archival purposes.[18]

A total of 18 years were spent on building the new collection. The Research Bureau was not successful in securing copies of trial records from individual Allied governments, because the latter proved unwilling to cooperate, with the exception of the Philippines and France. The Philippine government agreed to provide duplicates of the records of all Manila proceedings. A total of 160,000 pages of Manila trial records came into possession of the Ministry of Legal Affairs by 1964. As for the French government, its cooperation was limited to sharing copies of charge sheets and judgments.[19] Research and fieldwork within Japan, meanwhile, bore fruits. The members of the Research Bureau found out that regardless of the Allied authorities' policies prohibiting retention of personal copies, quite a few individual Japanese managed to smuggle back parts of the trial records and were prepared to turn them over to the Ministry of Legal Affairs. Moreover, Toyoda Kumao and his army counterpart, Inoue Tadao, were able to carry out interviews with as many as 700 individuals – who consisted of former accused and defense lawyers in the main – and include the records of interviews in the collection.[20] The project was brought to completion in 1973.

Quite unfortunately, the outcome of painstaking fieldwork by Toyoda, Inoue, and their associates was sealed and kept out of public view for more than three decades, apparently out of consideration for the privacy of convicted war criminals and their families.[21] One needed to wait until 1999 when the entire set was transferred to the National Archives of Japan, Tokyo, to be considered for possible declassification. After initial years of seeming hesitation, the Japanese national archives began taking steps to declassify the collection.[22] Varying degrees of restriction still apply, such as redaction of names of accused, and at times, even the names of victims. But the accessibility of the collection has improved markedly in the last half-decade. The increasing openness of the Japanese archives is presently spurring research interest among historians of Asia in utilizing these new sources.

Archival situations outside Japan have also changed for the better in the intervening decades. The American, Australian, and British national archives declassified the entirety of their trial records in the mid-1970s, and the records are accessible to public ever since. The National Diet Library at Tokyo, Japan, shortly acquired from the U.S. archives a duplicate of the entire American and Philippine war crimes trial records as well as the Tamura and Toyoda proceedings, so that they could be made readily accessible to the Japanese public. These records are presently either on microfiche or on microfilm, and are open to the public at *kensei shiryō shitsu* (the Constitutional Government Source Room) at the Diet Library, irrespective of the declassification status of duplicate materials in possession of the National Archives of Japan.[23] Meanwhile, the National Archives of Australia has taken steps to radically improve accessibility to the records of Australian war crimes trials; they scanned and uploaded the entire set to the archives' Web site.[24] Australia thus far is the only former Allied nation to disclose its entire trial records online. This speaks not only to the Australian archives' commitment to openness and transparency but also the great importance Australia attaches to promoting historical studies of war crimes trials.[25]

The impact of declassified trial records in these countries has been felt profoundly since the late 1970s in Japan, where existing oral-history materials had not been able to satisfy a wide range of research needs, interests, and demands. Kamisaka Fuyuko, an independent researcher and a prolific writer, emerged as a pioneer, as she made extensive use of the U.S. archival records to reconstruct the lives of individual war criminals and published her research outcomes in multiple books.[26] Other independent researchers followed suit although their research scope was generally limited to single cases.[27] Professional historians such as Utsumi Aiko, Hayashi Hirofumi, and Nagai Hitoshi took new research initiatives, too, using declassified trial records. (Some examples of their research pieces have been discussed in this book.) The fruits of research by these pioneers came to set new standards in Japanese scholarship of war crimes trials. Their works continue to define war crimes studies in Japan to this day.

In sum, with a vast corpus of trial records having become accessible within and outside Japan, the studies of post-WWII Allied war crimes trials presently hold out an enormous research potential for the future. These trials are an "old" topic, but it is still a young field that awaits new lines of investigation, interpretation, and assessment. Put differently, *now* is the good time to carry out a systematic analysis of these varied sources and herein lies the importance of carrying out the studies of historical war crimes trials today. It remains to be seen as to how and when all of the trial records can be declassified and made accessible, including those of Chinese, Dutch, French, and Soviet trials. But at least this much is clear: researchers today are vastly better positioned to undertake a comprehensive study of the Allied war crimes trials than their predecessors from a generation or two earlier. The major challenge for them is no longer to fill in the information void the way the Japanese people and their government had to in earlier decades. Rather, present-day researchers are tasked with analyzing, interpreting, and assessing the trial records they now have access to, *so that* they can determine the continuing relevance of these historical trials to deepening our understanding of World War II, war crimes, and the issues of justice, responsibility, and the rule of law in the present century. Long and arduous research lies ahead, but this author believes that the payoff is sufficiently great to make the tasks of analyzing, interpreting, and assessing these records rewarding.

This book now rests its case with the hope that it has shown satisfactorily by way of case studies the breadth, depth, and complexity of the post-WWII Allied war crimes trials. If it has managed to persuade some of its readers into joining this field, I shall say, "Welcome aboard."

Notes

SPECIAL SYMBOLS USED IN THE NOTES

When page numbers in the transcripts of court proceedings are referred to in this book, they are preceded by "R." For example, "Exhibit 3: Statement of Gen. Imamura Hitoshi," p. 3, Imamura Trial, R37," means page 3 within "Exhibit 3: Statement of Gen. Imamura Hitoshi," introduced at page 37 of the transcripts of court proceedings of the Imamura Trial. In the case of the **British trial records,** a separate single sequential pagination is often applied (presumably by clerical staff of the Allied war crime courts) to mark up all the documents contained in one case folder *in addition to* the sequential pagination already used in the transcripts of court proceedings. I make use of the former sequential pagination when citing those documents that are not incorporated into the transcripts of court proceedings (such as charge sheets, review reports, and abstracts of evidence). In such instances, I indicate the sequential page number by attaching the prefix "SP." For example, "'Charge Sheet,' Ishida Trial, SP8–10," means the charge sheet appearing between pages 8 and 10 of the single sequential pagination applied in the case file of the Ishida Trial. Some court exhibits use the symbol § to mark paragraph numbers. In such cases, the paragraph numbers are indicated in the notes to the text, using this symbol. For example, "'Exhibit DT: Affidavit of Toyoda Soemu,' p. 7, §12, Toyoda Trial, R4058," means page 7, paragraph 12, in "Exhibit DT: Affidavit of Toyoda Soemu," introduced at page 4058 of the transcripts of court proceedings at the Toyoda Trial.

SHORT CITATIONS

Short citations of published sources are handled in the usual fashion. For example, "A. Frank Reel, *The Case of General Yamashita*, (Chicago, IL: University of Chicago Press, 1949)" becomes "Reel, *Case of General Yamashita*."

When court exhibits are cited on more than one occasion, all subsequent citations appear in shortened form. By illustration, the first citation of a court exhibit looks like this: "'Exhibit I: Report on Employment of War Prisoners in SIAM-BURMA Railway,' Ishida Trial, R8." All subsequent citations of the same exhibit will appear as "Exhibit I, p. #, Ishida Trial." The number following "p." is the page number within the exhibit. Some court exhibits are compilations of documents, such as "Exhibit 12: Laws, Rules, and Regulations Pertaining to Prisoners of War" that was introduced at the Tamura Trial (discussed in Chapter 2). Short citations for this type of court exhibits retain in parentheses the name of a document referred to *within* the exhibit. By illustration, short citations of Exhibit 12 can look like this: "Exhibit 12, p. 3 ('Organization of the Prisoner of War Information Bureau, Imperial Ordinance No. 1246, December 27, 1941'), Tamura Trial"; or like this: "Exhibit 12, p. 30 ('Disposal of Prisoners of War, Army Ministry Notification, Asia, Confidential, No. 1456'), Tamura Trial." Both citations refer to the same exhibit, but specify different elements, viz., a document titled "Organization of the Prisoner of War Information Bureau" on the one hand, and one titled "Disposal of Prisoners of War" on the other. In both instances, the number following "p." is the page number within the exhibit.

INTRODUCTION

1. This conference resulted in the publication of Yuki Tanaka, Tim L. H. McCormack, and Gerry Simpson, eds., _Beyond Victor's Justice? The Tokyo War Crimes Trial Revisited_, International Humanitarian Law Series (Leiden, Netherlands: Martinus Nijhoff, 2010).

2. Representative publications that offer accounts of the Pacific War and that are readily accessible to general readers include, but are not limited to, the following: John Toland, _The Rising Sun: The Decline and Fall of the Japanese Empire, 1936–1945_ (New York, NY: Random House, 1970); John Costello, _The Pacific War: 1941–1945_ (New York, NY: Rawson, Wade, 1981); Ronald Specter, _Eagle against the Sun: The American War with Japan_ (New York, NY: Free Press, 1985); and William B. Hopkins, _The Pacific War: The Strategy, Politics, and Players That Won the War_ (Minneapolis, MN: Zenith Press, 2008).

3. There is voluminous Japanese-language historical literature that offers syntheses of war, war crimes, and problems associated with Japanese colonialism during World War II in the Asia-Pacific region. Classic examples are the following: Ienaga Saburō, _Taiheiyō sensō_ [The Pacific War] (Tokyo: Iwanami shoten, 1968); Rekishigaku kenkyūkai [History Research Association], ed., _Taiheiyō sensōshi_ [The history of the Pacific War], 6 vols. (Tokyo: Aoki shoten, 1973); Eguchi Keiichi, _Jūgonen sensō shōshi_ [A concise history of the Fifteen-Year War] (Tokyo: Aoki shoten, 1986); and Fujiwara Akira and Imai Seiichi, eds., _Jūgonen sensōshi_ [The history of the Fifteen-Year War], 4 vols. (Tokyo: Aoki shoten, 1988). Ienaga's _Taiheiyō sensō_ is available in English translation: Ienaga Saburō, _The Pacific War, 1931–1945: A Critical Perspective on Japan's Role in World War II_, trans. Frank Baldwin (New York, NY: Pantheon Books, 1978).

4. Other articles in which Cohen explores jurisprudence of post-WWII war crimes trials are the following: "Bureaucracy, Justice, and Collective Responsibility in the World War II War Crimes Trials," _Rechtshistorisches Journal_ [The journal of legal history]18 (1999), pp. 313–42; "Military Justice from WWII to Guantanamo: Fair Trials, Judicial Murder, and International Standards in WWII Crimes Trials in Asia," in _Summa Dieter Simon zum 70. Geburtstag_, ed. Rainer Maria Kiesow, Regina Ogorek, and Spiros Simitis (Frankfurt am Main, Germany: Vittorio Klostermann, 2005), pp. 59–80; "The Singapore War Crimes Trials and Their Relevance Today," _Singapore Law Review_ 31 (2013), pp. 1–38; "Weibo zhanzhenzui panjue caoan: Dongjing shenpan panjue de lingyi shijiao" [An alternative Tokyo Judgment: The Draft Webb Judgment on war crimes], in _2013 Dongjing shenpan xueshu taolunhui lunji_ [The compilation of essays from the symposium on the Tokyo Trial] (Shanghai, China: Shanghai jiaotong daxue chubanshe, in press); and "The Historiography of the Historical Foundations of Theories of Responsibility in International Criminal Law," in _Historical Origins of International Criminal Law_, vol. 1, ed. Morten Bergsmo, Cheah Wui Ling, and Yi Ping (New York, NY: Torkel Opsahl Academic EPublisher, in press).

5. "Japanese Instrument of Surrender," in _Documents on the Tokyo International Military Tribunal: Charter, Indictment and Judgments_, ed. Neil Boister and Robert Cryer (Oxford, New York: Oxford University Press, 2008), p. 3.

6. Article 10 of the "Potsdam Declaration (Proclamation Defining Terms for Japanese Surrender, 26 July, 1945)," in Boister and Cryer, *Documents on the Tokyo International Military Tribunal*, pp. 1–2.
7. India and the Philippines received invitation to take part in the Tokyo Trial after the establishment of the International Military Tribunal for the Far East.
8. For discussion of how the two additional international proceedings were planned and held in Tokyo, see Yuma Totani, *The Tokyo War Crimes Trial: The Pursuit of Justice in the Wake of World War II* (Cambridge, MA: Harvard University Asia Center, 2008), pp. 69–77. The two international proceedings are also known as the "GHQ Trials" and alternatively as the "Maru-no-uchi Trials" in the Japanese-language scholarship. The abbreviation "GHQ" refers to the general headquarters of the convening authority, the Supreme Commander for the Allied Powers, while the word "Maru-no-uchi" refers to the name of the district at which the trials were held. The Toyoda Trial is additionally known as the "Aoyama Trial" due to subsequent relocation of the courtroom to the Aoyama district in Tokyo. Tōkyō saiban handobukku henshū iinkai [The Tokyo Trial Handbook Compilation Committee], ed., *Tōkyō saiban handobukku* [The Tokyo Trial handbook] (Tokyo: Aoki shoten, 1989), pp. 76–8.
9. "Special Orders No. 1, General Headquarters, Supreme Commander for the Allied Powers (October 27, 1948)." This document is included in "Records of the Trial of Accused War Criminal Hiroshi Tamura, Tried by a Military Tribunal Appointed by the Supreme Commander of the Allied Powers, Tokyo, Japan, 1948–1949" (College Park, MD: National Archives and Records Administration [NARA hereafter]), microfilm, M1728, 3 rolls. The same document is contained in "Records of the Trial of Accused War Criminal Soemu Toyoda, Tried by a Military Tribunal Appointed by the Supreme Commander of the Allied Powers, Tokyo, Japan, 1948–1949" (College Park, MD: NARA), microfilm, M1729, 7 rolls.
10. Hōmu daijin kanbō shihō hōsei chōsabu [The Judiciary and Legislation Investigation Bureau, Secretariat of the Ministry of Legal Affairs], ed., *Sensō hanzai saiban gaishiyō* [A concise historical overview of war crimes trials] (August 1973), Hōmu-Hei-11-4B-23-6334, National Archives of Japan, p. 266. See also Tōkyō saiban handobukku henshū iinkai, *Tōkyō saiban handobukku*, pp. 219–24. There are differences in the data gathered by the Japanese government (the Ministry of Legal Affairs) and the records kept by individual Allied governments. The numbers provided in this book are based on the Japanese data alone and are not necessarily definitive figures. The difficulty of determining the exact numbers of trials and accused is discussed in Philip R. Piccigallo, *The Japanese on Trial: Allied War Crimes Operations in the East, 1945–1951* (Austin: University of Texas Press, 1979), pp. 263–5; and Hayashi Hirofumi, *BC-kyū senpan saiban* [Class BC war crimes trials] (Tokyo: Iwanami shoten, 2005), pp. 61–2. For the information regarding the locations of Allied war crimes trials, see Hayashi, *BC-kyū senpan saiban*, pp. 62–3.
11. For related discussion, see Totani, *Tokyo War Crimes Trial*, pp. 22–3.
12. For the summary of the American war crimes trials held at Yokohama and Manila, see "History of Nonmilitary Activities of the Occupation of Japan: Trials of Class 'B' and 'C' War Criminals," in SCAP Monograph Drafts, 1945–1951, entry UD

1598, RG 331, SCAP, Civil Property Custodian, Legal Section, Box 3676, NARA. For a thematic analysis of the U.S. Yokohama trials, see Yokohama bengoshikai [Yokohama Bar Association], *Hōtei no seijōki: BC-kyū senpan Yokohama saiban no kiroku* [The Stars and Stripes in the courtroom: Records of Class BC war crimes trials at Yokohama] (Tokyo: Nihon hyōronsha, 2004).

13. For an authoritative study of the British war crimes trials, see Hayashi Hiro-fumi, *Sabakareta sensō hanzai: Igirisu no tai-Nichi senpan saiban* [War crimes tried: The British war crimes trials against the Japanese] (Tokyo: Iwanami sho-ten, 1998).

14. For studies of the Australian war crimes program, see the following: Caroline Pappas, "Law and Politics: Australia's War Crimes Trials in the Pacific, 1943–1961," PhD diss., University of New South Wales, 1998; Michael Carrel, "Australia's Prosecution of Japanese War Criminals," PhD diss., University of Melbourne, 2005; Dean Aszkielowicz, "After the Surrender: Australia and the Japanese Class B and C War Criminals, 1945–1958," PhD diss., Murdoch University, 2013; and D. C .S. Sissons, "The Australian War Crimes Trials and Investigations (1942–51)," posted at the Web site of the War Crimes Studies Center at the University of California, Berkeley, accessed December 17, 2007, http://www.ocf.berkeley.edu/~changmin/documents/Sissons%20Final%20 War%20Crimes%20Text%2018-3-06.pdf.

    For a definitive study of the Australian war crimes trials, refer to the *The Australian War Crimes Trials Law Reports Series, 1945–51* (forthcoming), edited by Narrelle Morris and Timothy L. H. McCormack, and a supplementary thematic volume, *Australia's War Crimes Trials, 1945–51* (in press), edited by Georgina Fitzpatrick, Timothy L. H. McCormack, and Narrelle Morris.

15. For comprehensive studies of the Philippine trials, see Nagai Hitoshi, *Firipin to tai-Nichi senpan saiban, 1945–1953* [The Philippines and war crimes trials against the Japanese, 1945–1953] (Tokyo: Iwanami shoten, 2010); Nagai Hitoshi, *Firipin BC-kyū senpan saiban* [Philippine Class BC war crimes trials] (Tokyo: Kōdansha, 2013); and Sharon Chamberlain, "Justice and Reconciliation: Postwar Philippine Trials of Japanese War Criminals in History and Memory," PhD diss., George Washington University, 2010.

16. For studies of the Chinese war crimes trials, see Ikō Toshiya, "Chūgoku kokumin seifu no Nihon shobatsu hōshin no tenkai" [The development of policies on the punishment of Japanese war criminals by the Republic of China], in *Gendai rekishigaku to Nankin jiken* [Studies of modern history and the Nanjing Incident], ed. Kasahara Tokushi and Yoshida Yutaka (Tokyo: Kashiwa shobō, 2006), pp. 94–124; and Iwakawa Takashi, *Kotō no tsuchi to narutomo: BC-kyū senpan saiban* [Even if to become the soil of an isolated island: Class BC war crimes trials] (Tokyo: Kōdansha, 1995), pp. 438–616. For the first book-length study of Chinese trials, see Barak Kushner, *Men to Devils and Devils to Men: Japanese War Crimes and Chinese Justice* (Cambridge, MA: Harvard University Asia Center, 2015).

17. For data concerning convicted war criminals, see Hayashi, *BC-kyū senpan saiban*, pp. 61–2; Tōkyō saiban handobukku henshū iinkai, *Tōkyō saiban handobukku*, p. 219–20.

18. The last Allied war crimes trial in this region ended at the Australian Manus court on April 9, 1951. Tōkyō saiban handobukku henshū iinkai, *Tōkyō saiban handobukku*, p. 222.

19. Iwakawa, *Kotō no tsuchi to narutomo*, p. 621; Hayashi, *BC-kyū senpan saiban*, pp. 112–13. For accounts of trials and incarcerations by the Soviet authorities, see Matsumura Tomokatsu, "Saiban to kangoku" [Trial and detention], in *Saiban, kangoku, bōchō: Soren shūjin seisaku no uramen. senpan, yokuryūsha ga taiken shita repōto* [Trial, detention, espionage: The backstories of the Soviet prisoner policies. Reports on experiences of convicted war criminals and internees] (Tokyo: Nikkan rōdō tsūshinsha, 1958), pp. 3–90; Zenkoku ken'yūkai rengōkai hensan iinkai [The All-Japan Union for the Friends-of-Kenpei Association Compilation Committee], ed., *Nihon kenpei seishi* [The official history of the Japanese military police] (Tokyo: Kenbun shoin, 1976), pp. 1277–84; Satō Ryōichi, *Gyakutai no kiroku* [Records of abusive treatment] (Tokyo: Shio shobō, 1953) pp. 161–5; Kinoshita Hideaki, *Yokuryū seikatsu jūichi-nen: Soren no jissō* [Eleven years of life in internment: Reality of the Soviet Union] (Tokyo: Nikkan kōgyō shinbunsha, 1957), pp. 1–112; Kitazaki Manabu, *Shiberiya no hada* [The skin of Siberia] (Tokyo: Jiyū Ajia sha, 1955), pp. 122–38; and Maeno Shigeru, *Ikeru shikabane: Soren gokusō jūichinen* [Living corpse: Eleven years in Soviet prison] (Tokyo: Shunjūsha, 1961). *Ikeru shikabane* was reprinted as a pocket-size publication in 1979 under the title, *Soren gokusō jūichinen* [Eleven years in Soviet prison], 4 vols. (Tokyo: Kōdansha gakujutsu bunko, 1979).

20. For the Allied policy on the handling of the Japanese emperor as a war criminal, see Totani, *Tokyo War Crimes Trial*, chapter 2.

21. For the record of the Khabarovsk Trial, see *Materials on the Trial of Former Servicemen of the Japanese Army Charged with Manufacturing and Employing Bacteriological Weapons* (Moscow: Foreign Language Publishing House, 1950). For discussion of the Soviet initiative to put the Japanese emperor on trial, see Totani, *Tokyo War Crimes Trial*, pp. 59–62.

22. For a concise account of the People's Trials held by the Communist Chinese, see Adachi Tamenari, "Jinmin saiban" [People's Trials], in *Manshū kenkoku no yume to genjitsu* [Dream and reality in the establishment of the Manchukuoan state], ed. Kokusai zenrin kyōkai [The International Good-Neighbor Society] (Tokyo: Kenkōsha, 1975), pp. 415–22. For a first-person narrative concerning the People's Trials, see Ogawa Hitoo, *Shokei sarenakatta senpan: jinmin saiban no ura de. aru senpan no shuki* [A war criminal not executed: Behind the People's Trials. A memoir of a war criminal] (Tokyo: Nicchū shuppan, 1979).

23. For an overview of the trials held by the Communist Chinese, see Zenkoku ken'yūkai rengōkai hensan iinkai, *Nihon kenpei seishi*, pp. 1284–9; Iwakawa, *Kotō no tsuchi to narutomo*, pp. 541–70; and Toyoda Masayuki, "Chūka jinmin kyōwakoku no senpan saiban" [War crimes trials by the People's Republic of China], two installments, *Kikan sensō sekinin kenkyū* [The report on Japan's war responsibility] 17 (Fall 1997), pp. 67–73; 18 (Winter 1997), pp. 46–53. Those individuals who faced criminal prosecutions at Chinese courts underwent a unique reeducational program in the years preceding the actual trials. The program had a tremendous impact on the accused's understanding of personal guilt and, after repatriation, they came to take the lead in educating the Japanese public about Japanese military violence during the Sino-Japanese armed conflict (1937–1945). For more information on their activities, see Chūgoku kikansha renrakukai [The Association of Soldiers Repatriated from China], ed.,

Kaettekita senpan tachi no kōhansei [The latter half of the lives of repatriated war criminals] (Tokyo: Ryokufū shuppan, 1996).

24. "Netherlands Law Concerning Trials of War Criminals," in *Law Reports of Trials of War Criminals*, ed. United Nations War Crimes Commission, vol. 11 (London, UK: His Majesty's Stationery Office, 1949), pp. 86–110; "Chinese Law Concerning Trials of War Criminals," in *Law Reports of Trials of War Criminals*, vol. 14 (1949), pp. 152–60; and "French Law Concerning Trials of War Criminals by Military Tribunals and by Military Government Courts in the French Zone of Germany," in *Law Reports of Trials of War Criminals*, vol. 3 (1948), pp. 93–102.

25. This author has made use of the lists of country-by-country synopses of war crimes trials, compiled by a research group of the Japanese Ministry of Legal Affairs in the early 1970s and presently deposited at the National Archives of Japan. The research group is known as the Judiciary and Legislation Investigation Bureau, Secretariat of the Ministry of Legal Affairs (Hōmu daijin kanbō shihō hōsei chōsabu). (See the Conclusion for the origin and activities of this group.) Reference information of the synopses is as follows: "Beikoku sensō hanzai saiban gaikenhyō" [The table showing synopses of American war crimes trials], Hōmu-Hei-11-4B-15-7126; "Eikoku sensō hanzai saiban gaikenhyō" [The table showing synopses of British war crimes trials], Hōmu-Hei-11-4B-15-7128; "Gōshū sensō hanzai saiban gaikenhyō" [The table showing synopses of Austra-lian war crimes trials], Hōmu-Hei-11-4A-21-7129; "Waran sensō hanzai saiban gaikenhyō" [The table showing synopses of Dutch war crimes trials], Hōmu-Hei-11-4B-15-7130; "Hikoku sensō hanzai saiban gaikenhyō" [The table showing synopses of Philippine war crimes trials], Hōmu-Hei-11-4A-21-7132; "Futsukoku sensō hanzai saiban gaikenhyō" [The table showing synopses of French war crimes trials], Hōmu-Hei-11-4B-24-7134; and "Chūgoku sensō hanzai saiban gaikenhyō" [The table showing synopses of Chinese war crimes trials], Hōmu-Hei-11-4A-24-7135. For the narrative account of the origins of these synopses and other related reference materials, see Toyoda Kumao, *Sensō saiban yoroku* [Titbits of war trials] (Tokyo: Taiseisha, 1986), chapter 17 and especially pp. 471–4. In addition, this author put the following sources to use when selecting cases for this book project: (1) synopses of trials contained in individual case files of Australian and British war crimes trials, which are available at the National Archives of Australia and the National Archives at Kew, Surrey, Richmond, U.K. (U.K. National Archives hereafter), respectively; (2) review reports of the U.S. Yokohama war crimes trials, titled "Reviews of the Yokohama Class B and Class C war crimes trials by the 8th Army Judge Advocate, 1946–1949" (College Park, MD: NARA), microfilm, M1112, 5 rolls; and (3) the final report on U.S. war crimes tri-als, titled "History of Nonmilitary Activities of the Occupation of Japan: Trials of Class 'B' and 'C' War Criminals," in SCAP Monograph Drafts, 1945–1951. With respect to Australian war crimes trials, I am indebted to Narrelle Morris, who kindly shared with me the finding aid she was compiling in conjunction with the *The Australian War Crimes Trials Law Reports Series, 1945–51.*

26. United Nations War Crimes Commission, comp., *History of the United Nations War Crimes Commission and the Development of the Laws of War* (London, UK: His Majesty's Stationery Office, 1948). The records of the United Nations War

Crimes Commission have been declassified in recently years and are presently available online. Visit the Web site of the United Nations War Crimes Commission Project, http://www.unwcc.org.

27. "History of Nonmilitary Activities of the Occupation of Japan: Trials of Class 'B' and 'C' War Criminals," in SCAP Monograph Drafts, 1945–1951, pp. 42–3.

28. Paragraphs 22 and 23 of "Allied Land Forces, South East Asia War Crimes Instruction No. 1," in *Sensō hanzai saiban kankei hōreishū* [The compilation of legal documents on war crimes trials], ed. Hōmu daijin kanbō shihō hōsei chōsabu [The Judiciary and Legislation Investigation Bureau, Secretariat of the Ministry of Legal Affairs] (Tokyo: Hōmu daijin kanbō shihō hōsei chōsabu, 1963–1965), vol. 1, pp. 216–17. See also the organizational chart in Appendix A of "Allied Land Forces, South East Asia War Crimes Instruction No. 1," in Hōmu daijin kanbō shihō hōsei chōsabu, *Sensō hanzai saiban kankei hōreishū*, vol. 1, p. 251. See also Tōkyō saiban handobukku henshūiinkai, *Tōkyō saiban handobukku*, pp. 87–8, 114.

29. George Hubbard Blakeslee, *The Far Eastern Commission: A Study in International Cooperation: 1945 to 1952* (Washington, DC: Department of State, 1953), p. 17.

30. Ibid., p. 32.

31. For a limited discussion of the Far Eastern Commission's role in determining the overall framework of the Allied war crimes program in the Asia-Pacific region, see Totani, *Tokyo War Crimes Trial*, pp. 28, 55–7, 59–61. For the general history and workings of the Far Eastern Commission regarding the Allied occupation of Japan, see Blakeslee, *Far Eastern Commission*.

32. Paragraph 5, "Royal Warrant: Regulations for the Trial of War Criminals (A.O. 81/1945)," in *Sensō hanzai saiban kankei hōreishū*, Hōmu daijin kanbō shihō hōsei chōsabu, vol. 1, p. 89. Emphasis added. This is referred to as the "Royal Warrant" hereafter.

33. Paragraph 38, "Allied Land Forces, South East Asia War Crimes Instruction No. 1," in Hōmu daijin kanbō shihō hōsei chōsabu, *Sensō hanzai saiban kankei hōreishū*, vol. 1, p. 231.

34. Paragraph 5 (4), "Australian War Crimes Act," in *BC-kyū senpan Gōgun Rabauru saiban shiryō* [Sources on Australian military Class BC war crimes trials at Rabaul], ed. Chaen Yoshio (Tokyo: Fuji shuppan, 1990), p. 168. Emphasis added. For an analysis of the Australian War Crimes Act, see "Australian Law Concerning Trials of War Criminals by Military Courts," in United Nations War Crimes Commission, *Law Reports of Trials of War Criminals*, vol. 5 (1948), pp. 94–101.

35. Article 2, "Regulations Governing the Trial of War Criminals" (September 24, 1945), in *BC-kyū Beigun Manira saiban shiryō* [Sources on American military Class BC war crimes trials at Manila], ed. Chaen Yoshio (Tokyo: Fuji shuppan, 1986), p. 124. Emphasis added.

36. MacArthur delegated his authority as convening authority to Lt. Gen. Robert Eichelberger, commanding officer of the U.S. 8th Army, relative to the U.S. Yokohama trials, and to Lt. Gen. Wilhem D. Styer, commanding general of the U.S. Army Forces, Western Pacific, relative to the U.S. Manila trials.

37. Article 1 (b), "Regulations Governing the Trials of Accused War Criminals" (December 5, 1945), in "History of Nonmilitary Activities of the Occupation of Japan: Trials of Class 'B' and 'C' War Criminals," in SCAP Monograph Drafts,

1945–1951, p. 215. The term "SCAP Regulations" was introduced in the report by the United Nations War Crimes Commission for the purpose of distinguishing them from the regulations applicable to the Yamashita Trial. The latter was referred in the UNWCC report as "Pacific September Regulations." For more information, see "United States Law and Practice Concerning Trials of War Criminals by Military Commissions, Military Government Courts and Military Tribunals," in *Law Reports of Trials of War Criminals*, vol. 3 (1948), pp. 103–20. The same terminology will be used hereafter in referring to these two sets of U.S. regulations (i.e., Pacific September Regulations and SCAP Regulations).

38. Articles 2 and 6, "Regulations Governing the Trial of War Criminals" (January 21, 1946), pp. 82–6; and article 2, "United States Pacific Fleet Commander Marianas" (April 5, 1946), p. 98. Both documents are included in Chaen, *BC-kyū Beigun Manira saiban shiryō*, pp. 194–7 and pp. 197–8, respectively. The former regulations, which governed the American war crimes trials in Shanghai, will hereafter be referred to as the "China Regulations."

39. "Executive Order No. 68: Establishing a National War Crimes Office and Prescribing Rules and Regulations Governing the Trial of Accused War Criminals," in *BC-kyū senpan Firipin saiban shiryō* [Sources on Philippine Class BC war crimes trials], ed. Chaen Yoshio (Tokyo: Fuji shuppan, 1987), pp. 149–56. Hereafter the "Philippine Regulations."

40. I am indebted to David Cohen who alerted me to differences between fair-trial protections and due-process protections. For discussion concerning due-process protections, see the decision of the U.S. Supreme Court relative to the Yamashita Trial. The full text of the U.S. Supreme Court decision, including two dissenting opinions, can be found online, "In re Yamashita – 327 U.S. 1 (1946)," Justia.com, US Supreme Court Center, http://supreme.justia.com/cases/federal/us/327/1/case.html. For an in-depth analysis and discussion of what constituted fair trial in the post-WWII war crimes trials in the Pacific region, see Cohen, "Military Justice from WWII to Guantanamo: Fair Trials, Judicial Murder, and International Standards in WWII Crimes Trials in Asia"; and Cohen, "The Singapore War Crimes Trials and Their Relevance Today." The full text of the Geneva Convention Relative to the Treatment of Prisoners of War can be found as "Convention on Treatment of Prisoners of War, Geneva, July 27, 1929," in *The Law of War: A Documentary History*, ed. Leon Friedman (New York, NK: Random House, 1972), vol. 1, pp. 488–522. This convention is also referred to as the Geneva Prisoner-of-War Convention hereafter. There are various online sources that host the Geneva Prisoner-of-War Convention and other international conventions relating to the laws and customs of war. Visit, for instance, the Web site of the International Committee of the Red Cross at http://www.icrc.org. For the full text of the Geneva Prisoner-of-War Convention specifically, visit http://www.icrc.org/ihl/INTRO/305?OpenDocument.

41. Paragraph 8 (v), Royal Warrant; rule 14, "Statutory Rules 1945, No. 164, Regulations under the War Crimes Act"; article 13 (a) and (c), Pacific September Regulations; article 5 (a) (1) and (3), SCAP Regulations; article 13 (a) (c), China Regulations; and article 5 (a) (1) and (3), Philippine Regulations. For the "Statutory Rules 1945, No. 164, Regulations under the War Crimes Act," this author made use of the copy contained in Chaen, *BC-kyū senpan Gōgun Rabauru saiban shiryō*, pp. 176–83.

42. Paragraph 5 of the Royal Warrant reads, "The Convening Officer should normally appoint at least one officer having one of the legal qualifications mentioned in Rule of Procedure 93 (b) as President or as a member of the Court. But if no such officer is appointed, and in default of a person deputed by H. M. Judge Advocate General to act as Judge Advocate, the Convening Officer shall by order appoint a person having one of the said legal qualifications to act as Judge Advocate at the trial." Paragraph 43 (g) of "Allied Land Forces, South East Asia War Crimes Instruction No. 1" defines the duties of a law member as follows: "(i) in the absence of a shorthand writer he will normally make the record of the proceedings. (ii) he will be permitted to put without restriction such questions as he thinks proper to any witness before the court. (iii) he should be consulted before any decision is taken on any point of law and procedure arising at the trial. (iv) in the absence of a legal member the above duties shall be carried out by the J. A. if appointed." For rules providing for appointment of a judge advocate at Australian war crimes courts, see rules 5 and 6, "Statutory Rules 1945, No. 164, Regulations under the War Crimes Act." As for regulations applicable to American trials, article 8 of Pacific September Regulations simply reads, "If feasible, one or more members of a commission should have had legal training," and thus did not require a law member. The same is repeated in article 8 of China Regulations. Article 3 (c) of SCAP Regulations reads differently, however: "One specially qualified member shall be designated as the law member whose ruling is final insofar as concerns the commission on an objection to the admissibility of evidence offered during the trial." The same is repeated in article 3 (c) of the Philippine Regulations.

43. The quoted passage appears in article 5 (h) of SCAP Regulations. Equivalent provisions can be found in article 21, Pacific September Regulations; article 21, China Regulations; and article 5 (h), Philippine Regulations. As for the British and Australian regulations regarding review of trials, see paragraphs 10 and 11, Royal Warrant; and rules 17 and 18, "Statutory Rules 1945, No. 164, Regulations under the War Crimes Act."

44. Paragraph 7, Royal Warrant; paragraph 49, "Allied Land Forces, South East Asia War Crimes Instruction No. 1"; rule 10, "Statutory Rules 1945, No. 164, Regulations under the War Crimes Act"; article 14 (b) and (c), Pacific September Regulations; article 5 (b) (2) and (3), SCAP Regulations; article 14 (b) and (c), China Regulations; article 5 (b) (2) and (3), Philippine Regulations.

45. "Regulations Governing the Trials of Accused War Criminals (October 27, 1948)," contained in "Records of the Trial of Accused War Criminal Hiroshi Tamura." The same is also included in "Records of the Trial of Accused War Criminal Soemu Toyoda." Regulations applicable to the trials of Tamura and Toyoda are referred to as "Regulations of Subsequent Proceedings" hereafer.

46. "Senso saiban sanko shiryo: Bei-Yokohama, Ei-Shingaporu saiban bengonin Abe Taro shi yori choshu jiko" [Sources related to war crimes trials: Matters pertaining to the interview of Mr. Abe Taro, defense lawyer at the U.S. Yokohama and U.K. Singapore trials], in "Niigata, Nagano chiho shuccho hokokusho No. 49, Showa 37-nendo" [Report on fieldwork in Niigata and Nagano, no. 49, year 1962], Homu-Hei-11-4A-21-6576, National Archives of Japan, pp. 36–7.

47. "Senso saiban sanko shiryo: Ei-Shingaporu, Bei-Yokohama saiban bengonin Fujiiwa Mutsuro shi shoken" [Sources related to war crimes trials: Matters

pertaining to the interview of Mr. Fujiiwa Mutsurō, defense lawyer at U.K. Singapore and U.S. Yokohama trials], in "Fukuoka, Saga chihō shucchō chōsa hōkokusho, No. 52, Shōwa 37-nendo" [Report on fieldwork in Fukuoka and Saga, no. 52, year 1962], Hōmu-Hei-11–4A-21–6579, National Archives of Japan, p. 23.

48. Article 9 (b), "Charter of the International Military Tribunal for the Far East," in Boister and Cryer, *Documents on the Tokyo International Military Tribunal*, p. 9.

49. "Majority Judgment," in Boister and Cryer, *Documents on the Tokyo International Military Tribunal*, p. 77. Emphasis added.

50. Paragraph 50, "Allied Land Forces, South East Asia War Crimes Instruction No. 1," Hōmu daijin kanbō shihō hōsei chōsabu, *Sensō hanzai saiban kankei hōreishū*, vol. 1, p. 241.

51. Article 5 (b) (4), SCAP Regulations; article 5 (b) (4), Philippine Regulations; and article 6 (b) (4), Regulations of Subsequent Proceedings. Emphasis added. The word *substance* was absent in the equivalent provision in Pacific September Regulations, which were applicable to the Yamashita Trial. According to article 14 (d), the accused was entitled to "have the charges and specifications, the proceedings and any documentary evidence translated when he is unable otherwise to understand them."

52. "Rules of Procedure and Outline of Procedure for Trials of Accused War Criminals" (February 5, 1946), in "History of Nonmilitary Activities of the Occupation of Japan: Trials of Class 'B' and 'C' War Criminals," in SCAP Monograph Drafts, 1945–1951, p. 227.

53. Ibid., pp. 227–8.

54. Paragraph 8 (i), Royal Warrant. Emphasis added. The identical provision is included in paragraph 9 (1), Australian War Crimes Act.

55. Friedman, *Law of War*, p. 509. Emphasis added. I am indebted to David Cohen, who alerted me to this particular article in the Geneva Prisoner-of-War Convention.

56. Paragraph 8 (i), Royal Warrant.

57. Article 16, Pacific September Regulations.

58. Article 5 (1), SCAP Regulations.

59. Article 5 (d) (1), Philippine Regulations; and article 6 (f) (1), Regulations of Subsequent Proceedings.

60. Article 16, Pacific September Regulations; article 5 (d), SCAP Regulations; article 16, China Regulations; and article 5 (d) (1), Philippine Regulations. Maj. Robert W. Kerr, chief prosecutor at the Yamashita Trial, once commented that the procedural rules applicable at the U.S. military commission "were in fact derived from the Regulations for the Trial of War Criminals promulgated by Royal Warrant" and that "the Canadian and Australian regulations governing trials of war criminals closely follow the British regulations." In this regard, "the Anglo-Saxon nations generally are following the same procedure, and applying the same rules of evidence, in their separate prosecutions of Japanese war criminals." Kerr made this comment in a memorandum dated March 4, 1946, in which he expressed his disapproval of the dissenting opinion of Justice Wiley Rutledge at the U.S. Supreme Court ("In re Yamashita"). This memorandum can be located in "Preliminary Inventory to the United States Army Forces in the Western

Pacific, Military Commission Records, 1945–1946," collection number XX191, Hoover Institution Library and Archives, Stanford University, Stanford, CA.

61. Article 5 (d) (7), SCAP Regulations; and article 5 (d) (5), Philippine Regulations.

62. "Amendments to Regulations Governing the Trials of Accused War Criminals" (December 27, 1946), in "History of Nonmilitary Activities of the Occupation of Japan: Trials of Class 'B' and 'C' War Criminals," in SCAP Monograph Drafts, 1945–1951, p. 223.

63. Article 5 (d) (5), Philippine Regulations.

64. I am indebted to David Cohen who alerted me to the nature of the rules governing the present-day international criminal courts. For the rules of evidence applicable to the International Criminal Court (ICC), see articles 64 (9) and 69 of the Rome Statute, and Rules 63–75 of the ICC Rules of Procedure and Evidence. Documents related to ICC in general are available at the ICC Web site. http://www.icc-cpi.int/en_menus/icc/Pages/default.aspx. The full text of the ICC Rules of Procedure and Evidence is available at http://www.icc-cpi.int/iccdocs/ PIDS/legal-texts/RulesProcedureEvidenceEng.pdf. For the rules of evidence applicable to the International Criminal Tribunal for the Former Yugoslavia and the International Criminal Tribunal for Rwanda, see Rules 89–98 of the Rules of Procedure and Evidence. Documents related to ICTY and ICTR in general are available at the respective Web sites, http://www.icty.org, http://www .unictr.org. For the Rules of Procedure and Evidence specifically, visit http:// www.icty.org/x/file/Legal%20Library/Rules_procedure_evidence/IT032Rev49_ en.pdf (ICTY) and http://www.unictr.org/Portals/0/English/Legal/Evidance/ English/130410amended%206_26.pdf (ICTR).

65. "Note by C-in-C ALFSEA on Trials of Minor War Criminals in SEAC" (November 20, 1945), in "War Crimes: Policy, Sentences of Military Courts and Correspondence," reference number WO203/5596, U.K. National Archives. Emphasis in the original.

66. See United Nations War Crimes Commission, *Law Reports of Trials of War Criminals,* vol. 2, *The Belsen Trial* (1947); Raymond Philips, *Trial of Josef Kramer and Forty-Four Others (The Belsen Trial)* (London, UK: William Hodge, 1949).

67. "Headquarters Supreme Allied Commander South East Asia. Procedure for War Criminals Trials in SEAC" (November 17, 1945), in "War Office: South East Asia Command: Military Headquarters Papers, Second World War. SOUTH EAST ASIA COMMAND. War Crimes: Policy," reference number WO203/5594, U.K. National Archives.

68. "Extracts from SAC's 296th Meeting on 20th November, 1945," appended to "Note by C-in-C ALFSEA on Trials of Minor War Criminals in SEAC" (November 20, 1945), in "War Crimes: Policy, Sentences of Military Courts and Correspondence," reference number WO203/5596, U.K. National Archives. Emphasis in the original text.

69. Ibid.

CHAPTER 1

1. The records of three trials analyzed in this chapter are obtained from NARA. The full citation information is as follows: "Records of Trials of Accused Japanese War Criminals Tried at Manila, Philippines, by a Military Commission Convened

by the Commanding General of the United States Army in the Western Pacific, 1945–1947" (College Park, MD: NARA), microfilm, M1727, Rolls 29–33 (*This microfilm publication does not include court exhibits or the judgment.); "Masaharu Homma," entry UD 1322, RG 331, SCAP, Legal Section, Prosecution Division, USA vs. Japanese War Criminals Name Files, 1945–1949, Boxes 1671–2 and 1684–6; and "Shigenori Kuroda," entry UD 1323, RG 331, SCAP Legal Section, Prosecution Division, Philippines vs. Various Japanese War Criminals Case File, 1947–1949, Boxes 1699–1702. The records of the three trials will be referred to hereafter as the "Yamashita Trial," the "Honma Trial," and the "Kuroda Trial." I am indebted to Sharon Chamberlain, who made digital photographic copies of the transcripts of the court proceedings of the Honma Trial and the Kuroda Trial.

2. Yamashita Trial, R4062.
3. "Charge," Yamashita Trial, R31. The charge against Yamashita came with the bill of 64 particulars and a supplementary one that contained additional 59 particulars.
4. "In re Yamashita – 327 U.S. 1 (1946)," (see Introduction, note 40).
5. Some of the cases at the U.S. Yokohama courts were also related to Japanese war crimes in the Philippine theater.
6. The other charge against Honma read that the accused "unlawfully refused to grant quarter to the Armed Forces of the United States of America and its Allies." He was found not guilty of this charge. Honma Trial, R23.
7. One of the four other judges of the U.S. military commission was Maj. Gen. Basilio J. Valdes of the Philippine Army.
8. Honma Trial, R3365.
9. The full text of the U.S. Supreme Court decision, including two dissenting opinions, can be found online, "Application of Homma – 327 U.S. 759 (1946)," at Justia.com, US Supreme Court Center, http://supreme.justia.com/cases/federal/us/327/1/case.html.
10. "Charge," Kuroda Trial, R11.
11. "Rationale," pp. 3–4, Kuroda Trial, R3074.
12. For brief biographical information of Tanaka, see Fukukawa Hideki, ed., *Nihon rikugun shōkan jiten* [Dictionary of Japanese army generals] (Tokyo: Fuyō shobō shuppan, 2001), p. 451.
13. "Gen. Yamashita Loses Appeal," *Washington Post*, February 5, 1946, p. 1.
14. "Yamashita Appeal Denied, Six to Two, by Supreme Court," *New York Times*, February 5, 1946, p. 1.
15. Maj. Robert W. Kerr, chief prosecutor at the Yamashita Trial, expressed in a prepared memorandum his personal dissatisfaction with the U.S. Supreme Court decision and the nature of the press coverage. "Memorandum – Subject: The Dissenting Opinions in Ex Parte Yamashita (March 4, 1946)." A copy of this letter is in "Miscellaneous Trial Materials" (folder name), contained in collection number XX191, Hoover Institution Library and Archives (see Introduction, note 60).
16. This publication includes in the appendix the full text of the U.S. Supreme Court decisions. The Japanese translation of this book was published in 1952. *Yamashita saiban* (The Yamashita Trial), trans. Shimojima Muraji, 2 vols. (Tokyo: Nihon kyōbunsha, 1952).
17. Representative publications that discuss the Yamashita Trial are A. Frank Reel, *The Case of General Yamashita* (Chicago, IL: University of Chicago

Press, 1949); Telford Taylor, *Nuremberg and Vietnam: The American Tragedy* (Chicago, IL: Quadrangle Books, 1970); Richard Lael, *The Yamashita Precedent: War Crimes and Command Responsibility* (Wilmington, DE: Scholarly Resources, 1982); and Allan A. Ryan, *Yamashita's Ghost: War Crimes, MacArthur's Justice, and Command Accountability* (Lawrence: University Press of Kansas, 2012). For comprehensive bibliographical information on English-language publications on the Yamashita Trial, refer to Jeanie M. Welch, *The Tokyo Trial: A Bibliographic Guide to English-Language Sources* (Westport, CT and London, UK: Greenwood Press, 2002), pp. 134–56. On jurisprudence, see David Cohen, "Beyond Nuremberg: Individual Responsibility for War Crimes," in *Human Rights in Political Transitions: Gettysburg to Bosnia*, ed. Carla Hesse and Robert Post (New York, NY: Zone Books, 1999), pp 53–92. As for Japanese-language publications on the Yamashita Trial, see, for instance, Utsunomiya Naotaka, *Kaisō no Yamashita saiban* [The Yamashita Trial in remembrance] (Tokyo: Shirogane shobō, 1975). Utsunomiya was a wartime subordinate of Yamashita, and served as an assistant defense lawyer at the Yamashita Trial, along with Mutō Akira, former chief of staff of Yamashita.

18. "Application of Homma – 327 U.S. 759 (1946)."
19. For contemporaneous Japanese-language newspaper reporting on the Allied war crimes trials, see Utsumi Aiko and Nagai Hitoshi, eds., *Shinbun shiryō ni miru Tōkyō saiban, BC-kyū saiban* [The Tokyo Trial, Class BC trials as seen in newspaper sources], 2 vols. (Tokyo: Gendai shiryō shuppan, 2000).
20. "Testimony of Homma Masaharu," Honma Trial, R3047.
21. Ibid., R3048. For the official Japanese history of the Philippine invasion, see Bōei kenshūjo senshishitsu [Military History Room, Defense Research Institute], ed., *Senshi sōsho: 2. Hitō kōryaku sakusen* [War history series: Vol. 2. The invasion of the Philippine Islands] (Tokyo: Asagumo shinbunsha, 1966).
22. Honma spent part of his military career in the West, mostly in Britain, as a result of which he gained fluency in English. (For an account of his military career leading up to the Pacific War, see Honma Trial, R3029–36.) He provided the entirety of his court testimony in English, although from the midpoint of the cross-examination, he appears to have switched to taking questions in Japanese translation. All of his answers were rendered in English, without mediation of court interpretation. Honma Trial, R3028, 3180.
23. "Testimony of Homma Masaharu," Honma Trial, R3050.
24. The landing of the main force on December 22 was preceded by the landing of a detachment on Luzon on December 10. "Testimony of Homma Masaharu," Honma Trial, R3047–50.
25. "Testimony of Homma Masaharu," Honma Trial, R3053.
26. Ibid., R3054.
27. Ibid., R3056–7.
28. "Exhibit 18: Front Page of Manila Bulletin, Extra Edition, December 26, 1941, Regarding the Declaration of Manila as 'Open City,'" Honma Trial, R264.
29. Fukukawa, *Nihon rikugun shōkan jiten*, p. 595.
30. "Testimony of Homma Masaharu," Honma Trial, R3063.
31. Ibid., R3058.
32. Ibid., R3061.
33. Ibid., R2845–6.

34. Ibid., R3063.
35. Ibid.
36. Ibid., R3062.
37. Ibid., R3150.
38. Ibid., R3063–4. The reinforcement consisted of the 4th Division and three detachments known as the Kawaguchi, Kawamura, and Nagano Detachments. "Testimony of Nakajima Yoshio," Honma Trial, R2568.
39. "Testimony of Homma Masaharu," Honma Trial, R3065.
40. Ibid., R3065, 3075. According to the record kept by Gen. King's staff officer, Col. Charles S. Lawrence, approximately 74,800 individuals surrendered. About 10,500 of them were American officers, enlisted men and civilians. The remainder of surrendered soldiers are presumably Filipinos. "Exhibit 305: Statement of Col. Charles S. Lawrence," Honma Trial, R1431.
41. "Testimony of Wachi Takeji," Honma Trial, R2462–4, 2515. The details of the plan of prisoner-of-war evacuation, approved by Honma, are explained in the testimony of Wada Moriya. Wada was a staff member of the Second Department of the 14th Army in charge of the line of communications work, including matters concerning prisoners of war. "Testimony of Wada Moriya," Honma Trial, R2672–5.
42. "Testimony of Homma Masaharu," Honma Trial, R3047.
43. "Exhibit 8: Concerning the Scope of Command of Lt. General Homma, Statement of T. Katsube, Chief of Liaison Section, Central Liaison Office, Japanese Government," Honma Trial, R196.
44. "Testimony of Homma Masaharu," Honma Trial, R3081–2.
45. Ibid., R3092. See R3088 for reference to the location of the headquarters at the time of the Battle of Corregidor. Prior to Lamao, Honma kept his headquarters at Balanga in the northeast of Bataan, between April 8 and 28, 1942. "Testimony of Homma Masaharu," Honma Trial, R3080. See also "Testimony of Takatsu Toshimitsu," Honma Trial, R134.
46. "Testimony of Homma Masaharu," R3093.
47. Ibid., R3082–5. Wainwright offers a personal account of defeat and subsequent internment in his memoir. See Jonathan Mayhew Wainwright, *General Wainwright's Story: The Account of Four Years of Humiliating Defeat, Surrender, and Captivity* (New York, NY: Doubleday, 1946).
48. "Testimony of Homma Masaharu," Honma Trial, R3095.
49. Ibid., R3098.
50. Kuroda Shigenori explained the mission of the 14th Army as an occupation force as follows: "The commanding general of the 14th Army was given by the Imperial Headquarters the political and strategic missions in the Philippines. Until the independence of the Republic of the Philippines – 13 October 1943 – the army was in charge of the military administration in the Philippines. At the same time, it was also in charge of the defensive operations of the Philippines to be taken care of by land troops." "Testimony of Kuroda Shigenori," Kuroda Trial, R1374.
51. "Testimony of Capt. William P. Cain," Honma Trial, R1284, 1298–9.
52. "Testimony of Master Sergeant James Baldassarre," Honma Trial, R838; "Testimony of Maj. Gen. Takatsu Toshimitsu," Honma Trial, R134–5; "Testimony of Nakajima Yoshio," Honma Trial, R2583.

53. "Testimony of Pedro L. Felix," and "Testimony of Eduardo T. Vargas," Honma Trial, R1010–67. This instance of atrocity is listed in specification 13-b.
54. "Exhibit 310: Statement of Maj. Robert Conn," Honma Trial, R1440.
55. Exhibit 305, Honma Trial, R1426. Tsuneyoshi's speech to the same effect was recorded in a number of other accounts of former prisoners of war at Camp O'Donnell, including Brig. Gen. James R. N. Weaver. "Exhibit 304: Testimony [Deposition] of Brig. Gen. James R. N. Weaver," Honma Trial, R1415.
56. "Exhibit 307: Approximate Unit Strength, 2 April 1942, Luzon Forces," Honma Trial, R1431. The Japanese data showed 16,871 deaths and 16,091 patients out of a total of 68,575 prisoners of war at O'Donnell as of June 10, 1942. "Testimony of Horiguchi Shusuke," Honma Trial, R2865.
57. "Testimony of Lt. Col. Jacobo Zobe," Honma Trial, R1509–10. This Itō is possibly Itō Akira, who commanded the 22nd Field Artillery Regiment of the 16th Division under the 14th Army during the invasion of the Philippines. Fukukawa, *Nihon rikugun shōkan jiten*, pp. 86–7.
58. "Testimony of Jose Abad Santos, Jr.," Honma Trial, R1863; "Exhibit 376: Letter by President Manuel L. Quezon to Jose Abad Santos, Sr. (March 17, 1942)," Honma Trial, R1865. Quezon escaped from Mindanao to Australia first and then to the United States. For biographical information on Judge Santos, see Ramon C. Aquino, *A Chance to Die: A Biography of José Abad Santos, Late Chief Justice of the Philippines* (Quezon City, Philippines: Alemar-Phoenix, 1967).
59. "Testimony of Jose Abad Santos, Jr.," Honma Trial, R1871–2; "Testimony of Wachi Takeji," Honma Trial, R2492–5; "Exhibit G: Affidavit of Benigno Aquino," Honma Trial, R3027. Jose Abad Santos Jr. testified that he was taken into custody of the Kawaguchi Unit alongside his father, and that one day, his father informed him of the impending execution on the allegation of his "setting fires to Cebu City." After the death of his father, Santos Jr. was flown to Tokyo with Japanese escorts. He eventually served as personal secretary of Jorge Vargas. "Testimony of Jose Abad Santos, Jr.," Honma Trial, R1873, 1877–9.
60. "Testimony of Homma Masaharu," Honma Trial, R3126; "Testimony of Wachi Takeji," Honma Trial, R2494–5; "Exhibit F: Affidavit of Jose Laurel," Honma Trial, R3024–5; Exhibit G, Honma Trial, R3025–7. Judge Santos's brother alleged that Honma expressed animosity against the judge, but his account was at odds with those offered by Jose Laurel and Benigno Aquino. "Testimony of Salvador Santos," Honma Trial, R1884.
61. "Testimony of Jorge B. Vargas," Kuroda Trial, R2023.
62. "Testimony of Homma Masaharu," Honma Trial, R3124.
63. "Exhibit 16: Copy of the Tribune, Monday, January 5, 1942," Honma Trial, R258.
64. "Testimony by Homma Masaharu," Honma Trial, R3158.
65. Ibid., R3161–2.
66. According to Kōketsu Atsushi, *kenpei* was modeled on the French gendarmerie and established by *Kenpei jōrei* (Gendarmarie Ordinance, dated March 1881), as one of the seven branches of the Imperial Japanese Army. Its primary mission was to enforce law within the army. However, it also took on a wide range of responsibilities of law enforcement by its additional institutional affiliation with the Navy Ministry, the Ministry of Home Affairs, and the Ministry of Legal Affairs. Kōketsu Atsushi, "Kenpei," in *Nihon daihyakka zensho (Nipponika)* [The

Japan Encyclopedia (Nipponica)], available at the Web site of JapanKnowledge Lib at http://japanknowledge.com/library/en. Accessed August 22, 2014. For a comprehensive account of the history of *kenpei* and its activities, see Zenkoku ken'yūrengōkai hensan iinkai, *Nihon kenpei seishi.* The word *kenpei* is translated as "military police," and the word *kenpeitai* as "military police force" throughout this book. During World War II, *kenpei* took charge of law enforcement mainly in the army-occupied territories. As for administration of navy-occupied territories, the Imperial Japanese Navy deployed its own military police force, known as *tokubetsu keisatsutai* (special police force, also known in its abbreviated form, *tokkeitai*).

67. "Testimony of Ohta Seiichi," Honma Trial, R2619. Prior to the start of the Pacific War, Fort Santiago was utilized as an American military post, serving as a guardhouse or an Intelligence Section (G-2) facility, according to the accounts of two prosecution witnesses. "Testimony of Joaquin Pardo de Tavera," Honma Trial, R497–8; "Testimony of Nelson Vance Sinclair," Honma Trial, R532.

68. The "water treatment" is described in the Tokyo Judgment as follows. "The victim was bound or otherwise secured in a prone position; and water was forced through his mouth and nostrils into his lungs and stomach until he lost consciousness. Pressure was then applied, sometimes by jumping upon his abdomen to force the water out. The usual practice was to revive the victim and successively repeat the process." Boister and Cryer, *Documents on the Tokyo International Military Tribunal*, p. 557. Detailed descriptions of other torture methods, commonly used by the *kenpeitai*, can be found in the Tokyo Judgment, pp. 557–60.

69. For the prosecution's evidence of atrocities at Fort Santiago, see Honma Trial, R488–594; Yamashita Trial, R11172–1241; and Kuroda Trial, R929–83, 1040–1201.

70. "Testimony of Gaston Willoquet," Honma Trial, R1918–22.

71. The main part of the prosecution's evidence related to the Chinese consulate case can be found in Honma Trial, R1903–65. This case is stipulated in specification 20.

72. W.O. Matsuda Junzō, a prosecution witness and a former member of the Special Section of the *kenpeitai* at Fort Santiago in charge of gathering intelligence, could not verify whether the report prepared by the section regarding the Chinese consulate case reached Honma."Testimony of Matsuda Junzo," Honma Trial, R1943–5. Col. Ōta Seiichi, another prosecution witness and formerly head of the 14th Army *kenpeitai* directly subordinate to Honma, testified that this case "should have" been reported to Honma by his staff members, but he did not know if the report was indeed made to Honma. "Testimony of Ohta Seiichi," Honma Trial, R2627. Nishiharu Hideo, formerly chief of the Legal Department of the 14th Army and directly subordinate to Honma (also appearing as a prosecution witness), denied any knowledge of the arrest and execution of the Chinese consulate members. "Testimony of Nishiharu Hideo," Honma Trial, R1957–8.

73. "Testimony of Felisa Cu Loo," Honma Trial, R1913–14.

74. "Testimony of Honma Masaharu," Honma Trial, R3198.

75. Bōei kenshūjo senshishitsu, *Senshi sōsho: 2. Hitō kōryaku sakusen*, p. 555.

76. Ibid. See also "Exhibit V: Extracts from General Headquarters, Southwest Pacific, Military Intelligence Section, General Staff, 'Guerrilla Resistance Movements in the Philppines,'" Yamashita Trial, R3390. Extracts from this exhibit

were read at R3436–47. As no copies of court exhibits are included in the microfilm publication of the Yamashita Trial, this author made use of the physical copy
available at the Hoover Institution Library and Archives, Stanford University,
Stanford, CA, "Preliminary Inventory to the United States. Army. Forces in the
Western Pacific. Military Commission Records, 1945–1946," collection number
XX191. For published source materials and narrative accounts of wartime guer-
rilla activism in the Philippines, see Charles A. Willoughby, *The Guerrilla Resis-
tance Movement in the Philippines, 1941–1945* (New York, NY: Vantage Press,
1972); Ray C. Hunt and Bernard Norling, *Behind Japanese Lines: An American
Guerrilla in the Philippines* (Lexington: The University Press of Kentucky, 1986);
Robert Lapham and Bernard Norling, *Guerrillas in the Philippines, 1942–1945*
(Lexington: The University Press of Kentucky, 1996); and Bernard Norling, *The
Intrepid Guerrillas of North Luzon* (Lexington: The University Press of Ken-
tucky, 1999).

77. "Testimony of Kuroda Shigenori," Kuroda Trial, R1607.
78. Ibid., R1653.
79. "Testimony of Yamashita Tomoyuki," Yamashita Trial, R3520.
80. Ibid., R3544–5.
81. "The Final Argument of Defense," Yamashita Trial, R3928.
82. "Testimony of Yamashita Tomoyuki," Yamashita Trial, R3553–5.
83. Ibid., R3545.
84. For the Japanese official history of the Battle of Leyte, see Bōei kenshūjo sensh-
    ishitsu, *Senshi sōsho: 41. Shōgō rikugun sakusen (1) Reite kessen* [War history
    series: Vol. 41. Army plan Shō, (1) The decisive battle at Leyte] (Tokyo: Asa-
    gumo shinbunsha, 1966).
85. "Testimony of Yamashita Tomoyuki," Yamashita Trial, R3656.
86. Yamashita became a prisoner of war of the U.S. Army at Baguio, Luzon Island,
    on September 4, 1945. He was served with the charge on September 25, and ar-
    raigned at the Manila court on October 8 the same year.
87. During the Yamashita Trial, witness testimony on rape was taken in closed ses-
    sion. This was due to suggestions from the prosecution that "it would not be in
    the public interest" to do so in open court, and should be done in closed session
    "in fairness to the young women who will then testify." Yamashita Trial, R402.
    The record of the closed session (where eight witnesses testified and nine exhib-
    its were introduced in evidence) can be found at Yamashita Trial, R499–563.
    The same permission was granted with respect to taking evidence of rape at the
    Honma Trial. See Honma Trial, R2188–2242.
88. Actual locations of atrocities against the civilian population as identified in
    specifications are Batan Island, Batangas Province, Bulacan Province, Cagayan
    Province, Cavite Province, Cebu, La Union Province, Laguna Province, Mind-
    anao, Mountain Province, Nueva Vizcaya Province, Panay, Pouson Island, and
    Rizal Province.
89. No. 52 in the bill of particulars, Yamashita Trial, R53.
90. Locations of civilian internment as identified in specifications are the Santo
    Tomas Internment Camp, the Los Baños Internment Camp in Laguna Province,
    and the Old Bilibid Prison Camp.
91. Locations of prisoner-of-war internment as identified in specifications are the
    Cabanatuan Camp, the Old Bilibid Prison Camp, the Sakura Prisoner-of-War
    Camp at Fort McKinley, and Nichols Field.

92. "The Opening Statement of the Prosecution," Yamashita Trial, R99–100.
93. "Testimony of Narciso Lapus," Yamashita Trial, R938.
94. "Testimony of Joaquin S. Galang," Yamashita Trial, R1069.
95. Bislumino Romero, Ricarte's grandson, who claimed to have had intimate knowledge of Yamashita-Ricarte conversations in his capacity as his grandfather's interpreter and who took the stand as a defense witness, cast doubt on credibility of Lapus and Galang. See "Testimony of Bislumino Romero," Yamashita Trial, R2014–28. The defense also presented in evidence American intelligence reports regarding the two Filipino prosecution witnesses. The reports raised doubts about the motives of these witnesses and their credibility. "Exhibit E: CIC Report Concerning Narciso Lapus," Yamashita Trial, R2971; "Exhibit F: CIC Report Concerning Joaquin Galang," Yamashita Trial, R2978; "Exhibit G: Report Concerning Lapus," Yamashita Trial, R2982–5; and "Exhibit H: Report Concerning Galang," Yamashita Trial, R2987–90. See also "The Final Arguments of Defense," Yamashita Trial, R3977–80.
96. "Testimony of Norman James Sparnon," Yamashita Trial, R3391.
97. Ibid., R3391–5, 3450–1. Sparnon first appeared as a prosecution witness (R106–130), but was recalled to testify as a defense witness in the later part of the Yamashita Trial.
98. "Testimony of Okochi Denshichi," Yamashita Trial, R2534.
99. Ibid., R2534–6, 2538. For brief biographical information of Iwabuchi, see Fukukawa Hideki, ed., *Nihon riku-kaigun jinmei jiten* [The encyclopedia of names of individuals in the Japanese army and navy] (Tokyo: Fuyō shobō, 1999), p. 72.
100. "Testimony of Okochi Denshichi," Yamashita Trial, R2539–43.
101. Ibid., R2549–50.
102. Ibid., R2540.
103. "Testimony of Yokoyama Shizuo," Yamashita Trial, R 2664.
104. Ibid., R2671–2.
105. Ibid., R2672–3, 2682–3.
106. Ibid., R2681, 2683.
107. "Testimony of Okochi Denshichi," Yamashita Trial, R2544.
108. Ibid., R2545.
109. Ibid., R2555–6.
110. "The Final Arguments of Defense," Yamashita Trial, R3966–7. Notwithstanding Reel's assertion, Justice Murphy of the U.S. Supreme Court wrote a few months later (in his dissenting opinion relative to Yamashita's habeas corpus petition) that "no one denies that inaction or *negligence* may give rise to liability, civil or criminal." Reel, *Case of General Yamashita*, p. 285. Emphasis added. Negligence is a recognized standard of liability according to the Model Penal Code, a statutory text developed by the American Law Institute in the 1960s. Section 2.03 ("General Requirements of Culpability") of the code reads that "a person is not guilty of an offense unless he acted purposely, knowingly, recklessly or negligently, as the law may require, with respect to each material element of the offense." The definition of "purposely," "knowingly," "recklessly," and "negligently" is provided in the same section. For the full text of the Model Penal Code, visit the Web site of "Model Penal Code Annotated" at Criminal Law Web. http://www.law-lib.utoronto.ca/bclc/crimweb/web1/mpc/mpc.html. I am indebted to David Cohen who introduced me to this text. For the discussion

of present-day jurisprudence on the requirement of knowledge under the law of command responsibility, see Guénaël Mettraux, *The Law of Command Responsibility* (Oxford and New York: Oxford University Press, 2009), pp. 193–228. See Chapter 3, note 87, for related discussion.

111. "The Final Arguments of Defense," Yamashita Trial, R3967.
112. Ibid., R3911–2.
113. Ibid., R3918.
114. Ibid., R3927.
115. "Testimony of Yamashita Tomoyuki," Yamashita Trial, R3646; "The Final Arguments of Defense," Yamashita Trial, R3924–6.
116. "Testimony of Yamashita Tomoyuki," Yamashita Trial, R3650.
117. Ibid., R3653.
118. Ibid., R3656.
119. "Statement of the Commission Concluding the Trial of Tomoyuki Yamashita, General, Imperial Japanese Army (December 7, 1945)," p. 3. As a copy of the judgment is not included in the microfilm publication of the Yamashita Trial, this author made use of the physical copy available at the Hoover Institution Library and Archives, Stanford University, Stanford, CA, "Preliminary Inventory to the United States. Army. Forces in the Western Pacific. Military Commission Records, 1945–1946," collection number XX191.
120. Ibid., pp. 4–5. Emphasis added.
121. Ibid., p. 5.
122. Ibid., p. 6. Emphasis added.
123. "In re Yamashita," in Reel, *Case of General Yamashita*, p. 285.
124. Ibid., pp. 280–1.
125. "Charge" and "Additional Charge," Honma Trial, R23–4.
126. Specification 13. "Specifications," Honma Trial, R27–30.
127. Locations of prisoner-of-war internment and work details as indicated in specifications were Camp O'Donnell, Cabanatuan Prison Camp, Bilibid Prison Camp, Bacolod POW [Prisoner of War] and Civilian Internment Camp, Camp Keithley, Nichols Field, Lumban Camp, and Pasay Elementary School, and work details at Wawa, the Gapan Bridge, Tayabas, and the Capumpit Bridge.
128. Locations of civilian internment that are named in the specifications are Bacolod POW and Civilian Internment Camp, Negros Island, Camp John Hay and Santo Tomas.
129. Specification 4. "Specifications," Honma Trial, R26.
130. "Closing Argument on Behalf of the Prosecution," Honma Trial, R3344.
131. "The Prosecution's Reply to the Defense Motion for a Not-Guilty Verdict," Honma Trial, R2433–4.
132. "Testimony of Takatsu Toshimitsu," Honma Trial, R153. Lt. Col. Kitayama Michio, formerly a staff officer in charge of communications and railroads of the 14th Army, similarly testified that the general indifference to prisoners of war "prevailed all through the army." "Testimony of Kitayama Michio," Honma Trial, R209.
133. Fukukawa, *Nihon rikugun shōkan jiten*, p. 237.
134. "Testimony of Homma Masaharu," Honma Trial, R3072, 3080; "Testimony of Takatsu Toshimitsu," Honma Trial, R134.
135. "Testimony of Homma Masaharu," Honma Trial, R3073.

136. Ibid., R3080.
137. Ibid., R3076–7. See also "Testimony of Wachi Takeji," Honma Trial, R2552–3. The alleged lack of transportation vehicles was disputed by Maj. Gen. Earnest P. King and his subordinate officer, Lt. Col. Chester Lee Johnson. According to their accounts, they turned over American vehicles to the Japanese with an understanding that they be used for prisoner-of-war transfer. However, the Japanese authorities failed to take action accordingly. "Exhibit 296: Statement by Lt. Col. Chester Lee Johnson," Honma Trial, R1281–3. See also "Exhibit 425: Affidavit of Earnest P. King," Honma Trial, R3285–8.
138. "Testimony of Homma Masaharu," Honma Trial, R3144.
139. Ibid., R3145.
140. "Testimony of Horiguchi Shusuke," Honma Trial, R2868.
141. Ibid., R2885.
142. "Testimony of Homma Masaharu," Honma Trial, R3113. See also R3145, 3231.
143. "The Closing Argument on Behalf of the Defense," Honma Trial, R3331.
144. "Testimony of Wachi Takeji," Honma Trial, R2515.
145. Ibid., R2513–14. For more information regarding the circumstances of this personnel change, see "Testimony of Wachi Takeji," Honma Trial, R2557; "Testimony of Wada Moriya," Honma Trial, R2700–1; "Testimony of Homma Masaharu," Honma Trial, R3231.
146. "Testimony of Col. Nemesio Catalan," Honma Trial, R1482–3; "Testimony of Wachi Takeji," Honma Trial, R2487–8; "Testimony of Homma Masaharu," Honma Trial, R3117–18, 3230–1; "Testimony of Wada Moriya," Honma Trial, R2696–7.
147. "Testimony of Col. Nemesio Catalan," Honma Trial, R1479.
148. "The Closing Argument on Behalf of the Defense," Honma Trial, R3316. See also R2422–3 for the prosecution's argument.
149. "Exhibit I: Compilation of Reports of Cases Tried by the Courts-Martial between January 1942 and August 1942," Honma Trial, R3099. See also "Testimony of Homma Masaharu," Honma Trial, R3104–5, 3192.
150. "The Closing Argument on Behalf of the Defense," Honma Trial, R3316.
151. "Testimony of Wachi Takeji," Honma Trial, R2541.
152. Ibid., R2451.
153. Ibid., R2558.
154. "Testimony of Ohta Seiichi," Honma Trial, R2619–20. Ōta testified that he was responsible also for the *kenpeitai* headquarters in Tokyo. Honma Trial, R2624.
155. "Testimony of Homma Masaharu," Honma Trial, R3069.
156. Ibid., R3156. Terauchi is referred to as "Count Terauchi," as he was a member of modern Japanese aristocracy. A hereditary peerage was introduced in Japan in 1885 and abolished after World War II. Terauchi was the eldest son of Terauchi Masatake, a decorated Meiji-era army general. For biographical information on Terauchi Hisaichi, see Jōhō Yoshio, *Gensui Terauchi Hisaichi* [General Terauchi Hisaichi] (Tokyo: Fuyō shobō, 1978).
157. "Testimony of Homma Masaharu," Honma Trial, R3156–7.
158. "The Closing Argument on Behalf of the Defense," Honma Trial, R3341.
159. The Court revised the period of Honma's tenure as commanding general of the 14th Army to read between December 10, 1941, and August 4, 1942, not "8 December 1941 and 15 August 1942" as it originally appeared in the charge sheet. Honma Trial, R3365.

160. "United States vs. MASAHARA [Masaharu] HOMMA" (review report by 1st Lt. Henry H. Willmott, JAGD, Assistant Staff Judge Advocate, with concurrence of Col. Ashton M. Haynes, JAGD, Staff Judge Advocate, with a note of approval of the sentence by Lt. Gen. W. D. Styer, U.S. Army Commanding, the United States Army Forces Western Pacific, Office of the Commanding General, February 19, 1946, pending the action of the Supreme Commander for the Allied Powers, dated February 18, 1946), in "Headquarters Philippines-Ryukyus Command. Review by Office of the Staff Judge Advocate, vol. I, entry UD 1274, RG 331, SCAP, Records of the SCAP Legal Section, Administrative Division, 8th Army Reviews, 1946–1950, Box 1381, NARA.
161. Ibid., p. 9.
162. Ibid., p. 8.
163. Ibid. See also Honma Trial, R105-a.
164. "United States vs SEIICHI OHTA" (review report by Lt. Col. Bernard A. Brown, JAGD, Chief, War Crimes Sub-Section, with concurrence of Col. Ashton M. Haynes, JAGD, Staff Judge Advocate, with a note of approval of the sentence by Lt. Gen. W. D. Styer, U.S. Army Commanding, the United States Army Forces Western Commander for the Allied Powers, dated January 11, 1946), in "Headquarters Philippines-Ryukyus Command. Review by Office of the Staff Judge Advocate, vol. I, entry UD 1274, RG 331, SCAP Records of the SCAP Legal Section, Administrative Division, 8th Army Reviews, 1946–1950, Box 1381, NARA, p. 1. For the record of the trial of Ōta, see "Seiichi Ohta," entry UD 1321, RG 331, SCAP, Records of the SCAP Legal Section, Prosecution Division, US vs. Japanese War Criminal Case Files, 1945–1949, Box 1554, NARA.
165. For the record of the trial of Kawane, see "Case Docket No. 304: Kurataro Hirano, Yoshitaka Kawane," entry UD 1865, RG 331, SCAP Judge Advocate Section, War Crimes Division, Records of Trial File, 1945–1949, Boxes 9534-5, 9589–90, NARA. For short biographical information on Kawane, see Fukukawa, *Nihon rikugun shōkan jiten*, p. 237.
166. For the record of the trial of Tsuneyoshi, see "Case Docket No. 230: Yoshio Tsuneyoshi," entry UD 1865, RG 331, SCAP Judge Advocate Section, War Crimes Division, Records of Trial File, 1945–1949, Box 9580, NARA.
167. "Review of the Staff Judge Advocate" (Tsuneyoshi case, no. 230, dated May 24, 1949), in "Reviews of the Yokohama Class B and Class C War Crimes Trials by the 8th Army Judge Advocate, 1946–1949" (College Park, MD: NARA), microfilm, M1112, roll 3, p. 16. To verify Hirano's given name, I referred to Greg Bradsher, ed., *Japanese War Crimes and Related Topics: A Guide to Records at the National Archives* (College Park, MD: NARA, n.d.). This guide is supplied in a CD attached to Greg Bradsher, et al., *Researching Japanese War Crimes Records: Introductory Essays* (Washington, DC: NARA for the Nazi War Crimes and Japanese Imperial Government Records Interagency Working Group, 2006). It is also available online, http://www.archives.gov/iwg/japanese-war-crimes. Hirano's case file is "Case Docket No. 304: Kurataro Hirano, Yoshitaka Kawane," entry UD 1865, RG 331, SCAP Judge Advocate Section, War Crimes Division, Records of Trial File, 1945–1949, Boxes 9534-5, 9589–90, NARA.
168. "The Prosecution Opening Statement," Kuroda Trial, R24-5.

169. "Testimony of Willard H. Waterous," Kuroda Trial, R441–70. For the same witness's testimony at the Honma Trial, see Honma Trial, R755–80, 1592–6, 1744–53, 2035–53.

170. Wachi served as chief of staff for the successive commanding generals of the 14th Army. He was removed from the position at the end of March 1944, after which Lt. Gen. Isayama Haruki was appointed to serve in the same position. "Exhibit 94: Affidavit of Wachi Takeji," Kuroda Trial, R564. For Isayama's brief biographical information, see Fukukawa, *Nihon riku-kaigun jinmei jiten*, p. 37.

171. "The Prosecution Opening Statement for the Philippine Phase," Kuroda Trial, R576–7.

172. For the record of the Kōno Trial, see "Takeshi Kono," entry UD 1321, RG 331, SCAP, Records of the SCAP Legal Section, Prosecution Division: US vs. Japanese War Criminal Case Files, 1945–1949, Box 1563, NARA.

173. "Exhibit 117 (Philippine Phase): Testimony of Dr. Fermin G. Carem," p. 854, Kuroda Trial, R1295.

174. "Testimony of Kuroda Shigenori," Kuroda Trial, R1532–4.

175. "Testimony of Kawai Tadaharu," Kuroda Trial, R1214.

176. Ibid., R1214–15.

177. Ibid., R1213.

178. For the record of the Matsuzaki Trial, see "Hideichi Matsuzaki," entry UD 1323, RG 331, SCAP, Records of the SCAP Legal Section Prosecution Division: Philippines vs. Various Japanese War Criminals Case Files, 1947–1949, Box 1691, NARA.

179. "Testimony of Matsuzaki Hideichi," Kuroda Trial, R1243.

180. Ibid., R1240.

181. Ibid., R1275.

182. "Testimony of Kuroda Shigenori," R1324–1782. Kuroda spent three years of his formative years in Britain, as a result of which he gained fluency in English. During his trial, he testified in Japanese. By the Court's decision, however, he was required to take all questions in English. Kuroda Trial, R1328.

183. The defense documentary evidence comprised organizational charts, maps, extracts from Philippine newspapers, the Japanese army ministry regulations, a report on the conditions of Allied assaults in the Philippines (prepared by the Japanese First Demobilization Bureau, the former Army Ministry), affidavits, sworn statements, and excerpts from preceding U.S. and Philippine trials held at Manila.

184. Capt. Pedro A. Serran, chief defense counsel, informed the court that "the accused himself has lost his voice and physically unfit so that we will be proceeding by presenting documentary evidence at this stage of the trial." Kuroda Trial, R1426. For the entirety of Kuroda's testimony, see Kuroda Trial, R1324–1425, 1513–1762. For the testimony of Yamashita and Honma respectively, see Yamashita Trial, R3518–3660, 3865–3904, and Honma Trial, R3028–3235.

185. "Testimony of Kuroda Shigenori," Kuroda Trial, R1617.

186. Ibid., R1374–5.

187. Ibid., R1615.

188. Ibid., R1616–17.

189. Ibid., R1614–15.

190. Ibid., R1674. For an in-depth study of the Japanese police and justice systems prior to and during World War II, see, for instance, Richard H. Mitchell,

Janus-Faced Justice: Political Criminals in Imperial Japan (Honolulu: University of Hawai'i Press, 1992). For an overview of crimes and criminal justice systems in Japan before, during, and after the Pacific War, see Shinichi Tsuchiya and Minoru Shikita, *Crime and Criminal Policy in Japan from 1922–1988: Analysis and Evaluation of the Shōwa Era* (Tokyo: Japan Criminal Policy Society, 1990). The latter publication was originally written in Japanese as Tsuchiya Shinichi, *Shōwa no keiji seisaku* [Criminal policy in the Shōwa period].

191. "Testimony of Kuroda Shigenori," Kuroda Trial, R1675–6.
192. Ibid., R1610–11.
193. Ibid., R1648.
194. Ibid., R1727. Emphasis added.
195. "Testimony of Tomas Morato," Kuroda Trial, R1782.
196. Ibid., R1784.
197. "Testimony of Jorge B. Vargas," Kuroda Trial, R2018–19.
198. Ibid., R2016.
199. "Testimony of Camilo Osias," Kuroda Trial, R2042.
200. Ibid., R2033.
201. Ibid., R2043–4.
202. Ibid., R2063. Emphasis added.
203. "Testimony of Kuroda Shigenori," Kuroda Trial, R1384–6.
204. "Exhibit 93 (Defense Phase): Excerpts from the Collection of Laws and Regulations Concerning Prisoners of Wars – Ordinance concerning POW Camps (Dec. 23, 1941, Imperial Ordinance No. 1182)," Kuroda Trial, R2065. The Japanese translation can be found in Chaen Yoshio, ed., *Furyo ni kansuru shohōki ruijū (Jūgonen sensō gokuhi shiryōshū, 11)* [The compilation of various rules concerning prisoners of war (Secret sources of the Fifteen-Year War, vol. 11)] (Tokyo: Fuji shuppan, 1988), pp. 17–8.
205. Exhibit 93 (Defense Phase), p. 1, Kuroda Trial.
206. Kuroda Trial, R2065–9
207. "Testimony of Kuroda Shigenori," Kuroda Trial, R1656.
208. Ibid., R1667–8.
209. The phrase "Commander in Chief of the Imperial Japanese Forces in the Philippines" in the charge sheet was changed to "Commanding General of the 14th Army, later the 14th Army Group, the Army of Occupation in the Philippines, and Head of the Japanese Military Administration in the Philippines" in the decision. Kuroda Trial, R3084. The accused was found not guilty of specifications that the prosecution had already withdrawn or failed to substantiate. See Kuroda Trial, R573, 1315. See also "Testimony of Wachi Takaji," Kuroda Trial, R565–6.
210. "Rationale," pp. 6–7, Kuroda Trial, R3074.
211. Japan signed and ratified the Hague Convention No. 4 of 1907 but not all other signatories did. This convention contained the so-called "general participation clause," by which "the Convention would be binding only if all the Belligerents were parties to it." Boister and Cryer, *Documents on the Tokyo International Military Tribunal*, pp. 102, 104. As for the Geneva Convention Relative to the Treatment of Prisoners of War of 1929, Japan signed it but did not ratify it. In the wake of the outbreak of the Pacific War, however, the Japanese government informed the Allied governments that "while she [Japan]

was not formally bound by the Convention, she would apply the Convention, 'mutatis mutandis,' toward American, British, Canadian, Australian and New Zealand prisoners of war." Boister and Cryer, *Documents on the Tokyo International Military Tribunal*, p. 106. The Tokyo Tribunal weighed the legal effect of these and other international conventions concerning the laws of war, and reached the following conclusion. "Reference has been made in an earlier part of this judgment to the effect of the various conventions in relation to the treatment of prisoners of war and civilian internees and to the obligations of belligerents in that respect. Whatever view may be taken of the assurance or undertaking of the Japanese Government to comply with the Geneva Prisoner of War Convention '<u>mutatis mutandis</u>' the fact remains that under the customary rules of war, acknowledged by all civilized nations, all prisoners of war and civilian internees must be given humane treatment. It is the grossly inhumane treatmet by the Japanese military forces . . . that is particularly reprehensible and criminal. [A] person guilty of such inhumanities cannot escape punishment on the plea that he or his government is not bound by any particular convention. The general principles of the law exist independently of the said conventions. The conventions merely reaffirms the pre-existing law and prescribe detailed privosions for its application." Boister and Cryer, *Documents on the Tokyo International Military Tribunal*, p. 578.

212. "Rationale," p. 8, Kuroda Trial.
213. Ibid., p. 9.
214. Ibid., p. 10.
215. Ibid., p. 11.
216. Ibid., pp. 12–13.
217. Chamberlain, *Justice and Reconciliation*, pp. 113–17. For a study of Philippine policy on clemency and repatriation of Japanese war criminals, see also Beatrice Trefalt, "Hostages to International Relations? The Repatriation of Japanese War Criminals from the Philippines," *Japanese Studies*, vol. 31, no. 2 (September 2011): pp. 191–209. For a contemporary Japanese-language account of Kuroda's repatriation, see Tsuji Yutaka, *Montenrupa: Hitō yūshū no kiroku* [Muntinlupa: Records of imprisonment in the Philippines] (Tokyo: Asahi shinbunsha, 1952), pp. 19–25.
218. "Testimony of Camilo Osias," Kuroda Trial, R2048–9. Emphasis added.
219. For Osias's autobiography, see Camilo Osias, *The Story of a Long Career of Varied Tasks* (Quezon City, Philippines: Manlapaz, 1971). For a pathbreaking study of wartime Philippine collaborators, see David Joel Steinberg, *Philippine Collaboration in World War II* (Ann Arbor, MI: University of Michigan Press, 1962).

CHAPTER 2

1. Richard Harding Davis et al., *The Russo-Japanese War: A Photographic and Descriptive Review of the Great Conflict in the Far East* (New York, NY: P. F. Collier & Son, 1905), p. 101. I would like to express my heartfelt gratitude to Ferdinand Martignetti, who presented me with a copy of this rare book when I had a brief teaching stint at Harvard University back in 2005. I have put this book to use in my class many times ever since, and it also inspired me to write the introductory segment of this chapter as I have.

2. Ibid., Introduction.

3. For a historical study of war correspondents from the mid-nineteenth century to the Vietnam War, see Phillip Knightley, *The First Casualty: From the Crimea to Vietnam: The War Correspondent as Hero, Propagandist, and Myth Maker* (New York, NY and London, UK: Harcourt Brace Jovanovich, 1975). For analysis of Japanese news reporting at the turn of the century, see Katayama Yoshitaka, *Nichi-Ro sensō to shinbun: "sekai no naka no Nihon" o dō ronjitaka* [The Russo-Japanese War and newspapers: How was "Japan in the world" debated?] (Tokyo: Kōdansha, 2009); Hirama Yōichi, *Nichi-Ro sensō o sekai wa dō hōjitaka* [How did the world report on the Russo-Japanese War?] (Tokyo: Fuyō shobō shuppan, 2010); and Inoue Yūko, *Nisshin, Nichi-Ro sensō to shashin hōdō* [The Sino-Japanese War, the Russo-Japanese War, and photojournalism] (Tokyo: Yoshikawa kōbunkan, 2012).

4. For accounts of the treatment of Japanese and Russian prisoners of war in connection with the Russo-Japanese War, see Utsumi Aiko, *Nihongun no horyo seisaku* [Prisoner-of-war policies of the Japanese military] (Tokyo: Aoki shoten, 2005), pp. 72–124; Fukiura Tadamasa, *Horyotachi no Nichi-Ro sensō* [The Russo-Japanese War from the perspective of prisoners of war] (Tokyo: Nihon hōsō shuppan kyōkai, 2005); Ōkuma Hideji, *Nichi-Ro sensō no uragawa "daini no kaikoku": Nihon rettō ni jōrikushita Roshiagun horyo shichiman-nin* ["The second opening of the country" behind the scenes of the Russo-Japanese War: 70,000 Russian prisoners of war who landed on the Japanese archipelago] (Tokyo: Sairyūsha, 2011); and Miyawaki Noboru, *Roshia-hei horyo ga aruita Matsuyama: Nichi-Ro sensō ka no kokusai kōryū* [The city of Matsuyama in which the Russian prisoners of war walked: International exchange during the Russo-Japanese War] (Matsuyama: Ehime shinbunsha, 2005).

5. Publications that document the Japanese mistreatment of Allied prisoners of war during the Pacific War are many. A key reference is Van Waterford, *Prisoners of the Japanese in World War II: Statistical History, Personal Narratives and Memorials Concerning POWs in Camps and on Hellships, Civilian Internees, Asian Slave Laborers and Others Captured in the Pacific Theater* (Jefferson, NC, and London, UK: McFarland, 1994). For a narrative account of prisoner-of-war experiences with broad coverage of the Pacific theater, see Gavan Daws, *Prisoners of the Japanese: POWs of World War II in the Pacific* (New York, NY: William Morrow, 1994).

6. Tachikawa Kyōichi, "Kyūgun ni okeru horyo no toriatsukai: Taiheiyō sensō no jōkyō o chūshin ni" [Treatment of prisoners of war by the former army: Centering on the circumstances of the Pacific War], *Bōei kenkyūjo kiyō* [Bulletin of the National Institute for Defense Studies] 10, no. 1 (September, 2007): p. 89.

7. The Tokyo Tribunal heard a single joint case against twenty-eight defendants. The charges were crimes against peace, murder, war crimes, and crimes against humanity. The number of defendants was reduced to twenty-five during the court proceedings, due to two deaths and one case of mental unfitness to stand trial. For more discussion of the charges and the Tribunal's findings, see Totani, *Tokyo War Crimes Trial*.

8. Most of the record of the Tamura Trial is included in "Records of the Trial of Accused War Criminal Hiroshi Tamura, Tried by a Military Tribunal Appointed by the Supreme Commander of the Allied Powers, Tokyo, Japan,

1948–1949" (College Park, MD: NARA), microfilm, M1728, 3 rolls. A section of the trial record that is missing in the M1728 series can be found in "Transcripts from the Case of the United States of America vs. Soemu Toyoda and Hiroshi Tamura, 1946–1948" (College Park, MD: NARA), microfilm, M1661, rolls 1–2. The record of the Tamura Trial will be referred to as the "Tamura Trial" hereafter in the notes, and in the text.

9. "Majority Judgment," in Boister and Cryer, *Documents on the Tokyo International Military Tribunal*, pp. 304–5.

10. Ibid., p. 532. For the Japanese original, I refer to *Kyokutō kokusai gunji saiban sokkiroku* [Transcripts of court proceedings at the International Military Tribunal for the Far East], vol. 10 (Tokyo: Yūshūdō shoten, 1968), p. 766.

11. Hirota's brief biographical information can be found in the indictment contained in Boister and Cryer, *Documents on the Tokyo International Military Tribunal*, pp. 64–5.

12. "Majority Judgment," in Boister and Cryer, *Documents on the Tokyo International Military Tribunal*, p. 532. For the Japanese original, see *Kyokutō kokusai gunji saiban sokkiroku*, vol. 10, p. 767.

13. Hiranuma's brief biographical information can be found in the indictment contained in Boister and Cryer, *Documents on the Tokyo International Military Tribunal*, p. 64.

14. "Majority Judgment," in Boister and Cryer, *Documents on the Tokyo International Military Tribunal*, p. 532. Emphasis added. For the Japanese original, see *Kyokutō kokusai gunji saiban sokkiroku*, vol. 10, p. 767.

15. "Majority Judgment," in Boister and Cryer, *Documents on the Tokyo International Military Tribunal*, p. 534. The full text of the Lytton Report is available online at the Web site of Sōgo bijinesusha (a Japanese publisher), "The Report of the Commission of Inquiry," accessed April 5, 2014, http://www.business-sha. co.jp/wp-content/uploads/Lytton_Commission.pdf. For the Japanese original the quoted passage, see *Kyokutō kokusai gunji saiban sokkiroku*, vol. 10, p. 767.

16. "Majority Judgment," in Boister and Cryer, *Documents on the Tokyo International Military Tribunal*, p. 534. The Pingdingshan Massacre has been extensively researched in Japan, especially in connection with a reparation lawsuit fought by survivors at a Japanese court in 1990–2006. For an overview of the case, see Heichōzan jiken soshō bengodan [The Lawyers' Association for the Litigation on the Pingdingshan Incident], *Heichōzan jiken to wa nandattanoka: saiban ga tsumuida Nihon to Chūgoku no shimin no kizuna* [What was the Pingdingshan Incident? The strengthening of ties between the Japanese and Chinese citizens through the trial] (Tokyo: Kōbunken, 2008). For a source book, see Inoue Hisashi and Kawakami Shirō, *Heichōzan jiken shiryōshū* [Sources of the Pingdingshan Incident] (Tokyo: Kashiwa shobō, 2012).

17. "Majority Judgment," in Boister and Cryer, *Documents on the Tokyo International Military Tribunal*, p. 535.

18. Ibid., p. 535.

19. Ibid., p. 538.

20. Ibid., p. 541.

21. Ibid., p. 535.

22. For studies of collaboration in wartime China, see Timothy Brook, *Collaboration: Japanese Agents and Local Elites in Wartime China* (Cambridge, MA: Harvard

University Press, 2007); and John Hunter Boyle, *China and Japan at War, 1936–1945: The Politics of Collaboration* (Stanford, CA: Stanford University Press, 1972).

23. Nishinarita Yutaka, *Chūgokujin kyōsei renkō* [Chinese forced deportation] (Tokyo: Tōkyō daigaku shuppankai, 2002), pp. 88, 307. The mass deportation of Chinese people for forced labor has been studied extensively in Japan. Major publications include, but are not limited to, the following: Nishinarita, *Chūgokujin kyōsei renkō*; Sugihara Tōru, *Chūgokujin kyōsei renkō* [Chinese forced deportation] (Tokyo: Iwanami shoten, 2002); Nozoe Kenji, *Kigyō no sekinin: Chūgokujin kyōsei renkō no genba kara* [Corporate responsibility for war: From the scenes of Chinese forced deportation] (Tokyo: Shakai hyōronsha, 2009); and Ishitobi Jin, *Chūgokujin kyōsei renkō no kiroku: Nihonjin wa Chūgokujin ni nani o shitaka* [Records of Chinese forced deportation: What the Japanese did to the Chinese] (Tokyo: San'ichi shobō, 1997). Published source materials include: Tanaka Hiroshi, Utsumi Aiko, and Ishitobi Jin, eds., *Shiryō Chūgokujin kyōsei renkō no kiroku* [Sources: Records on Chinese forced deportation] (Tokyo: Akashi shoten, 1987); Tanaka Hiroshi, Utsumi Aiko, and Niimi Takashi, *Shiryō Chūgoku kyōsei renkō no kiroku* [Records of Chinese forced deportation] (Tokyo: Akashi shoten, 1990); and Tanaka Hiroshi and Matsuzawa Tetsuya, *Chūgokujin kyōsei renkō shiryō: "Gaimushō hōkokusho" zen-5-bunsatsu hoka* [Sources on Chinese forced deportation: "Reports by the Ministry of Foreign Affairs," 5 volumes and others] (Tokyo: Gendai shokan, 1995). For a comprehensive study of Chinese reparation lawsuits at Japanese courts in general, see Chūgokujin sensō higai baishō seikyū jiken bengodan [The Lawyers' Association for Reparation Lawsuits by Chinese Victims of the War], *Sajōno shōheki: Chūgokujin sengo hoshō saiban 10-nen no kiseki* [Barrier on the sand: The ten-year trajectory of postwar Chinese reparation trials] (Tokyo: Nihon hyōronsha, 2005).

24. "Majority Judgment," in Boister and Cryer, *Documents on the Tokyo International Military Tribunal*, p. 539.

25. Ibid., p. 540.

26. Ibid., p. 535. Known as the Hanaoka Incident, this particular case of forced labor and mistreatment of Chinese people sent to Akita Prefecture was brought to trial at the U.S. Yokohama Trial. "Case Docket No. 74: Kingoro Fukuda, et al.," entry UD 1865, RG 331, SCAP Judge Advocate Section, War Crimes Division, Records of Trial File, 1945–1949, Boxes 9613–14, NARA, College Park, MD. The trial record has recently been published in Japan by Hanaoka kenkyūkai [The Hanaoka Research Group], ed., *Hanaoka jiken Yokohama hōtei kiroku: BC-kyū senpan saiban no daihyōteki jirei* [The Yokohama court record on the Hanaoka Incident: A representative case in the Class BC war crimes trials] (Tokyo: Sōwasha, 2006). Civil litigation in the postwar period resulted in the out-of-court settlement between the Chinese plaintiffs and the Kashima Construction Company. For more information, see Ishitobi Jin, *Hanaoka jiken: "Kashima kōshō" no kiseki* [The Hanaoka Incident: The trajectory of the "Kashima Negotiation"] (Tokyo: Sairyūsha, 2010); Niimi Takashi, *Kokka no sekinin to jinken: guntai kiritsu ron, anzen hairyo gimu no hōri* [State responsibility and human rights: Legal principles on military discipline and obligations for a safety guarantee] (Tokyo: Yui shobō, 2006); Naitō Mitsuhiro

and Furukawa Atsushi, *Tōhoku Ajia no hō to seiji* [Law and politics in North-east Asia] (Tokyo: Senshū daigaku shuppankyoku, 2005); and Sengo hoshō mondai kokkai gijiroku henshū iinkai [The Committee for the Compilation of Parliamentary Records on Postwar Reparation Issues], ed., *Shiryō: sengo hoshō mondai kokkai gijiroku* [Sources: Parliamentary records on postwar reparation issues] (Tokyo: Sengo hoshō mondai kokkai gijiroku henshū iinkai, 1993).

27. "Majority Judgment," in Boister and Cryer, *Documents on the Tokyo International Military Tribunal*, p. 540. While this instance of massacre involved navy personnel, the army appears to have had jurisdiction over the island and took charge of the investigation.

28. For related discussion, see Totani, *Tokyo War Crimes Trial*, pp. 152–5.

29. "Exhibit 12: Laws, Rules, and Regulations Pertaining to Prisoners of War – Ordinance of Prisoner of War Units (Imperial Ordinance No. 1182, December 23, 1941)," p. 5, Tamura Trial, R85. (In short citations of Exhibit 12 in the following notes, the number following "p." is the page number within the exhibit, the same as for other exhibits, and the title in parentheses is a heading on that page.) This document was introduced in evidence also at the Kuroda Trial (and is discussed in part in Chapter 1). The Japanese original can be found in Chaen Yoshio, ed., *Furyo ni kansuru shohōki ruijū* (*Jūgonen sensō gokuhi shiryōshū*, 11) [The compilation of various rules concerning prisoners of war (Secret sources of the Fifteen-Year War, vol. 11)] (Tokyo: Fuji shuppan, 1988), pp. 17–18.

30. Exhibit 12, p. 10 ('Detailed Regulations for the Treatment of Prisoners of War, Army Ministry Notification No. 29, April 21, 1943, as amended by Army Ministry Notification No. 58, 1943'), Tamura Trial. For the Japanese original, see "Furyo toriatsukai saisoku" (Shō-18-4-21, Riku-tatsu-29), in Chaen, *Furyo ni kansuru shohōki ruijū*, pp. 24–9.

31. Exhibit 12, p. 6 ('Regulations for the Treatment of Prisoners of War, Army Ministry Notification No. 22, December 14, 1904, as amended by the Army Ministry Notification No. 167, 1904; No. 7, 1905; No. 31, 1914; Army Ministry Notification, HQs, 30 and 57, 1943'), Tamura Trial. For the Japanese original, see "Furyo toriatsukai kisoku" (Mei-37-2-14, Riku-tatsu-22), in Chaen, *Furyo ni kansuru shohōki ruijū*, p. 19. The date of issuance of Notification No. 22 in the original version in Japanese appears as February 14, 1904.

32. Exhibit 12, p. 3 ('Organization of the Prisoner of War Information Bureau, Imperial Ordinance No. 1246, December 27, 1941'), Tamura Trial.

33. "Exhibit 56: Statement of Sanada Joichiro," p. 3, Tamura Trial, R172. For Sanada Jōichirō's biographical information, see Fukukawa, *Nihon rikugun shōkan jiten*, p. 355.

34. Article 14. The full text of the Hague Convention No. 4 Respecting the Laws and Customs of War on Land can be found as "Laws and Customs of War on Land (Hague, IV)," in Friedman, *Law of War*, vol. 1, pp. 308–23. The text can be found online by visiting the Web site of the International Committee of the Red Cross at http://www.icrc.org/applic/ihl/ihl.nsf/INTRO/195.

35. Exhibit 12, p. 3 ('Organization of the Prisoner of War Information Bureau, Imperial Ordinance No. 1246, December 27, 1941'), Tamura Trial.

36. Friedman, *Law of War*, vol. 1, pp. 488–522.

37. "Majority Judgment," in Boister and Cryer, *Documents on the Tokyo International Military Tribunal*, p. 576.

38. Ibid., p. 577.

39. Exhibit 56, p. 3, Tamura Trial. See also Exhibit 12, p. 4 ('Regulations for the Treatment of Prisoners of War, Army Ministry Notification Asia, Confidential, No. 1034, March 31, 1942'), Tamura Trial. For the Japanese original, see "Furyo toriatsukai ni kansuru kitei" (Shō-17-3-31, Riku-A-Mitsu-1034), in Chaen, *Furyo ni kansuru shohōki ruijū*, pp. 15–16.

40. "Exhibit 16: Notification to the Chief of the POW Control Bureau from the Adjutant (November 22, 1942')," Tamura Trial, R121.

41. "Exhibit 59: Extract from Monthly Report No. 5 on Prisoners of War, POW Information Bureau (Vol. UA-1)," Tamura Trial, R221.

42. A reprint of "Laws, Rules and Regulations Concerning Prisoners of War" (*Furyo ni kansuru shohōki ruijū*), the November 1943 edition, is available in Chaen, *Furyo ni kansuru shohōki ruijū*, pp. 1–259. Regarding the distribution of this material within the army, I referred to the trial record "Rimpei Kato, Okikatsu Arao, Goro Isoya, Choho Mononobe, Hiroshi Nukata, Bunro Saheki, Mitsuo Tomita, Yahei Toyama, Tadakatsu Wakamatsu," entry UD 1321, RG 331, SCAP, Records of the SCAP Legal Section, Prosecution Division: US vs. Japanese War Criminal Case Files, 1945–1949, Boxes 1637–8, NARA, College Park, MD, especially the prosecution's opening statement, R51, and "Exhibit 9: Affidavit of Yotsumoto Masanori (June 4, 1948)," p. 1, R62.

43. Exhibit 56, p. 6, Tamura Trial.

44. "Majority Judgment," in Boister and Cryer, *Documents on the Tokyo International Military Tribunal*, pp. 531–2.

45. Exhibit 12, p. 39 ('Disposal of Prisoners of War, Army Ministry Notification, Asia, Confidential, No. 1456'), Tamura Trial. For the Japanese original, see "Nanpō ni okeru furyo no shori yōryō no ken" (Shō-17-5-5, Hyō-Sō-Kō-34), in Chaen, *Furyo ni kansuru shohōki ruijū*, pp. 57–8.

46. Racial segregation in Japanese prisoner-of-war policy has been discussed extensively in Japanese-language scholarship to date. An authoritative study can be found in Utsumi, *Nihongun no horyo seisaku*, pp. 167–515.

47. "Exhibit 60: Instructions of War Minister Hideki Tojo to the Newly-Appointed Commanders of the Prisoner of War Camps (July 7, 1942)," Tamura Trial, R222. This exhibit was introduced at the Tokyo Trial as Prosecution Exhibit No. 1963. A reprint of the Japanese original can be found in Utsumi Aiko and Nagai Hitoshi, eds., *Tōkyō saiban: horyo kankei shiryō* [The Tokyo Trial: Sources related to prisoners of war], vol. 2, (Tokyo: Gendai shiryō shuppan, 2012), p. 127. Substantially the same instruction was repeated in "Exhibit 61: Instructions of War Minister Hideki Tojo Following his Visit to Zentsuji (May 30, 1943)," Tamura Trial, R224.

48. For accounts of prisoner-of-war sea transfer and related war crimes by the Japanese during the Pacific War, see Gregory F. Michno, *Death on the Hell-ships: Prisoners at Sea in the Pacific War* (Annapolis, MD: Leo Cooper, 2001); and Raymond Lamont-Brown, *Ships from Hell: Japanese War Crimes on the High Seas* (Stroud, UK: Sutton Publishing, 2002). For an Allied war crimes trial that contains detailed documentation of organizational aspects of war crimes related to prisoner-of-war shipment, see "Rimpei Kato, Okikatsu Arao, Goro Isoya, Choho Mononobe, Hiroshi Nukata, Bunro Saheki, Mitsuo Tomita, Yahei Toyama, Tadakatsu Wakamatsu," entry UD 1321, RG 331, SCAP, Records of

the SCAP Legal Section, Prosecution Division: US vs. Japanese War Criminal Case Files, 1945–1949, Boxes 1637–8, NARA, College Park, MD. I am indebted to Sharon Chamberlain, who made a digital photographic copy of the transcripts of the court proceedings of the U.S. Yokohama Trial of Katō et al. For a study of hellship trials held at the British Singapore court, see Wui Ling Cheah, "Post-World War II British 'Hell-Ship' Trials in Singapore: Omissions and the Attribution of Responsibility," *Journal of International Criminal Justice* 8 (2010), pp. 1035–58.

49. Exhibit 12, p. 40 ('Transportation of Prisoners of War, War Ministry, Asia, Confidential Report No. 5104, December 10, 1942'), Tamura Trial.
50. "Exhibit 66: Suggestions Regarding Improvement of Health Conditions of Prisoners of War Camps (Investigation Squad of Army Medical College)," Tamura Trial, R231.
51. Ibid., pp. 1–3.
52. "Exhibit 64: Excerpt from the War Prisoners' Information Bureau's Monthly Report (March 20, 1944) – Re Improvement of PW Administration (Army Asia, Secret No. 696, March 3, 1944)," Tamura Trial, R229.
53. "Charge" and "Specifications," Tamura Trial, R3–7.
54. Ibid.
55. "The Prosecution's Opening Statement," Tamura Trial, R67–8.
56. "Defense Motion for Finding of Not Guilty," Tamura Trial, R1241.
57. Exhibit 56, p. 4, Tamura Trial.
58. Ibid., p. 6.
59. "Testimony of Sanada Joichiro," Tamura Trial, R216.
60. Ibid., R175.
61. Ibid., R204.
62. "Exhibit 358: Affidavit of Sugai Toshimaro," p. 1, Tamura Trial, R953.
63. "Testimony of Sugai Toshimaro," Tamura Trial, R960.
64. Ibid., R958.
65. "Testimony of Hoda Haruo," Tamura Trial, R1075–6.
66. Ibid., R1089.
67. "Exhibit 429: Affidavit of Hoda Haruo," p. 6, Tamura Trial, R1048.
68. Ibid., p. 4.
69. Ibid., p. 6.
70. For Emoto's biographical information, see "Exhibit 134: Interrogation of Emoto Shigeo," Tamura Trial, R444. The prisoner-of-war camp group in Hokkaidō consisted of the main camp in Hakodate, three branch camps, and a dispatch camp. The prisoner-of-war population ranged between 1,000 and 1,300 during Emoto's service as area camp commandant. See Exhibit 134 for more information. For the record of the trial of Hatakeyama, see "Case Docket No. 203: Toshio Hatakayama [Hatakeyama]," entry UD 1865, RG 331, SCAP Judge Advocate Section, War Crimes Division, Records of Trial File, 1945–1949, Box 9521, NARA, College Park, MD.
71. Exhibit 134, p. 4, Tamura Trial.
72. Ibid., p. 6.
73. Ibid., pp. 8–10.
74. Ibid., p. 10.

75. Ibid., p. 12.
76. "Testimony of Emoto Shigeo," Tamura Trial, R498.
77. Tamura Trial, R1269.
78. Tamura Trial, R1382–3.
79. "Tonai tō kyojū no sensō saiban jukeisha tō ni taisuru mensetsu chōsa
    hōkokusho, No. 48 (Shōwa 37.3.12 – 8.17), Shōwa 37-nendo" [Report on inter-
    views and investigations of convicted war criminals etc. with residence
    in Tokyo, etc., No. 48 (March 12–August 17, 1962), Year 1962], Hōmu-Hei-11-
    4B-23-6575, National Archives of Japan, p. 26.
80. Ibid., p. 27.
81. Tamura Trial, R1382–3. Verdict of the court.

CHAPTER 3

1. The records of three trials analyzed in this chapter were obtained from the U.K.
   National Archives. The record group is known as "WO 235 – Judge Advocate
   General's Office: War Crimes Case Files, Second World War." The citation
   information of the three trials is as follows: "WO235/963 – Defendant Ishida
   Eiguma, Place of Trial Singapore"; "WO235/1034 – Defendant Banno Hiroteru,
   Place of Trial Singapore"; and "WO235/943 – Defendant Kudo Hikosaku, Place
   of Trial Singapore". The three trials will be referred hereafter as the "Ishida
   Trial," the "Banno Trial," and the "Kudō Trial."
2. For the American strategic plans on China in the initial months of the Pacific
   War, see Grace Person Hayes, *The History of the Joint Chiefs of Staff in World
   War II: The War against Japan* (Annapolis, MD: Naval Institute Press, 1982),
   pp. 71–81, 198–249.
3. Rekishigaku kenkyūkai [History Research Association], ed., *Taiheiyō sensōshi:
   4. Taiheiyō sensō, 1. 1940–1942* [The history of the Pacific War: Vol. 4. The
   Pacific War, 1. 1940–1942], pp. 44–9; Louis Allen, *Burma: The Longest War
   1941–45* (London, UK, and Melbourne, Australia: J.M. Dent & Sons, 1984),
   p. 7; Frank McLynn, *The Burma Campaign: Disaster into Triumph 1942–1945*
   (New Haven, CT, and London, UK: Yale University Press, 2011), pp. 5–6, 19,
   53. There are a number of narrative accounts of the war in the CBI theater. For
   representative publications, see Allen, *Burma: The Longest War 1941–1945*;
   and Sir William Slim, *Defeat into Victory: Battling Japan in Burma and India,
   1942–1945* (London, UK: The Print Society, 1956). For an account of the
   Asia-Pacific War with an emphasis on China, see Rana Mitter, *Forgotten Ally:
   China's World War II 1937–1945* (Boston, MA: Houghton Mifflin Harcourt,
   2013). For the Japanese grand strategy concerning the invasion of Burma,
   see, for instance, Bōei kenshūjo senshishitsu, ed., *Senshi sōsho: 5. Biruma
   kōryakusen* [War history series: Vol. 5. The invasion of Burma] (Tokyo: Asagumo shinbunsha, 1967).
4. There are innumerable publications on the Burma-Siam Death Railway to
   date. For published primary-source documents, see Paul H. Kratoska, *The
   Thailand-Burma Railway, 1942–1946: Documents and Selected Writings*,
   6 vols. (London, UK and New York, NY: Routledge, 2006); and T.R. Sareen,
   Building the Siam-Burma Railway during World War II (A Documentary

Study) (Delhi: Kalpaz, 2005). These publications contain reproductions of some evidence that the British prosecutors put to use at the trials analyzed in this chapter.

5. "Abstract of Evidence," p. 9, Ishida Trial, SP885.
6. "Exhibit I: Affidavit by Robert Crawford," Kudō Trial, R34.
7. According to a report produced by British medical officers (dated November 23, 1945), Terauchi was "suffering from advanced arteriosclerosis with cerebral degeneration." The report reads that Terauchi's staff found him to be "in full possession of his faculties and carrying out all his duties up to April 10th 1945," when he "developed a partial paralysis of his left side and some difficulty with his speech." He came to have great difficulty understanding reports made to him since around November 18, 1945, onwards. "Examination of Field Marshal TERAUCHI on November 23rd 1945," in "War Crimes: Policy," reference number WO203/5595, U.K. National Archives. For Terauchi's biography, see Jōhō, *Gensui Terauchi Hisaichi.*
8. "Exhibit I: Report on Employment of War Prisoners in SIAM-BURMA Railway," Ishida Trial, R8. For information concerning war crimes investigations by the postwar Japanese government authorities, see the introductory essay in Nagai Hitoshi, ed., *Sensō hanzai chōsa shiryō: furyo chōsa chūō iinkai chōsa hōkokusho tsuzuri* [Sources on war crimes investigations: The compilation of investigation reports by the central committee for investigations concerning prisoners of war] (Tokyo: Higashi shuppan, 1995). The original Japanese version of the report, titled, "Tai, Biruma rensetsu tetsudō kensetsu ni tomonau furyo shiyō jōkyō chōsho," is reprinted in Nagai, *Sensō hanzai chōsa shiryō,* pp. 343–463. A copy of the Japanese original can be found also in "BC-kyū (Igirisu saiban kankei) Shingapōru saiban, dai-96-1-gō jiken (5-mei)" [Class BC (relative to British trials) Singapore trial, case no. 96–1 (5 accused)], Hōmu-Hei-11-4B-35-4441, National Archives of Japan; and "BC-kyū (Igirisu saiban kankei) Shingapōru saiban, dai-96-2-gō jiken (5-mei)" [Clas BC (relative to British trials) Singapore trial, case no. 96–2 (5 accused)], Hōmu-Hei-11-4B-35-4442, National Archives of Japan.
9. "Exhibit E: Opening Address by the Prosecution," p. 1, Ishida Trial, R5.
10. Exhibit I, p. 1, Ishida Trial.
11. Ibid., p. 10. According to Utsumi's *Nihongun no horyo seisaku,* the order to expedite the railway construction was issued in March 1943. Utsumi, *Nihongun no horyo seisaku,* p. 436.
12. Exhibit I, p. 11, Ishida Trial.
13. Ibid., p. 12. For Wakamatsu's brief biographical information, see Fukukawa, *Nihon rikugun shōkan jiten,* p. 804.
14. Exhibit I, p. 1, Ishida Trial.
15. Ibid., p. 34.
16. Ibid., p. 1.
17. Friedman, *Law of War,* vol. 1, p. 314. Emphasis added.
18. Ibid., vol. 1, p. 501. Emphasis added.
19. "Majority Judgment," in Boister and Cryer, *Documents of the Tokyo International Military Tribunal,* pp. 575–9. See also Chapter 1, note 211.
20. Exhibit I, p. 34, Ishida Trial.
21. Ibid.

22. Ibid., p. 35.
23. Ibid., p. 36. Emphasis added.
24. Ibid., p. 29.
25. Ibid.
26. Ibid., pp. 30–1.
27. Ibid., p. 38.
28. Ibid.
29. Ibid.
30. Sugiyama Hajime gensui denki kankōkai [The Committee for the Publication of General Sugiyama Hajime's Biography], ed., *Sugiyama Hajime den* [Biography of Sugiyama Hajime] (Tokyo: Hara shobō, 1969), pp. 272–81.
31. On the circumstances of Tōjō's attempted suicide, see Jōhō Yoshio, *Tōjō Hideki* [Tōjō Hideki] (Tokyo: Fuyō shobō, 1974), pp. 421–42.
32. Exhibit I, p. 38, Ishida Trial. Emphasis added.
33. "Constitution of the Empire of Japan." Available at the Web site of the National Diet Library, http://www.ndl.go.jp/constitution/e/etc/c02.html.
34. Emperor Hirohito's wartime words and deeds are documented extensively in a wide variety of Japanese-language published sources. The best source material to date would be Nakao Yūji, ed., *Shōwa tennō hatsugen kiroku shūsei* [The compilation of the records of statements made by Emperor Shōwa], 2 vols. (Tokyo: Fuyō shuppan, 2003). Emperor Hirohito made a retrospective account of the war in early 1946 in which he justified his role in the Asia-Pacific War. For its full text, see Terasaki Hidenari and Mariko Terasaki Miller, eds., *Shōwa tennō dokuhakuroku: Terasaki Hidenari, goyō gakari nikki* [The monologue of Emperor Shōwa, and the diary of an imperial attendant, Terasaki Hidenari] (Tokyo: Bungei shunjū, 1991). For an English-language biography of Emperor Hirohito, including his years during the Pacific War, see Herbert Bix, *Hirohito and the Making of Modern Japan* (New York, NY: HarperCollins, 2002).
35. "Ei Shingapōru saiban jiken bangō dai-96-gō, Tai-Men tetsudō Ishida kēsu shiryō, kyōjutsusha Ishida Eiguma. Shōwa 35-nen, 3-gatsu 14-ka" (British Singapore trial, case no. 96: Sources on the Burma-Siam Railway Ishida Case. Interviewee: Ishida Eiguma. March 14, 1960), in "BC-kyū (Igirisu saiban kankei) Shingapōru saiban, dai-96-gō jiken (5-mei)" (Class BC [relative to British trials] Singapore trial, case no. 96 [5 Accused])," Hōmu-Hei-11-4B-35-4442, National Archives of Japan, p. 391.
36. The Speedo Period covered the months between February and July 1943. The order to postpone the deadline by two months was issued in July 1943. "War Crimes Courts" (review report, prepared by the Department of Judge Advocate General, South East Asia Land Forces, dated March 6, 1947), p. 3, Ishida Trial, SP13.
37. "Testimony of Harry Jones," Ishida Trial, R40–1.
38. "Exhibit BM: Record by Stanley Septimus Pavillard," p. 8, Ishida Trial, R162.
39. Ibid., p. 9.
40. "Testimony of John Kendal Gale," Ishida Trial, R63.
41. "Exhibit O: Affidavit of Lt. Col. Charles Henry Kappe," p. 28, Banno Trial, R83.
42. "Exhibit S: 'F' Force Report on Activities of AIF 'F' Force in Thailand by Lt. Col. C. H. Kappe," p. 55, Banno Trial, R84.

43. "Testimony of John Kendall Gale," Ishida Trial, R89.
44. "Testimony of Maj. Rowland Lyne," Ishida Trial, R113.
45. Exhibit BM, p. 11, Ishida Trial.
46. "Testimony of John Kendall Gale," Ishida Trial, R62.
47. Ibid., R16.
48. "Testimony of Stanley Septimus Pavillard," Ishida Trial, R178.
49. "Testimony of Yanagita Shoichi," Ishida Trial, R320.
50. Exhibit S, p. 1, Banno Trial.
51. Ibid., p. 58.
52. Ibid. For reference to Lt. Col. S. W. Harris, see also "Exhibit K: Unsworn Statement of Lt. Col. Cyril Wild. Subject: 'F' Force Case – Korean guard TOYOYAMA KISEI," p. 1, Banno Trial, R82.
53. Exhibit S, p. 58, Banno Trial.
54. For accounts of the Battle of the Somme, See Lyn MacDonald, *Somme* (London, UK: M. Joseph, 1983); and C. E. W. Bean, *The Australian Imperial Force in France, 1916* (St. Lucia, Queensland, Australia: University of Queensland Press, 1982). For a somber assessment of the historical significance of the Battle of Pozières for Australian soldiers, their families, and the Australian people in general, see Scott Bennet, *Pozieres: The Anzac Story* (Melbourne: Vision Australia Information Service, 2012).
55. "Testimony of Ishida Hidekuma," Ishida Trial, R221.
56. Ibid., R250.
57. Exhibit E, p. 4, Ishida Trial.
58. "Testimony of Ishida Hidekuma," Ishida Trial, R250.
59. "Charge Sheet," Ishida Trial, SP8–10. The implications of the use of the term, "concerned," at the British war crimes trials are discussed in Nina H. B. Jørgensen, "On Being 'Concerned' in a Crime: Embryonic Joint Criminal Enterprise?" in *Hong Kong's War Crimes Trials*, ed. Suzannah Linton (Oxford UK: Oxford University Press, 2013), pp. 137–67.
60. "The Closing Address for the Prosecution," Ishida Trial, R499–500.
61. Ibid., R507–8.
62. "Testimony of Ishida Hidekuma," Ishida Trial, R233. Emphasis added.
63. Ibid., R244.
64. Findings and sentences, Ishida Trial, R515–6, 522–3.
65. "Testimony of Banno Hiroteru," Banno Trial, R106. Banno had been tried by the Dutch authorities at Medan, Sumatra, prior to being brought to the U.K. Singapore court. The charge against him was mistreatment of prisoners of war at the Medan prisoner-of-war camp, where he had served as camp commandant in the early months of the Pacific War. He was found guilty, but received a light penalty of four years (which was subsequently remitted to two years). "Oranda sensō saiban gaikenhyō," Hōmu-Hei-11-4A-21-7130, p. 37. National Archives of Japan. This trial is titled "Medan Dutch trial no. 11" in the collection of war crimes trial records deposited at the National Archives of Japan.
66. "Testimony of Banno Hiroteru," Banno Trial, R117. Fukukawa, *Nihon rikugun shōkan jiten*, pp. 41–2.
67. "Testimony of Banno Hiroteru," Banno Trial, R106.
68. "Testimony of Garret George Richwood," Banno Trial, R40.
69. "Exhibit J: Affidavit of Lt. Col. Cecil Tats Hutchinson," p. 6, Banno Trial, R82.

70. "Testimony of Col. Charles Henry Kappe," Banno Trial, R202.
71. Ibid.
72. Ibid., R289.
73. "Exhibit F: History of the 'F' Force," Banno Trial, R16. The prosecution read excerpts from this document throughout the court proceedings, interspersing them with other exhibits and witness testimony.
74. Utsumi Aiko has researched and written extensively on Korean *gunzoku* and the postwar Allied criminal prosecutions against them. Her representative publications are as follows: *Chōsenjin BC-kyū senpan no kiroku* [Records of Korean Class BC war criminals] (Tokyo: Keisō shobō, 1982); and *Kimu wa naze sabakaretanoka: Chōsenjin BC-kyū senpan no kiseki* [Why was Kim tried? The trajectory of Korean Class BC war criminals] (Tokyo: Asahi shinbun shuppansha, 2008).
75. "Exhibit G: Sworn Statement of Capt. R. W. Pearce," p. 1, Banno Trial, R81.
76. Ibid., p. 3.
77. Ibid., p. 2.
78. Ibid., p. 3.
79. For further biographical information on Cyril Wild, see James Bradley, *Cyril Wild: The Tall Man Who Never Slept* (Fontwell, West Sussex, UK: Woodfield, 1991).
80. Exhibit K, pp. 1–2, Banno Trial.
81. Ibid., p. 2.
82. "Charge Sheet," Banno Trial, SP377.
83. Banno Trial, R375, 379.
84. "The Closing Statement by the Prosecution," Banno Trial, R348.
85. Ibid., R351.
86. Ibid., R353–4.
87. Ibid., R357. The prosecution uses the word "negligence," but his closing argument on accused Banno rather suggests that he meant to say the accused disregarded his duty, either *knowingly* or *recklessly*, but not *negligently*. Section 2.02 of the Model Penal Code reads as follows: "Minimum Requirements of Culpability . . . (a) Purposely . . . (b) Knowingly. A person acts knowingly with respect to a material element of an offense when: (i) if the element involves the nature of his conduct or the attendant circumstances, he is aware that his conduct is of that nature or that such circumstances exist; and (ii) if the element involves a result of his conduct, he is aware that it is practically certain that his conduct will cause such a result. (c) Recklessly. A person acts recklessly with respect to a material element of an offense when he consciously disregards a substantial and unjustifiable risk that the material element exists or will result from his conduct. The risk must be of such a nature and degree that, considering the nature and purpose of the actor's conduct and the circumstances known to him, its disregard involves a gross deviation from the standard of conduct that a law-abiding person would observe in the actor's situation. (d) Negligently. A person acts negligently with respect to a material element of an offense when he should be aware of a substantial and unjustifiable risk that the material element exists or will result from his conduct. The risk must be of such a nature and degree that the actor's failure to perceive it, considering the nature and purpose of his conduct and the circumstances known to him, involves a gross deviation from the standard of care that a reasonable person would observe in the actor's

situation." In this scheme of things, the mode of liability applicable to Banno seems to be *knowingly* or *recklessly* but not *negligently*. For the full text of the Model Penal Code, visit the Web site of Criminal Law Web, "Model Penal Code Annotated," http://www.law-lib.utoronto.ca/bclc/crimweb/web1/mpc/mpc.html (see Chapter 1, note 110).

88. "Statement of Toyoyama Kisei," Banno Trial, R292–3.
89. "War Crimes Trial" (review report, prepared by the Department of Judge Advocate General, South East Asia Land Forces, dated December 19, 1946), p. 6, Banno Trial, SP356.
90. "Testimony of Watanabe Mutsuo," Kudō Trial, R158.
91. Ibid. This Kitagawa is possibly Kitagawa Masataka, an army medical officer who served as chief of the water supply for the Southern Army. Fukukawa, *Nihon rikugun shōkan jiten*, p. 255.
92. "Testimony of Watanabe Mutsuo," Kudō Trial, R158.
93. Ibid.
94. Ibid., R162–3.
95. "Testimony of Ishida Hidekuma," Kudō Trial, R148.
96. "Exhibit W: Affidavit of Lt. Col. Horace Claude Benson," pp. 1–2, Kudō Trial, R60. The word "coolie" is no longer in use in Japanese or English due to its derogatory connotation. However, this term commonly appears in historical records. For instance, one can find a series of official documents, issued by the military attaché at the Japanese embassy in Thailand during the Pacific War, in which the word "*kūrī*" (i.e. coolie) is used when referring to civilian laborers to be utilized for the Burma-Siam railway construction project. Yoshikawa Toshiharu, *Taimen tetsudō: kimitsu bunsho ga akasu Ajia Taiheiyō sensō* [The Burma-Siam Railway: The Asia-Pacific War as revealed in secret documents] (Tokyo: Yūzankaku, 2011), pp. 193–235.
97. Exhibit W, p. 6, Kudō Trial.
98. Ibid., p. 15.
99. "Exhibit V: Affidavit of Joseph Francis McGarity," p. 2, Kudō Trial, R60.
100. Exhibit I, p. 1, Kudō Trial.
101. Ibid., p. 3.
102. "Charge Sheet," Kudō Trial, SP30.
103. "Exhibit J: Affidavit by Robert Henry Cuthbert," p. 4, Kudō Trial, R34.
104. "Exhibit M: Affidavit by Kenneth Glyn Prickett," pp. 2–4, Kudō Trial, R34.
105. "Exhibit O: Affidavit by Pte. David Ralph Boardman," Kudō Trial, and "Exhibit Q: Affidavit by Capt. Peterson," Kudō Trial, R34.
106. Kudō Trial, R383A-384, 390. The court found no evidence to justify the conviction of co-accused 2nd Lt. Yaguchi Sanya. He was acquitted.
107. "Exhibit BQ: The Closing Address for the Prosecution," p. 13, Kudō Trial, R383A.
108. Exhibit M, p. 3, Kudō Trial.
109. Exhibit BQ, pp. 13–15, Kudō Trial.

CHAPTER 4

1. The trial records of four trials analyzed in this chapter were obtained from the Web site of the National Archives of Australia. http://www.naa.gov.au. The full citation information is as follows: "War Crimes – Military Tribunal – HIROTA

Akira (Major-General) AWC 2120: Unit – 8th Army Group, Japanese Forces: Place and Date of Tribunal – Rabaul, 19–21, 24–29 and 31 March, 3 April 1947," series no. A471, control symbol 81654, Parts A, B, C, and D; "War Crimes, Proceeding of a Military Tribunal. Lt Gen Adachi Matazo [Hatazō]," series no. A471, control symbol 81652, Parts A, B, and C; "War Crimes – Military Tribunal – KATO Rinpei (Lieutenant-General) AWC 2959: Unit – Chief of Staff, 8th Japanese Army Group: Place and Date of Tribunal – Rabaul, 28 and 29 April 1947," series no. A471, control symbol 81065; and "War Crimes – Military Tribunal – IMAMURA Hitoshi (General) AWC 2121: Unit – 8th Japanese Army Group: Place and Date of Tribunal – Rabaul, 1, 2, 5, 9, 12, 13, 15 and 16 May 1947," series no. A471, control symbol 81635, Parts A, B, C, D, E, and F. The records of the four trials will be referred hereafter as the "Hirota Trial," the "Adachi Trial," the "Katō Trial," and the "Imamura Trial," respectively. I am indebted to Steven Bullard, who kindly provided me with a CD-ROM version of the records of these trials.

2. For the Japanese official history of the South Pacific campaigns by the Japanese ground forces in 1942 and early 1943, see Bōei kenshūjo senshishitsu, *Senshi sōsho: 14. Minami Taiheiyō rikugun sakusen (1) Pōto Moresubī, Ga-tō shoki sakusen* [War history series: Vol. 14. The army strategy in the South Pacific. (1) The initial strategy relative to Port Moresby and Guadalcanal]; and *Senshi sōsho: 28. Minami Taiheiyō rikugun sakusen (2) Gadarukanaru, Buna sakusen* [War history series: Vol. 28. The army strategy in the South Pacific. (2) Strategies relative to Guadalcanal and Buna]. Extracts from the two volumes have been rendered in English translation by Steven Bullard and are available under the title, *Japanese Army Operations in the South Pacific Area: New Britain and Papua Campaigns, 1942–43* (Canberra: Australian War Memorial, 2007).

3. "Exhibit A: Certified Maps Showing Imamura's Area of Responsibility and a List of Units and All Relative Information of Units under His Command as G. O. C. 16th Army and G. O. C. 8 Army Group," p. 3, Imamura Trial, R4.

4. For a definitive account of the Australian army campaigns in the South Pacific, see the following series of publications by the Australian War Memorial: Lionel Wigmore, *The Japanese Thrust*, Australia in the War of 1939–1945, Series One (Army), vol. 4 (Canberra: Australian War Memorial, 1957); Dudley McCarthy, *South-West Pacific Area – First Year: Kokoda to Wau*, Australia in the War of 1939–1945, Series One (Army), vol. 5 (Canberra: Australian War Memorial, 1959); David Dexter, *The New Guinea Offensive*, Australia in the War of 1939–1945, Series One (Army), vol. 6 (Canberra: Australian War Memorial, 1961); and Gavin Long, *The Final Campaigns*, Australia in the War of 1939–1945, Series One (Army), vol. 7 (Canberra: Australian War Memorial, 1963). For a concise account of the ground warfare in the South Pacific, see Eric Bergerud, *Touched with Fire: The Land War in the South Pacific* (New York, NY: Penguin Books, 1996). I am indebted to Steven Bullard, who kindly shared with me the digital version of the *Australia in the War of 1939–1945* series. For debates on the Japanese war plan against Australia in the South Pacific region, see Steven Bullard, "Japanese Strategy and Intentions towards Australia," in *Australia 1942: In the Shadow of War*, ed. Peter J. Dean (Cambridge, UK: Cambridge University Press, 2013), pp. 124–39.

5. Rekishigaku kenkyūkai, *Taiheiyō sensōshi: 5. Taiheiyō sensō,* 2. 1942–1945 [The history of the Pacific War: Vol. 5. The Pacific War, 2. 1942–1945], pp. 43–53.

6. "The Opening Address by the Defense," Adachi Trial, R51.

7. "Exhibit 3: Statement of Gen. Imamura Hitoshi," p. 3, Imamura Trial, R37. For the Australian army's operational goals in the handling of Rabaul, see Long, *The Final Campaigns,* pp. 241–70.

8. Imamura was tried at the Dutch war crimes court, too, subsequent to the case at the Australian Rabaul proceedings. For Imamura's personal accounts of experiencing the Australian and Dutch war crimes trials, see Imamura Hitoshi, *Yūshū kaikoroku* [Memoirs of imprisonment] (Tokyo: Akita shoten, 1966). Excerpts from this publication was reprinted in his autobiography, published in 1970. Imamura Hitoshi, *Ichi gunjin rokujū-nen no aika* [An army officer's elegy on his sixty years] (Tokyo: Fuyō shobō, 1970).

9. One of the responsibility trials not discussed in this chapter is that of Gen. Baba Masao (Rabaul trial no. 176). His case concerned mistreatment and deaths of Allied prisoners of war in Borneo in connection with the Sandakan-Ranau Death Marches. The record of the Baba Trial can be accessed at the Web site of the National Archives of Australia. "War Crimes – Military Tribunal – BABA Masao (Lieutenant-General): Unit – 27th Japanese Army: Date and Place of Tribunal – Rabaul, 28 May and 2 June 1947," series no. A471, control symbol 81631, Parts A and B. National Archives of Australia, http://www.naa.gov.au.

10. "Exhibit 16: Statement by Imamura Hitoshi," p. 1, Hirota Trial, R88. Narrelle Morris kindly shared with me a digital copy of this and some other exhibits, which are missing in the record of the Hirota Trial but which she has been able to locate among the seas of archival records deposited at the Australian War Memorial, Canberra. The reference number is AWM54, 1010/9/92.

11. Ibid.

12. "Exhibit 8: Statement of Kagoshima Takeshi," p. 1. Imamura Trial, R75.

13. "Exhibit 17: Statement of Kanda Masatane," p. 1, Hirota Trial, R97. AWM54, 1010/9/92, Australian War Memorial. A copy obtained from Narrelle Morris.

14. Fukukawa, *Nihon rikugun shōkan jiten,* p. 499.

15. Exhibit 16, p. 1, Hirota Trial.

16. Exhibit 3, p. 9, Imamura Trial.

17. Exhibit 16, p. 1, Hirota Trial.

18. Exhibit 3, p. 9, Imamura Trial.

19. For more information about Lt. Col. Woo Yien, see Georgina Fitzpatrick, "Rabaul," in Fitzpatrick, et al., *Australia's War Crimes Trials, 1945–51* (in press).

20. "Exhibit E: Declarations of Lt. Col. Woo Yien and Capt. Lee Chi Yung," p. 1, Hirota Trial, R5.

21. "Exhibit F: Declaration of Maj. Chen Kwok Leong and Lt. Yung Chiu Chung," p. 1, Hirota Trial, R5.

22. Exhibit E, p. 1, Hirota Trial.

23. "Exhibit T: Report by Col. Woo Yien," p. 1. Hirota Trial, R14. A duplicate of the same document (of better digital quality) can be found in the record of the Imamura Trial. "Exhibit X: Report by Col. Woo Yien," Imamura Trial, R18.

24. On fortification of Japanese-controlled central Pacific islands, see Mark R. Peattie, *Nan'yō: The Rise and Fall of the Japanese in Micronesia, 1885–1945* (Honolulu: University of Hawai'i Press, 1988), chapters 8 and 9. For accounts of

Micronesians' experiences of the Pacific War, see Laurence Marshall Carucci, Suzanne Falgout, and Lin Poyer, eds., *The Typhoon of War: Micronesian Experiences of the Pacific War* (Honolulu: University of Hawai'i Press, 2001); and *Memories of War: Micronesians in the Pacific War* (Honolulu: University of Hawai'i Press, 2008).

25. "Exhibit AD: Statements by Chu Yo Soo, Chiang Hai See, and Wha Poi Fouck," and "Exhibit AE: Statement of Luin Yun," Adachi Trial, R39.

26. Exhibit AE, p. 1, Adachi Trial.

27. Exhibit T, pp. 1–2, Hirota Trial; Exhibit X, pp. 1–2, Imamura Trial.

28. "Exhibit Z: Statement of Ho Wen," p. 1, Imamura Trial, R26.

29. "Exhibit 11: Statement by Miyama Yozo," p. 1, Adachi Trial, R97.

30. "Exhibit 7: Statement by Hosoda Hiromu," p. 1, Imamura Trial, R73.

31. Kaori Maekawa, "The Heiho during the Japanese Occupation of Indonesia," in *Asian Labor in the Wartime Japanese Empire: Unknown Histories*, ed. Paul H. Kratoska (Armonk, New York, and London, UK: M.E. Sharpe, 2005), pp. 180–5. See also Kaori Maekawa, "Forgotten Soldiers in the Japanese Army: Asian Personnel in Papua New Guinea," symposium paper for the Remembering the War in New Guinea project, Australian War Memorial, accessed April 14, 2014, http://ajrp.awm.gov.au/AJRP/remember.nsf.

32. "Exhibit 8: Statement of Kagoshima Takashi," p. 1, Imamura Trial, R75. For recruitment of Indonesians for *heiho* companies, see Maekawa Kaori, "The Heiho during the Japanese Occupation of Indonesia," in Kratoska, *Asian Labor in the Wartime Japanese Empire*, pp. 185–91.

33. Exhibit 8, p. 2, Imamura Trial. According to studies by Hayashi Hirofumi and Utsumi Aiko, the Southern Army had actually adopted the policy to organize the Indian prisoners of war into work parties as early as March 1, 1942. See Hayashi Hirofumi, *Senpan saiban no kenkyū: senpan saiban seisaku no keisei kara Tōkyō saiban, BC-kyū saiban made* [A study of war crimes trials: From the formation of policies on war crimes trials to the Tokyo Trial and Class BC war crimes trials] (Tokyo: Bensei shuppan, 2010), pp. 260, 277; and Utsumi, *Nihongun no horyo seisaku*, p. 201.

34. "Exhibit 8: Statement by General Imamura," p. 1, Adachi Trial, R91.

35. "Testimony of Kuroda Shigenori," Imamura Trial, R22.

36. "Disposal of Prisoners of War (War Ministry, Asia, Confidential Report No. 1456, May 6, 1942; War Ministry, Asia, Confidential Report No. 1404, May 2, 1942; Communication and Transportation Report No. 434, May 5, 1942)," in "Exhibit 12: Laws, Rules, and Regulations Pertaining to Prisoners of War," p. 39, Tamura Trial, R85. This document is contained on roll 1 of the record of the Tamura Trial (see Chapter 2, note 8). Emphasis added.

37. "Testimony of Kuroda Shigenori," Imamura Trial, R22.

38. Ibid., R24.

39. "Exhibit 9: Statement by Kuroda Shigenori," p. 2, Adachi Trial, R94.

40. Adachi Trial, R103. The gist of Nan-Sō-San No. 1470 was provided in the translation of Exhibit 9 (Statement by Kuroda Shigenori) based off the witness's memory. The Japanese original is contained in "Exhibit 10: The Original of Nan-So-San No. 1470, Included in the 8th Army Group File Copy, 'Regulations Concerning Labourers,'" Adachi Trial, R96. This exhibit was translated into English and introduced as "Exhibit 12: Translation of Exhibit 10 – Nan-So-San

No. 1470," Adachi Trial, R103. The defense objected to Exhibit 12 on account of translation errors, however, which led the court to have the court interpreter to provide a definitive translation.

41. "Testimony of Kuroda Shigenori," Adachi Trial, R95.
42. "Testimony of Kagoshima Takashi," Imamura Trial, R75–6.
43. For a more recent study of the INA, see Peter Ward Fay, *The Forgotten Army: India's Armed Struggle for Independence, 1942–45* (Ann Arbor, MI: University of Michigan Press, 1993). For a study of a broad range of Asian armies that emerged during decolonization processes in the British Far East during and after World War II, see C. A. Bayly and T. N. Harper, *Forgotten Armies: The Fall of British Asia, 1941–1945* (Cambridge, MA: Belknap Press of Harvard University Press, 2005); and *Forgotten Wars: Freedom and Revolution in Southeast Asia* (Cambridge, MA: Harvard University Press, 2007). Bayly and Harper explore not only the formation of Asians-only combat units during the Pacific War, but also that of the "armies" of Asian workers.
44. For Fujiwara's own recollection of the INA movement, see Fujiwara Iwaichi, *F kikanchō no shuki: Ajia kaihō o yume mita tokumu kikanchō no shuki* [The F Agency: Memoirs of a special agent chief who dreamt of Asian liberation] (Tokyo: Bajiriko, 2012). The original version was published by Hara shobō in 1976. The English translation is also available. Fujiwara Iwaichi, *F kikan: Japanese Army Intelligence Operations in Southeast Asia During World War II* (Hong Kong: Heinemann Asia, 1983).
45. For biographical accounts of Rash Behari Bose, see Nakajima Takeshi, *Nakamura-ya no Bōsu: Indo dokuritsu undō to kindai Nihon no Ajiashugi* [Bose of Nakamuraya: The Indian independence movement and Asianism in modern Japan] (Tokyo: Hakusuisha, 2005).
46. Fay, *Forgotten Army*, pp. 384–5. At present, Bose's ashes are purportedly kept at the Renkōji Buddhist Temple in Suginami Ward, Tokyo, Japan. At the precinct of the Renkōji Temple, a bust of Subhas Chandra Bose greets visitors from India and others who remember him to this day. For related information, visit the Renkōji Web site (Nichirenshū Tōkyō saibu shūmusho [The Religious Affairs Institute of the Nichiren Sect of Buddhism, Western Tokyo], accessed April 6, 2014, at http://www.tokyo-saibu.com/list/suginami_renkoji/index.html.
47. "Testimony of Kuroda Shigenori," Imamura Trial, R24.
48. For instance, see "Testimony of Chint Singh," Adachi Trial, R6–19, 27–36a; "Exhibit D: Statement by Major Charles Edward James," Imamura Trial, R7.
49. For more information about Chint Singh, see Georgina Fitzpatrick, "Rabaul," in Fitzpatrick, et al., *Australia's War Crimes Trials, 1945–51* (in press).
50. "Testimony of Chint Singh," Adachi Trial, R17.
51. Exhibit 8, p. 1, Adachi Trial.
52. These are rough estimates based on numbers given in "Testimony of Chint Singh," Adachi Trial, R18; Exhibit D, p. 1, Imamura Trial; and "Exhibit E: Sworn Statement by Subedar Ganpatrao Suriyawanso," p. 1, Imamura Trial, R7. No exhaustive data of the special-duty companies were presented at the Rabaul proceedings. For detailed information regarding areas, unit names, commanders, strengths and ethnicity of special service companies in East New Guinea, Solomon, and Bismarck Islands, see Table 4 in Maekawa, "Forgotten Soldiers in the Japanese Army."

53. "Testimony of Chint Singh," Adachi Trial, R17–8. The breakdown of the number of survivors in New Guinea, as given by Chint Singh, is as follows. No. 16 Special-Duty Company had one survivor out of the original strength of 560; No. 17 Special-Duty Company had zero survivor out of the original strength of 560; No. 18 Special-Duty Company had two survivors out of the original strength of 565; No. 19 Special-Duty Company had seven survivors including Chint Singh out of the original strength of 539; and No. 26 Special-Duty Company had two survivors out of the original strength of 309.

54. Mohan Singh, *Leaves from My Diary* (Lahore: Free-World Publications, 1946), p. 18.

55. Mohan Singh, *Soldiers' Contribution to Indian Independence: The Epic of the Indian National Army* (New Delhi: Army Educational Stores, 1974), p. 234.

56. Article 103 (f) of the Rules of Procedure, in Australia Military Board, *Australian Edition of Manual of Military Law, 1941 (Including Army Act and Rules of Procedure as Modified and Adapted by the Defence Act 1903–1939 and the Australian Military Regulations)* (Canberra: L. F. Johnston, Commonwealth Government Printer, 1941), p. 607. I am indebted to Tim McCormack who kindly shared with me a copy of this volume.

57. Hirota Trial, R124.

58. Imamura Trial, R119; Friedman, *Law of War*, p. 323

59. Imamura Trial, R119. Article 6 (b) in the Charter of the International Military Tribunal at Nuremberg reads as follows: "War crimes: namely, violations of the laws or customs of war. Such violations shall include, but not be limited to, murder, ill-treatment or *deportation to slave labour or for any other purpose of civilian population of or in occupied territory*, murder or ill-treatment of prisoners of war or persons on the seas, killing of hostages, plunder of public or private property, wanton destruction of cities, towns or villages, or devastation not justified by military necessity." Friedman, *Law of War*, vol. 1, p. 887. Emphasis added. The full text of the Nuremberg Charter is also available at the website Web site of the International Committee of the Red Cross. "Agreement for the Prosecution and Punishment of the Major War Criminals of the European Axis, and Charter of the International Military Tribunal. London, 8 August 1945," http://www.icrc.org/ihl.nsf/FULL/350.

60. Imamura Trial, R142.

61. Adachi Trial, R135.

62. "War Crimes Trial, Rabaul" (June 11, 1947), in "War Crimes – Miscellaneous Correspondence re Criminals, Suspects and Trials (1) MISC 18 part 1 – War Crimes – Miscellaneous Correspondence re Criminals, Suspects and Trials (2) War Crimes (American Court) – Adm. TOYODA Soemu," series no. MP742/1, control symbol 336/1/1865, National Archives of Australia.

63. Their combat missions ended in disaster due to poor planning of operations and logistics by their Japanese military superiors. The INA saga in the Burma campaign may be traced in Allen, *Burma: The Longest War*, pp. 150–314; and Fay, *The Forgotten Army*, pp. 273–437.

64. The record of the first Red Fort trial has been published. Moti Ram, ed., *Two Historic Trials in Red Fort: An Authentic Account of the Trial by a General Court Martial of Captain Shah Nawaz Khan, Captain PK Sahgal and Lt GS*

Dhillon; and the Trial by a European Military Commission of Emperor Bahadur Shah (New Delhi: Moti Ram, 1946).

65. Singh, *Soldiers' Contribution to Indian Independence*, pp. 367–8. Mohan Singh is likely to have heard about the public outcry over the Red Fort Trial rather than seeing it himself, since he was still detained in Singapore at the time of the INA trials.

66. "Trial of Japanese War Criminal – Maj-Gen Hirota Akira" (review report, prepared by the Judge Advocate General, Australian Military Forces, dated June 5, 1947), p. 1, Hirota Trial.

67. "Exhibit AC: Interrogation of Maj. Hirota Akira," p. 3, Hirota Trial, R98. Narrelle Morris kindly shared with me a digital copy of this exhibit, which is missing in the record of the Hirota Trial but which she has been able to locate at the National Archives of Australia. Series no. MP742/1, control symbol 336/1/1266.

68. "Exhibit G: R55 [Rabaul Trial No. 55]," Hirota Trial, R6.

69. "Testimony of Shimura Yuzo"; "Testimony of Okabayashi Eikyu"; "Testimony of Takebayashi Tsuruichi"; "Testimony of Yanagawa Uetane"; and "Testimony of Furuya Eisuke," Hirota Trial, R17–31. The statements of these five witnesses were also presented in evidence. "Exhibit X: Statement of Shimura Yuzo"; "Exhibit Y: Statement of Okabayashi Eikyu"; "Exhibit Z: Statement of Takabayashi [Takebayashi] Tsuruichi"; "Exhibit AA: Statement of Yangawa Uetane"; and "Exhibit AB: Statement of Furuya Eisuke," Hirota Trial, R33–4.

70. "Testimony of Hirota Akira," Hirota Trial, R48–9.

71. Ibid., R50–1.

72. "Exhibit 1: Statement of Hirota Akita," p. 2, Hirota Trial, R38. AWM54, 1010/9/92, Australian War Memorial. A copy obtained from Narrelle Morris.

73. "Exhibit 9: Supply Depot's Case," p. 1, Hirota Trial, R42. AWM54, 1010/9/92, Australian War Memorial. A copy obtained from Narrelle Morris.

74. Exhibit 16, p. 1, Hirota Trial.

75. Ibid., p. 5.

76. Ibid., p. 3.

77. Ibid., pp. 2–3.

78. Ibid., p. 3.

79. Hirota Trial, R120. Emphasis added. The quoted passage can be found in "In re Yamashita," in Reel, *Case of General Yamashita*, p. 283.

80. Hirota Trial, R120.

81. Brock did not use this particular term. For discussion of strict liability at the Yamashita Trial, see Cohen, "Beyond Nuremberg".

82. Hirota Trial, R121. Emphasis in the original. The quoted passage can be found in "In re Yamashita," in Reel, *Case of General Yamashita*, pp. 262–3.

83. Hirota Trial, R121. Emphasis added.

84. Ibid., R144.

85. "War Crimes Trial – Lt.-Gen. Adachi Hatazo" (review report, prepared by the Judge Advocate General, Australian Military Forces, dated June 13, 1947), p. 1, Adachi Trial.

86. The background of the "MO" Operation is provided in "Exhibit 1: Statement of Lt. Gen. Adachi Hatazo (No. 1)," Adachi Trial, R52. For the Japanese army's official account of the "MO" Operation (*"mō-gō sakusen"* in original Japanese), see Bōei kenshūjo senshishitsu, ed., *Senshi sōsho: 84. Minami Taiheiyō rikugun*

sakusen. (5) Aitape, Puriaka, Rabauru [War history series: vol. 84. The army strategy in the South Pacific. (5) Aitape, Puriaka, Rabaul] (Tokyo: Asagumo shinbunsha, 1975), pp. 11–225.

87. Adachi was first headquartered at Rabaul, New Britain. He moved to New Guinea in March 1943 to establish the 18th Army headquarters at Madang, and then at Boiken in April 1944. He remained in Boiken until February 1945 when his headquarters were moved to Numbok in the Alexander Ranges. "Exhibit C: Statement of Lt. Gen. Adachi Hatazo," p. 1, Adachi Trial, R4.

88. Exhibit 1, p. 2, Adachi Trial.

89. Ibid., pp. 2–3.

90. Ibid., p. 3.

91. Ibid., pp. 4–5.

92. Ibid., p. 5.

93. "Exhibit C: Interrogation of Lt. Gen. Yoshihara Kane," p. 2, Katō Trial, R4.

94. "Testimony of Adachi Hatazo," Adachi Trial, R72–3; "Exhibit 3: Lt. Gen. Adachi Hatazo's Statement (No. 3)," pp. 1–2, Adachi Trial, R53.

95. Exhibit 3, p. 2, Adachi Trial.

96. Exhibit C, p. 2, Katō Trial.

97. "Testimony of Adachi Hatazo," Adachi Trial, R61. The Japanese original of "Rikugun keihō sōsoku" [The army criminal code, general rules], April 10, Meiji 41, Law no. 46, can be found in published source books. See, for instance, *Heibonsha roppō zensho* [The Heibonsha compilation of six laws], The Showa 16 Revised Edition (Tokyo: Heibonsha, 1931), p. 450.

98. "Exhibit 5: Lt. Gen. Adachi Hatazo's Statement," p. 4, Adachi Trial, R53.

99. "Testimony of Lt. Col. Tanaka Kengoro," Adachi Trial, R105.

100. "Testimony of Adachi Hatazo," Adachi Trial, R60.

101. Exhibit 1, p. 5, Adachi Trial.

102. "Testimony of Adachi Hatazo," Adachi Trial, R64.

103. "Testimony of Chint Singh," Adachi Trial, R6–20, 27–36a; See also "Exhibit K: Excerpts from Rabaul Trial No. 17," Adachi Trial, R23. This exhibit consists of court exhibits that were used at the trial of Mitsuba. See note 107 below.

104. "Testimony of Chint Singh," Adachi Trial, R27–8.

105. "Exhibit K: Declaration of Jamadar Chint Singh," Adachi Trial.

106. Ibid.

107. "War Crimes – Military Tribunal – MITSUBA Hisaneo [Hisanao] (Captain) AWC 2211: MARAI Koichi (Lieutenant) AWC 2212: IMAMURA Kazuhiko (Lieutenant) AWC 2213: HIBINO Kazuo (Lance Corporal) AWC 2228: Unit – Special Water Duty Company: Place and Date of Tribunal – Rabaul, 15–18 March 1946," series no. A471, control symbol 80749, National Archives of Australia. Excerpts from the record of this trial were presented as Exhibit K at the Adachi Trial. Mitsuba was a lieutenant during the war but he identified himself as a captain during the Rabaul proceedings, indicating that he was promoted at some point before the end of the war.

108. Adachi Trial, R152.

109. Ibid. The quoted passage can be found in Reel, *Case of General Yamashita*, p. 280.

110. Adachi Trial, R153.

111. Ibid., R156.

112. "Report of Court of Inquiry, Rabaul, September 23, 1947," and "Letter Addressed to Maj. Upson," in "War Crimes – Trial of Lt/Gen. Adachi Hatazo," series no. MP742/1, control symbol 336/1/1264. National Archives of Australia. The translation of Adachi's letter to Upson is included in the Report of Court of Inquiry, which made a report on the circumstances of Adachi's death. For Adachi's much longer versions of farewell notes, addressed to Gen. Imamura and other members of the 18th Army, see Bōei kenshūjo senshishitsu, *Senshi sōsho: Minami Taiheiyō rikugun sakusen. (5) Aitape, Puriaka, Rabauru*, pp. 451–4. *Senshi sōsho* indicates that the Imperial General Headquarters sanctioned the "MO" Operation on Adachi's insistence, despite awareness of its inadvisability.
113. "Record of Military Court" (summary of the case), Katō Trial.
114. "Exhibit A: Exhibit G of the Trial of Haranaka and Katagiri," Katō Trial, R3.
115. "Exhibit 2: Statement of Gen. Imamura Hitoshi," p. 1, Katō Trial, R19.
116. "Exhibit 6: Excerpt from Japanese Army Regulations, Volume 1," Katō Trial, R29. The Japanese original can be found in the same exhibit.
117. Katō Trial, R48.
118. These numbers are based on Japanese sources. Tōkyō saiban handobukku henshū iinkai, *Tōkyō saiban handobukku*, p. 222.
119. For accounts of hellships, see Michno, *Death on the Hellships*, and Lamont-Brown, *Ships from Hell*.
120. U.S. Yokohama Trial Docket No. 346 (United States of America vs. Katō Rinpei and 8 others). The full trial record can be found in "Rimpei Kato, Okikatsu Arao, Goro Isoya, Choho Mononobe, Hiroshi Nukata, Bunro Saheki, Mitsuo Tomita, Yahei Toyama, Tadakatsu Wakamatsu," entry UD 1321, RG 331, SCAP, Records of the SCAP Legal Section, Prosecution Division: US vs. Japanese War Criminal Case Files, Boxes 1637–8, NARA. For a study of the British Singapore trials concerning the hellship cases, see Cheah, "Post-World War II British 'Hell-Ship' Trials in Singapore."
121. "The Opening Address by the Defense," Imamura Trial, R36.
122. Imamura Trial, R147.
123. Ibid., R145.
124. Ibid.
125. "Record of Military Court" (summary of the case), Imamura Trial.
126. Imamura Trial, R136.
127. Ibid., R148.
128. "War Crimes Trial, Rabaul" (June 11, 1947), in "War Crimes – Miscellaneous Correspondence re Criminals, Suspects and Trials (1) MISC 18 part 1 – War Crimes – Miscellaneous Correspondence re Criminals, Suspects and Trials (2) War Crimes (American Court) – Adm. TOYODA Soemu," series no. MP742/1, control symbol 336/1/1865. National Archives of Australia.

CHAPTER 5

1. The records of two trials analyzed in this chapter are obtained from the U.K. National Archives. The record group is known as "WO 235 – Judge Advocate General's Office: War Crimes Case Files, Second World War." The full citation information of the cases is as follows: "WO 235/961 – Defendant Ichikawa Seigi, Place of Trial Rangoon"; and "WO 235/1004 – Defendant Nishimura

Takoma [Takuma], Place of Trial Singapore." The two trials will be referred to hereafter as the "Ichikawa Trial" and the "Nishimura Trial." The transcripts of the court proceedings for the Ichikawa Trial start with page 1 for *each* of the prosecution's case and the defense case. To avoid confusion, the page numbers in the transcripts relative to the prosecution's case will follow the usual format ("Ichikawa Trial, R#") while the page numbers relative to the defense case will be marked as "Ichikawa Trial (defense case), R#."

2. "BC-kyū (Igirisu saiban kankei) Shingapōru saiban dai-12-gō jiken" [Class BC (relative to British trials) Singapore trial, case no. 12], p. 77. Hōmu-Hei-11-4A-17-4359, National Archives of Japan.

3. Ibid., p. 36. For the general history of these islands leading up to the Pacific War, see L. P. Mathur, *History of the Andaman and Nicobar Islands, 1756–1966* (Delhi: Sterling Publishers, 1968).

4. The full record of this trial can be found at the U.K. National Archives. "Defendant Itzuki [Itsuki] Toshio, Place of Trial Singapore." The reference number is WO 235/834.

5. The Itsuki Trial is discussed in the following publications: Kimura Kōichirō, *Wasurerareta sensō sekinin: Kānikobaru-tō jiken to Taiwanjin gunzoku* [Forgotten war responsibility: The Car Nicobar Incident and Taiwanese auxiliary forces] (Tokyo: Aoki shoten, 2001); and Iwakawa Takashi, *Kami o shinzezu: BC-kyū senpan no bohimei* [I do not believe in God: The epitaph of Class BC war criminals] (Tokyo: Chūō kōronsha, 1978), pp. 225–36.

6. "BC-kyū (Igirisu saiban kankei) Shingapōru saiban dai-12-gō jiken" [Class BC (relative to British trials) Singapore trial, case no. 12], pp. 46-7. Hōmu-Hei-11-4A-17-4359, National Archives of Japan.

7. Ibid., p. 61.

8. Ibid., p. 63.

9. Article 61 of the Geneva Prisoner-of-War Convention. Friedman, *Law of War*, vol. 1, p. 508.

10. Tōkyō saiban handobukku henshū iinkai, *Tōkyō saiban handobukku*, p. 221.

11. "Testimony of Timothy Tun Nyein," Ichikawa Trial, R221.

12. The Kalagon Massacre has been explored at some length in Hayashi, *Sabakareta sensō hanzai*, pp. 253–62.

13. The Singapore Massacre has been explored in the following publications: Hayashi Hirofumi, *Shingapōru kakyō shukusei: Nihongun wa Shingapōru de nani o shitanoka* [The purge of Chinese in Singapore: What did the Japanese military do in Singapore?] (Tokyo: Kōbunken, 2007); Ralph P. Modder, *The Singapore Chinese Massacre: 18 February to 4 March 1942* (Singapore: Horizon Books, 2004); and Nakajima Masato, *Bōsatsu no kōseki: Shingapōru kakyō gyakusatsu jiken* [Traces of premeditated murder: The Singapore Chinese Massacre] (Tokyo: Kōdansha, 1985). For an analysis of the Nishimura Trial relative to the Singapore Massacre, see Hayashi, *Sabakareta Sensō hanzai*, pp. 209–27.

14. Fukukawa, *Nihon rikugun shōkan jiten*, p. 397.

15. Hayashi, *Sabakareta sensō hanzai*, p. 225. For Tsuji's own account of his life as a fugitive, see Tsuji Masanobu, *Senkō sanzenri* [Going underground for three thousand miles] (Tokyo: Mainichi shinbunsha, 1950).

16. "Testimony of Saw Kaw Ku," Ichikawa Trial, R1–46.

17. For Saw Kaw Ku's background, see, "Testimony of Supe-An," Ichikawa Trial, R94; and "Testimony of Timothy Tun Nyein," Ichikawa Trial, R217–8.

18. "Testimony of Saw Kaw Ku," Ichikawa Trial, R37.

19. Ibid., R38. According to the study by Hayashi Hirofumi, Abbey belonged to the British special operation force known as Unit 136, which engaged in propaganda and unconventional warfare in the Pacific theater. Hayashi, *Sabakareta sensō hanzai*, pp. 178–81, 253.

20. "Testimony of Saw Kaw Ku," Ichikawa Trial, R4–5.

21. Ibid., R6.

22. Ibid., R7.

23. Ibid., R8–18.

24. Ibid., R24.

25. Ibid., R25.

26. Ibid., R27.

27. Ibid., R28.

28. Ibid., R30.

29. Ibid., R33.

30. "Testimony of Tara Bibi," Ichikawa Trial, R150.

31. "Testimony of Mohd Eusof," Ichikawa Trial, R114–5. The same witness also testified the number of missing as "about 174 men, 195 or 196 women, and 266 or 267 children." Ichikawa Trial, R121.

32. Ibid., R128.

33. Ibid., R122.

34. "Testimony of Sulaiman," Ichikawa Trial, R153.

35. "Testimony of Hakijan," Ichikawa Trial, R155–47, 162–5.

36. Ichikawa Trial, R162. Emphasis added.

37. "Testimony of Hakijan," Ichikawa Trial, R155. There is a notation in the trial transcripts that this witness "did not appear to speak any particular language" and that her father was to serve as an interpreter. After a defense objection, witness Sulaiman was brought in "to assist the interpretation." Hakijan's father was "allowed to stay in court." This presumably means that this witness's father no longer served as her interpreter.

38. "Judgment," p. 5, Ichikawa Trial. The judgment appears at SP541–550 (10 pages). There is no pagination in the original.

39. "Exhibit E: Statement of Sakamaki Saburo," p. 1, Ichikawa Trial, R168.

40. "Exhibit D: Statement of Ichikawa Seigi," p. 1, Ichikawa Trial, R168.

41. Ibid., p. 2.

42. "Exhibit G: Statement of Midorikawa Hisashi," p. 1, Ichikawa Trial, R168.

43. "Testimony of Ichikawa Seigi," Ichikawa Trial (defense case), R2.

44. Ibid., R3. This part of the testimony was initially translated as "I received orders to the effect that I was to kill the villagers or Kalagon and to burn the whole village." In the retranslated version, the word "orders" is replaced by "instructions," and "I was to kill" was changed to read, "I must kill."

45. Ibid., R9.

46. Ibid., R20.

47. Ibid., R9.

48. Ibid., R30

49. "Judgment," p. 7, Ichikawa Trial.

50. "Testimony of Tsukada Misao," Ichikawa Trial (defense case), R116.
51. Ibid., R118–9.
52. Ibid., R128.
53. Ibid., R125. This particular dialogue is hand-written in the trial record.
54. Ibid.
55. "Testimony of Katayama Toru," Ichikawa Trial (defense case), R144–6, 148–57.
56. "Testimony of Tsukada Misao," Ichikawa Trial (defense case), R149. Emphasis added.
57. "Judgment," pp. 3–4, Ichikawa Trial. After the trial, Tsukada filed a petition on behalf of the convicted, pleading once again that he was the one responsible for ordering the killing of villagers as well as the abduction of women. The reviewing authority was critical of Tsukada's petition, however, commenting that "it is not . . . necessary to consider who issued the order, although it can be said that the equivocations of Col. TSUKADA when giving evidence contrast unfavourably with the definite statements in his petition." This quote appears in the review report, p. 5, prepared by the Department of Judge Advocate General, Allied Land Forces, S.E.A. The first page is missing in the file. Ichikawa Trial, SP16.
58. "Judgment," p. 1, Ichikawa Trial. Emphasis added. The original of the quoted passage can be found in Great Britain War Office, *Manual of Military Law 1929 Amendments (No. 12): Chapter XIV. The Laws and Usages of War on Land* (London, UK: His Majesty's Stationery Office, 1942), pp. 85–6. This chapter was removed from the *Manual* for revision and reissued separately in 1936 as Amendments No. 12. For the rest of the *Manual*, see Great Britain War Office, *Manual of Military Law 1929*. Reprinted December 1939 (London, UK: His Majesty's Stationery Office, 1949. This version does not include Amendments No. 12. The verbatim stipulation of the quoted passage can be found also in the Australia Military Board, *Australian Edition of Manual of Miltiary Law 1941*, p. 291.
59. "Judgment," p. 1, Ichikawa Trial. *Manual of Military Law 1929 Amendments (No. 12)* includes the following stipulation: "459. What kinds of acts should be resorted to as reprisals is a matter for the consideration of the injured party. Acts done by way of reprisals must not, however, be excessive, and must not exceed the degree of violation committed by the enemy" (p. 86). A note to this stipulation provides some examples of legitimate forms of reprisals from the time of the Franco-German War (1870–1871) and during World War I.
60. "Testimony of Tsukada Misao," Ichikawa Trial (defense case), R130.
61. "Judgment," p. 2, Ichikawa Trial.
62. Ibid. Emphasis added. For the original text, see Lord Wright, "War Crimes under International Law," *The Law Quarterly Review*, vol. 62, no. 1 (January 1946), p. 45.
63. "Judgment," p. 3, Ichikawa Trial.
64. "Testimony of Yanagisawa Izumi," Ichikawa Trial (defense case), R58.
65. Ibid., R61.
66. Ibid., R62–3. Emphasis added.
67. "Testimony of Midorikawa Hisashi," Ichikawa Trial (defense case), R67.
68. Ibid., R70.
69. Ibid., R67.
70. Ibid., R66.

71. "Judgment," p. 4, Ichikawa Trial. Paragraph 6 of the Royal Warrant read as follows: "The accused shall not be entitled to object to the President or any member of the Court or the Judge Advocate or to offer any special plea to the jurisdiction of the Court." Hōmu daijin kanbō shihō hōsei chōsabu, *Sensō hanzai saiban kankei hōreishū*, vol. 1, p. 89.
72. "Judgment," p. 4, Ichikawa Trial.
73. "Testimony of Midorikawa Hisashi," Ichikawa Trial (defense case), R72.
74. "Judgment," p. 4, Ichikawa Trial.
75. "Military Court for the Trial of War Criminals" (summary of the case), Ichikawa Trial, SP4.
76. "Testimony of Sugita Ichiji," Nishimura Trial, R8.
77. Ibid., R10; "Exhibit Q: Statement of Hashizume Isamu," p. 2, Nishimura Trial, R121. A copy of the original report in Japanese can be found as "Shingapōru ni okeru kakyō shodan jōkyō chōsho" [Report on circumstances of the disposition of ethnic Chinese in Singapore], in Nagai, *Sensō hanzai chōsa shiryō*, pp. 87–149. The same report can be found also in "BC-kyū (Igirisu kankei) Shingapōru saiban dai-118-gō" [Class BC (relative to British trials) Singapore trial, case no. 118], Hōmu-Hei-11-4B-35-4465.
78. Shinozaki Mamoru, *Shingapōru senryō hiroku* [A secret record of the occupation of Singapore] (Tokyo: Hara shobō, 1976), p. 175.
79. "Testimony of Sugita Ichiji," Nishimura Trial, R8.
80. Ibid. Prior to the Japanese invasion of British Malaya, local residents formed several armed volunteer forces to defend their territories. The main ones are the Straits Settlements Volunteer Forces (SSVF), which consisted of two battalions (based in Singapore), one in Penang, and another in Malacca in Malay Peninsula. There were also: (1) a separate Malayan regiment, headquartered at Port Dickson, and (2) the so-called Dalforce, the Singapore Overseas Chinese Volunteer Army. According to Hayashi Hirofumi, the Japanese army did not appear to have accurate information about these various volunteer forces in British Malaya, and was unable to distinguish one from the other. Hayashi, *Shingapōru kakyō shukusei*, pp. 40–1.
81. "Testimony of Sugita Ichiji," Nishimura Trial, R9.
82. Ibid., R17.
83. Exhibit Q, p. 3, Nishimura Trial.
84. Ibid., pp. 3–4.
85. "Exhibit S: Statement of Hishikari Takafumi," p. 2, Nishimura Trial, R121.
86. "Exhibit R: Statement of Ichikawa Tadashi," p. 1, Nishimura Trial, R121.
87. Ibid., pp. 1–2.
88. "Testimony of Shinozaki Mamoru," Nishimura Trial, R19.
89. Ibid., R20–1.
90. Ibid., R24.
91. Ibid., R25.
92. Ibid., R32.
93. In addition to court testimony by witnesses, the prosecution presented in evidence eight statements by British prisoners of war.
94. "Testimony of Khoo Ah Lim," Nishimura Trial, R57–9.
95. "Testimony of Lee Keng Jin," Nishimura Trial, R62.
96. Ibid., R63–4.
97. Ibid., R67.

98. "Testimony of Lim Peng Keoi," Nishimura Trial, R73–4.
99. "Testimony of Chua Choon Guan," Nishimura Trial, R82–3.
100. "Testimony of Cheng Kwang Yu," Nishimura Trial, R84–7.
101. "Testimony of Low Sze Thang," Nishimura Trial, R35–7.
102. "Testimony of Ng Kim Song," Nishimura Trial, R39–41.
103. "Testimony of Puay Ah Boh," Nishimura Trial, R42.
104. "Testimony of Yeo Hung Chung," Nishimura Trial, R47.
105. Ibid., R48.
106. "Testimony of Tan Hai Suar," Nishimura Trial, R52.
107. "Testimony of Nishimura Takuma," Nishimura Trial, R141. For Obata's bio-
     graphical information, see Fukukawa, *Nihon rikugun shōkan jiten*, p. 196.
108. "Testimony of Nishimura Takuma," Nishimura Trial, R142.
109. Ibid., R143.
110. Ibid., R141. This Kobayashi is probably Kobayashi Takashi, who served as com-
     mander of the infantry of the Imperial Guards Division at the time of the Ma-
     layan invasion. Fukukawa, *Nihon rikugun shōkan jiten*, p. 312.
111. "Testimony of Nishimura Takuma," Nishimura Trial, R145.
112. Ibid., R146.
113. Ibid., R147.
114. "Testimony of Kawamura Saburo," Nishimura Trial, R162. Kawamura served
     as commander of the Singapore Guard Unit only briefly, between February 18
     and March 18 of 1942. "Testimony of Kawamura Saburo," Nishimura Trial,
     R151, 160.
115. Ibid., R152–3.
116. Ibid., R154–5.
117. Ibid., R159.
118. Ibid., R160.
119. "Testimony of Oishi Masayuki," Nishimura Trial, R172.
120. Ibid., R180.
121. Ibid., R183.
122. "Testimony of Yokota Yoshitaka," Nishimura Trial, R190.
123. Ibid., R193.
124. Ibid.
125. "Ei-Shingapōru saiban jiken bangō dai-117-gō, kakyō shukusei kēsu shiryō"
     [British Singapore trial, case no. 117: Sources relative to the case of the Chi-
     nese purge], in Hōmu-Hei-11-4A-20-4465, National Archives of Japan, p. 378.
126. Ibid.
127. Ibid., p. 379.
128. Ibid.
129. Ibid., p. 383.
130. Zenkoku ken'yūkai rengōkai hensan iinkai, *Nihon kenpei seishi*, p. 1299.
131. Ibid., pp. 1299–1300.
132. Ibid., p. 1300.
133. "Military Court for the Trial of War Criminals" (summary of the case),
     Nishimura Trial, SP12.
134. "War Crimes Trial" (review report, prepared by Brigadier F. G. T. Davis,
     Department of Judge Advocate General, South East Asia Land Forces, dated
     May 5, 1947), Nishimura Trial, SP21–4.
135. Ibid., p. 2.

136. Ibid., p. 3.
137. The charge against Nishimura concerned the killing of surrendered Allied soldiers over the course of the Malayan invasion. For details of the Australian trial, see "War Crimes – Military Tribunal – NISHIMURA Takuma (Lieutenant General): NONAKA Shoichi (Captain): Date and Place of Tribunal – Manus, 19 June and 22 June 1950," series no. A471, control symbol 81942, National Archives of Australia. There are a couple of books that trace the fate of Nishimura in the hands of British and Australian war crimes prosecutors. Nakata Seiichi, *Saigo no senpan shikeishū Nishimura Takuma chūjō to aru kyōkaishi no kiroku* [The last death-sentenced war criminal: Records of Lieutenant General Nishimura Takuma and a prison chaplain] (Tokyo: Heibonsha, 2011); and Ian Ward, *Snaring the Other Tiger* (Singapore: Media Masters, 1996). The latter publication is available in Japanese translation as well. *Shōgun wa naze korosaretaka: Gōshū senpan saiban, Nishimura Takuma chūjō no higeki* [Why was the general killed? The tragedy of Lieutenant General Nishimura Takuma in the Australian war crimes trial], trans. Suzuki Masanori (Tokyo: Hara shobō, 2005).
138. "War Crimes Trial" (review report, prepared by Brigadier F. G. T. Davis, Department of Judge Advocate General, South East Asia Land Forces, dated May 5, 1947), p. 4, Nishimura Trial.
139. The letter is reproduced in Kawamura Saburō, *Jūsan kaidan o agaru: senpan shokeisha no kiroku* [Going up the thirteen steps: Records of an executed war criminal] (Tokyo: Atō shobō, 1952), pp. 170–6. It is not clear if Kawamura's letter was ever delivered to Mountbatten.
140. Ibid., p. 171.
141. Ibid., p. 173.
142. Ibid., p. 174.
143. Ibid., p. 176.

CHAPTER 6

1. Most of the record of the trial analyzed in this chapter is included in "Records of the Trial of Accused War Criminal Soemu Toyoda, Tried by a Military Tribunal Appointed by the Supreme Commander of the Allied Powers, Tokyo, Japan, 1948–1949" (College Park, MD: NARA), microfilm, M1729, 7 rolls. Some sections of the record missing in this publication can be found in "Transcripts from the Case of the United States of America vs. Soemu Toyoda and Hiroshi Tamura, 1946–1948" (College Park, MD: NARA), microfilm, M1661, rolls 1–4. The record of the Toyoda Trial will be referred to as the "Toyoda Trial" hereafter in the notes, and in the text. The international military tribunal that tried the case will be referred to as the "Toyoda Tribunal" or the "tribunal" (the latter when it is obvious from the context which tribunal is meant). In the text, the "Toyoda Trial" will continue to be used to describe the trial itself.
2. "The Defense Summation," Toyoda Trial, R4637.
3. Shimanouchi Tatsuoki, *Tōkyō saiban* [The Tokyo Trial] (Tokyo: Nihon hyōronsha, 1984), p. 265.
4. The Mitsubishi No. 11 Building was vacated, as it was slated for use of other branches of occupation authorities. Ibid., p. 249.
5. Ibid., p. 265.

6. Ibid., pp. 262–3. The tribunal similarly acknowledged in the judgment the competent work of court staff in the making of the Toyoda Trial. See "Judgment," Toyoda Trial, R4999.
7. Shimanouchi, *Tōkyō saiban*, pp. 259–61.
8. Ibid., p. 262.
9. During the defense summation for Toyoda, Furness made a brief comment on his personal impression of the Honma Trial. "I did take part in the Homma trial," Furness stated, "and I can only say that we felt that he was not guilty and, since he has been mentioned so often in summation, that I held and still hold him in affectionate respect and memory." But he went on to comment on the substance of the Honma Trial as follows: "His case, however, was not nearly as clear a case as this [against Toyoda]. He [Honma] was definitely in the chain of command; he was present; he did issue orders. The question was whether he enforced the orders enough, issued enough orders. He was cleared on the only charge of personal dishonor, the refusal of quarter at Corregidor. Few people, including the Supreme Commander, seem to realize that he was found not guilty on that count of the indictment." Toyoda Trial, R4922.
10. Shimanouchi, *Tōkyō saiban*, p. 262.
11. For the navy assistance in the Toyoda Trial, see the memoir by Toyoda Kumao, a high-ranking official of the navy's demobilization bureau. Toyoda, *Sensō saiban yoroku*, pp. 299–314. See also the Conclusion, regarding his postwar activities as an official for the Ministry of Legal Affairs.
12. This author uses the term "equality of arms" in the meaning of the defense having "sufficient, adequate facilities" and facing "no 'substnative disadvantage'" (p. 259), to draw upon definitions discussed in Charles C. Jalloh and Amy DiBella, "Equality of Arms in International Criminal Law: Continuing Challenges," in *The Ashgate Research Companion to International Criminal Law: Critical Perspectives*, ed. William A. Schabas, Yvonne McDermott, and Niamh Hayes (Farnham, Surrey, England, and Burlington, VT: Ashgate, 2013), pp. 251–88. This article can be obtained from the Web site of Social Science Research Network (SSRN) at http://ssrn.com/abstract=2314587.
13. John O'Brien led the Australian Scientific Mission to Japan (1945–1946) and headed the science and technology division of Gen. MacArthur's staff in Tokyo (1945–1951). I am indebted to Steve Bullard who alerted me to O'Brien's biographical information contained in *Australian Dictionary of Biography*. For further detail, see A. J. Sweeting, "O'Brien, John William Alexander (1908–1980)," in *Australian Dictionary of Biography* (National Centre of Biography, Australian National University), accessed July 2, 2013, http://adb.anu.edu.au/biography/obrien-john-william-alexander-11275/text20117.
14. "Judgment," Toyoda Trial, R5004.
15. Ibid.
16. Toyoda Trial, R11.
17. Ibid., R1066.
18. Ibid., R1186.
19. "Judgment," Toyoda Trial, R5002.
20. Shimanouchi, *Tōkyō saiban*, p. 252.
21. Count 55 of indictment, in Boister and Cryer, *Documents on the Tokyo International Military Tribunal*, p. 33.

22. "Majority Judgment," in Boister and Cryer, *Documents on the Tokyo International Military Tribunal*, pp. 603–4, 617–8, 627–8.
23. Toyoda testified between July 14 and 20, 1949.
24. Shimanouchi, *Tōkyō saiban*, pp. 265–6.
25. Toyoda was appointed commander-in-chief of the Combined Naval Forces on April 25, 1945, and also commander-in-chief of the Naval Escort Command on May 1, 1945. "Exhibit DT: Affidavit of Toyoda Soemu," p. 1, §1, Toyoda Trial, R4058.
26. Toyoda offers a personal account of his upbringing and the naval war in the Pacific War. See Toyoda Soemu, *Saigo no teikoku kaigun* [The last of the Imperial Navy] (Tokyo: Sekai no Nippon sha, 1950). This publication is available also in English: *Toyoda Speaks: The Last of the Japanese Imperial Navy* (Tokyo: Sekai no Nippon sha, 1951). For an overview of Japanese naval atrocities during World War II, see Mark Felton, *Slaughter at Sea: The Story of Japan's Naval War Crimes* (Annapolis, MD: Naval Institute Press, 2007).
27. "The Charge and Specifications," Toyoda Trial, R9–11.
28. Toyoda Trial, R38, 45, 53, 497–8, 790.
29. The machine gun was introduced in Exhibit 403 at Toyoda Trial, R630. Exhibit 406 contained drawings of the gun emplacement. Toyoda Trial, R641.
30. "The Prosecution's Summation," Toyoda Trial, R4437.
31. Ibid.
32. Ibid.
33. Ibid., R4444. Emphasis added.
34. Ibid., R4487.
35. "Testimony of Okawachi Denshichi," Toyoda Trial, R115–6, 261–85; "Exhibit 167: Affidavit of Okawachi Denshichi," Toyoda Trial, R116; "Exhibit 168: Further Affidavit of Okawachi Denshichi," Toyoda Trial, R262. Ōkōchi's name appears in the record of the Toyoda Trial as "Okawachi [Ōkawachi]." This is another possible phonetic rendering of the ideographs used for the name, "Ōkōchi." The correct reading should be "Ōkōchi," however, as shown in Nihon kindai shiryō kenkyūkai [The Research Group on Sources of Modern Japan], ed., *Nihon riku-kaigun no seido, soshiki, jinji* [System, organization, and personnel of the Japanese army and navy] (Tokyo: Tōkyō daigaku shuppankai, 1971), p. 87.
36. Toyoda Trial, R277.
37. Ibid., R278.
38. "Majority Judgment," in Boister and Cryer, *Documents on the Tokyo International Military Tribunal*, pp. 564–5, 616, 619.
39. "Review of the Staff Judge Advocate" (Ichioka Case, no. 339, dated March 30, 1949), in "Reviews of the Yokohama Class B and Class C War Crimes Trials by the 8th Army Judge Advocate, 1946–1949" (College Park, MD: NARA), microfilm, M1112, roll 5. For the full record of the Ichioka Trial, see "Hisashi Ichioka, et 43," entry UD 1321, RG 331, SCAP, Records of the SCAP Legal Section, Prosecution Division: US vs. Japanese War Criminal Case Files, 1945–1949, NARA.
40. All accused at the Ichioka Trial initially pleaded not guilty to the charge and specifications, but some of the accused subsequently changed their plea to guilty. Vice Adm. Nakazawa Tasuku – who maintained the plea of not

guilty – is said to have complained to Toyoda's defense counsel about being advised to plead guilty. "I will not be able to die with no regrets if we are forced into this type of compromise trial [*dakyō saiban*] for no reason." Shimanouchi, *Tōkyō saiban*, p. 255.

41. "Judgment," Toyoda Trial, R5004. Emphasis added.

42. Article 6 of the "Charter of the International Military Tribunal," available online at the Web site of the Avalon Project: Documents in Law, History and Diplomacy at the Yale Law School Lillian Goldman Law Library, http://avalon .law.yale.edu/imt/imtconst.asp. Article 5 of the "Charter of the International Military Tribunal for the Far East (26 April 1946)," in Boister and Cryer, *Documents on the Tokyo International Military Tribunal*, p. 8.

43. For the relevant part in the Nuremberg judgment, see the section titled, "The Law Relating to War Crimes and Crimes against Humanity." The full text of the Nuremberg judgment is available online at the Web site of the Avalon Project: Documents in Law, History and Diplomacy at the Yale Law School Lillian Goldman Law Library. http://avalon.law.yale.edu/subject_menus/judcont.asp.

44. "Majority Judgment," in Boister and Cryer, *Documents on the Tokyo International Military Tribunal*, p. 85.

45. Jesse Deitch devoted nearly a half of the prosecution's summation to summarizing the defense witnesses' testimony and enumerating inconsistencies in each, to argue that they were liars and prevaricators. "The Prosecution's Summation," Toyoda Trial, R4501–81.

46. For instance, Deitch criticized Navy Capt. Imagawa Fukuo, saying that "the witness understood English and undoubtedly changed his testimony because of the long-winded argument he heard when Mr. Blakeney objected to the translation." Ibid., R4511. Deitch raised similar criticism against Rear Adm. Yokoyama Ichize, who had used English in his official capacity during and after the war, but who "said he did not think he could understand [English]" and "insisted upon testifying in Japanese." Ibid., R4513.

47. "The Defense Summation," Toyoda Trial, R4715.

48. Ibid., R4614.

49. Ibid., R4631–5. This episode concerned organizational charts of the navy. The prosecution presented Exhibit 2 (the chart showing the Japanese naval organization, introduced at R34) but withheld corrections that the Second Demobilization Bureau subsequently supplied.

50. Ibid., R4698–4700. This episode concerns the prosecution's handling of the interrogation record pertaining to Toyoda's policy on the defense of Manila and transfer of naval land forces to the army on the eve of the Battle of Manila. "Exhibit 4: Statement of Toyoda Soemu," Toyoda Trial, R55.

51. "Judgment," Toyoda Trial, R5019.

52. "The Defense Summation," Toyoda Trial, R4639.

53. Ibid., R4646.

54. Ibid., R4640.

55. Ibid., R4641. Emphasis added. See note 9 above for related information.

56. Ibid.

57. Ibid., R4640.

58. "Judgment," Toyoda Trial, R5005. Emphasis added.

59. Ibid.

60. Ibid., R5005–6. Emphasis added.
61. Toyoda Trial, R1186. Emphasis added.
62. "Exhibit E: Fleet Ordinance (November 30, 1914)," Toyoda Trial, R1194. For the Japanese original of the Fleet Ordinance (*Kantairei*), see Naikaku insatsu-kyoku [The Cabinet Printing Office], ed., *Taishō nenkan hōrei zensho. Taishō 3-nen, 4. gunrei, seirei, ritsuryō, kakurei, shōrei* [The Taishō-era compendium of laws. Taishō 3, vol. 4. military laws, regulations, legal codes, cabinet ordinances, ministerial ordinances] (Tokyo: Hara shobō, 1986), pp. 75–82. The same text can be found also in Kaigun daijin kanbō [The Secretariat of the Navy Ministry] ed., *Kaigun seido enkaku, kan-3 (ge-kansei)* [The history of the navy system, vol. 3 (part 2. organization)] (Tokyo: Kaigun daijin kanbō insatsu, 1939), pp. 1452–5.
63. "The Defense Summation," Toyoda Trial, R4649.
64. Exhibit E, p. 3, Toyoda Trial; Naikaku insatsukyoku, *Taishō nenkan hōrei zensho. Taishō 3-nen, 4. gunrei, seirei, ritsuryō, kakurei, shōrei*, p. 77.
65. "Exhibit I: Affidavit of Yoshida Zengo," p. 2, Toyoda Trial, R1200.
66. Exhibit E, p. 2, Toyoda Trial; Naikaku insatsukyoku, *Taishō nenkan hōrei zensho. Taishō 3-nen, 4. gunrei, seirei, ritsuryō, kakurei, shōrei*, p. 77.
67. Ibid.
68. "Exhibit F: Regarding the Administrative Competence of the Combined Fleet. Secretariat No. 3567 (November 24, 1924)," Toyoda Trial, R1195. The Japanese original of this text can be found in Kaigun daijin kanbō, *Kaigun seido enkaku, kan-3 (ge-kansei)*, pp. 1479–80.
69. "Exhibit K: Affidavit of Kobayashi Seizo," p. 2, §5, Toyoda Trial, R1223.
70. Exhibit DT, p. 62, §101, Toyoda Trial.
71. "Exhibit BR: Regarding Control of Administration of Occupied Areas by Fleet Commanders and Special Guard District Commanders. Restricted Order (Nairei) No. 1538 (November 26, 1941)," Toyoda Trial, R2028. Emphasis added. The Japanese original of this text can be found in "Nairei, Shōwa 16-nen 10-gatsu – Shōwa 16-nen 12-gatsu" [Restricted Ordinances, October 1941 – December 1941], call number: 0-Hōrei-Nairei-13, National Institute for Defense Studies, Center for Military History Archive.
72. "Exhibit L: Affidavit of Takada Toshitane," p. 4, §5-B, Toyoda Trial, R1241.
73. "Exhibit G: Re: Special Stipulations Regarding the Organization of the Combined Fleet As Defined In the Fleet Ordinance. Restricted Order (Nairei) No. 619 (April 10, 1942)," Toyoda Trial, R1196. Emphasis added. The Japanese original of this text can be found in "Nairei 2-kan, Shōwa 17-nen 4-gatsu – Shōwa 17-nen 6-gatsu [Restricted Ordinances, vol. 2, April 1942 – June 1942], call number: 0-Hōrei-Nairei-15, National Institute for Defense Studies.
74. For organizational charts of the Japanese army and navy during the Asia-Pacific War, see Bōei kenshūjo senshishitsu, ed., *Senshi sōsho. 102. Riku-kaigun nenpyō fu heiki, hyōgo no kaisetsu* [War history series: The army and navy chronology, with an appendix containing the annotation on weaponry and military terms] (Tokyo: Asagumo shinbunsha, 1980), pp. 460–535.
75. "Exhibit T: Daikaishi No. 38 (January 3, 1942)," Toyoda Trial, R1584. The Japanese original of this text is included in "Daikaishi 1/9 (1-gō kara 100-gō made)" [General Staff Directives 1/9 (from no. 1 to no. 100)], call number: 1-Chūō-Meirei-20, National Institute for Defense Studies.

76. "Exhibit A: General Staff Directive [Daikaishi] No. 189 (January 13, 1943)," p. 2, Toyoda Trial, R357.
77. Ibid., p. 4. Emphasis added. The Japanese original of this text is included in "Daikaishi 3/9 (181-gō kara 210-gō made)" [General Staff Directives 3/9 (from no. 181 to no. 210)], call number: 1-Chūō-Meirei-22, National Institute for Defense Studies.
78. Exhibit A, p. 4, Toyoda Trial.
79. "Testimony of Okawachi Denshichi," Toyoda Trial, R264, 271–2.
80. "Exhibit M: General Staff Directive No. 463 (September 23, 1944)," Toyoda Trial, R1431. The Japanese original of this text is included in "Daikaishi 8/9 (451-gō kara 510-gō made)" [General Staff Directives 8/9 (from no. 451 to no. 510)], call number: 1-Chūō-Meirei-27, National Institute for Defense Studies.
81. "Exhibit N: General Staff Directive No. 477 (October 23, 1944)," p. 1, Toyoda Trial, R1432. The Japanese original of this text is included in "Daikaishi 8/9 (451-gō kara 510-gō made)" [General Staff Directives 8/9 (from no. 451 to no. 510)], call number: 1-Chūō-Meirei-27, National Institute for Defense Studies.
82. "Exhibit D: General Staff Directive Nos. 504 and 505 (February 5, 1945)." p. 1, Toyoda Trial, R1050. The Japanese original of these texts is included in "Daikaishi 8/9 (451-gō kara 510-gō made)" [General Staff Directives 8/9 (from no. 451 to no. 510)], call number: 1-Chūō-Meirei-27, National Institute for Defense Studies. The 10th Fleet was organized by combining the 1st and 2nd Southern Expeditionary Fleets on February 5, 1945. "The Defense Summation," Toyoda Trial, R4739, 4741.
83. "Exhibit CV: Naval Districts Ordinance. Military Ordinance pertaining to the Navy No. 5 (August 23, 1923)," p. 1, Toyoda Trial, R3475. This ordinance underwent several revisions through 1944. The Japanese original of this text can be found in Kaigun daijin kanbō, *Kaigun seido enkaku, kan-3 (ge-kansei)*, pp. 37–8.
84. Exhibit DT, p. 3, §5; and p. 4, §8, Toyoda Trial.
85. Ibid., p. 7, §12.
86. Ibid., p. 3, §5.
87. Ibid., p. 7, §12.
88. Ibid., p. 4, §6.
89. Ibid., p. 2, §3.
90. For Toyoda's argument regarding his lack of knowledge about mistreatment at the Ōfuna prisoner-of-war camp, see ibid., p. 7, §12 – p. 11, §19.
91. "Exhibit BP: Naval General Staff Ordinance. Military Ordinance Pertaining to the Navy No. 5 (September 27, 1933)," Toyoda Trial, R2027. The same ordinance is dated September 26, 1933 in the Japanese original. Kaigun daijin kanbō [The Secretariat of the Navy Ministry], ed., *Kaigun seido enkaku, kan-2 kansei (jō)* [The history of the navy system, vol. 2. organization (part 1)] (Tokyo: Kaigun daijin kanbō insatsu, undated), pp. 951–2. This ordinance underwent revision three times afterwards.
92. Exhibit DT, p. 67, §108, Toyoda Trial. Emphasis added.
93. For specific tasks of the Navy General Staff, see "Exhibit EC: Regulations for Liaison between the Navy Ministry and the Naval General Staff. Restricted Order (Nairei) No. 294 (October 1, 1933, revised by No. 483 of 1934)," Toyoda Trial, R4058.
94. "Testimony of Ozawa Jizaburo," Toyoda Trial, R3945.
95. Exhibit DT, pp. 67–8, §108, Toyoda Trial.

96. "Judgment," Toyoda Trial, R5002. Emphasis added.
97. Ibid., R5015.
98. Ibid., R5018–19.
99. Ibid., R5019. Emphasis added.
100. Ibid.
101. Exhibit DT, p. 78, §124, Toyoda Trial. Emphasis added.

CONCLUSION

1. There are numerous Japanese-language publications that offer accounts of personal experiences of the Allied war crimes trials. The ones with broad coverage of cases and personalities are the following: Sugamo isho hensan iinkai [The Sugamo Committee for the Compilation of Wills], ed., *Seiki no isho* [The Will of the century] (Tokyo: Sugamo isho hensan iinkai kankō jimusho, 1953); Sugamo hōmu iinkai [The Sugamo Legal Affairs Committee], ed., *Senpan saiban no jissō* [Reality of war crimes trials] (Tokyo: Fuji shuppansha, 1952); and Chaen Yoshio and Shigemitsu Kazuyoshi, eds., *Hokan: senpan saiban no jissō* [Supplementary sources: Reality of war crimes trials] (Tokyo: Fuji shuppan, 1987). For a bibliography of Japanese-language publications up to the early 1980s, see Sumitani Osachi, Utsumi Aiko, and Akazawa Shirō, eds., "Tōkyō saiban, BC-kyū sensō hanzai, sensō sekinin kankei shiyō bunken mokuroku" [Index to published sources concerning the Tokyo Trial, Class BC war crimes, and war responsibility], *Shisō*, no. 719 (May 1985), 28 pages. This article appears at the back end of the journal.
2. For more information on prewar and wartime Japanese criminal justice systems, see Mitchell, *Janus-Faced Justice*. For a thematic analysis of criminal justice in the Shōwa era (1926–1989), see Tsuchiya and Shikita, *Crime and Criminal Policy in Japan*.
3. At least in the case of the Tokyo Trial, some of the contemporary trial observers regarded the Tokyo Trial as a practical lessen for learning court practices of the Anglo-American justice system. Totani, *Tokyo War Crimes Trial*, pp. 194–5 and, 205–7. On legal reform in occupied Japan, see the following publications: Alfred C. Oppler, *Japan's Courts and Law in Transition* (Tokyo: Foreign Affairs Association of Japan, 1952); Alfred C. Oppler, *Legal Reform in Occupied Japan: A Participant Looks Back* (Princeton, NJ: Princeton University Press, 1976); and Washington Law Review, ed., *Legal Reforms in Japan during the Allied Occupation: A Collection of Essays* (Seattle, WA: Washington Law Review, 1977). For a comprehensive source book, see Naitō Yorihiro, *Shūsengo no shihō seido kaikaku no keika: Ichiji tōkyokusha no tachiba kara* [Progress in the reform of the legal system after the end of the war: From the viewpoint of a person in charge], 4 vols. (Tokyo: Shinzansha, 1997–1998). Oppler's *Legal Reform in Occupied Japan* is available in Japanese translation as well: *Nihon senryō to hōsei kaikaku* [Occupation of Japan and legal reform], trans. Naitō Yorihiro, Naya Hiromi, and Takachi Shigeyo (Tokyo: Nihon hyōronsha, 1990).
4. Kuroda Trial, R3071 (see Chapter 1, note 1).
5. "Rationale," p. 11, Kuroda Trial.
6. Tōkyō saiban handobukku henshū iinkai, *Tōkyō saiban handobukku*, p. 82.
7. The Australian military authorities at Manus and the U.S. Navy at Guam allowed part or the whole of the trial records to be taken back to Japan. Toyoda, *Sensō saiban yoroku*, p. 470.

8. For a compilation of news reporting concerning the Allied war crimes trials, see Utsumi and Nagai, eds., *Shinbun shiryō ni miru Tōkyō saiban, BC-kyū saiban.*

9. Major publications in the early postwar years that document death-row inmates' views on the trial experiences include, but are not limited to, the following: Kadomatsu Shōichi, *Kōshukei* [Death by hanging] (Tokyo: Jīpusha, 1950); Okada Tasuku, *Sugamo no jūsan kaidan: senpan shokeisha no kiroku* [The thirteen steps at Sugamo: A record of an executed war criminal] (Tokyo: Atō shobō, 1952); Matsuo Saburō, *Kōshudai no hibiki: aru interi senpan shikeishū no shuki* [The sound of the gallows: Memoirs of a convicted "intelligentsia" war criminal on death row] (Tokyo: Sekaisha, 1952); Sugimatsu Fujio, ed., *Shishite sokoku ni ikin: 4 senpan shikeishū no isho* [Die to live in the homeland: Wills of four war criminals on death row] (Tokyo: Sōjusha, 1952); Yukawa Yōzō, ed., *Asu no asa no "9-ji": senpan shikeisha no ishoshū* [Tomorrow morning at nine o'clock: A collection of wills by executed war criminals] (Tokyo: Nihon shūhōsha, 1952); Okamoto Torao, ed., *Nokosareta hitobito: Hitō senpan shikeishū no shuki* [People left behind: Memoirs of war criminals on death row in the Philippines] (Tokyo: Suma shobō, 1952); Shiojiri Kōmei, ed., *Aru isho ni tsuite* [About a will] (Tokyo: Shinchōsha, 1948); and Shiojiri Kōmei, ed., *Sokoku e no isho: senpan shikeishū no shuki* [Wills for the homeland: Memoirs of war criminals on death row] (Tokyo: Mainichi shinbunsha, 1952). Accounts of death-row inmates and other convicted war criminals from the viewpoints of prison chaplains were published in the early years of the postwar period as well. See Hanayama Nobukatsu, *Heiwa no hakken* [Discovery of peace] (Tokyo: Asahi shinbunsha, 1949); and Kagao Hidenobu, *Montenrupa ni inoru: Hitō senpan shikeishū to tomo ni* [Praying at Muntinlupa: Together with war criminals on death row in the Philippines] (Tokyo: Fuji shoen, 1952). For a contemporaneous account of war crimes trials from the standpoint of Japanese defense lawyers, see Sōmiya Shinji, *Anbon-tō senpan saibanki* [Records of war crimes trials at Ambon] (Tokyo: Hōritsu shinpōsha, 1946).

10. Sugamo isho hensan iinkai, *Seiki no isho*, p. 743. The reprint of *Seiki no isho* was published in 1984. For an in-depth analysis of the discourse of *Seiki no isho*, see Ushimura Kei, *Saikō: "Seiki no isho" to Tōkyō saiban: tai-Nichi senpan saiban no seishinshi* [Reconsideration: *Seiki no isho* and the Tokyo Trial; Intellectual history of war crimes trials against the Japanese] (Tokyo: PHP shuppan, 2004), pp. 15–47.

11. An abridged version containing a selection of some 100 pieces from *Seiki no isho* was published for a much broader circulation in later years. See Sugamo isho hensan iinkai [The Sugamo Committee for the Compilation of Wills], ed., *Shi to eikō: senpan shikeishū no shuki* [Death and glory: Memoirs of war criminals on death row] (Tokyo: Nagashima shobō, 1957). The national association of former *kenpeitai* members in later decades published their own version of compilation of wills by fellow *kenpeitai* officers. Zenkoku ken'yūkai rengōkai hensan iinkai [The All-Japan Union for the Friends-of-Kenpei Association Compilation Committee], ed., *Junkoku kenpei no isho* [The wills of patriotic military police] (Tokyo: Kenbun shoin, 1982).

12. *Senpan saiban no jissō* does not include any accounts of Chinese war crimes trials. The information on Australian trials is also limited, covering only those cases held at Singapore and Hong Kong.

13. *Senpan saiban no jissō*, pp. 661–87.
14. Chaen and Shigematsu, *Hokan: senpan saiban no jissō*, p. 193.
15. The first printing of *Senpan saiban no jissō* in 1952 amounted to 200 copies only, just enough to be distributed to lawmakers, former defense lawyers at the Tokyo Trial, and other individuals. The Sugamo inmates hoped that these people would make use of the publication to influence public opinion in favor of early release of convicted war criminals. The book apparently met a cool reception, however, as few Japanese in those years were prepared to support an agenda in conflict with the Allied war crimes policy and more specifically the Treaty of Peace with Japan (September 8, 1951). Ibid., p. 191. Article 11 of the peace treaty read, "Japan accept[s] the judgments of the International Military Tribunal for the Far East and of other Allied War Crimes Courts both within and outside Japan, and will carry out the sentences imposed thereby upon Japanese nationals imprisoned in Japan." (The full text of the Treaty of Peace with Japan is available at the Web site of the United Nations Treaty Collection: https://treaties.un.org/doc/Publication/UNTS/Volume%20136/volume-136-I-1832-English.pdf.) That said, other contemporaneous publications by Sugamo inmates did circulate and animate the public debate on the possibility of convicted war criminals' early release. Some of the impactful publications in the 1950s include the following: Atō shobō [Atō Publisher], ed., *Ware shinubeshiya: BC-kyū senpansha no kiroku* [Should I die? Records of Class BC war criminals] (Tokyo: Atō shobō, 1952); Satō Ryōichi, *Gyakutai no kiroku*; Iizuka Kōji, ed., *Arekara 7-nen: gakuto senpan no gokuchū kara no tegami* [Seven years since then: Letters from student war criminals in prison] (Tokyo: Kōbunsha, 1953); and Riron henshūbu [Theory Editor Section], ed., *Kabe atsuki heya: BC-kyū senpan no jinseiki* [A room with thick walls: Life stories of Class BC war criminals] (Tokyo: Nihon tosho sentā, 1992; originally published in 1953). Katō Tetsutarō, a Sugamo inmate and an avid writer in those years, later gained fame as a result of a film adaptation of his personal accounts of his experience as a convicted war criminal. (Katō subsequently initiated a copyright lawsuit against the script writer of the said film, however.) For more information, see Katō Tetsutarō, *Watashi wa kai ni naritai: aru BC-kyū senpan no sakebi* [I would like to be a seashell: Cry of a Class BC war criminal] (Tokyo: Shunjūsha, 1994).
16. Other representative publications by former convicted war criminals and defense lawyers in later years include the following: Yano Kenzō, *Gokuchūki: himeraretaru shūsen zangyaku monogatari* [Prison notes: A secret story of postwar atrocity] (Tokyo: Chōbunsha, 1962); Nogi Harumichi, *Kaigun tokubetsu keisatsutai: Anbon-tō BC-kyū senpan no shuki* [The navy special military police force: Personal notes by a Class BC war criminal at Ambon] (Tokyo: Taihei shuppansha, 1975); Matsuura Yoshinori, *Shinjitsu o uttaeru: Rabauru senpan bengonin no nikki* [Appealing the truth: The diary of a lawyer for war crimes trials at Rabaul] (Tokyo: Genshū shuppansha, 1997); and Tarumoto Jūji, *Aru senpan no shuki: Taimen tetsudō kensetsu to senpan saiban* [Personal notes of a war criminal: The construction of the Burma-Siam Railway and war crimes trials] (Tokyo: Gendai shiryō shuppan, 1999). Excerpts of *Senpan saiban no jissō*, meanwhile, gained greater circulation in the intervening years. See Saka Kuniyasu, ed., *Shijitsu kiroku sensō saiban* [Historical records of war crimes trials], 5 vols. (Tokyo: Tōchōsha, 1967–8); Sugamo hōmu iinkai [The Sugamo Legal

Affairs Committee], ed., *Haruka naru minami Jūjisei: senpan saiban no jissō* [The Southern Cross afar: Reality of war crimes trials] (Tokyo: Sannō shobō, 1968); and Kawano Kyōsuke, ed., *Jinmon, gōmon, shokei* [Interrogation, torture, execution] (Tokyo: Akita shoten, 1970). A supplementary volume of *Senpan saiban no jissō* was also published in later years. Chaen and Shigematsu, *Hokan: senpan saiban no jissō*. In the West, studies have been made recently regarding repatriation, clemency, release, and othe related issues on the post-trial treatment of convicted Japanese war criminals. See Dean Aszkielowicz, "Repatriation and the Limits of Resolve: Japanese War Criminals in Australian Custody," *Japanese Studies*, vol. 31, no. 2 (September 2011), pp. 211–28; Robert Cribb, "Avoiding Clemency: The Trial and Transfer of Japanese War Criminals in Indonesia, 1946–1949," *Japanese Studies*, vol. 31, no. 2 (September 2011), pp. 151-70; Beatrice Trefalt, "A Peace Worth Having: Delayed Repatriations and Domestic Debate Over the San Francisco Peace Treaty," *Japanese Studies*, vol. 27, no. 2 (September 2007), pp. 173–87; Trefalt, "Hostages to International Relations"; Sandra Wilson, "After the Trials: Class B and C Japanese War Criminals and the Post-War World," *Japanese Studies*, vol. 31, no. 2 (September 2011), pp. 141–9; and Sandra Wilson, "Prisoners in Sugamo and Their Campaign for Release, 1952–1953," *Japanese Studies*, vol. 31, no. 2 (September 2011), pp. 191–90. These scholars' co-authored book manuscript, *Japanese War Criminals, 1945–1958: From Arrest to Release,* is presently under consideration for publication.

17. Toyoda, *Sensō saiban yoroku*, p. 460.
18. Ibid., pp. 465–6.
19. Ibid., p. 471.
20. Ibid., p. 472.
21. Parts of the collection that the Ministry of Legal Affairs compiled were published in subsequent years. For instance, excerpts from the collection appear in multivolume source books by Chaen Yoshio, published between 1983 and 1999. This particular series suffers from poor editorial work, however, which diminishes its value as source material. The titles contained in the series are as follows: Chaen Yoshio, ed., *Nihon BC-kyū senpan shiryō* [Japanese sources on Class BC war crimes trials] (Tokyo: Fuji shuppan, 1983); *BC-kyū Beigun Manira saiban shiryō*; *BC-kyū senpan Beigun Shanhai tō saiban shiryō* [Sources on American military Class BC war crimes trials at Shanghai etc.] (Tokyo: Fuji shuppan, 1989); *BC-kyū senpan Chūgoku Futsukoku saiban shiryō* [Sources on Chinese and French Class BC war crimes trials] (Tokyo: Fuji shuppan, 1992); *BC-kyū senpan Eigun saiban shiryō* [Sources on British military Class BC war crimes trials] (Tokyo: Fuji shuppan, 1988); *BC-kyū senpan Firipin saiban shiryō*; *BC-kyū senpan Gōgun Manusu tō saiban shiryō* [Sources on Australian Class BC war crimes trials at Manus etc.] (Tokyo: Fuji shuppan, 1991); *BC-kyū senpan Gōgun Rabauru saiban shiryō*; *BC-kyū senpan Waran saiban shiryō zenkan tsūran* [Sources on Dutch Class BC war crimes trials and an overview of all volumes] (Tokyo: Fuji shuppan, 1992); *BC-kyū senpan gunji hōtei shiryō Kanton hen* [Sources on Class BC war crimes military trials at Guangdong] (Tokyo, Fuji shuppan, 1984); *BC-kyū senpan Yokohama saiban shiryō* [Sources on Class BC war crimes trials at Yokohama] (Tokyo: Fuji shuppan, 1985).
22. Handō Kazutoshi, *"BC-kyū saiban" o yomu* [Reading the "Class BC trials"] (Tokyo: Nihon keizai shinbun shuppansha, 2010), p. 33.

23. For information concerning declassification status of trial records at the former Allied countries around 1989, see Tōkyō saiban handobukku henshū iinkai, *Tōkyō saiban handobukku*, pp. 146–7.

24. Visit http://www.naa.gov.au.

25. At present, the International Criminal Court (ICC) Legal Tools Database is partnering with research centers worldwide in order to build an online portal for hosting the records of the past and the present international criminal proceedings. For more information, visit its Web site at http://www.legal-tools.org.

26. Kamisaka Fuyuko, *Seitai kaibō: kyūshū daigaku igakubu jiken* [Vivisection: The case of the Medical Department at Kyūshū University] (Tokyo: Mainichi shinbunsha, 1979); *Sugamo Purizun 13-gō teppi* [The iron doors at Sugamo Prison No. 13] (Tokyo: Shinchōsha, 1981); *Sugamo: senpan kōshukei* [Sugamo: Death by hanging of a war criminal] (Tokyo: Mineruva shobō, 1981); *Nokosareta tsuma: Yokohama saiban BC-kyū senpan hiroku* [Wives left behind: Secret records of the Yokohama Class BC war criminals] (Tokyo: Chūō kōronsha, 1983); and *Kai ni natta otoko: Naoetsu horyo shūyōjo jiken* [A man who became a seashell: The case of the Naoetsu Prisoner-of-War Internment Camp] (Tokyo: Bungei shunjū, 1986).

27. See, for instance, Kimura, *Wasurerareta sensō sekinin*; and Nagano Tameyoshi, *Rabauru gunji hōtei: aru Nihonjin no saiban kiroku* [The Rabaul military court: Trial records of a Japanese] (Tokyo: Keisō shuppan sābisu sentā, 1982).

Works Cited

Archives

Australian War Memorial. Canberra.
Hoover Institution Library and Archives. Stanford University, Stanford, CA.
Imperial War Museums. London.
National Archives. Kew, Richmond, Surrey, UK.
National Archives and Records Administration. College Park, MD.
National Archives of Australia. Melbourne.
National Archives of Japan. Tokyo.
National Diet Library. Tokyo.
National Institute for Defense Studies, Center for Military History Archive. Tokyo.

Microfilm Sources

New York Times. Ann Arbor, MI: University Microfilms.
"Records of the Trial of Accused War Criminal Hiroshi Tamura, Tried by a Military Tribunal Appointed by the Supreme Commander of the Allied Powers, Tokyo, Japan, 1948–1949." 3 rolls. M1728. College Park, MD: National Archives and Records Administration.
"Records of the Trial of Accused War Criminal Soemu Toyoda, Tried by a Military Tribunal Appointed by the Supreme Commander of the Allied Powers, Tokyo, Japan, 1948–1949." 7 rolls. M1729. College Park, MD: National Archives and Records Administration.
"Records of Trials of Accused Japanese War Criminals Tried at Manila, Philippines, by a Military Commission Convened by the Commanding General of the United States Army in the Western Pacific, 1945–1947." 34 rolls. M1727. College Park, MD: National Archives and Records Administration.
"Reviews of the Yokohama Class B and Class C War Crimes Trials by the 8th Army Judge Advocate, 1946–1949." 5 rolls. M1112. College Park, MD: National Archives and Records Administration.
"Transcripts from the Case of the United States of America vs. Soemu Toyoda and Hiroshi Tamura, 1946–1948." 4 rolls. M1661. College Park, MD: National Archives and Records Administration.
Washington Post. New Haven, CT: Research Publications, Inc.

Online Sources

Australian Dictionary of Biography, National Centre of Biography, Australian-National University
http://adb.anu.edu.au/biography

Australian War Memorial
http://www.awm.gov.au

The Avalon Project: Documents in Law, History and Diplomacy, Yale Law School, Lillian Goldman Law Library
http://avalon.law.yale.edu

International Criminal Court
http://www.icc-cpi.int/en_menus/icc/Pages/default.aspx

International Criminal Court (ICC) Legal Tools Database
http://www.legal-tools.org

International Committee of the Red Cross
http://www.icrc.org

International Criminal Tribunal for the Former Yugoslavia
http://www.icty.org

International Criminal Tribunal for Rwanda
http://www.unictr.org

JapanKnowledge Lib
http://japanknowledge.com/library/en

Justia.com, U.S. Supreme Court Center
http://supreme.justia.com

Model Penal Code Annotated
http://www.law-lib.utoronto.ca/bclc/crimweb/index.html

National Archives of Australia
http://www.naa.gov.au

National Archives and Records Administration
http://www.archives.gov

National Diet Library
http://www.ndl.go.jp

Nichirenshū Tōkyō saibu shūmusho [The Religious Affairs Institute of the Nichiren
    Sect of Buddhism, Western Tokyo]
http://www.tokyo-saibu.com

Remembering the War in New Guinea, Australian War Memorial
http://ajrp.awm.gov.au/AJRP/remember.nsf

Sōgō bijinesusha (a Japanese publisher)
http://www.business-sha.co.jp

United Nations Treaty Collection
https://treaties.un.org

United Nations War Crimes Commission Project
http://www.unwcc.org

War Crimes Studies Center, University of California, Berkeley
http://socrates.berkeley.edu/~warcrime

Other Published Sources

Adachi Tamenari. "Jinmin saiban" [People's Trials]. In *Manshū kenkoku no yume to genjitsu* [Dream and Reality in the Establishment of the Manchukuoan State].

Edited by Kokusai zenrin kyōkai [The International Good-Neighbor Society]. Tokyo: Kenkōsha, 1975, pp. 415–22.

Allen, Louis. *Burma: The Longest War, 1941–45.* London, UK and Melbourne, Australia: J. M. Dent, 1984.

Aquino, Ramon C. *A Chance to Die: A Biography of José Abad Santos, Late Chief Justice of the Philippines.* Quezon City, Philippines: Alemar-Phoenix Publishing House, 1967.

Aszkielowicz, Dean. "After the Surrender: Australia and the Japanese Class B and C War Criminals, 1945–1958." PhD diss., Murdoch University, 2013.

————. "Repatriation and the Limits of Resolve: Japanese War Criminals in Australian Custody." *Japanese Studies,* vol. 31, no. 2 (September 2011): pp. 211–28.

Atō shobō [Atō Publisher], ed. *Ware shinubeshiya: BC-kyū senpansha no kiroku* [Should I die? Records of Class BC war criminals]. Tokyo: Atō shobō, 1952.

Australia Military Board. *Australian Edition of Manual of Military Law, 1941 (Including Army Act and Rules of Procedure as Modified and Adapted by the Defence Act 1903–1939 and the Australian Military Regulations).* Canberra: L. F. Johnston, Commonwealth Government Printer, 1941.

Bayly, C. A., and T. N. Harper. *Forgotten Armies: The Fall of British Asia, 1941–1945.* Cambridge, MA: Belknap Press of Harvard University Press, 2005.

————. *Forgotten Wars: Freedom and Revolution in Southeast Asia.* Cambridge, MA: Harvard University Press, 2007.

Bean, C. E. W. *The Australian Imperial Force in France, 1916.* St. Lucia, Queensland, Australia: University of Queensland Press, 1982.

Bennet, Scott. *Pozieres: The Anzac Story.* Melbourne: Vision Australia Information Service, 2012.

Bergerud, Eric. *Touched with Fire: The Land War in the South Pacific.* New York: Penguin Books, 1996.

Bergsmo, Morten, Cheah Wui Ling, and Yi Ping, eds. *Historical Origins of International Criminal Law,* vol. 1. New York: Torkel Opsahl Academic EPublisher, in press.

Bix, Herbert. *Hirohito and the Making of Modern Japan.* New York: HarperCollins, 2000.

Blakeslee, George Hubbard. *The Far Eastern Commission: A Study in International Cooperation: 1945 to 1952.* Washington, DC: Department of State, 1953.

Bōei kenshūjo senshishitsu [Military History Room, Defense Research Institute], ed. *Senshi sōsho* [War history series]. 102 vols. Tokyo: Asagumo shinbunsha, 1966–80.

Boister, Neil, and Robert Cryer, eds. *Documents on the Tokyo International Military Tribunal: Charter, Indictment and Judgments.* Oxford and New York: Oxford University Press, 2008.

Boyle, John Hunter. *China and Japan at War, 1936–1945: The Politics of Collaboration.* Stanford, CA: Stanford University Press, 1972.

Bradley, James. *Cyril Wild: The Tall Man Who Never Slept.* Fontwell, West Sussex, UK: Woodfield, 1991.

Bradsher, Greg, ed. *Japanese War Crimes and Related Topics: A Guide to Records at the National Archives.* Supplied in a CD attached to Bradsher, *Researching Japanese War Crimes Records* (see below). Available also at the Web site of the National Archives and Records Administration, http://www.archives.gov/iwg/japanese-war-crimes.

Bradsher, Greg, et al. *Researching Japanese War Crimes Records: Introductory Essays*. Washington, DC: National Archives and Records Administration for the Nazi War Crimes and Japanese Imperial Government Records Interagency Working Group, 2006.

Brook, Timothy. *Collaboration: Japanese Agents and Local Elites in Wartime China*. Cambridge, MA: Harvard University Press, 2007.

Bullard, Steven, trans. *Japanese Army Operations in the South Pacific Area: New Britain and Papua Campaigns, 1942–43*. Canberra: Australian War Memorial, 2007.

————. "Japanese Strategy and Intentions towards Australia." In *Australia 1942: In the Shadow of War*. Edited by Peter J. Dean. Cambridge, MA: Cambridge University Press, 2013, pp. 124–39.

Carrel, Michael. "Australia's Prosecution of Japanese War Criminals." PhD diss., University of Melbourne, 2005.

Carucci, Laurence Marshall, Suzanne Falgout, and Lin Poyer, eds. *Memories of War: Micronesians in the Pacific War*. Honolulu: University of Hawai'i Press, 2008.

————, eds. *The Typhoon of War: Micronesian Experiences of the Pacific War*. Honolulu: University of Hawai'i Press, 2001.

Chaen Yoshio, ed. *BC-kyū senpan Beigun Manira saiban shiryō* [Sources on American military Class BC war crimes trials at Manila]. Tokyo: Fuji shuppan, 1986.

————, ed. *BC-kyū senpan Beigun Shanhai tō saiban shiryō* [Sources on American military Class BC war crimes trials at Shanghai etc.]. Tokyo: Fuji shuppan, 1989.

————, ed. *BC-kyū senpan Chūgoku Futsukoku saiban shiryō* [Sources on Chinese and French Class BC war crimes trials]. Tokyo: Fuji shuppan, 1992.

————, ed. *BC-kyū senpan Eigun saiban shiryō* [Sources on British military Class BC war crimes trials]. Tokyo: Fuji shuppan, 1988.

————, ed. *BC-kyū senpan Firipin saiban shiryō* [Sources on Philippine Class BC war crimes trials]. Tokyo: Fuji shuppan, 1987.

————, ed. *BC-kyū senpan Gōgun Manusu tō saiban shiryō* [Sources on Australian military Class BC war crimes trials at Manus etc.]. Tokyo: Fuji shuppan, 1991.

————, ed. *BC-kyū senpan Gōgun Rabauru saiban shiryō* [Sources on Australian military Class BC war crimes trials at Rabaul]. Tokyo: Fuji shuppan, 1990.

————, ed. *BC-kyū senpan gunji hōtei shiryō Kanton hen* [Sources on Class BC war crimes military trials at Guangdong]. Tokyo: Fuji shuppan, 1984.

————, ed. *BC-kyū senpan Waran saiban shiryō zenkan tsūran* [Sources on Dutch Class BC war crimes trials and an overview of all volumes]. Tokyo: Fuji shuppan, 1992.

————, ed. *BC-kyū senpan Yokohama saiban shiryō* [Sources on Class BC war crimes trials at Yokohama]. Tokyo: Fuji shuppan, 1985.

————, ed. *Furyo ni kansuru shohōki ruijū (Jūgonen sensō gokuhi shiryōshū, 11)* [The compilation of various rules concerning prisoners of war (Secret sources of the Fifteen-Year War, vol. 11)]. Tokyo: Fuji shuppan, 1988.

————, ed. *Nihon BC-kyū senpan shiryō* [Japanese sources on Class BC war crimes trials]. Tokyo: Fuji shuppan, 1983.

Chaen Yoshio and Shigemitsu Kazuyoshi, eds. *Hokan: senpan saiban no jissō* [Supplementary sources: Reality of war crimes trials]. Tokyo: Fuji shuppan, 1987.

Chamberlain, Sharon. "Justice and Reconciliation: Postwar Philippine Trials of Japanese War Criminals in History and Memory." PhD diss., George Washington University, 2010.

Cheah, Wui Ling. "Post-World War II British 'Hell-Ship' Trials in Singapore: Omissions and the Attribution of Responsibility." *Journal of International Criminal Justice* 8 (2010): pp. 1035–58.

Chūgoku kikansha renrakukai [The Association of Soldiers Repatriated from China], ed. *Kaettekita senpan tachi no kōhansei* [The latter half of the lives of repatriated war criminals]. Tokyo: Ryokufū shuppan, 1996.

Chūgokujin sensō higai baishō seikyū jiken bengodan [The Lawyers' Association for Reparation Lawsuits by Chinese Victims of the War]. *Sajō no shōheki: Chūgokujin sengo hoshō saiban 10-nen no kiseki* [Barrier on the sand: The ten-year trajectory of postwar Chinese reparation trials]. Tokyo: Nihon hyōronsha, 2005.

Cohen, David. "Beyond Nuremberg: Individual Responsibility for War Crimes." In *Human Rights in Political Transitions: Gettysburg to Bosnia.* Edited by Carla Hesse and Robert Post. New York: Zone Books, 1999, pp. 53–92.

————. "Bureaucracy, Justice, and Collective Responsibility in the World War II War Crimes Trials." *Rechtshistorisches Journal* [The Journal of Legal History] 18 (1999): pp. 313–42.

————. "The Historiography of the Historical Foundations of Theories of Responsibility in International Criminal Law." In *Historical Origins of International Criminal Law,* vol. 1. Edited by Morten Bergsmo, Cheah Wui Ling, and Yi Ping. New York: Torkel Opsahl Academic EPublisher, in press.

————. "Military Justice from WWII to Guantanamo: Fair Trials, Judicial Murder, and International Standards in WWII Crimes Trials in Asia." In *Summa Dieter Simon zum 70. Geburtstag.* Edited by Rainer Maria Kiesow, Regina Ogorek, and Spiros Simitis. Frankfurt am Main: Vittorio Klostermann, 2005, pp. 59–80.

————. "The Singapore War Crimes Trials and Their Relevance Today." *Singapore Law Review* 31 (2013): pp. 1–38.

————. "Weibo zhanzhenzui panjue caoan: Dongjing shenpan panjue de lingyi shijiao" [An alternative Tokyo Judgment: The draft Webb judgment on war crimes]. In *2013 Dongjing shenpan xueshu taolunhui lunji* [The compilation of essays from the symposium on the Tokyo Trial]. Shanghai, China: Shanghai jiaotong daxue chubanshe, in press.

Costello, John. *The Pacific War: 1941–1945.* New York: Rawson, Wade, 1981.

Cribb, Robert. "Avoiding Clemency: The Trial and Transfer of Japanese War Criminals in Indonesia, 1946–1949." *Japanese Studies,* vol. 31, no. 2 (September 2011): pp. 151–70.

Davis, Richard Harding, Frederick Palmer, James F. J. Archibald, Robert L. Dunn, Ellis Ashmead Bartlett, James H. Hare, Henry James Whigham, and Victor K. Bulla. *The Russo-Japanese War: A Photographic and Descriptive Review of the Great Conflict in the Far East.* New York: P. F. Collier, 1905.

Daws, Gavan. *Prisoners of the Japanese: POWs of World War II in the Pacific.* New York: William Morrow, 1994.

Dexter, David. *The New Guinea Offensive.* Australia in the War of 1939–1945. Series One (Army), vol. 6. Canberra: Australian War Memorial, 1961.

Eguchi Keiichi, *Jūgonen sensō shōshi* [A concise history of the Fifteen-Year War]. Tokyo: Aoki shoten, 1986.

Fay, Peter Ward. *The Forgotten Army: India's Armed Struggle for Independence, 1942–45.* Ann Arbor, MI: University of Michigan Press, 1993.

Felton, Mark. *Slaughter at Sea: The Story of Japan's Naval War Crimes.* Annapolis, MD: Naval Institute Press, 2007.

Fitzpatrick, Georgina, Timothy L. H. McCormack, and Narrelle Morris, eds. *Australia's War Crimes Trials, 1945–51.* Leiden, the Netherlands: Brill, in press.

Friedman, Leon, ed. *The Law of War: A Documentary History.* 2 vols. New York: Random House, 1972.

Fujiwara Akira and Imai Seiichi, eds. *Jūgonen sensōshi* [The history of the Fifteen-Year War]. 4 vols. Tokyo: Aoki shoten, 1988.

Fujiwara Iwaichi. *F kikanchō no shuki: Ajia kaihō o yume mita tokumu kikanchō no shuki* [The F Agency: Memoirs of a special agent chief who dreamt of Asian liberation]. Tokyo: Bajiriko, 2012.

_____. *F kikan: Japanese Army Intelligence Operations in Southeast Asia during World War II.* Hong Kong: Heinemann Asia, 1983.

Fukiura Tadamasa. *Horyotachi no Nichi-Ro sensō* [The Russo-Japanese War from the perspective of prisoners of war]. Tokyo: Nihon hōsō shuppan kyōkai, 2005.

Fukukawa Hideki, ed. *Nihon riku-kaigun jinmei jiten* [The encyclopedia of names of individuals in the Japanese army and navy]. Tokyo: Fuyō shobō, 1999.

_____. *Nihon rikugun shōkan jiten* [Dictionary of Japanese army generals]. Tokyo: Fuyō shobō shuppan, 2001.

Geneva Convention Relative to the Treatment of Prisoners of War. See "Convention on Treatment of Prisoners of War, Geneva, July 27, 1929." In *The Law of War: A Documentary History*, edited by Leon Friedman, vol. 1 (New York: Random House, 1972), pp. 488–522. Also called Geneva Prisoner-of-War Convention in the text of this book. Available online at the Web site of the International Committee of the Red Cross, http://www.icrc.org/ihl/INTRO/305?OpenDocument.

Great Britain War Office. *Manual of Military Law 1929.* Reprinted December 1939. London, UK: His Majesty's Stationery Office, 1940.

_____. *Manual of Military Law 1929 Amendments (No. 12): Chapter XIV. The Laws and Usages of War on Land.* London, UK: His Majesty's Stationery Office, 1942.

Hague Convention No. 4 Respecting the Laws and Customs of War on Land. See "Laws and Customs of War on Land (Hague, IV)." In *The Law of War: A Documentary History*, edited by Leon Friedman, vol. 1 (New York: Random House, 1972), pp. 308–23. Also called Hague Convention No. 4 in the text of this book. Available online at the Web site of the International Committee of the Red Cross, http://www.icrc.org/applic/ihl/ihl.nsf/INTRO/195.

Hanaoka kenkyūkai [The Hanaoka Research Group], ed. *Hanaoka jiken Yokohama hōtei kiroku: BC-kyū senpan saiban no daihyōteki jirei* [The Yokohama court record on the Hanaoka Incident: A representative case in the Class BC war crimes trials]. Tokyo: Sōwasha, 2006.

Hanayama Nobukatsu. *Heiwa no hakken* [Discovery of peace]. Tokyo: Asahi shinbunsha, 1949.

Handō Kazutoshi. *"BC-kyū saiban" o yomu* [Reading the "Class BC trials"]. Tokyo: Nihon keizai shinbun shuppansha, 2010.

Hayashi Hirofumi. *BC-kyū senpan saiban* [Class BC war crimes trials]. Tokyo: Iwanami shoten, 2005.

_____. *Sabakareta sensō hanzai: Igirisu no tai-Nichi senpan saiban* [War crimes tried: The British war crimes trials against the Japanese]. Tokyo: Iwanami shoten, 1998.

_____. *Senpan saiban no kenkyū: senpan saiban seisaku no keisei kara Tōkyō saiban, BC-kyū saiban made* [A study of war crimes trials: From the formation of policies on war crimes trials to the Tokyo Trial and Class BC war crimes trials]. Tokyo: Bensei shuppan, 2010.

_____. *Shingapōru kakyō shukusei: Nihongun wa Shingapōru de nani o shitanoka* [The purge of Chinese in Singapore: What did the Japanese military do in Singapore?]. Tokyo: Kōbunken, 2007.

Hayes, Grace Person. *The History of the Joint Chiefs of Staff in World War II: The War against Japan.* Annapolis, MD: Naval Institute Press, 1982.

Heibonsha roppō zensho [The Heibonsha compilation of six laws]. The Showa 16 Revised Edition. Tokyo: Heibonsha, 1931.

Heichōzan jiken soshō bengodan [The Lawyers' Association for the Litigation on the Pingdingshan Incident]. *Heichōzan jiken to wa nandattanoka: saiban ga tsumuida Nihon to Chūgoku no shimin no kizuna* [What was the Pingdingshan incident? The strengthening of ties between the Japanese and Chinese citizens through the trial]. Tokyo: Kōbunken, 2008.

Hirama Yōichi. *Nichi-Ro sensō o sekai wa dō hōjitaka* [How did the world report on the Russo-Japanese War?]. Tokyo: Fuyō shobō shuppan, 2010.

Hōmu daijin kanbō shihō hōsei chōsabu [The Judiciary and Legislation Investigation Bureau, Secretariat of the Ministry of Legal Affairs], ed. *Sensō hanzai saiban kankei hōreishū* [The compilation of legal documents on war crimes trials]. 2 vols. Tokyo: Hōmu daijin kanbō shihō hōsei chōsabu, 1963–1965.

Hopkins, William B. *The Pacific War: The Strategy, Politics, and Players That Won the War.* Minneapolis, MN: Zenith Press, 2008.

Hunt, Ray C., and Bernard Norling. *Behind Japanese Lines: An American Guerrilla in the Philippines.* Lexington: University Press of Kentucky, 1986.

Ienaga Saburō. *Taiheiyō sensō* [The Pacific War]. Tokyo: Iwanami shoten, 1968.

_____. *The Pacific War, 1931–1945: A Critical Perspective on Japan's Role in World War II.* Translated by Frank Baldwin. New York: Pantheon Books, 1978.

Ikō Toshiya. "Chūgoku kokumin seifu no Nihon shobatsu hōshin no tenkai" [The development of policies on the punishment of Japanese war criminals by the Republic of China]. In *Gendai rekishigaku to Nankin jiken* [Studies of modern history and the Nanjing Incident]. Edited by Kasahara Tokushi and Yoshida Yutaka. Tokyo: Kashiwa shobō, 2006, pp. 94–124.

Imamura Hitoshi. *Ichi gunjin rokujū-nen no aika* [An army officer's elegy on his sixty years]. Tokyo: Fuyō shobō, 1970.

_____. *Yūshū kaikoroku* [Memoirs of imprisonment]. Tokyo: Akita shoten, 1966.

Iizuka Kōji, ed. *Arekara 7-nen: gakuto senpan no gokuchū kara no tegami* [Seven years since then: Letters from student war criminals in prison]. Tokyo: Kōbunsha, 1953.

Inoue Hisashi and Kawakami Shirō. *Heichōzan jiken shiryōshū* [Sources of the Pingdingshan Incident]. Tokyo: Kashiwa shobō, 2012.

Inoue Yūko. *Nisshin, Nichi-Ro sensō to shashin hōdō* [The Sino-Japanese War and the Russo-Japanese War, and photojournalism]. Tokyo: Yoshikawa kōbunkan, 2012.

Ishitobi Jin. *Chūgokujin kyōsei renkō no kiroku: Nihonjin wa Chūgokujin ni nani o shitaka* [Records of Chinese forced deportation: What the Japanese did to the Chinese]. Tokyo: San'ichi shobō, 1997.

_____. *Hanaoka jiken: "Kashima kōshō" no kiseki* [The Hanaoka Incident: The trajectory of the "Kashima Negotiation"]. Tokyo: Sairyūsha, 2010.

Iwakawa Takashi. *Kami o shinzezu: BC-kyū senpan no bohimei* [I do not believe in God: The epitaph of Class BC war criminals]. Tokyo: Chūō kōronsha, 1978.

_____. *Kotō no tsuchi to narutomo: BC-kyū senpan saiban* [Even if to become the soil of an isolated island: Class BC war crimes trials]. Tokyo: Kōdansha, 1995.

Jalloh, Charles C. and Amy DiBella. "Equality of Arms in International Criminal Law: Continuing Challenges." In *The Ashgate Research Companion to International Criminal Law: Critical Perspectives*, edited by William A. Schabas, Yvonne McDermott, and Niamh Hayes. Farnham, Surrey, England, and Burlington, VT: Ashgate, 2013, pp. 251–88. This article is avaialble at the Web site of Social Science Research Network (SSRN) at http://ssrn.com/abstract=2314587.

Jōhō Yoshio. *Gensui Terauchi Hisaichi* [General Terauchi Hisaichi]. Tokyo: Fuyō shobō, 1978.

_____. *Tōjō Hideki* [Tōjō Hideki]. Tokyo: Fuyō shobō, 1974.

Jørgensen, Nina, H. B. "On Being 'Concerned' in a Crime: Embryonic Joint Criminal Enterprise?" In *Hong Kong's War Crimes Trials*. Edited by Suzannah Linton. Oxford: Oxford University Press, 2013, pp. 137–67.

Kadomatsu Shōichi. *Kōshukei* [Death by hanging]. Tokyo: Jīpusha, 1950.

Kagao Hidenobu. *Montenrupa ni inoru: Hitō senpan shikeishū to tomo ni* [Praying at Muntinlupa: Together with war criminals on death row in the Philippines]. Tokyo: Fuji shoen, 1952.

Kaigun daijin kanbō [The Secretariat of the Navy Ministry], ed. *Kaigun seido enkaku, kan-2 kansei (jō)* [The history of the navy system, vol. 2. organization (part 1)]. Tokyo: Kaigun daijin kanbō insatsu, undated.

_____, ed. *Kaigun seido enkaku, kan-3 (ge-kansei)* [The history of the navy system, vol. 3 (part 2. organization)]. Tokyo: Kaigun daijin kanbō insatsu, 1939.

Kamisaka Fuyuko. *Kai ni natta otoko: Naoetsu horyo shūyōjo jiken* [A man who became a seashell: The case of the Naoetsu Prisoner-of-War Internment Camp]. Tokyo: Bungei shunjū, 1986.

_____. *Nokosareta tsuma: Yokohama saiban BC-kyū senpan hiroku* [Wives left behind: Secret records of the Yokohama Class BC war criminals]. Tokyo: Chūō kōronsha, 1983.

_____. *Seitai kaibō: Kyūshū daigaku igakubu jiken* [Vivisection: The case of the Medical Department at Kyūshū University]. Tokyo: Mainichi shinbunsha, 1979.

_____. *Sugamo Purizun 13-gō teppi* [The iron doors at Sugamo Prison No. 13]. Tokyo: Shinchōsha, 1981.

_____. *Sugamo: senpan kōshukei* [Sugamo: Death by hanging of a war criminal]. Tokyo: Mineruva shobō, 1981.

Katayama Yoshitaka. *Nichi-Ro sensō to shinbun: "sekai no naka no Nihon" o dō ronjitaka* [The Russo-Japanese War and newspapers: How was "Japan in the world" debated?]. Tokyo: Kōdansha, 2009.

Katō Tetsutarō. *Watashi wa kai ni naritai: aru BC-kyū senpan no sakebi* [I would like to be a seashell: Cry of a Class BC war criminal]. Tokyo: Shunjūsha, 1994.

Kawamura Saburō. *Jūsan kaidan o agaru: senpan shokeisha no kiroku* [Going up the thirteen steps: Records of an executed war criminal]. Tokyo: Atō shobō, 1952.

Kawano Kyōsuke, ed. *Jinmon, gōmon, shokei* [Interrogation, torture, execution]. Tokyo: Akita shoten, 1970.

Kimura Kōichirō. *Wasurerareta sensō sekinin: Kānikobaru-tō jiken to Taiwanjin gunzoku* [Forgotten war responsibility: The Car Nicobar Incident and Taiwanese auxiliary forces]. Tokyo: Aoki shoten, 2001.

Kinoshita Hideaki. *Yokuryū seikatsu jūichi-nen: Soren no jissō* [Eleven years of life in internment: Reality of the Soviet Union]. Tokyo: Nikkan kōgyō shinbunsha, 1957.

Kitazaki Manabu. *Shiberiya no hada* [The skin of Siberia]. Tokyo: Jiyū Ajia sha, 1955.

Knightley, Phillip. *The First Casualty: From the Crimea to Vietnam: The War Correspondent as Hero, Propagandist, and Myth Maker*. New York and London: Harcourt Brace Jovanovich, 1975.

Kratoska, Paul H., ed. *Asian Labor in the Wartime Japanese Empire: Unknown Histories*. Armonk, NY, and London, UK: M. E. Sharpe, 2005.

_____. *The Thailand-Burma Railway, 1942–1946: Documents and Selected Writings*. 6 vols. London and New York: Routledge, 2006.

Kushner, Barak. *Men to Devils and Devils to Men: Japanese War Crimes and Chinese Justice*. Cambridge, MA: Harvard University Asia Center, 2015.

Kyokutō kokusai gunji saiban sokkiroku [Transcripts of court proceedings at the International Military Tribunal for the Far East]. 10 vols. Tokyo: Yūshūdō shoten, 1968.

Lael, Richard. *The Yamashita Precedent: War Crimes and Command Responsibility*. Wilmington, DE: Scholarly Resources, 1982.

Lamont-Brown, Raymond. *Ships from Hell: Japanese War Crimes on the High Seas*. Stroud, UK: Sutton Publishing, 2002.

Lapham, Robert, and Bernard Norling. *Guerrillas in the Philippines, 1942–1945*. Lexington: The University Press of Kentucky, 1996.

Lawson, Konrad M. "Wartime Atrocities and the Politics of Treason in the Ruins of the Japanese Empire, 1936–1953." PhD diss., Harvard University, 2012.

Lebra, Joyce C. *Jungle Alliance: Japan and the Indian National Army*. Singapore: Donald Moore for Asia Pacific Press, 1971.

Linton, Suzannah, ed. *Hong Kong's War Crimes Trials*. Oxford: Oxford University Press, 2013.

Long, Gavin. *The Final Campaigns*. Australia in the War of 1939–1945. Series One (Army), vol. 7. Canberra: Australian War Memorial, 1963.

Lord Wright. "War Crimes under International Law." *The Law Quarterly Review*, vol. 62, no. 1 (January 1946): pp. 40–52.

MacDonald, Lyn. *Somme*. London: M. Joseph, 1983.

Maekawa, Kaori. "Forgotten Soldiers in the Japanese Army: Asian Personnel in Papua New Guinea." Symposium paper for the Remembering the War in New Guinea Project. Available at the Web site of the Australian War Memorial, http://ajrp.awm.gov.au/AJRP/remember.nsf.

_____. "The Heiho during the Japanese Occupation of Indonesia." In *Asian Labor in the Wartime Japanese Empire: Unknown Histories*. Edited by Paul H. Kratoska. Armonk, NY, and London, UK: M. E. Sharpe, 2005, pp. 179–196.

Maeno Shigeru. *Ikeru shikabane: Soren gokusō jūichinen* [Living corpse: Eleven years in Soviet prison]. Tokyo: Shunjūsha, 1961.

_____. *Soren gokusō jūichinen* [Eleven years in Soviet prison]. 4 vols. Tokyo: Kōdansha gakujutsu bunko, 1979.

Materials on the Trial of Former Servicemen of the Japanese Army Charged with Manufacturing and Employing Bacteriological Weapons. Moscow: Foreign Language Publishing House, 1950.

Mathur, L. P. *History of the Andaman and Nicobar Islands, 1756–1966*. Jullundur and Delhi: Sterling, 1968.

Matsumura Tomokatsu. "Saiban to kangoku" [Trial and detention]. In *Saiban, kangoku, bōchō: Soren shūjin seisaku no uramen. senpan, yokuryūsha ga taiken shita repōto* [Trial, detention, espionage: The backstories of the Soviet prisoner policies. Reports on experiences of convicted war criminals and internees]. Tokyo: Nikkan rōdō tsūshinsha, 1958, pp. 3–90.

Matsuo Saburō. *Kōshudai no hibiki: aru interi senpan shikeishū no shuki* [The sound of the gallows: Memoirs of a convicted "intelligentsia" war criminal on death row]. Tokyo: Sekaisha, 1952.

Matsuura Yoshinori. *Shinjitsu o uttaeru: Rabauru senpan bengonin no nikki* [Appealing the truth: The diary of a lawyer for war crimes trials at Rabaul]. Tokyo: Genshū shuppansha, 1997.

McCarthy, Dudley. *South-West Pacific Area – First Year: Kokoda to Wau.* Australia in the War of 1939–1945. Series One (Army), vol. 5. Canberra: Australian War Memorial, 1959.

McLynn, Frank. *The Burma Campaign: Disaster into Triumph 1942–45.* New Haven, CT and London, UK: Yale University Press, 2011.

Mettrau, Guénaël. *The Law of Command Responsibility.* Oxford and New York: Oxford University Press, 2009.

Michno, Gregory F. *Death on the Hellships: Prisoners at Sea in the Pacific War.* Annapolis, MD: Leo Cooper, 2001.

Mitchell, Richard H. *Janus-Faced Justice: Political Criminals in Imperial Japan.* Honolulu: University of Hawai'i Press, 1992.

Mitter, Rana. *Forgotten Ally: China's World War II 1937–1945.* Boston: Houghton Mifflin Harcourt, 2013.

Miyawaki Noboru. *Roshia-hei horyo ga aruita Matsuyama: Nichi-Ro senso ka no kokusai kōryū* [The city of Matsuyama in which the Russian prisoners of war walked: International exchange during the Russo-Japanese War]. Matsuyama: Ehime shinbunsha, 2005.

Morris, Narrelle, and Timothy L. H. McCormack, eds. *The Australian War Crimes Trials Law Reports Series, 1945–51.* Leiden, Netherlands: Martinus Nijhoff Publishers, forthcoming 2016.

Modder, Ralph P. *The Singapore Chinese Massacre: 18 February to 4 March 1942.* Singapore: Horizon Books, 2004.

Moti Ram, ed. *Two Historic Trials in Red Fort: An Authentic Account of the Trial by a General Court Martial of Captain Shah Nawaz Khan, Captain PK Sahgal and Lt GS Dhillon; and the Trial by a European Military Commission of Emperor Bahadur Shah.* New Delhi: Moti Ram, 1946.

Nagai Hitoshi. *Firipin to tai-Nichi senpan saiban, 1945–1953* [The Philippines and war crimes trials against the Japanese, 1945–1953]. Tokyo: Iwanami shoten, 2010.

———. *Firipin BC-kyū senpan saiban* [Philippine Class BC war crimes trials]. Tokyo: Kōdansha, 2013.

———, ed. *Sensō hanzai chōsa shiryō: furyo kankei chōsa iinkai chōsa hōkokusho tsuzuri* [Sources on war crimes investigations: The compilation of investigation reports by the central committee for investigation concerning prisoners of war]. Tokyo: Higashi shuppan, 1995.

Nagano Tameyoshi. *Rabauru gunji hōtei: aru Nihonjin no saiban kiroku* [The Rabaul military court: Trial records of a Japanese]. Tokyo: Keisō shuppan sābisu sentā, 1982.

Naikaku insatsukyoku [The Cabinet Printing Office], ed. *Taishō nenkan hōrei zensho. Taishō 3-nen, 4. gunrei, seirei, ritsuryō, kakurei, shōrei* [The Taishō-era compendium of laws. Taishō 3, vol. 4. military laws, regulations, legal codes, cabinet ordinances, ministerial ordinances]. Tokyo: Hara shobō, 1984–1997.

Naitō Mitsuhiro and Furukawa Atsushi. *Tōhoku Ajia no hō to seiji* [Law and politics in Northeast Asia]. Tokyo: Senshū daigaku shuppankyoku, 2005.

Naitō Yorihiro. *Shūsengo no shihō seido kaikaku no keika: Ichiji tōkyokusha no tachiba kara* [Progress in the reform of the legal system after the end of the war: From the viewpoint of a person in charge]. 4 vols. Tokyo: Shinzansha, 1997–1998.

Nakajima Masato. *Bōsatsu no kōseki: Shingapōru kakyō gyakusatsu jiken* [Traces of premeditated murder: The Singapore Chinese Massacre]. Tokyo: Kōdansha, 1985.

Nakajima Takeshi. *Nakamura-ya no Bōsu: Indo dokuritsu undō to kindai Nihon no Ajiashugi* [Bose of Nakamuraya: The Indian independence movement and Asianism in modern Japan]. Tokyo: Hakusuisha, 2005.

Nakao Yūji, ed. *Shōwa tennō hatsugen kiroku shūsei* [The compilation of the records of statements made by Emperor Shōwa]. 2 vols. Tokyo: Fuyō shuppan, 2003.

Nakata Seiichi. *Saigo no senpan shikeishū: Nishimura Takuma chūjō to aru kyōkaishi no kiroku* [The last death-sentenced war criminal: Records of Lieutenant General Nishimura Takuma and a prison chaplain]. Tokyo: Heibonsha, 2011.

Niimi Takashi. *Kokka no sekinin to jinken: guntai kiritsu ron, anzen hairyo gimu no hōri* [State responsibility and human rights: Legal principles on military discipline and obligations for a safety guarantee]. Tokyo: Yui shobō, 2006.

Nihon kindai shiryō kenkyūkai [The Research Group on Sources of Modern Japan], ed. *Nihon riku-kaigun no seido, soshiki, jinji* [System, organization, and personnel of the Japanese army and navy]. Tokyo: Tōkyō daigaku shuppankai, 1971.

Nishinarita Yutaka. *Chūgokujin kyōsei renkō* [Chinese forced deportation]. Tokyo: Tōkyō daigaku shuppankai, 2002.

Nogi Harumichi. *Kaigun tokubetsu keisatsutai: Anbon-tō BC-kyū senpan no shuki* [The navy special military police force: Personal notes by a Class BC war criminal at Ambon]. Tokyo: Taihei shuppansha, 1975.

Norling, Bernard. *The Intrepid Guerrillas of North Luzon.* Lexington: The University Press of Kentucky, 1999.

Nozoe Kenji. *Kigyō no sekinin: Chūgokujin kyōsei renkō no genba kara* [Corporate responsibility for war: From the scenes of Chinese forced deportation]. Tokyo: Shakai hyōronsha, 2009.

Ogawa Hitoo. *Shokei sarenakatta senpan: jinmin saiban no ura de. aru senpan no shuki* [A war criminal not executed: Behind the People's Trials. A memoir of a war criminal]. Tokyo: Nicchū shuppan, 1979.

Okada Tasuku. *Sugamo no jūsan kaidan: senpan shokeisha no kiroku* [The thirteen steps at Sugamo: A record of an executed war criminal]. Tokyo: Atō shobō, 1952.

Okamoto Torao, ed. *Nokosareta hitobito: Hitō senpan shikeishū no shuki* [People left behind: Memoirs of war criminals on death row in the Philippines]. Tokyo: Suma shobō, 1952.

Ōkuma Hideji. *Nichi-Ro sensō no uragawa "daini no kaikoku": Nihon rettō ni jōrikushita Roshiagun horyo shichiman-nin* ["The second opening of the country" behind the scenes of the Russo-Japanese War: 70,000 Russian prisoners of war who landed on the Japanese archipelago]. Tokyo: Sairyūsha, 2011.

Oppler, Alfred C. *Japan's Courts and Law in Transition*. Tokyo: Foreign Affairs Association of Japan, 1952.

_____. *Legal Reform in Occupied Japan: A Participant Looks Back*. Princeton, NJ: Princeton University Press, 1976.

_____. *Nihon senryō to hōsei kaikaku* [Occupation of Japan and legal reform]. Translated by Naitō Yorihiro, Naya Hiromi, and Takachi Shigeyo. Tokyo: Nihon hyōronsha, 1990.

Osias, Camilo. *The Story of a Long Career of Varied Tasks*. Quezon City, Philippines: Manlapaz, 1971.

Pappas, Caroline. "Law and Politics: Australia's War Crimes Trials in the Pacific, 1943–1961." PhD diss., University of New South Wales, 1998.

Peattie, Mark R. *Nan'yō: The Rise and Fall of the Japanese in Micronesia, 1885–1945*. Honolulu: University of Hawai'i Press, 1988.

Philips, Raymond. *Trial of Josef Kramer and Forty-Four Others (The Belsen Trial)*. London: William Hodge, 1949.

Piccigallo, Philip R. *The Japanese on Trial: Allied War Crimes Operations in the East, 1945–1951*. Austin: University of Texas Press, 1979.

Reel, A. Frank. *The Case of General Yamashita*. Chicago, IL: University of Chicago Press, 1949.

_____. *Yamashita saiban* [The Yamashita Trial]. Tranlated by Shimojima Muraji. 2 vols. Tokyo: Nihon kyōbunsha, 1952.

Rekishigaku kenkyūkai [History Research Association], ed. *Taiheiyō sensōshi* [The history of the Pacific War]. 6 vols. Tokyo: Aoki shoten, 1973.

Riron henshūbu [Theory Editor Section], ed. *Kabe atsuki heya: BC-kyū senpan no jinseiki* [A room with thick walls: Life stories of Class BC war criminals]. Tokyo: Nihon tosho sentā, 1992.

Ryan, Allan A. *Yamashita's Ghost: War Crimes, MacArthur's Justice, and Command Accountability*. Lawrence: University Press of Kansas, 2012.

Saka Kuniyasu, ed. *Shijitsu kiroku sensō saiban* [Historical records of war crimes trials]. 5 vols. Tokyo: Tōchōsha, 1967–1968.

Sareen, T. R. *Building the Siam-Burma Railway during World War II (A Documentary Study)*. Delhi: Kalpaz, 2005.

Satō Ryōichi, ed. *Gyakutai no kiroku* [Records of abusive treatment]. Tokyo: Shio shobō, 1953.

Sengo hoshō mondai kokkai gijiroku henshū iinkai [The Committee for the Compilation of Parliamentary Records on Postwar Reparation Issues], ed. *Shiryō: sengo hoshō mondai kokkai gijiroku* [Sources: Parliamentary records on postwar reparation issues]. Tokyo: Sengo hoshō mondai kokkai gijiroku henshū iinkai, 1993.

Shimanouchi Tatsuoki. *Tōkyō saiban* [The Tokyo Trial]. Tokyo: Nihon hyōronsha, 1984.

Shinozaki Mamoru. *Shingapōru senryō hiroku* [A secret record of the occupation of Singapore]. Tokyo: Hara shobō, 1976.

Shiojiri Kōmei, ed. *Aru isho ni tsuite* [About a will]. Tokyo: Shinchōsha, 1948.

_____, ed. *Sokoku e no isho: senpan shikeishū no shuki* [Wills for the homeland: Memoirs of war criminals on death row]. Tokyo: Mainichi shinbunsha, 1952.

Singh, Mohan. *Leaves from My Diary*. Lahore: Free-World Publications, 1946.

_____. *Soldiers' Contribution to Indian Independence: The Epic of the Indian National Army*. New Delhi: Army Educational Stores, 1974.

Slim, Sir William. *Defeat into Victory: Battling Japan in Burma and India, 1942–1945.* London: The Print Society, 1956.

Sissons, D. C. S. "The Australian War Crimes Trials and Investigations (1942–51)." Available at the Web site of the War Crimes Studies Center at the University of California, Berkeley, http://www.ocf.berkeley.edu/~changmin/documents/Sissons%20Final%20War%20Crimes%20Text%2018-3-06.pdf.

Sōmiya Shinji. *Anbon-tō senpan saibanki* [Records of war crimes trials at Ambon]. Tokyo: Hōritsu shinpōsha, 1946.

Specter, Ronald. *Eagle against the Sun: The American War with Japan.* New York: Free Press, 1985.

Steinberg, David Joel. *Philippine Collaboration in World War II.* Ann Arbor: University of Michigan Press, 1962.

Sugamo hōmu iinkai [The Sugamo Legal Affairs Committee], ed. *Haruka naru minami jūjisei: senpan saiban no jissō* [The Southern Cross afar: Reality of war crimes trials]. Tokyo: Sannō shobō, 1968.

————, ed. *Senpan saiban no jissō* [Reality of war crimes trials]. Tokyo: Fuji shuppansha, 1952.

Sugamo isho hensan iinkai [The Sugamo Committee for the Compilation of Wills], ed. *Seiki no isho* [The will of the century]. Tokyo: Sugamo isho hensan iinkai kankō jimusho, 1953.

————, ed. *Shi to eikō: senpan shikeishū no shuki* [Death and glory: Memoirs of war criminals on death row]. Tokyo: Nagashima shobō, 1957.

Sugihara Tōru. *Chūgokujin kyōsei renkō* [Chinese forced deportation]. Tokyo: Iwanami shoten, 2002.

Sugimatsu Fujio, ed. *Shishite sokoku ni ikin: 4 senpan shikeishū no isho* [Die to live in the homeland: Wills of four war criminals on death row]. Tokyo: Sōjusha, 1952.

Sugiyama Hajime gensui denki kankōkai [The Committee for the Publication of General Sugiyama Hajime's Biography], ed. *Sugiyama Hajime den* [Biography of Sugiyama Hajime]. Tokyo: Hara shobō, 1969.

Sumitani Osachi, Utsumi Aiko, and Akazawa Shirō, eds. "Tōkyō saiban, BC-kyū sensō hanzai, sensō sekinin kankei shiyō bunken mokuroku" [Index to published sources concerning the Tokyo Trial, Class BC war crimes, and war responsibility]. Shisō, no. 719 (May 1985): 28 pages. This article appears at the back end of the journal.

Tachikawa Kyōichi. "Kyūgun ni okeru horyo no toriatsukai: Taiheiyō sensō no jōkyō o chūshin ni" [Treatment of prisoners of war by the former army: Centering on the circumstances of the Pacific War]. *Bōei kenkyūjo kiyō* [Bulletin of the National Institute for Defense Studies] 10, no. 1 (September 2007): pp. 74–100.

Takeda, Kayoko. *Interpreting the Tokyo War Crimes Tribunal: A Sociopolitical Analysis.* Ottawa: University of Ottawa Press, 2010.

Tanaka Hiroshi and Matsuzawa Tetsuya, eds. *Chūgokujin kyōsei renkō shiryō: "Gaimushō hōkokusho" zen-5-bunsatsu hoka* [Sources on Chinese forced deportation: "Reports by Ministry of Foreign Affairs," 5 volumes and others]. Tokyo: Gendai shokan, 1995.

Tanaka Hiroshi, Utsumi Aiko, and Ishitobi Jin, eds. *Shiryō Chūgokujin kyōsei renkō no kiroku* [Sources: Records on Chinese forced deportation]. Tokyo: Akashi shoten, 1987.

Tanaka Hiroshi, Utsumi Aiko, and Niimi Takashi, eds. *Shiryō Chūgoku kyōsei renkō no kiroku* [Records of Chinese forced deportation]. Tokyo: Akashi shoten, 1990.

Tanaka, Yuki, Tim L. H. McCormack, and Gerry Simpson, eds. *Beyond Victor's Justice? The Tokyo War Crimes Trial Revisited.* International Humanitarian Law Series. Leiden, the Netherlands: Martinus Nijhoff, 2010.

Tarumoto Jūji. *Aru senpan no shuki: Taimen tetsudō kensetsu to senpan saiban* [Personal notes of a war criminal: The construction of the Burma-Siam Railway and war crimes trials]. Tokyo: Gendai shiryō shuppan, 1999.

Taylor, Telford. *Nuremberg and Vietnam: The American Tragedy.* Chicago, IL: Quadrangle Books, 1970.

Terasaki Hidenari and Mariko Terasaki Miller, eds. *Shōwa tennō dokuhakuroku: Terasaki Hidenari, goyō gakari nikki* [The monologue of Emperor Shōwa, and the diary of an imperial attendant, Terasaki Hidenari]. Tokyo: Bungei shunju, 1991.

Tōkyō saiban handobukku henshū iinkai [The Tokyo Trial Handbook Compilation Committee], ed. *Tōkyō saiban handobukku* [The Tokyo Trial handbook]. Tokyo: Aoki shoten, 1989.

Toland, John. *The Rising Sun: The Decline and Fall of the Japanese Empire, 1936–1945.* New York: Random House, 1970.

Totani, Yuma. *The Tokyo War Crimes Trial: The Pursuit of Justice in the Wake of World War II.* Cambridge, MA: Harvard University Asia Center, 2008.

Toyoda Kumao. *Sensō saiban yoroku* [Titbits of war trials]. Tokyo: Taiseisha, 1986.

Toyoda Masayuki. "Chūka jinmin kyōwakoku no senpan saiban" [War crimes trials by the People's Republic of China]. *Kikan sensō sekinin kenkyū* [The report on Japan's war responsibility], no. 17 (Fall 1997): pp. 67–73.

————. "Chūka jinmin kyōwakoku no senpan saiban" [War crimes trials by the People's Republic of China], *Kikan sensō sekinin kenkyū* [The report on Japan's war responsibility], no. 18 (Winter 1997): pp. 46–53.

Toyoda Soemu. *Saigo no teikoku kaigun* [The last of the Imperial Navy]. Tokyo: Sekai no Nippon sha, 1950.

————. *Toyoda Speaks: The Last of the Japanese Imperial Navy.* Tokyo: Sekai no Nippon sha, 1951.

Trefalt, Beatrice. "Hostages to International Relations? The Repatriation of Japanese War Criminals from the Philippines." *Japanese Studies*, vol. 31, no. 2 (September 2011): pp. 191–209.

————. "A Peace Worth Having: Delayed Repatriations and Domestic Debate Over the San Francisco Peace Treaty." *Japanese Studies*, vol. 27, no. 2 (September 2007): pp. 173–87.

Tsuchiya Shinichi. *Shōwa no keiji seisaku* [Criminal policy in the Shōwa period]. Tokyo: Tachibana shobō, 1991.

Tsuchiya, Shinichi, and Minoru Shikita. *Crime and Criminal Policy in Japan from 1922–1988: Analysis and Evaluation of the Shōwa Era.* Tokyo: Japan Criminal Policy Society, 1990.

Tsuji Masanobu. *Senkō sanzenri* [Going underground for three thousand miles]. Tokyo: Mainichi shinbunsha, 1950.

Tsuji Yutaka. *Montenrupa: Hitō yūshū no kiroku* [Muntinlupa: Records of imprisonment in the Philippines]. Tokyo: Asahi shinbunsha, 1952.

United Nations War Crimes Commission, comp. *History of the United Nations War Crimes Commission and the Development of the Laws of War.* London: His Majesty's Stationery Office, 1948.

————, ed. *Law Reports of Trials of War Criminals.* 15 vols. London: His Majesty's Stationery Office, 1947–1949.

Ushimura Kei. *Saikō: "Seiki no isho" to Tōkyō saiban: tai-Nichi senpan saiban no seishinshi* [Reconsideration: *Seiki no isho* and the Tokyo Trial; Intellectual history of war crimes trials against the Japanese]. Tokyo: PHP shuppan, 2004.

Utsumi Aiko. *Chōsenjin BC-kyū senpan no kiroku* [Records of Korean Class BC war criminals]. Tokyo: Keisō shobō, 1982.

————. *Kimu wa naze sabakaretanoka: Chōsenjin BC-kyū senpan no kiseki* [Why was Kim tried? The trajectory of Korean Class BC war criminals]. Tokyo: Asahi shinbun shuppansha, 2008.

————. *Nihongun no horyo seisaku* [Prisoner-of-war policies of the Japanese military]. Tokyo: Aoki shoten, 2005.

Utsumi Aiko and Nagai Hitoshi, eds. *Shinbun shiryō ni miru Tōkyō saiban, BC-kyū saiban* [The Tokyo Trial, Class BC trials as seen in newspaper sources]. 2 vols. Tokyo: Gendai shiryō shuppan, 2000.

————, eds. *Tōkyō saiban: horyo kankei shiryō* [The Tokyo Trial: Sources related to prisoners of war]. 3 vols. Tokyo: Gendai shiryō shuppan, 2012.

Utsunomiya Naotaka. *Kaisō no Yamashita saiban* [The Yamashita Trial in remembrance]. Tokyo: Shirogane shobō, 1975.

Wainwright, Jonathan Mayhew. *General Wainwright's Story: The Account of Four Years of Humiliating Defeat, Surrender, and Captivity.* New York: Doubleday, 1946.

Ward, Ian. *Shōgun wa naze korosaretaka: Gōshū senpan saiban, Nishimura Takuma chūjō no higeki* [Why was the general killed? The tragedy of Lieutenant General Nishimura Takuma in the Australian war crimes trial]. Translated by Suzuki Masanori. Tokyo: Hara shobō, 2005.

————. *Snaring the Other Tiger.* Singapore: Media Masters, 1996.

Washington Law Review, ed. *Legal Reforms in Japan during the Allied Occupation: A Collection of Essays.* Seattle: Washington Law Review, 1977.

Waterford, Van. *Prisoners of the Japanese in World War II: Statistical History, Personal Narratives and Memorials Concerning POWs in Camps and on Hellships, Civilian Internees, Asian Slave Laborers and Others Captured in the Pacific Theater.* Jefferson, NC and London, UK.: McFarland, 1994.

Welch, Jeanie M. *The Tokyo Trial: A Bibliographic Guide to English-Language Sources.* Westport, CT and London, UK Greenwood Press, 2002.

Wigmore, Lionel. *The Japanese Thrust.* Australia in the War of 1939–1945. Series One (Army), vol. 4. Canberra: Australian War Memorial, 1957.

Willoughby, Charles A. *The Guerrilla Resistance Movement in the Philippines, 1941–1945.* New York: Vantage Press, 1972.

Wilson, Sandra. "After the Trials: Class B and C Japanese War Criminals and the Post-War World." *Japanese Studies*, vol. 31, no. 2 (September 2011): pp. 141–9.

————. "Prisoners in Sugamo and Their Campaign for Release, 1952–1953." *Japanese Studies*, vol. 31, no. 2 (September 2011): pp. 171–90.

Yamada Akira. *Shōwa tennō no gunji shisō to senryaku* [Military thought and strategies of Emperor Shōwa]. Tokyo: Azekura shobō, 2002.

Yano Kenzō. *Gokuchūki: himeraretaru shūsen zangyaku monogatari* [Prison notes: A secret story of postwar atrocity]. Tokyo: Chōbunsha, 1962.

Yokohama bengoshikai [Yokohama Bar Association]. *Hōtei no seijōki: BC-kyū senpan Yokohama saiban no kiroku* [The Stars and Stripes in the courtroom: Records of Class BC war crimes trials at Yokohama]. Tokyo: Nihon hyōronsha, 2004.

Yoshikawa Toshiharu. *Taimen tetsudō: kimitsu bunsho ga akasu Ajia Taiheiyō senso* [The Burma-Siam Railway: The Asia-Pacific War as revealed in secret documents]. Tokyo: Yūzankaku, 2011.

Yukawa Yōzō, ed. *Asu no asa no "9-ji": senpan shikeisha no ishoshū* [Tomorrow morning at nine o'clock: A collection of wills by executed war criminals]. Tokyo: Nihon shūhōsha, 1952.

Zenkoku ken'yūkai rengōkai hensan iinkai [The All-Japan Union for the Friends-of-Kenpei Association Compilation Committee], ed. *Junkoku kenpei no isho* [The wills of patriotic military police]. Tokyo: Kenbun shoin, 1982.

————, ed. *Nihon kenpei seishi* [The official history of the Japanese military police]. Tokyo: Kenbun shoin, 1976.

Index